Radical Approaches to Politica
Roads Less Traveled

Rainer Eisfeld

Radical Approaches to Political Science: Roads Less Traveled

With an Introduction by Klaus von Beyme

Barbara Budrich Publishers
Opladen • Berlin • Toronto 2012

A CIP catalogue record for this book is available from
Die Deutsche Bibliothek (The German Library)

© 2012 by Barbara Budrich Publishers, Opladen, Berlin & Toronto
www.barbara-budrich.net
ISBN   978-3-8474-0028-8
eISBN   978-3-86649-536-4

Das Werk einschließlich aller seiner Teile ist urheberrechtlich geschützt. Jede Verwertung außerhalb der engen Grenzen des Urheberrechtsgesetzes ist ohne Zustimmung des Verlages unzulässig und strafbar. Das gilt insbesondere für Vervielfältigungen, Übersetzungen, Mikroverfilmungen und die Einspeicherung und Verarbeitung in elektronischen Systemen.

Die Deutsche Bibliothek – CIP-Einheitsaufnahme
Ein Titeldatensatz für die Publikation ist bei Der Deutschen Bibliothek erhältlich.

Verlag Barbara Budrich 🅑 Barbara Budrich Publishers
Stauffenbergstr. 7. D-51379 Leverkusen Opladen, Germany

86 Delma Drive. Toronto, ON M8W 4P6 Canada
www.barbara-budrich.net

Jacket illustration by disegno, Wuppertal, Germany – www.disenjo.de
Printed in Europe on acid-free paper by
paper&tinta, Warsaw

Contents

Acknowledgments

Roads Less Traveled, the second part of this book's title, derives from an inspired suggestion by my Canadian colleague and friend Leslie Pal (Carleton University, Ottawa), who suggested that it alludes to "...searching where others have not. Plus, it alliterates nicely with the title's first part." Les and I look back on a two-year experience of close cooperation in preparing the volume *Political Science in Central-East Europe*, which we co-edited and which was published by Barbara Budrich in 2010. Collaborating with Les has been a truly marvelous experience, for which I remain intensely grateful. Once again, I am deeply indebted to him for his resourceful ingenuity, as well as for his generous permission to include our jointly authored introductory piece to the aforementioned volume in this collection.

Klaus von Beyme, who wrote the book's introduction, and I first met at the 1979 IPSA World Congress in Moscow – an exercise in "peaceful coexistence" held at Lomonosov University, whose students were not permitted to attend the sessions' often spirited debates. When we stepped out of an elevator in the (since demolished) Rossija Hotel, Beyme's tightly packed travel bag burst open and spilled its contents on the hotel lobby's floor. Without further ado, we both knelt and started dumping his clothing back into the bag. I like to picture the introduction to the present book, which I very greatly appreciate, as a late sequel to that act of spontaneous collaboration. In his succeeding years, Beyme has been devoting an increasing amount of sophisticated thinking to ways in which political science relates to the social and cultural world around it. Whoever wishes to extend inquiries beyond the discipline's traditional confines, may draw encouragement from him.

With his concept of "interest-group liberalism", Theodore J. Lowi, who graciously offered the assessment printed on the back cover, deeply influenced my thinking while I was writing my dissertation. Hardly did I surmise at the time that, 35 years later, Ted and I would cooperate on a book reviewing pluralist approaches to democratic theory and practice, which I would edit for IPSA's 'World of Political Science' series. The most moving moment, however, occurred in 1999 during the UNESCO World Conference on Science in Budapest, where Ted Lowi, then IPSA President, chaired a session on "Science and Democracy" and invited me as rapporteur. During our spare time, we traveled by tram to Budapest's huge Rákoskeresztúr Cemetery with its beautiful headstones and crypts (many now in need of restoration), where several of Ted's ancestors lie entombed.

Since my retirement in 2006, the University of Osnabrück has continued to provide resources which have proved crucial to my academic pursuits, and for which I remain deeply grateful. The decisive first step in arranging for such support was taken by Michael Bommes, who served as the department's dean at the time. Michael, who held a chair in migration studies, and who played a key part in connecting German research with international scholarship on migration, sadly became afflicted with a severe illness and passed away much too early two years ago. I will continue to preserve his memory.

Finally, Vera Bröcker taught me again that, to paraphrase Sir Arthur C. Clarke, advanced computer know-how is indistinguishable from magic. I remain very much indebted to her for her sustained and good-humoured support.

Introduction

Klaus von Beyme

"Radical" in German sounds "more radical" than in the Anglo-Saxon tradition and in French ideologies because German liberalism since the 19th century was rarely radical. Radicalism as a characterization of a way of thought in political science implies two aspects:

- A *normative position* that is not satisfied with a focus on individuals' political behavior and on institutions, as it has been predominating since the behavioral revolution in the United States.
- A rather *moderate leftist position* as an engaged political scientist.

After the Second World War, the critical Frankfurt School in the tradition of Adorno, Horkheimer and later Habermas was the incarnation of such a normative position of committed leftist social scientists. Not by chance, Rainer Eisfeld took his PhD in Frankfurt and wrote his first German-language books on "Pluralism between Liberalism and Socialism" (1972) and, dealing with the leftist experiment in Portugal, on "Socialist Pluralism in Europe". Two of his shorter works on Portugal are included in this volume (Chapter V, 1 and 2).

In this tradition, Eisfeld is a "radical liberal" who never opted for one of the authoritarian branches of socialism or communism. Eisfeld had some sympathies for the "Praxis movement" in Yugoslavia. One of his articles on "Pluralism as a Critical Political Theory" was published in the journal *Praxis International* in 1986 – edited by Seyla Benhabib and Svetozar Stojanovič – which oriented itself towards "Marxist humanism" and "democratic socialism" (Chapter I, 4 in this volume). Eisfeld based his assumptions originally on Harold Laski's ideas of a dynamic theory centering on the fundamentally associative character of society and aiming at an egalitarian basis for redistributing material advantages between social groups and classes.

Later Rainer Eisfeld moved closer to German versions of "neopluralism" in the tradition of Ernst Fraenkel who had developed his ideas as an émigré in the United States and later taught in Berlin. Neopluralism became the ideological opposition to authoritarian Communism in East Germany and in the Soviet Union. After the collapse of Communism, these ideas won relevance for the new systems in their transition to democracy. Eisfeld did not overlook the problem that an oligarchic structure of society may result in a "limited pluralism" as a consequence of the internationalization of capital. In his studies, Robert Dahl's analyses of the "dilemmas of pluralist democracy" frequently emerge as a normative point of reference.

Eisfeld is a rather unorthodox representative of political science. His pluralism is proved already by his multidisciplinary approach. According to Mattei Dogan's and Robert Pahre's *Creative Marginality* (Boulder 1990), innovations mostly take place at the intersections of social sciences. This insight is pertinent to Eisfeld's oeuvre: He has a strong interest in history and in the popular arts.

Great attention was paid by him to the development of German political science under the Weimar Republic and the Nazi regime. Eisfeld's book on those exiled German social scientists who in spite of their fate were quite right-wing-oriented, some even close to the Nazi movement, caused a vehement debate in Germany. "The ambivalent response to the 1933 Nazi seizure of power", which derives from it, is included in this volume (Chapter II.2). His historical interests are also demonstrated in his analyses "From Hegelianism to Neo-Pluralism" (Chapter III.1) and of the "Mitteleuropa" myth (Chapter III.2).

Finally, that part of the Frankfurt tradition which corresponds to Rainer Eisfeld's interest in arts and literature, shows up in the book's pieces on the myth of the Western, and on fantasies about Mars (Chapter IV, 1 and 2). Elsewhere, he has written about teenagers' dreams in the 1950s.

I hope that this engrossing pluralistic volume may find the interested readers which it richly deserves.

I.
Political Science
Taking Sides – Why, How?

When, in 1949, the inclusion of political science into the curricula of West Germany's universities was first discussed, the discipline, for the Munich University's rector, might be compared only to theology – "always a matter of belief". Half a century later, prominent political scientists expressed their own severe misgivings. Giovanni Sartori, for one, contended that political science "is a largely useless science that does not supply knowledge for use". Former IPSA Secretary General John Trent, in 2011, voiced the key question for the readers of European Political Science: "Is political science out of step with the world, and if so what might be done about it?" To the controversial debate in the same EPS issue, I contributed the following fairly unequivocal opinion.

How Political Science Might Regain Relevance And Obtain an Audience: A Manifesto for the 21st Century

In July 2009, at the IPSA World Congress in Santiago de Chile, John Trent (2009) raised a number of critical questions about the relevance of our discipline. About three months later, on 5 November 2009, the U.S. Senate rejected Coburn Amendment 2631 to the 2010 Commerce, Justice & Science Appropriations Act. The Amendment would have prohibited the National Science Foundation 'from wasting federal research funding on political science projects'.[1] 62 senators voted 'nay'; 36, though, voted 'yea'. Among the reasons for his motion, Senator Thomas Coburn (R, OK) included the statement that scarce funds should be spent on endeavours 'yield[ing] breakthroughs and discoveries that can improve the human condition'. The implication was evident.

The Coburn Amendment triggered a 19 October 2009 *New York Times* article. Writer Patricia Cohen (2009) quoted Joseph S. Nye to the effect that political science may be 'moving in the direction of saying more and more about less and less'. She also cited *Perspectives on Politics* editor Jeffrey C. Isaac, who held that political scientists 'should do a better job... of doing more relevant work'.

The Coburn Amendment and the U.S. Senate vote, the *New York Times* write-up and John Trent's assessment all highlight a number of preoccupations about our discipline, among which are the discipline's compartmentalization, its quest for relevance and for an audience, and – in the earlier instances at least implicitly – the continuing tension between normative and

---

1   http://www.senate.gov/legislative/LIS/roll_call_lists/roll_call_vote;   http:/coburn.senate. gov/ public/index.cfm?_FuseAction=RightNow, both accessed 5/27/2010.

empirical approaches. These challenges contrast conspicuously with the recent advances that political science has made in quantitative terms. During the 1990s, as the discipline established its institutional footing across the European continent's central and eastern regions, the total number of academic staff engaged in political science roughly doubled in Europe. The European Consortium for Political Research (ECPR), established in 1970 and easily the discipline's most important European association in terms of promoting cross-national cooperation, acquired new institutional members from countries such as Albania and Bulgaria, Croatia and Slovenia, Latvia and Lithuania, Poland and the Czech Republic and, not least, Russia. The European Confederation of Political Science Associations (ECPSA), founded in late 2007 to promote the discipline's common interests in teaching, research and funding, consists of at present 19 member organizations, ranging from the Russian to the British, from the Hungarian to the German, from the Slovenian to the Spanish Political Science Associations. Regional and inter-regional cooperation is flourishing; numerous networks of political scientists are emerging across the continent.

Such progress stands at odds with the discipline's modest contribution to addressing the highly relevant issues of regulating financial and economic globalization, of making the best of regional and global migration, of not just combating terrorism, but promoting the reduction of its underlying grievances and causes. Central and Eastern Europe's nascent political science 'cultures' have been merging into an empirically-oriented 'mainstream' whose research has mainly focused on national political systems, comparative politics, European studies and international relations.

On the one hand, considerable advances have been made in these fields. On the other hand, however, *political studies have largely been reduced to a functionalist science of 'managing' parliamentary and party government.* Central and Eastern European political science is not alone in being been marked by an 'almost total absence of critical theory' (Hankiss 2002: 22).[2] There has been no systematic reflection of the 'state of the art' after the collapse of 'actually existing socialism'. At the heart of politics – including democratic politics – are issues of power and authority, of participation and of control over agenda-setting. Unfortunately, these issues no longer figure at the centre of the discipline's attention.

In a period of globalization-induced financial and economic crises, too few political scientists concern themselves with examining the political behaviour of business and the structural connections between business and government – in other words, with a renewed and reinvigorated *political economy*. In an era of increasing ethno-cultural pluralisation, there is a lack of studies which can blend political, psychological, cultural, and economic

---

2   See also Eisfeld and Pal (2010).

aspects, to advance integration and cultural cross-fertilization. In short, we lack a *political science of recognition* that can adequately address issues of cultural segmentation and ensuing socio-political cleavages. In a context of millennialist violence, the discipline needs to offer well-reasoned concepts against adopting anti-terrorist policies which, relying solely on repression, threaten fundamental democratic values without actually offering prospects of success. We need to develop *concepts for a social defence against terrorism* that can pay heed to the satisfaction of basic needs, to a more equitable distribution of political resources, to cultural recognition, and to broader civic participation.

Bringing these pressing regional and global challenges closer to their solution is a political project that involves many years (history), levels (structure), and players (agency). It is these challenges which any political science – not just *European* political science – now needs to address. That the discipline flourishes solely in a democratic environment bears repeating (even if authoritarian regimes have demonstrated a use for truncated versions, adapted to their purposes). Political science should, therefore, *(re-) define itself as a science of democracy*, as it did with particular emphasis subsequent to the Great Depression and World War II, to Fascism and Stalinism.

2009 Economics Nobel Laureate Elinor Ostrom has attested a 'neglect of the citizen' to the present discipline. In an interview, she illustrated her criticism with the following observation: 'Once while waiting at a meeting of the Political Science Association I was asked why I was reading a book on peasants. Political science was about presidents, parties, and Congress'. (Toonen 2010: 197).[3] As a science of democracy, political studies should redirect their principal concerns, addressing the afore-mentioned challenges not least in a determined effort 'to help citizens prepare themselves for various possible futures' (Hankiss 2002: 22).[4] Otherwise, 'perplexity, distrust, fear and intol-

---

3   The political scientist who remains unconvinced by the mere reference to Professor Ostrom's reading habits could do worse than glance at the following sentences: 'Reading and writing letters for illiterate peasants made me understand that poverty takes many cruel forms other than occasional hunger... I sensed how my intrusion must have inhibited them and saw how inarticulate they were... I also remember the shock of discovering at an early age that illiteracy or semi-literacy were not a product of casual neglect but part of the established social order... As I ended an afternoon reading session in a gathering of pea-sants eager to listen to the speeches of President Roosevelt promising freedom, I was suddenly seized by a rural Republican Guard... He threatened to beat me up if I persisted in disturbing the minds of local people with that "Communist poison", as he put it. I swore to myself that I would one day be able to explain the motivations and the power behind that rural guard' (Figueiredo 1975: 10-12]. This report might spur the scholar to further peruse, e. g., Cutileiro (1971).

4   Cf. also Maxwell (1984:, 46, 51, 66) who defines the academic community's 'basic task' as promoting rational thinking and problem-solving in 'the rest of the human world' so that it may, over time, become capable of 'rational social action'. While I evidently consider this idea sound enough, some readers may find Maxwell's extensive from-knowledge-to-wisdom argument a bit contrived.

erance' may overwhelm large segments of society, (ibid.: 20),[5] making them strike out against democratic principles and practices.

Citizens grapple with a plethora of economic, political, and cultural challenges; it is vital that they understand public policies designed to provide solutions. *Political science should support these citizens in their searches,* acting 'as an aid, refiner, extender' of lay inquiry (Lindblom 1990: 216 – 17)[6]. Whenever necessary, it should *play the uncomfortable part of a critical, even an oppositional force;* it should be critical of power structures skewed in favour of economically-privileged minorities or culturally-privileged majorities. It should stand in opposition to prevailing socio-political 'fads'.

Efforts at teamwork across sub-fields, across disciplines, and across countries are essential to make the most of existing specialization. *Normative notions should emerge as an indispensable part of the discipline, though definitely not at the cost of empirical rigour.*[7] The discipline needs to go beyond theories of what 'good *governance*' should be (this 'Bismarckian' notion has more to do with administrative 'efficiency' and the pursuit of the *Rechtsstaat* ideal, than with parliamentary or other forms of democracy). *Political science should develop 'visions' of how a 'good society' might be designed and politically attained* – a society which recognizes ethno-cultural heterogeneity, which is able to defend itself socially against terrorism, and which can draw consequences from the insights of political economy. In the doing, it needs to *incorporate history, structure and agency* – historical changes and their dynamics;[8] embedded socio-economic and political power relations; individuals, associations, parties, and social movements as players.

This brings up a second and related point. In trying to understand some of the deeper causes of the present financial and economic crisis, political scientists have begun to realize that the ongoing process of financial and economic globalization has not occurred without political intervention. Quite the contrary, it is precisely *pro-market* state intervention which has been on the increase. With regard to both public services – including welfare benefits – and regulation, governments have been restricting their performance in a determined fashion. Under the impact of an increasingly hegemonic neo-liberal discourse, administrations led by social democratic parties have joined their liberal-conservative counterparts in opting for privatization and deregulatory policies. Government and market players alike have offered competing

---

5   Cf. Theodor Geiger's (1930) exemplary depiction of 'desperation' and 'panic' induced by the Great Depression that prompted Germany's middle classes to largely vote for the Nazis. See also Geiger (1932: 118, 121).
6   See also Lupia (2000: 12).
7   A „regression' to „more diffuse' theories with „less empirical content' [Feyerabend (1976: 212)] is not implied. 'Removing intellectual rubbish' [ibid.: 25] may, however, be part of the job.
8   Smith (1997: 273).

recipes for the 'slimming down' of states; they are bent on cutting expenditures and supervision.

This is established wisdom;[9] I am not presenting any new insights. My point is that *the trend of pro-market intervention needs to be reversed*, and that *political science needs to intervene in the debate*. Capitalist economies, certainly including financial institutions, require tough regulation. To be effective, such supervision must be internationally coordinated and endowed with robust powers to enforce strict standards.

But, again, the political problems go deeper. If globalization has acted as a constraint on redistributive and regulatory policies, the downsizing of social security budgets and the reduction of resources available for allocation by representatives to constituents have weakened the legitimacy of democratic states. Due to the influence of multinational investors and of foreign competitive pressures, there has been a reduction in both the power and the accountability of democratic legislatures and administrations. The net result has been a weakening of citizen loyalty and of grassroots commitment to democratic processes.[10] *The danger that more and more individuals might react against democracy is not the least reason why political science should be partisan* in conflicts between business interests and democratic government.

Franklin Roosevelt's New Deal, the 'Roosevelt Revolution' after 1933, did not restore, for the United States, prosperity in peacetime. But it did succeed (besides alleviating the suffering of millions of unemployed) in establishing organized labour and organized agriculture as political players alongside business in bargaining for political benefits. Capitalism, it appeared, might be reformed; democracy broadened.[11]

We may be at another crucial juncture. By legislating New Dealish measures, democratically elected representatives need to demonstrate that business has not acquired veto power in economic and social policy-making. Political science must emerge visibly as their ally in this contest. Regulatory reforms may not be easy to achieve, but by making the case, our discipline will be meeting again, as stipulated above, 'the needs of (those) ordinary

---

9   Cf., e.g., Cerny (1997, 1999).

10   That is the sobering outcome of the studies conducted under the Norwegian Power and Democracy Project (1998-2003). Appointed by the government of Norway in early 1998, and headed by Øyvind Østerud (University of Oslo), the state-funded research group worked on the basis of a 1997 mandate by the Norwegian Parliament to compile a report on Power and Democracy within a period of five years. See Ringen (2004); Engelstad and Østerud (2004).

11   In the 1970s, Robert Dahl and Charles Lindblom, after having turned more skeptical and radical in their assessments, explained their earlier commitment to the ongoing political system thus: „The New Deal was not a remote historical episode. It provided grounds for thinking that reform periods would again occur with some frequency'; cf. Dahl and Lindblom (1976: XXX).

citizens' who should be the 'intended beneficiaries of (its) professional inquiry'.[12]

In other words, political science must address the public—the citizens whom it needs to win as an audience – and it must take sides in the doing. As a science of democracy, it is inevitably partisan. It should opt for acknowledging partisanship, explaining aims and implications.

References

Cerny, P.G. (1997): 'Paradoxes of the Competition State: The Dynamics of Political Globalization', *Government and Opposition* 32, 251-274.

Cerny, P. G. (1999): 'Globalization and the Erosion of Democracy', *European Journal of Poli- tical Research* 36, 1-26.

Cohen, P. (2009): 'Field Study: Just How Relevant Is Political Science?' *New York Times,* October 19; http:/www.nytimes.com/2009/books/20poli.html, accessed 5/27/2010.

Cutileiro, J. (1971): *A Portuguese Rural Society*, Oxford: Oxford University Press.

Dahl, R. A., and C. E. Lindblom (1976):'Preface', in: Re-Issue of *Politics, Economics and Wel-fare* (1953), Chicago: Chicago University Press, pp. xxi-xliv.

Eisfeld, R., and L. A. Pal (eds.) (2010): *Political Science in Central-East Europe: Diversity and Convergence,* Opladen: Barbara Budrich.

Engelstad, F. and Ø. Østerud (eds.) (2004) *Power and Democracy*, Aldershot: Ashgate.

Feyerabend, P. (1976): *Wider den Methodenzwang,* Frankfurt: Suhrkamp.

Figueiredo, A. de (1975): *Portugal: Fifty Years of Dictatorship*, Harmondsworth: Penguin Books.

Geiger, T. (1930): 'Panik im Mittelstand', *Die Arbeit* 7: 637-654.

Geiger, T. (1932): *Die soziale Schichtung des deutschen Volkes*, Stuttgart: Enke.

Hankiss, E. (2002): 'Brilliant Ideas or Brilliant Errors? Twelve Years of Social Science Research in Eastern Europe', in Max Kaase and Vera Sparschuh (eds.): *Three Social Science Disciplines in Central and Eastern Europe*, Berlin/Budapest: GESIS/Collegium Budapest, pp. 17-24.

Lindblom, C. E. (1990): *Inquiry and Change. The Troubled Attempt to Understand and Shape Society*, New Haven/London: Yale University Press.

Lupia, A. (2000) 'Evaluating Political Science Research: Information for Buyers and Sellers', P*S: Political Science and Politics* 33 (1): 7-13.

Maxwell, N. (1984): *From Knowledge to Wisdom*, Oxford/New York: Basil Blackwell.

Ringen, S. (2004): 'Wealth and Decay. The Norwegian Study of Power and Democracy', *Times Literary Supplement*, February 13, pp. 3-5.

Smith, R. M. (1997): 'Still Blowing in the Wind: The American Quest for a Democratic, Scien- tific Political Science', *Daedalus* 126 (1): 253-278.

---

12   Lindblom (1990: 257-258).

Toonen, Theo (2010): 'Resilience in Public Administration: The Work of Elinor and Vincent Ostrom from a Public Administration Perspective', *Public Administration Review* 70 (2): 193-202.

Trent, J. E. (2009): 'Political Science 2010: Out of Step with the World? Empirical Evidence and Commentary', paper presented at the 21st Political Science World Congress, 12-16 July, Santiago de Chile.

Is political science "with a regional stamp" a concept which makes sense? Maybe not in exactly the same way as American Studies or, closer to the topic, European Studies do. Still, the suggested focus on ethno-cultural diversity in Central-East Europe would tackle one of the region's perennial key issues on which, according to Canadian philosopher Will Kymlicka, there is "a great need for new work". As subsequently set out in more detail, the proposal was inspired by one of the major findings of Leslie Pal's and my co-edited 2010 book on the discipline's state of the art in Central-East Europe – that institutional cooperation and research networks are decidedly underdeveloped in and among the region's countries. A thematic focus might be needed, around which a major part of research efforts in several countries could crystallize. I expounded the idea at a conference held in Vilnius on the "Baltic-Black Sea Intermarum" as a "New Region of Europe", and the Lithuanian Foreign Policy Review *elected to publish my remarks in its No. 25 (2011) issue.*

Towards Creating a Discipline With a "Regional Stamp": Central-East European Political Science and Ethno-Cultural Diversity[1]

I

On our continent, political science has recently made conspicuous advances in quantitative terms. During the 1990s, with the discipline's institutionalization across Europe's central and eastern regions, total academic staff engaged in political science in Europe approximately doubled. The European Consortium for Political Research (ECPR), established in 1970 and easily the discipline's most important European association in terms of promoting cross-national cooperation, acquired new institutional members from Albania and Bulgaria through Croatia and Slovenia, Latvia and Lithuania to Poland, the Czech Republic and Russia. The European Confederation of Political Science Associations (ECPSA), founded in late 2007 to promote the discipline's common interests in teaching, research and funding, at present consists of 22 member organizations, including 8 from Central-East Europe.

However – and this may serve as a first caveat, – the ECPSA Executive Committee more than mirrors the numerical preponderance of Western European groups, with just two of its seven members coming from Central-East

---

1   This is the revised version of a paper read at the academic conference "A New Region of Europe: Regional Development Paradigms in the Baltic-Black Sea Intermarum", Vilnius, November 26-27, 2010.

Europe – more precisely, from Hungary and Slovenia. Similarly, engagement in CEPSA, the Central European Political Science Association established as early as 1994, has remained restricted to a core group of 8 organizations. The simple reason is that, in a number of Central-East European countries, either no political science association has formed, or existing associations are largely inactive. The degree and effectiveness of professional representation indicate considerable intra-regional disparities in our discipline's evolution. A discussion of the problem will follow below.

The considerable quantitative progress which, nevertheless, has been visible is at odds with the discipline's modest contribution to addressing the salient contemporary issues of regulating financial and economic globalization, of making the best of regional and global migration, of not just combating terrorism, but promoting the reduction of its underlying grievances and causes. In summing up the country reports, which Canadian political scientist Leslie Pal and this author have recently compiled in a book, it may be safely stated that the influence of university departments and foundations from Western Europe and the United States has encouraged the merger of Central and Eastern Europe's nascent political science "cultures" into an empirically oriented "mainstream" focusing on national political systems, comparative politics, European studies and international relations. Across the region, the discipline's dominant approach is institutionalist, with emphasis on current policy-making and on applied research. This tendency has been favoured by the emergence of numerous non-governmental research institutes and analytical centres ("think tanks"), often financed by Western foundations, with the professed mission of contributing to the consolidation of democracy.

On the one hand, considerable advances have been made in the fields just mentioned. On the other hand, political studies have largely been reduced to a functionalist science of "managing" parliamentary and party government. In a way, that is hardly surprising. Establishing a new political system means that, once institutionalized, political science will rather automatically turn to explaining the workings of that system. To a certain extent, political science in any country with new political institutions will be descriptive and institutionalist. The problem, obviously, is to what extent, and how can it grow beyond that focus?

In post-Communist Central and Eastern Europe, political science has been marked by an "almost total absence of critical theory".[2] No systematic reflection of the "state of the art" occurred after the collapse of "actually existing socialism". Instead, the discredit wrought upon Marxist-Leninist ideology and its anti-empirical normativism was rather automatically extend-

---

2 Hankiss E., "Brilliant Ideas or Brilliant Errors? Twelve Years of Social Science Research in Eastern Europe", in Kaase M., Sparschuh V., eds., *Three Social Science Disciplines in Central and Eastern Europe*, Berlin/Budapest: Social Science Information Centre (IZ)/Collegium Budapest, 2002, p. 17-24, quote on p. 22.

ed to normative conceptions of any kind. The baby was thrown out with the bath-water.

In large parts of the region, political science has been facing an additional problem: more often than not, the discipline is suffering from extreme theoretical and methodological fragmentation, accompanied by low research standards. In almost half of the 19 post-Communist societies included in Pal/Eisfeld's collected volume, the authors – without exception experts from the countries under survey – found individual and institutional cooperation deficient, research networks underdeveloped, professional interests insufficiently represented.[3]

Absence of internal cohesion has its analogy in a lack of sustained regional cooperation. By reason of the earlier transfer of resources and conceptual approaches, international links established by Central and East European political scientists are typically East-West. The sort of fragmentation just referred to often implies a divide between a minority of internationally connected and a majority of inward-looking academics.

Three major challenges, it would seem, are at present facing political science disciplines in the region: A paucity of normative theory-building (which is not meant to imply a regression to more diffuse conceptions with less empirical content); a need for a thematic focus, around which a major part of segmented research efforts in a number of countries might crystallize; and a comparatively informed, decidedly "regional stamp" of that focus, which might serve to strengthen the cross-border cooperation of political scientists.

II

The chapter started out by arguing that too few political scientists have so far concerned themselves with the increasing ethno-cultural "pluralization", in William Connolly's pertinent words, of already pluralist polities,[4] with millennialist terrorist violence, with the required robust international regulation of business and finance. Bringing these pressing regional and global challenges even remotely closer to their solution is a political project that involves many years (history), many levels (structure), and many players ("agency", in political science terminology). Addressing them requires the reemergence of normative notions as an indispensable part of the discipline, though – again – definitely not at the cost of empirical rigor in researching constraints and perspectives.

---

3   Eisfeld R., Pal L. A., "Political Science in Central-East Europe and the Impact of Politics: Factors of Diversity – Forces of Convergence", in id., eds., *Political Science in Central-East Europe: Diversity and Convergence*, Opladen/Farmington Hills: Barbara Budrich, 2010, p. 9-35, esp. 21-25.

4   Connolly W. E., *The Ethos of Pluralization*, Minneapolis/London: University of Minnesota Press, 1995, p. XIX-XXIV.

The discipline once again needs to go beyond conceptions of what "good *governance*" should be – a notion that should by no means be held in low regard, but which has more to do with administrative "efficiency" and the rule of law, than with parliamentary or other forms of democracy. Generally speaking, political science should develop "visions" how a "good *society*" might be designed and politically attained. In doing so, the discipline (as has just been emphasized) needs to incorporate history, structure and agency: historical changes and their dynamics;[5] embedded socio-economic and political power relations; individuals, associations, business corporations, political parties and social movements as players.

As Lithuanian scholars Dovilė Jakniūnaitė and Inga Vinogradnaitė have noted, in Central-East Europe, the evolving political science might reasonably start "challeng[ing] the 'mechanical' application" of Western concepts, looking for "a more elaborate conceptualization" of the region's own "experienced 'realities'".[6] Several reasons suggest selecting ethno-cultural pluralisation from among a number of such realities – and from among the triad of pressing issues earlier referred to in this paper – as a major, in fact, <u>the</u> major thematic focus of a political science with a "regional stamp".

In the first place, policies shaping the position of ethno-cultural minorities have been a perennial issue in Central and Eastern European countries since the Habsburg and Czarist empires. Secondly, "learning to live with the… institutionalization of ethno-cultural diversity" may well be considered "a key condition for [any] stable and just democracy".[7] Finally, "virtually all aspects of the transition from Communism to democracy… have displayed ethno-cultural dimensions which cannot be ignored".[8]

Most conspicuous among these, of course, were the civil wars in Serbia and Croatia, which shocked the world with their levels of brutality. The atrocities of "ethnic cleansing" dramatically disproved the hopes pronounced a decade and a half earlier, when cautious optimism in assessing societal levels of toleration had still seemed indicated: "A multi-lingual and multi-ethnic society like Yugoslavia may exhibit considerable frictions between its constituent units, but those frictions will not necessarily threaten the existence of the society itself".[9] Armenia, Georgia, Moldova, and Ukraine, for

---

5   Cf. Smith R. M., "Still Blowing in the Wind: the American Quest for a Democratic, Scientific Political Science", *Daedalus* 126, 1997, p. 253-278, esp. 273.
6   Jakniūnaitė, D., Vinogradnaitė, I., "Political Science in Lithuania: A Maturing Discipline", in Eisfeld, Pal, ibid., p. 177-191, quotes on p. 186-187.
7   Kymlicka W., Opalski M., eds., *Can Liberal Pluralism be Exported? Western Political Theory and Ethnic Relations in Eastern Europe*, Oxford: Oxford UP, 2001, p. 1.
8   Kymlicka W., "Preface and Acknowledgments", in Kymlicka, Opalski, ibid., p. XII-XVII, quote on p. XII.
9   Weale A., "Toleration, Individual Differences, and Respect for Persons", in Horton J., Mendus S., eds., *Aspects of Toleration*, London/New York: Methuen, 1985, p. 16-35, quote on p. 26.

their part, also experienced ethnically driven struggles. In the Ukrainian case, these were settled by the establishment of the Autonomous Republic of Crimea within Ukraine (60% Russians, 25% Ukrainians, 12% Crimean Tatars). In the other instances, conflicts continue to linger – Karabakh, Abkhazia, South Ossetia, Transnistria. In 1993, Czechoslovakia split over the question how to satisfy the demands of the Slovaks as the largest minority group.

In newly independent Slovakia, sizable minorities have emerged again: Hungarians (10% of the population) and Roma. Russian minorities account for 28% of the Latvian and 25% of the Estonian populations. Ukraine has a Russian population of some 17%, concentrated in the country's Eastern region. In Belarus, Russians comprise 11% of the population, and of the country's two official languages, Russian is much more widely used than Belarusian.

The present situation may be summed up as follows: The numerical proportion of the region's ethno-cultural minorities has considerably declined since the 1930s. Still, the socio-economic and political problems associated with such minorities have not abated proportionally.[10] On the contrary, ideological disorientation, economic anxiety and mounting social inequality have fueled the "rediscovery" of ethnicity as a source of belonging, of identity, of imagined "certainty in an uncertain world".[11]

III

A Central-East European political science focusing on ethno-cultural diversity might seek to advance integration and cultural cross-fertilization, in contrast to discrimination, segmentation, and ensuing socio-political cleavages. Some recent approaches in the region which might point the way toward such a project will now be provided.

The chapter earlier referred to the compact Russian minorities in Latvia and Estonia. Political science disciplines in these two Baltic states have been setting examples regarding comparative, policy-oriented studies on ethnocultural conflict and accommodation. In the case of the Tallinn University's Department of Government, this work has led to involvement in the conceptualization and drafting of Estonia's minority integration policy.[12] In Latvia, led by the non-governmental Latvian Center for Human Rights and Ethnic

10 Liebich A., "Ethnic Minorities and Long-Term Implications of EU Enlargement", in Zielonka J., ed., *Europe Unbound*, London: Routledge, 2002, p. 117-136, esp. p. 117.
11 Durando D., "The Rediscovery of Identity", *Telos* No. 97, 1993, 21-31, quote on p. 26.
12 Pettai V., "Political Science in Estonia: Advantages of Being Small", in Eisfeld, Pal, ibid., p. 119-133, esp. p. 123, 130.

Studies, several institutions have been focusing their research on the role of ethnicity in politics, minority rights and societal integration.[13]

In Ukraine, too, the discipline's evolution has included a focus on ethnopolitics, "born out of the specific need for political science to offer proposals for... preserving territorial unity", against the backdrop of the tendencies for ethnic separatism mentioned earlier.[14] Political science has not produced a comparable thrust in Bulgaria, with its Turkish (nearly 10%) and Roma (5%) populations, nor in Romania and Slovakia with their ethnic Hungarian minorities of 6.5 and 10% respectively.

A decade ago, the noted Canadian political philosopher Will Kymlicka, widely known for his work on multicultural societies, along with East European Studies specialist Magdalena Opalski, undertook the project of inviting a number of academics and writers from Central-East Europe to comment on a liberal-pluralist model of managing ethno-cultural diversity which Kymlicka had prepared. The commentators hailed from Russia, Hungary, Latvia, Estonia, the Czech Republic, Romania, Ukraine. None of the issues they raised and discussed have lost their saliency over the intervening years: perspectives for the further development of civil societies and civic cultures as counter-forces to ethnic nationalism; status and conceivable rights of ethno-cultural groups in relation to those of individuals on the one hand, and of civil and political associations on the other hand; instances of ethno-cultural minorities holding oppressive values vis-à-vis other – internal or external – minorities; different formal and (hardly less important) informal practices in the handling of language interests; pros and cons of federal arrangements and/or territorial autonomy as minority rights regimes.

The resulting volume remains a rich source of sophisticated observations on ethnic relations in the region, including public discourses at popular and elite levels; on the challenges and dilemmas facing attempts to apply the liberal-pluralist approach to Central-East Europe; and – in the two editors' concluding words – on "the immense potential of, and the great need for, new work in this area".[15]

The substantive context of the debate initiated by Kymlicka and Opalski was transition from Communism and consolidation of democracy in the region. In 2008, *Politics and Central Europe*, the journal of the Central European Political Science Association, in a thematic issue entitled "Values and Diversity in Contemporary Europe" shifted the focus to European integration, and, more specifically, toward the quest for an eventual European identity. In an environment characterized by the increasing value pluralism of European

---

13 Ikstens J., "Political Science in Latvia: Learning the Basics", in Eisfeld, Pal, ibid., p. 163-175, esp. p. 164-165.

14 Kruglashov A. M., "Ukrainian Political Science: From Quantity to Quality", in: Eisfeld, Pal, ibid., p. 291-304, quote on p. 294.

15 Kymlicka, Opalski, ibid., p. 9.

societies, how should cultural differences be reconciled? Should Europe seek consistency in the ways such issues were tackled by different countries?[16]

The example selected for discussion was religious symbols in the public space as a salient expression of cultural pluralisation. Two instances must suffice here to indicate the character of the problems scrutinized in the journal's issue. How might religious freedom of expression be guaranteed, and yet the discrimination of certain lifestyles by a specific religion be avoided? On what grounds should religious minorities be allowed to claim special treatment, up to being granted exemptions from general law?

While highly significant for the region, these questions are, of course, not peculiar to Central-East Europe. Rather, their treatment may be hoped to help putting in a better perspective challenges which have emerged across the entire European continent, and also to help dealing with them more reasonably, flexibly and equitably. A regional focus would absolutely not involve detaching political science from its West European or American counterparts, but would – quite the contrary – emphasize its particular contribution to a global scholarly effort.

This has been illustrated by a recent (June, 2010) St. Petersburg conference on "Ethno-Cultural Diversity and the Problem of Tolerance", jointly organized by the Russian Political Science Association, the non-governmental Saint Petersburg Centre for Humanities and Political Studies, and the International Political Science Association's Research Committee on Politics and Ethnicity. Several of the major presentations focused on a central feature of present societies, already mentioned earlier, which the migration component of globalization may be safely predicted to produce on an increasing, rather than a lessening, scale: the resort to ethnicity as a source of social identification and identity – not just for these societies' minorities, but also for their *majorities*.

How much heterogeneity will these majorities accept? How may cultural narratives be advanced, which promote mutual "recognition" and tolerance, rather than separation and conflict? Might "symbolic" politics help in developing such discourses – politics, for instance, which emphasize a civic "Rossiyskij" rather than an ethno-cultural "Russian" polity? Should political science, along the lines of the sociological role model, attempt to develop concepts replacing the idea of a single identity by the notion of "a set of identities", allowing the individual "to participate in various [cultural] communities"?[17]

The issues raised in the cases cited here concern a plethora of challenges with which both policy-makers and any number of individual citizens grap-

16   Strnadová L., "Editorial", *Politics in Central Europe* 4 (2), 2008, p. 2-7, esp. p. 5-6.
17   Kuznetsov A., "Political Science Before a Challenge of Ethno-Cultural Pluralism", in: *Ethno-cultural Diversity and the Problem of Tolerance in a Globalizing World* (Conference Proceedings), St. Petersburg: n. p., 2010, p. 96-110

ple. Political science should particularly support the latter in their search, "help[ing] citizens [to] prepare themselves for various possible futures".[18] Otherwise, "perplexity, distrust, fear" and the intolerance born out of distrust and fear may overwhelm large segments of society.[19]

Finally, the discipline should, whenever necessary – not merely, but certainly also in the Central-East European region, – play the admittedly uncomfortable part of a critical, even an oppositional force. It should be publicly critical of power structures skewed in favour of ethnically privileged majorities (or, for that matter, of politically and economically privileged minorities). In 2007, Estonian political scientists were among those who warned against the removal of the Bronze Soldier memorial in Tallinn, whose razing later sparked two days of violent protest among Russian-speaking youth.[20] If the xenophobic "All for Latvia" Party had been included in that country's next governing coalition, as originally announced by Prime Minister Valdis Dombrovskis, Latvian political scientists might have had reasons for a similar move.

In a region where "hybrid" regimes with more or less authoritarian elements have been emerging alongside consolidated democracies, a discipline, such as the one portrayed here, might emerge as a science of democracy. Such a science would be partisan insofar, as it would pursue research and teaching in a humanist spirit, emphasizing broad societal participation in the shaping of public policies, which would not least be informed by a vision of ethno-cultural non-domination and cross-fertilization.

---

18   Hankiss (note 1), p. 22.
19   Ibid., p. 20.
20   Pettai (note 11), p. 130.

Pluralism may well (re-)emerge as the discipline's dominant paradigm for inquiring into the 21ˢᵗ century's increasingly multi-ethnic, multi-cultural polities – endorsing, as it does (in Giovanni Sartori's pertinent words), the intrinsic worth of cultural diversity in "cross-fertilized" cultures. The concept has a long and diverse history: Between 1915 and 1925, English pluralists, focusing on the fundamentally associative character of society, had called for the democratic control of the various communities of which each individual is a part. From the 1950s to the 1970s, American group-centered pluralism "gave capitalist democracy a little theoretical apparatus which discriminated nicely between this system and other systems with which we as a nation were in rivalrous relations" (Douglas Rae, Yale University). Reacting to increasing criticism of the model's shortcomings on both theoretical and empirical grounds, a few of its main proponents during the 1980s and 1990s returned to pluralism the democratizing dimension which the English pluralists had first supplied. Simultaneously, a debate on the "recognition" and "inclusion" of ethno-cultural – analogous to political – pluralism began to set in, and has since been stepping up. The following chapter reviews a century of pluralist investigation into how economy, civil society and government have been interacting – and how they should interact, if securing broad democratic participation in the shaping of public policies remains a foremost concern. It was first published as a section of the author's edited book Pluralism. Developments in the Theory and Practice of Democracy *(Barbara Budrich Publishers, 2006). The volume's other parts were written by Philip G. Cerny, Avigail Eisenberg, and Theodore J. Lowi.*

Pluralism and Democratic Governance:
A Century of Changing Research Frameworks

I. A Pluralist Perspective on Capitalist Democracy
Empirical Diagnoses, Normative Visions, Legitimating Ideologies

Theorizing about the presumed pluralist structure of Western capitalist societies and about the access pluralist players have in fact, and should have, to the setting of public agendas commenced in earnest a century ago. Emerging in the early 20ᵗʰ century when it was finally recognized that the small, non-industrial community envisaged by "classical" political theory had, for most practical purposes, disappeared, the original variety of pluralism was constructed as a *critical* political theory (cf. Gettell 1924: 470), providing an approach both descriptive and prescriptive.

Even before World War I, business corporations and industrial combines – the first multinationals among them – had risen to prominence, underscoring the unequal distribution of power between labor and capital. However, if continuing entrepreneurial hegemony seemed assured, a century had also passed since Adam Smith's grim dictum that the laboring poor were destined, by "the progress of the division of labor", to remain "as stupid and ignorant as it is possible for a human creature to become" (Smith 1776: 366). After bitter struggles, a labor movement had emerged. Unions had been organized, and in most industrialized countries the right to strike had been won.

Concurrently, the 19th century's rigid class structure was already dissolving. The working class was segmenting into numerous blue- and white-collar strata – groups, in fact – differentiated by vocation and attitude, by income and education and, again, by grossly unequal influence and control both economically and politically.

The intellectual climate seemed to be ready for a "new" political concept, analytical no less than normative, reformulating the notions of freedom and democracy in a determined attempt at attaining the "good society" in the context provided by organized capitalism and the large nation state. The answer was a theory of associations, of positive, interventionist government and of a more participatory political system, with industrial democracy as a complement of political democracy. In 1915, the British Labor Party intellectual Harold J. Laski gave the name "pluralism" to the new approach, borrowing the term from the pragmatist philosophy of William James who had used it to describe the character of a "distributive" reality (in contrast to monist ideas, particularly Hegel's, about a unified "bloc universe").

Less than half a century later, "pressure politics", the lobbying activities by which organized groups, now including labor, were seeking to influence parties, legislatures, governments and administrative bureaucracies, had become increasingly topical. At the same time, against the backdrop of the Cold War, the need was felt for a comprehensive theoretical perspective designed to explain and justify the political systems of the "free world", meaning the United States and post-World War II Western Europe. Stripped of most of its prescriptive – certainly its anticapitalist – implications, reduced to a "legitimating discourse" (Merelman 2003: 9) and in tune with "realistic" Schumpeterian theories of democratic elitism prevalent at the time (see, e.g., Held 2003: 200), the concept of pluralism (supplemented now, more often than not, by the prefix 'liberal' or 'neo-', in contrast to 'radical') seemed to serve the purpose perfectly.

Another five decades later, nation-states in North America, Western Europe and elsewhere are being affected by growing economic-financial globalization and permeation no less than by increasing ethno-cultural pluralization and diversification, due to regional and global migratory movements. The pattern of societal cleavages and linkages is changing, the fragmentation of interests furthered, the role of the positive state is questioned, adherence to traditional institutional loyalties put in jeopardy. How, then, can we accept both economic globalization and the further pluralization of plural societies without, on the one hand, sacrificing electoral responsiveness and governmental accountability and, on the other, furthering a fundamentalization of group values that would, in Arthur Schlesinger's phrase, "disunite" society and polity?

Once again, the concept of pluralism may come to the rescue. Because the concept's endorsement of diversity is considered to include cultural multiplicity, a "revived pluralist perspective" now stands for "full and pluralist cultural inclusiveness" (McLennan 1995: 40) – for the assertion and public expression, the institutionalization even, of ethno-cultural differences, provided that basic rights and principles of justice remain respected and protected. However, it is precisely the extent of differentiated treatment to be accorded to ethnic groups, in order to protect and develop their special cultural characteristics and practices, which has been the subject of continuing controversy. So far, this debate has achieved nothing which even remotely resembles conceptual clarity.

The specific problem illustrates a general point. Every variety of political pluralism so far put forward has been critically challenged: Early radical pluralism by liberal pluralism, with the challenge returned later for good measure; liberal pluralism, in addition, by neo-corporatism; cultural pluralism by a liberal individualism arguing in favor of impartiality. *Actually, there have never been full-fledged "theories" of pluralism, but rather empirical and normative research programs focusing on the means, constraints, and perspectives of societal participation in the shaping of public policies.* Frameworks for these programs have included the web of social organizations which has increasingly been referred to as civil society, the linkages of individuals, associations and governments (ranging from the internal government of associations to the pressures exerted by such organizations on each other and on state administrations), the building of legitimacy, consensus and cohesion on the basis of conflictual interests, the validity of the traditional division into private and public spheres (with ensuing limitations on the applicability of democratic principles), inequalities in the availability of political resources, finally the powers and the rights of majorities and minorities.

In the final analysis, successive pluralist research programs have amounted to nothing less than a persistent inquiry into the theory and practice of democracy under changing socio-economic and socio-cultural conditions.

II. Underpinning Political by Economic Democracy: Harold Laski and the Emergence of Radical Pluralism

As noted at the outset, the first two decades of the 20th century "revealed new problems of economic and political power for which the older democrats, whether liberals or socialists, had no ready solutions" (Beer 1975: IX). American philosophical pragmatism, developed by William James and insisting, as it did, on a "pluralistic" – rather than a monistic – interpretation of the cosmos, assumed "vital significance" for the slowly emerging "pluralistic theory of the state" (Laski 1921: 169; id. 1917: 23): None of reality's elements "includes everything or dominates everything ... The pluralistic world is thus more like a federal republic, than an empire or a kingdom ... However much may be collected, ... something else is self-governed ... and unreduced to unity" (James 1909: 208). Translated into political terms, such a "pluralistic universe" could be construed as a polity where groups, associated for "essential social ends" and "eliciting individual loyalties", evolved naturally, possessing inherent rights not conceded by the state (Coker 1924: 89, 93).

Harold Laski went even further. With "group competing against group", the state, as he would maintain in a 1915 lecture delivered at Columbia University, had to prove its superiority "by virtue of its moral program". Only in this way could it claim obedience from its citizens. And in a typical turn, which heralded the further development of his position, Laski added: "A state may in theory exist to secure the highest life for its members. But when we come to the analysis of the hard facts it becomes painfully apparent that the good actually maintained is that of a certain section, not the community as a whole. I should be prepared to argue, for instance, that in England before the war the ideal of the trade unions was a wider ideal than that which the state had attained" (Laski 1917: 15, 23).

The ideas of the Fabian Society, that intellectual circle of "respectable" socialists – established, among others, by Sidney and Beatrice Webb and George Bernard Shaw – which took part in the formation of the British Labour Party, considerably influenced Harold Laski's thinking. So did the argument of the guild socialists ("young rebels" in the Fabian ranks, building on French anarcho-syndicalism), particularly G. D. H. Cole, who held that associations sprang up in society according to the logic of functional differentiation and that self-government, consequently, was identical with functional representation on every social level (see Eisfeld 1996: 269/270, 272 ss.). That definitely included the workplace, the factory, the enterprise – in a nutshell, "control of production" by worker organizations –, since individuals (having, by steps, been enfranchised in the political sphere) had remained "enslaved" by industrial autocracy in the economic sector (Cole 1918: 40, 103 ss.).

Like Cole, Harold Laski remained convinced that "no political democracy (could) be real" without being underpinned by "an economic democracy" (Laski 1919: 38). Like Cole, too, he initially envisioned that the body politic should be "divide(d) upon the basis of functions", resulting in a dual legislature: a vocational Congress – after a transition period of joint industrial control by labor and capital – and a territorial Parliament. "Joint questions" would have to be solved by "joint adjustment" (Laski 1919b: 74, 87 ss.). Avoiding the term "conflict", Laski made no provision for any mechanism whose role went beyond mere "coordination". A certain "weakness on the constructive side" (Ellis 1923: 596) was apparent.

In his 1925 magnum opus entitled a *Grammar of Politics*, Laski retained two central contentions:

(1) The structure of social organisation involves, not myself and the state, my groups and the state, but all these and their interrelationships ... The interest of the community is the total result of the whole pressure of social forces (Laski 1925: 141, 261).
(2) Exactly as the evolution of political authority has been concerned with the erection of limitations upon the exercise of power, so also with economic authority ... In a sense not less urgent than that in which Lincoln used it, no state can survive that is half-bond and half-free. The citizen ... must be given the power to share in the making of those decisions which affect him as a producer if he is ... to maximize his freedom (ibid.: 112/113).

Repudiating the institutional project of the guild socialists whose difficulties he had come to consider "insurmountable" (ibid.: 72), Laski now focused on that distinction which would remain pivotal to conceptions of democratizing society: the distinction between ownership of the means of production and their control (ibid.: 112):

Just as the holder of government bonds has no control ... over government policy, so it is possible to prevent interference with the direction of an industrial enterprise by the loaners thereto of capital ... The present system of private property does not in the least involve the present technique of industrial direction.

It required the Great Depression of 1929 and the circumstances of the formation of the British National Government in 1931 for Laski to move more clearly in a Marxian direction without, however, as has been erroneously suggested, "rejecting" pluralism (Deane 1955: 153). Rather, by combining pluralism and Marxism, he proposed in 1937 to transcend the capitalist system, envisaging not violent action but, in a term Laski was to coin during World War II, a "revolution by consent" (Laski 1925: XII):

The purpose of pluralism merges into a larger purpose ... The object of the pluralist must be the classless society ... If the main ground of conflict is thus removed, it becomes possible to conceive of a social organization in which the truly federal nature of society receives institutional expression. And in such a social organization, authority can be pluralistic both in form and expression.

In modern terms, Laski's pluralism aimed at a more participatory democracy and an employee-controlled economy, diminishing the discretionary exercise and grossly unequal distribution of organizational – political and economic – power. *'Radical' pluralism, as it came to be called (Apter 1977: 295), emphasized the substantial equality of political resources.*

III. The New Deal and the Cold War as Backdrops: Liberal Pluralism's Focus on the Status Quo

According to Harry Elmer Barnes, writing in the 1921 *American Political Science Review*, both Cole and Laski – besides searching "for some method of social improvement" – could be given credit for having played a part in that "cardinal contribution of sociology to politics": the interpretation of government as the "agency" through which interest groups either "realize their objects, or effect ... (an) adjustment of their aims with the opposing aspirations of other groups". However, Barnes also contended that the "most thorough and comprehensive exposition" of that view could be found not in the works of English pluralists or guild socialists, but in Arthur F. Bentley's *The Process of Government* (Barnes 1921: 495, 512).

Rejecting both individualism and institutionalism, Bentley in his 1908 treatise aimed at introducing the group as the central analytical category. Describing his effort as "strictly empirical ... 'positively' grasp(ing) social facts just for what they are", he went on to argue that every activity could be stated "either on the one side as individual, or on the other side as social group activity". In interpreting social processes, however, the former was "in the main of trifling importance", whereas the latter "is essential, first, last, and all the time" (Bentley 1908: 56, 176, 210, 214/215).

In the United States, Harold Laski's normative considerations were echoed, to a certain extent, by progressive thinkers such as Mary Follett – who argued that the economic philosophy of individualism had resulted in the "crushing of individuals", of "all – but a few" (Follett 1918: 170) – and John Dewey who, like Follett, called for the "positive state", contending that "a measure of the goodness of the state is the degree to which it relieves individuals from the waste of negative struggle" (Dewey 1927: 72; Follett 1918: 182, 184). For a "brief moment", it seemed as if American progressives and British socialist pluralists might join in "accept(ing) the pluralist agenda", and that there might be a realistic chance, after World War I, to construct "a new political and social order" (Stears 2002: 2/3, 261). However, concepts for industrial citizenship did not catch on. In the United States, corporations, "with the full support of Democratic and Republican administrations in Washington", pushed back industrial relations to the practices "of the late nineteenth century". In England, the guild socialist tendency all but disappeared after the trade unions' defeat in the General Strike of 1925. The British Labour Party, subsequently, subscribed to the nationalization, rather than to democratic control, of key industries (Stears 2002: 263, 268).

Still, the behavioral group approach propounded by Bentley, which Barnes judged "the most notable American contribution to political theory", was likewise "neglected" after Bentley's book had first come out (Barnes 1924: 493, 494 n. 18). Eight decades later, informed opinion continued to agree: Bentley's "immediate impact on the discourse of political science" was "minimal" (Gunnell 2004: 105). That situation would change, after a considerable number of pressure group studies had been published in the United States between World Wars I and II, and after the New Deal had finally established organized labor and organized agriculture as industry's "junior partners" in bargaining for political benefits. As more and more social interests organized and 'log-rolling' became the established legislative procedure, the "acceptance of groups as lying at the heart of the process of government" was judged conceptually "unavoidable" (Truman 1951: 46).

For David Truman who, echoing Bentley, would state that "we do not, in fact, find individuals otherwise than in groups", Bentley's analysis had served as "the principal bench mark" (Truman 1951: IX, 48). However, the political system, according to Truman, was not merely accounted for "by the 'sum' of organized interest groups". He included constitutionalism, civil liberties, and representative techniques such as the "rules of the game" among the norms according to which organized groups had to operate. Otherwise, they risked bringing large, still *un*organized "potential" groups into action, whose widely held attitudes and values Bentley had termed the system's "habit background" (Truman 1951: 51, 159, 524; Bentley 1908: 218).

In its entirety, the group concept resembled a modified marketplace model ('interest-group liberalism', in Theodore Lowi's term): "The notion of individual competition is replaced by a network of organizational competition ... This makes for a system of countervailing powers" (Apter 1977: 312, 314/315). That "central ingredient of a stable pluralist democratic system" (ibid.: 355/356), countervailing power, was supposedly guaranteed by a "natural self-balancing factor ... almost amount(ing) to a law" – in other words, Adam Smith's 'invisible hand' in new clothes: "Nearly every vigorous push in one direction stimulates an opponent or a coalition of opponents to push in the opposite direction" (Milbrath 1955: 365; see also Kornhauser 1961: 130). Resulting from ever-present counterbalancing tendencies, "tam(ing), civiliz(ing), ... and limit(ing) power to decent human purposes", competing "multiple centers of power" were supposed to resolve conflicts "to the mutual benefit of all parties" (Dahl 1967: 24).

The group theorists' 'analytical' (Latham 1952: 9) or 'sociological' (Lijphart 1968: 2n.) pluralism, while claiming to disregard considerations of a normative kind, was admittedly biased toward group leadership. It was, in fact, an elite model, according to which leaders of associations conducted the process of organized pressure and bargaining, thereby "control (ling) each other" (Dahl/Lindblom 1953: 23, 325/326). Control *among* leaders, however, provided but one significant attribute of the political process. A second was control *of* leaders by means of periodic elections, holding them accountable to party or interest group members, and to the electorate at large. "Civic trust in leaders, and leaders' responsiveness to potential interest group claims might be expected to do the rest" (McLennan 1995: 35/36).

The Cold War confrontation encouraged the introduction of a more or less explicitly normative element into the concept. The rise of fascism and, more importantly after 1945, of communism were interpreted to demonstrate the dangers of mass movements. Because in Western political systems leaders were assumed to have been "socialized into the dominant values ... of industrial society", politics of group leadership were supposed to ensure moderate, rational conflict, serving as a demarcation line domestically against radicalism and the "irrationality and chaos" of mass politics, internationally against totalitarianism (Rogin 1967: 10, 15; see also Nicholls 1974: 25).

Liberal pluralism "portrayed capitalist democracy in a favorable light and gave it a little theoretical apparatus which discriminated nicely between this system and other systems with which we as a nation were in rivalrous relations" (Douglas Rae, quoted by Merelman 2003: 50/51). Put otherwise, the static descriptive (see Rothman 1960: 31/32) and the anti-totalitarian normative dimension blended in a manner to ensure the "astonishing career" (Steffani 1980: 9) of pluralism as a "public philosophy" which "public men" grew accustomed to use rather instinctively both as guideline and justification for their policies (see Lowi 1967: passim, and id. 1979: 51 ss.). Substantiation of the argument is provided by two not untypical examples, both a decade and a continent apart: When the Portuguese "revolution of carnations" seemed to veer to the left during 1974/75, the European Community's Council of Heads of State and Government declared "that the EC, because of its political and historical tradition, can grant support only to a pluralist democracy" (Commission 1976: 8). And in the United States, the National Endowment for Democracy (NED) was set up by the early 1980s with a view to promoting "American-style pluralist societies" (*New York Times* 1984: B 10).

In politics as in political science, "pluralism's flexibility, adaptability, terminological simplicity" (Merelman 2003: 117; also ibid.: 123) helped to spread the discourse. The quote by Winfried Steffani referred to West Germany, where every major political party, as Steffani showed, professed to back "free and pluralist democracy". In post-World War II Germany, the experience by many of intellectual exile in the United States during the Nazi regime had favored the emergence of a 'neo'-pluralist concept largely analogous to the American model (and indeed influenced by David Truman's argument; cf. Eisfeld 1998: 394/395). The approach was judged in retrospect "probably the most important product of the early stage of (West-German) political science" (Blanke et al. 1975: 76):

Not only could 'neo'-pluralism lay claim to putting the theory of parliamentary democracy on a new footing; it also won wide acceptance beyond the discipline of political science. Explicitly substituting totalitarianism – "the construct beyond the 'Iron Curtain' and the Wall" (Fraenkel 1968: 165) – for monism as the principal counterpart to pluralism, it also served as a perfect Cold War term. Ernst Fraenkel who had initially embraced the notion with some hesitation (cf. id. 1957: 236), only to push it the more vigorously later, bluntly professed that neo-pluralism was "fighting – to say nothing of Hitler's shadow – the much less faded shadow of Stalin" (Fraenkel 1968: 187). The simplified 'neo'-pluralism/totalitarianism dichotomy would soon prove a major reason for questioning the model (Eisfeld 1972: 86; Kremendahl 1977: 209/210).

Liberal pluralists usually conceded that income, education and status were apt to determine, to a considerable extent, political activity, including control of leaders and access to government (Truman 1951: 265; Dahl/Lindblom 1953: 315). They also noted that these resources were not merely unequally distributed between business and labor (Truman 1951: ibid.), but that the system offered "unusual" opportunities for "pyramiding" such resources into structures of social power (Dahl 1963: 227). However, the prospects for "citizens weak in resources" to influence government – principally by associating with others – were not seriously questioned, because "probably no resource is uniformly most effective in American politics" (Dahl 1967: 378; see also id. 1963: 228). *Generally, it was formal equality of opportunity which liberal pluralism emphasized.*

IV. Democratizing Economy and Society: Dahl's and Lindblom's Transformation of Liberal Pluralism

During the late 1960s, when the Cold War had thawed, when radical dissent over ever more massive American bombing in Vietnam brought the "armies of the night" converging on Washington and Lyndon Johnson's vision of a Great Society succumbed to the exigencies of the same Vietnam War, the then president of the American Political Association felt bound to note that political scientists, "in some considerable measure, (had) worn collective blinkers". Their restricted vision had prevented them from recognizing major flaws in current interpretations of democracy, making them susceptible to "governmental interpretations of American interests ... both at home and abroad" (Easton 1969: 1057). David Easton therefore supported a rearrangement of research priorities "in the light of a better understanding of own value assumptions", including the construction of political alternatives, rather than "uncritically acquiesc(ing) in prevailing politics" (id.: 1058/1059, 1061). Robert Dahl and Charles Lindblom, having turned more skeptical and radical in their assessments, later explained their earlier commitment to the ongoing political system in sentences that read like a comment on Easton's statement: "The New Deal was not a remote historical episode. It provided grounds for thinking that reform periods would again occur with some frequency" (Dahl/Lindblom 1976: XXX; see also David Mayhew in a 1997 interview, quoted by Merelman 2003: 85: "Pluralism [was] a New Dealish philosophy"). In looking back on his career a few years earlier, German political scientist and sometime emigré Ernst Fraenkel likewise attributed his "development of a pluralist model of democracy" to "the experience of the 'Roosevelt Revolution'" when labor and agriculture had been recognized as political players alongside business (Fraenkel 1973: 26).

Looking for ways to remedy what Dahl eventually would identify as the "dilemmas of pluralist democracy", Dahl and Lindblom singled out the large business corporation – the "corporate leviathan" (Dahl 1970: 117) – as the major target for structural, participatory reforms. To a remarkable extent, liberal pluralist thinking (unlike Laski's radical pluralism) had previously failed to diagnose and analyze economic constraints. No systematic consequences had been drawn from the acknowledgment that oligopoly, "the most frequent market form of modern (capitalist) economies", and the resulting monopolistic competition are "group phenomena" (Latham 1952: 5). Instead, as shown by the quotes included above, it had been maintained as a general supposition that "organization begets counter-organization" (Latham 1952: 31).

In a manner reminiscent of Harold Laski's earlier argument, but more systematically, Dahl and Lindblom now focused their analysis on the transformation of the privately owned and managed firm into the joint-stock company, the ensuing divorce between property and control, and the exercise, by the large corporation, of power comparable to that of states: "The small family enterprise run by its owner became the large enterprise in which operation was separated from ownership. The ideology of the private enterprise of farmer and small merchant was transferred (, however,) more or less intact to the big corporation ... (even if) nothing could be less appropriate than to consider the giant firm a *private* enterprise" (Dahl 1970: 119/120; also Dahl/Lindblom 1976: XXVIII).

Nothing could be less appropriate, because business corporations – with regard to sales, assets, numbers of employees, the impact of their pricing, investment, and financing policies – had developed into *social and public* institutions, "political bodies" with an "internal government". As Dahl and Lindblom went on to emphasize, because of the persisting application of the ideology of private ownership to the large corporation "excessive weight (is given) to the particularistic interests of managers and investors" (Dahl/Lindblom 1976: XXIX). The ensuing "privileged position of business" – and of "corporate executives in particular" – involves the capacity to distort public policies, or – should undesirable measures nevertheless be legislated – to contract out from under the effects of such legislation (Dahl 1982: 40 ss.). Thus, it "restrict(s) polyarchical rules and procedures (i.e. those approximating democracy) to no more than a part of government and politics, and ... challenge(s) them even there" (Lindblom 1977: 172, 190).

Suggesting that corporate "rulers" were subject neither to effective internal control by stockholders, nor to adequate external control by governments and markets, Dahl went on to propose a determined effort at further democratization – the "enfranchisement" of blue- and white-collar employees, realizing industrial self-government in the sense originally propounded by Harold Laski (Dahl 1982: 199, 204; Dahl 1989: 327 ss., 331/332). Dahl's position may not have been one "with any clear sense of its connections to the past" (Gunnell 2004: 235), even if in one instance he did acknowledge that, by the late 1930s, he had "read Laski", and that he and Lindblom "were familiar with the British ... ideas about pluralism" (Dahl 1986: 234, 282 n. 11). At any rate, the following quote might have come straight from Laski's *Grammar of Politics*:

To say that people are entitled to the fruits of their labor is not to say that investors are entitled to govern the firms in which they invest" (Dahl 1989: 330).

In Germany, a distinct "Laski School" (Detjen 1988: 63) had emerged by this time whose exponents, not unlike Dahl and Lindblom, argued in favor of "democratizing" the economy and, by fusing everyday "social" with "political" activity, developing perceptions and qualifications conducive to a more participatory political process (Eisfeld 1972: 21, 103; Bermbach/Nuscheler 1973: 11; Nuscheler 1980: 158/159). Pointing to the legitimating functions of the established pluralist discourse (Eisfeld 1972: 85/86; Bermbach/Nuscheler 1973: 10; Nuscheler 1980: 157), these writers also took pains to emphasize the inequality of political resources and, consequently, the limited representativeness of interest groups – pluralism "as a smokescreen for the realpolitik of elite accommodation" (Garson 1978: 157).

In the United States, the indictment of pluralism's egalitarian shortcomings by Dahl and Lindblom amounted to an "internal transformation" of the concept by two of its leading exponents (McLennan 1995: 4). Earlier critiques of the model's shortcomings had served as forerunners. Liberal pluralists had argued that cross-cutting pressures from overlapping group memberships affecting an individual were apt to promote "compromise through bargaining" (Truman 1951: 162/163, 166; Dahl/Lindblom 1953: 329). In the last instance, conflicting group loyalties supposedly served to advance "a high degree of liberty *and* consent" (Kornhauser 1961: 80). Allusions to political apathy had at least surfaced as a quite different possible outcome in the texts of both Truman and Dahl/Lindblom, even if neither had pursued the implications for democratic politics. A more detailed examination based on the same empirical findings would conclude that apathy, in practice, may either mean frustration, the "compartmentalization of simultaneously maintained loyalties", or "non-rational adaptation" – in other words, inertia and docility (Mitchell 1963, as quoted by Lijphart 1968: 11; Eckstein 1966: 72 ss.).

Severe doubt was thus cast on the supposedly democratic effects of liberal pluralism's central provisions. In addition, it was demonstrated that the entire model of group interaction "breaks down" (Rothman 1960: 23) if the concept's reasoning is reversed, as Truman had done in his book's concluding chapter. Defining, as will be recalled, *potential* groups in terms of "widely held", but "unorganized" interests (i. e. attitudes), Truman had singled out "multiple memberships" in these *potential* groups as the political system's "balance wheel" – in other words, the polity's decisive factor (Truman 1951: 512, 514). He had thereby resorted to a "deus ex machina" which could be brought in "for any purpose" (Rothman 1960: 23; see also Lowi 1979: 37).

Closer examination of the countervailing-power hypothesis shattered a final corner-stone of liberal pluralism. Even if this particular debate largely focused on the specific economic form given to the argument by John Kenneth Galbraith– according to whom "in the typical American market", private economic power was supposed to generate "the countervailing power of those who are subject to it" (Galbraith 1956: 125, 151, 182) –, still it had something generally applicable to say about the "romantic" attribution of "proxy-mindedness" to organizational oligopolies (Stigler 1954: 9/10). The concept, as was shown, basically amounted to a philosophy of "perpetual stalemate" which made it conservative in impact and undemocratic in action (McCord Wright 1954: 14; see also Lowi 1967: 20). In addition, the critique of the countervailing-power scenario suggested other analyses that depicted today's large-scale organizations as "unwieldy", "unresponsive" – to changes in their environments – and "insensitive" – to the need for flexibility. Cumbersome and immune to internal or external control, they were charged with generating alienated, angry and/or apathetic individuals who "feed streams of hostility and aggressiveness into both domestic and international affairs" (McClelland 1965: 268).

If the liberal variety of pluralism emerged distinctly frayed from the melee, the debate had also emphasized the normative challenge posed by pluralism's inherent anti-monist, anti-hierarchical, participatory implications. Radical pluralist propositions, such as those put forward by Robert Dahl from the mid-1970s, have consequently merged into the larger, more comprehensive debate on democratization, a "spill-over" of democratic norms onto economy and society. The attribute "political" has thus been reconceptualized, now relating to any form of group decision-making. Pluralist democratization would be intended to make "all societal sectors more responsive to their members" and thereby society as a whole "more receptive" to its own pivotal value – the norm of political equality (Etzioni 1968: 6).

Actual evidence is ambiguous as to what extent such visions of increased citizen competence and control might be accepted, internalized, or practiced by increasing segments of "consumption-oriented, acquisitive (and) privatistic" societies (Dahl 1970: 135). Experiences with isolated "participatory environments" do not automatically promote general orientations furthering broad social change in a more egalitarian direction (see Greenberg 1981). The present situation not only warrants further research, but more participatory experimentation. This seems unlikely, however, as democratic governance is being delegitimized under the impact of the increasingly "hegemonic" neo-liberal discourse accepted by governmental and market players alike who rival each other in "reinvent(ing)" and reorganizing the state "along the lines of private industry" as a "quasi-'enterprise association'" bent on cutting outlays and proving competitiveness (Cerny 1997: 251, 256, 269; id. 1999: 2).

V. The Rise and Demise of the Neo-Corporatist Alternative

On top of the reemergence of radical pluralism, likewise taking "a less benign view of the democratic credentials of group politics" in comparison to liberal pluralists (Williamson 1989: 3), neo- or liberal corporatism was the second conceptual challenge to confront liberal pluralism during the early 1970s. By the mid-sixties, Stein Rokkan had already characterized "established" triangular interest representation in Norway as "corporate pluralist" – labor, farming and business interests maintaining existing inequalities by conspicuously excluding the unorganized from bargaining processes at the top, as "corporate pluralist" (Rokkan 1966: 105). Referring to the post-World War I involvement of organized business interests with public administrations in formulating economic policies to "recast bourgeois Europe", Charles Maier had also used the term "corporate pluralismto label such interplay (Maier 1974: 202 ss.; and id. 1975: 353/354, 543).

Neo-corporatists, with Philippe Schmitter and Gerhard Lehmbruch in the forefront, now focused more systematically on "institutionalized patterns" of policy formulation and implementation, in which organized business and organized labor "cooperate(d) with each other and with public authorities" at the leadership level, controlling and mobilizing group members in a top-down process (Lehmbruch 1979: 150, 152; Panitch 1979: 123; Jessop 1979: 200). Such patterns required the involved leaders' commitment "to the overall legitimacy of the existing economic system", expressed in their willingness to "confin(e) themselves to demands", or to push for compromises, compatible with steady economic growth (Jessop 1979: ibid.).

Consequently, the neo-corporatist school of thought has insisted that

(1) the "social and economic attributes around which interests organize" are "unequally distributed",
(2) that such "socio-economic inequalities are reflected in, and indeed reinforced by, the politics of organized interests", not least because
(3) certain associations, particularly organized business and organized labor, are "granted privileged access" to governmental decision-making processes,
(4) that political processes typically take the form of oligarchically structured "interest intermediation" through a "closed process of bargaining" among leaders, "consciously or not" guided by efforts at promoting system stabilization, rather than interest maximization, and implying
(5) that involved associations, far from providing "valuable route(s) to participation", allow leaders "a regulatory role over their members" (Williamson 1989: 2/3, 68/69).

Proponents of corporatism and liberal pluralism alike have usually conceded that pluralist and corporatist arrangements more often than not may occur in mixed combinations, with (West) Germany providing a typical example (see, e.g., Beyme 1979: 238, 241; Streeck 1983: 279). Both varieties may, in fact, not perform too differently, considering what liberal pluralism had to say about bargaining among leaders and about the possible "pyramiding" of unequally distributed political resources.

Because trade union leaders may be expected to face particularly difficult tasks in "delivering their members" on agreements reached, the involvement of social democratic parties as predominant players *able to secure trade union support* has been considered a salient requirement of corporatist structures (Panitch 1979: 129/130; Jessop 1979: 207/208). As conclusively demonstrated by recent French and German experience, that condition was linked, in its turn, to a "fair-weather" situation of high economic growth, allowing for high real wages and high welfare benefits. The social democratic/trade union alliance was eroded when governments led by social democratic parties, accepting the notion of international "competitiveness" as the new social and economic orthodoxy, joined conservative administrations in attempts at mediating the consequences of globalization by the pursuit of deregulatory and privatization policies (Cerny 1997: 258 ss.). Recent developments have not borne out optimistic contentions that social democratic corporatism could be expected to remain politically and economically viable, because it provided not just a profitable, but also a stable "home for business" (Garrett 1998: 155, 157).

Corporatism, moreover, had always remained very much a "Europeanist" concept. With regard to the United States, observers continued to note "the strength of corporate business in the circles of decision" (Salisbury 1979: 213) even in the brief historical moment when the Nixon administration, during the early 1970s, seemed to be endorsing a corporatist solution. After that attempt had been abandoned, it was diagnosed that precisely because of that political strength, "and the concomitant weakness of labor", no genuine interest in such an arrangement existed on the part of the American business elite (Salisbury 1979: 228).

In present-day European polities, too, with "pro-market state intervention on the increase", and governments ever more determinedly "underperforming" with regard to regulation and public services, tripartite neo-corporatist arrangements including trade unions are replaced by a more assertive reemergence of "overarching" corporate hegemony (Cerny 1999a: 19/20). Or one could use the term 'corporate pluralism', lately preferred by Theodore J. Lowi, for a constellation which radical pluralists had diagnosed much earlier. By transferring production facilities and investment outlays between countries, shifting profits via transfer-pricing, and moving large amounts of liquid assets, multinational companies had long been able to opt out of the effects of national economic policies. The monetary and fiscal tools of legislative and governmental interventionism were already proving inadequate. With the progress of globalization, the mere threat by large transnational corporations of moving capital or economic enterprise out of the country has now gained so much in credibility that it "radically eats into the capacity" of legislatures. To comply with the demands of international investors and foreign competitive pressures, welfare states "must be traded down to minimal safety nets". Corporate hegemony means that "business has acquired veto power in economic policy" (Hirst 2004: 155; Ringen 2004: 4).

VI. The Ethno-cultural Issue: Toward a Politics of Pluralist Inclusion?

In the increasingly multicultural Western-type societies which the migration component of globalization has entailed, mounting social inequalities and economic insecurities rank high among the factors which have been fueling the rediscovery of ethnicity as a source of belonging, of ostensible "certainty in an uncertain world" (Durando 1993: 26). As far back as three decades ago, analysts recorded a pronounced growth in tendencies by persons in many countries to insist on the significance of their groups' distinctiveness and, consequently, in the "salience of ethnic-based" (as against class-based, "which of course continue to exist") "forms of social identification and conflict" (Glazer/Moynihan 1975: 3, 7).

With these developments in mind, two arguments were advanced in favor of applying the norms of political pluralism to the problems posed by accepting ("recognizing") the cultural, religious, and linguistic heterogeneity of different ethnic groups, without inviting further societal segmentalization:

(1) Because pre-World War II strands of pluralist theory included the roles that associations play in individual self-development as a central theme, "striking similarities" were suggested to exist between these approaches and "the new theories of difference and identity" in a multicultural context. A 'reconstructed' normative theory of pluralism, it was argued, ought to provide for every individual's chance of both "engagement and disengagement with groups" to develop a "critical perspective" (Eisenberg 1995: 1, 3, 188, 190). Pluralism therefore should assess political systems not least "in terms of whether they contribute to the well-being of societal (i.e. ethno-cultural) groups".

(2) Because pluralism affirmed the belief "in the worth of diversity", the notion was held to "endorse", first and foremost, "cultural multiplicity" in the sense of a "cross-fertilized" rather than a "tribalized" culture (Sartori 1997: 60/61, 62).

Like political pluralism, the idea of cultural pluralism had also been inspired by William James' philosophy (see Menand 2001: 379, 388). When the term "cultural pluralism" was first introduced by Horace M. Kallen in 1924, immigrant subcultures were flourishing in the eastern United States, after nearly 15 million immigrants – mostly from southern and eastern Europe – had been admitted to the country between 1901 and 1920 (id. 2001: 381). Writing between 1915 and 1924, arguing against assimilationist pressures and "melting pot" conformity, Kallen offered his vision of a "commonwealth of cultures", a "federated republic" of different nationalities (Kallen 1924: 11, 116). Convinced that self-government was impossible without "self-realization", that the latter – in the sense of personal identity – hinged upon the assertion of ethnic differences, and that society's creativity would benefit from such heterogeneous strains, he proposed granting equal treatment to each ethnocultural tradition.

Cultural pluralism, as advocated by Kallen, evidently requires a measure of "structural" pluralism (Gordon 1975: 85, 88): To persist, ethnic groups, co-existing within the same society, must maintain some separation from each other. Policies of differentiated group treatment – e.g., affirmative action; official multilingualism; a composition of political agencies reflecting the existence of various ethnic groups – may work to reinforce both cultural and structural pluralism. To be effective, such policies need to show an awareness of the connection between cultural and economic power or, in other terms, between "workable" recognition and concomitant re-distributive measures (Phillips 2004: 71, 75). *Radical ethno-cultural pluralism* – to avoid Milton Gordon's rather confusing term "corporate pluralism", meant to denote that the approach focuses on group rights (see Gordon 1975: 106; id. 1981: 182 ss.) –, *in analogy to radical political pluralism, emphasizes equality of condition.*

Such pluralism is in opposition to public policies that remain neutral toward ethnocultural differences: Neutrality implies that discrimination on ethnic grounds is legally prohibited, while benefits are provided according to individual eligibility. "The unit of attribution for equity considerations is always and irrevocably the individual" (Gordon 1981: 184). For that model, Gordon has retained the term liberal pluralism (see id. 1975: 105/106; id. 1981: 184). *Again, it is equality of opportunity which the liberal-pluralist approach emphasizes.*

Most of the relevant debate has been centering on the controversial relation existing between "pluralism and liberal neutrality", as one volume's title has summarized the central issue (see Bellamy/Hollis 1999). Should liberal principles and procedures be reinterpreted in scope and character, or – as maintained by, e.g., Chandran Kukathas – "is there insufficient reason to abandon, modify or reinterpret liberalism", for "its very emphasis on *individual* rights ... bespeaks ... wariness of the power of the majority over minorities" (Kukathas 1997: 230)? Would not any determined movement in the direction of group rights imply that "the individual's claim to be considered only as an individual, regardless of race, color, or national origin", will be irrevocably reduced (Glazer 1997: 137)? Might the acceptance of such rights, even inadvertently, work to endanger individual autonomy, to bar individuals from "opting out" of their group by adopting ideas and practices running counter to their ethnocultural heritage? Obviously, "groups as well as the state might violate ... individual rights" (Van Dyke 1976/77: 368).

More basically, where Bentley and Truman had favored the group as the primary unit, they were arguing in *analytical* terms. If the individual could always be found within groups, as both insisted, these were groups "of his *choice*" (Goulbourne 1991: 224). Conceptions of ethnocultural recognition and inclusion have, however, tended to assign a *normative* priority to their groups. The inadvertent result might consist in confining individuals to a premodern, neo-feudal "*ascribed* group definition and status" (Goulbourne 1991: ibid.).

Should not, consequently – and so as to avoid the promotion of "ethnic sectarianism" (Waldron 1997: 113) –, compromises rather than clear-cut solutions be sought? Bellamy, for one, has argued in favor of a politics of continuing "negotiated compromise" as a central feature of democratic processes guided by a vision of "non-domination, mutual acceptance and accommodation" (Bellamy 1999: 138). Such compromises might most likely be worked out in those cases where a "definite assessment of the oppression, discrimination and persistent exclusion of (a particular) group is possible" and the conflict with liberal principles thus "less sharp" (Galeotti 1999: 50). A pluralist politics informed by a spirit of both political participation and social justice clearly would concede such groups "some" political standing and "some" legal rights (Walzer 1997: 149). Clearly, then, elements of the corporate model should be introduced into liberal pluralism – but to what extent?

Available options (which, of course, may overlap) include legal protection and public funding for the expression of cultural pecularities; federalism as a form of self-government; finally group-based political representation, up to the complex arrangements of consociationalism, which have been attracting "increasing attention" as devices for "overcoming ethnic cleavages by political accommodation" (Stanovcic 1992: 368; see also Kymlicka 1995: chs. 2, 7). A general argument advanced in favor of such politics of recognition/inclusion has been that, while "the sense of being a distinct nation within a larger country" is indeed "potentially destabilizing", the "denial of self-government rights is also destabilizing, since it encourages resentment and even secession" (Kymlicka 1995: 192). Put in optimistic terms (and contrasting with Arthur Schlesinger's fears quoted at the outset), group-differentiated citizenship may result in the ability of "the plural state, unlike the liberal state, ... to offer an emotional identity with the whole to counterbalance the emotional loyalties to ethnic and religious communities, which should prevent the fragmentation of society into narrow, selfish communalism" (Modood 1999: 88).

Consociationalism, identical with a high degree of group-based political representation, includes the following basic elements (Lijphart 1977: 25): Considerable autonomy for each involved group in the management of its internal affairs; application of a proportional standard in political representation, civil service appointments, and allocation of financial resources; right of mutual veto in governmental decision-making; finally, joint government by an either official or unofficial grand coalition of group leaders.

In a case study of consociational democracy in the Netherlands during the 1950s and 1960s, a number of significant negative consequences had been spelled out – elite predominance, the arcane character of negotiations, a large measure of political immobilism (Lijphart 1968: 111, 129, 131). At an even more basic level, group autonomy (as already indicated above) may involve internal restrictions on the right of individual members "to question and dissent from traditional practices" (Kymlicka 1995: 154) – barriers which run counter to a liberal conception of minority rights: Groups "cannot act rightly in ways that disempower individuals ... from living successfully outside their bounds" (Galston 2002: 104).

In addition, immobilism – which Lijphart concedes to be "the gravest problem" (Liphart 1977: 51) – may lead to morally reprehensible deadlocks

46

by "entrench(ing) an unjust status quo" (Bellamy/Hollis 1999: 75; see also Bellamy 1999: 127). The right of mutual veto in matters of public policy amounts to "concurrent", in John C. Calhoun's term, rather than numerical majority rule, and Calhoun's proposal for such a procedure was designed at the time to put America's pre-Civil War south in a position for "effectively block(ing) ... deliberation of the slavery question" (Bellamy/Hollis 1999: 74). Thus, expectations may not be met that a high degree of group-based political representation would contribute to a more vibrant democracy.

VII. The Challenge of Participatory Pluralism in a Globalizing World

The same issues have kept resurfacing during this overview of research on pluralism and democracy: A grossly unequal distribution of political resources; skewed power structures; a "centripetal politics" enacted – even before the advent of globalization – by a web of governmental-corporate centers proceeding in "partnership" (Ionescu 1975: 8/9). As a research framework for inquiring into these problems which will persist to haunt 21st century democracy, pluralism – it should be repeated – will be of continuing relevance if it reverts to the role of a "critical political theory" (Gettell 1924: 470). It must be critical, as it sporadically has been, about the status quo of concentrated economic and political power.

Such a radical pluralist approach may start from where early pluralists – Harold Laski and Mary Follett in particular – had left off in their attempt to define the social obligations of both business corporations and trade unions, and to surmount the unequal distribution of power between capital and labor (see Laski 1921: 97/98. 272 ss., 289 ss.; Follett 1918: 170). It may build on Robert Dahl's and Charles Lindblom's analyses and on Dahl's ensuing proposal to "achieve the best potentialities of pluralist democracy" by realizing what Dahl termed "a third democratic transformation": democratic internal government of economic enterprises (Dahl 1982: 47, 110, 170; id. 1989: 312, 327/328, 331/332).

Resorting to an analysis guided by a set of group-centered propositions, a radical pluralist approach is able to explain the segmentation of class structures into blue and white collar strata differentiated by vocation and attitude; the emergence of additional patterns of ethnocultural cleavages exacerbated by economic injustices; the continuing inequalities of economic influence and control, equivalent to so many structurally embedded participatory barriers; basic origins of social passivity and depoliticization; resulting unequal chances for the organized representation of interests; limits of redistributive and regulatory public policies before and since the onset of globalization; the weakening of state legitimacy due to the downsizing of public budgets and the reduction of resources available for allocation by representatives to constituents (e.g., Eisfeld 1986: 281/282; Putzel 2005: 12). The normative challenge posed by pluralist analysis thus becomes apparent: At the very moment in history when the power and the accountability of democratic governance are literally bleeding away, when – consequently – the reasons "for high levels of citizen loyalty to the state or active commitment to the democratic process" are disappearing fast (Hirst 2004: 155), a determined effort at democratization merits to be once again put high on the agenda of our thinking about democracy.

References

Apter, David E. (1977): Introduction to Political Analysis, Cambridge: Winthrop
Barnes, Harry Elmer (1921): "Some Contributions of Sociology to Modern Political Theory", *American Political Science Review* XV, 487-533.
Beer, Samuel H. (1975): "Introduction", in: Webb, Sidney/Webb, Beatrice, eds.: *A Constitution for the Socialist Commonwealth of Great Britain*, London: Longmans, Green, IX- XXXIII.
Bellamy, Richard (1999): *Pluralism and Liberalism*, London/New York: Routledge
Bellamy, Richard/Hollis, Martin, eds. (1999): *Pluralism and Liberal Neutrality*, Portland: Frank Cass.
Bellamy, Richard/Hollis, Martin (1999): "Consensus, Neutrality and Compromise", in: Bellamy/Hollis, op. cit., 54-78.
Bentley, Arthur F. (1949): *The Process of Government*, Evanston: Principia.
Bermbach, Udo/Nuscheler, Franz, eds. (1973): *Sozialistischer Pluralismus*, Hamburg: Hoffmann & Campe.
Beyme, Klaus von (1979): "Der Neo-Korporatismus und die Politik des begrenzten Pluralis-mus in der Bundesrepublik", in: Habermas, Jürgen, ed.: *Stichworte zur 'Geistigen Situation der Zeit*, Frankfurt: Suhrkamp, 229-247.
Blanke, Bernhard/Jürgens, Ulrich/Kastendiek, Hans (1975): *Kritik der Politischen Wissenschaft* 1, Frankfurt: Campus.
Cerny, Philip G. (1997): "Paradoxes of the Competition State: The Dynamics of Political Globalization", *Government and Opposition* 32, 251-274.
Cerny, Philip G. (1999): "Globalization and the Erosion of Democracy", *European Journal of Political Research* 36, 1-26.
Coker, Francis W. (1924): "Pluralistic Theories and the Attack on State Sovereignty", in: Merriam, Charles E./Barnes, Harry E., eds.: *A History of Political Theories*, Vol. 4, New York: Macmillan, 80-117.
Cole, G. D. H. (1918): *Self-government in Industry*, London: G. Bell and Sons.
Commission of the European Communities (1976): *Die Beziehungen zwischen der EG und Portugal*, Brussels: European Communities.
Dahl, Robert A. (1967): *Pluralist Democracy in the United States: Conflict and Consent*, Chicago: Rand McNally.

Dahl, Robert A. (1970): *After the Revolution? Authority in a Good Society*, New Haven: Yale University Press.

Dahl, Robert A. (1982): *Dilemmas of Pluralist Democracy*, New Haven: Yale University Press.

Dahl, Robert A. (1986): *Democracy, Liberty, and Equality*, Oslo: Norwegian University Press.

Dahl, Robert A. (1989): *Democracy and Its Critics*, New Haven: Yale University Press.

Dahl, Robert A./Lindblom, Charles E. (1953): *Politics, Economics and Welfare*, Chicago: Chicago University Press.

Dahl, Robert A./Lindblom, Charles E. (1976): "Preface", in: Re-Issue of Dahl/Lindblom, op. cit., XXI-XLIV.

Deane, Harold A. (1955): *The Political Ideas of Harold J. Laski*, New York: Columbia Univer-sity Press.

Detjen, Joachim (1988): *Neopluralismus und Naturrecht*, Paderborn: Schöningh

Dewey, John (1927): *The Public and its Problems*, Denver: Swallow.

Durando, Dario (1993): "The Rediscovery of Identity", *Telos*, No. 115, 117-144

Easton, David (1969): "The New Revolution in Political Science", *American Political Science Review* LXIII, 1051-1061.

Eckstein, Harry (1966): *Division and Cohesion in Democracy*, Princeton: Princeton University Press.

Eisenberg, Avigail E. (1995): *Reconstructing Political Pluralism*, Albany: SUNY Press.

Eisfeld, Rainer (1972): *Pluralismus zwischen Liberalismus und Sozialismus*, Stuttgart: Kohlhammer.

Eisfeld, Rainer (1986): "Pluralism as a Critical Political Theory", *Praxis International* 6, 277-293.

Eisfeld, Rainer (1996): "The Emergence and Meaning of Socialist Pluralism", *International Political Science Review* 17, 267-279.

Eisfeld, Rainer (1998): "From Hegelianism to Neo-pluralism: the Uneasy Relationship Between Private and Public Interest in Germany", *International Review of Sociology* 8, 389-396.

Ellis, Ellen D. (1923): "Guild Socialism and Pluralism", *American Political Science Review* XVII, 584-596.

Engelstad, Fredrik/Østerud, Øyvind, eds. (2004): *Power and Democracy*, Aldershot: Ashgate.

Etzioni, Amitai (1968): *The Active Society*, London/New York: Free Press.

Follett, Mary P. (1918): *The New State*, New York: Longmans, Green.

Fraenkel, Ernst (1957): "Pluralismus", in: Fraenkel, Ernst/Bracher, Karl Dietrich, eds.: *Fischer Lexikon Staat und Politik*, Frankfurt: S. Fischer, 234-236.

Fraenkel, Ernst (1968): *Deutschland und die westlichen Demokratien*, Stuttgart: Kohlhammer.

Fraenkel, Ernst (1973): "Anstatt einer Vorrede", in: id., *Reformismus und Pluralismus*, Falk Esche/Frank Grube, eds., Hamburg: Hoffmann & Campe, 11-26.

Galbraith, John Kenneth (1956): *American Capitalism. The Concept of Countervailing Power*, Boston: Houghton Mifflin.

Galeotti, Anna Elisabetta (1999): "Neutrality and Recognition", in: Bellamy/Hollis, eds., op. cit., 37-53.

Galston, William A. (2002): *Liberal Pluralism*, Cambridge/New York: Cambridge University Press.

Garrett, Geoffrey (1998): *Partisan Politics in the Global Economy*, Cambridge/New York: Cambridge University Press.

Garson, G. David (1978): *Group Theories of Politics*, Beverly Hills/London: Sage.

Gettell, Raymond G. (1924): *History of Political Thought*, London: Allen.

Glazer, Nathan (1997): "Individual Rights against Group Rights", in: Kymlicka, Will, ed., op. cit., 123-138.

Glazer, Nathan/Moynihan, Daniel P., eds. (1975): *Ethnicity*, Cambridge/London: Harvard Uni-versity Press.

Gordon, Milton M. (1975): "Toward a General Theory of Racial and Ethnic Group Relations", in: Glazer/Moynihan, eds., op. cit., 84-110.

Gordon, Milton M. (1981): "Models of Pluralism. The New American Dilemma", in: id., ed.: *America as a Multicultural Society*, Annals of the American Academy of Political and Social Science, Vol. 454, 178-188.

Goulbourne, Harry (1991): "Varieties of Pluralism: The Notion of a Pluralist Post-Imperial Great Britain", *New Community*, Vol. 17, 211-227.

Greenberg, Edward S. (1981): "Industrial Self-Management and Political Attitudes", *American Political Science Review* LXXV, 29-42.

Gunnell, John G. (2004): *Imagining the American Polity*, University Park: Pennsylva-nia Uni-versity Press .

Held, David (2003): *Models of Democracy*, Cambridge/Oxford: Polity/Blackwell.

Hirst, Paul (2004): "What is Globalization?", in: Engelstad/Østerud, op. cit., 151-168.

Ionescu, Ghita (1975): *Centripetal Politics: Government and the New Centres of Power*, London: Hart-Davis.

James, William (1909): *A Pluralistic Universe*, New York: Longmans, Green.

Jessop, Bob (1979): "Corporatism, Parliamentarism and Social Democracy", in: Schmitter/Lehmbruch, eds., op. cit., 185-212.

Kallen, Horace M. (1924): *Culture and Democracy in the United States*, New York: Boni & Liveright.

Kornhauser, William (1961): *The Politics of Mass Society*, Glencoe: Free Press.

Kremendahl, Hans (1977): *Pluralismustheorie in Deutschland*, Leverkusen: Heggen.

Kukathas, Chandras (1997): "Are there any Cultural Rights?", in: Kymlicka, Will, ed., op. cit., 228-256.

Kymlicka, Will (1995); *Multicultural Citizenship*, Oxford/New York: Clarendon Press.

Kymlicka, Will, ed. (1997): *The Rights of Minority Cultures*, Oxford/New York: Oxford University Press.

Laski, Harold J. (1917): *Studies in the Problem of Sovereignty*, New Haven: Yale University Press.

Laski, Harold J. (1919): *Authority in the Modern State*, New Haven: Yale University Press.

Laski, Harold J. (1921): *The Foundations of Sovereignty and Other Essays*, London: Harcourt, Brace.

Laski, Harold J. (1948): *A Grammar of Politics*, London: George Allen & Unwin.

Latham, Earl (1952): *The Group Basis of Politics*, Ithaca: Cornell University Press.

Lehmbruch, Gerhard (1979): "Liberal Corporatism and Party Government", in: Schmitter/Lehmbruch, op. cit., 147-183.

Lijphart, Arend (1968): *The Politics of Accommodation*, Berkeley/Los Angeles: California University Press.
Lijphart, Arend (1977): *Democracy in Plural Societies*, New Haven/London: Yale University Press.
Lindblom, Charles E. (1977): *Politics and Markets*, New York: Basic Books.
Lowi, Theodore J. (1967): "The Public Philosophy: Interest-Group Liberalism, *American Political Science Review* LXI, 5-24 .
Lowi, Theodore J. (1979): *The End of Liberalism*, New York: W. W. Norton.
Maier, Charles S. (1974): "Strukturen kapitalistischer Stabilität in den zwanziger Jahren: Errungenschaften und Defekte", in: Winkler, Heinrich August, ed.: *Organisierter Kapitalismus*, Göttingen: Vandenhoeck & Ruprecht, 195-213.
Maier, Charles S. (1975): *Recasting Bourgeois Europe*, Princeton: Princeton University Press.
McClelland, Charles A. (1965): "Systems Theory and Human Conflict", in: McNeil, Elton B., ed.: *The Nature of Human Conflict*, Englewood Cliffs: Prentice-Hall, 258-283.
McCord Wright, David (1954): "Contribution to the Discussion", *American Economic Review*, Papers & Proceedings, XLIV, 26-30.
McLennan, Gregor (1995): *Pluralism*, Buckingham: Open University Press.
Menand, Louis (2001): *The Metaphysical Club*, New York: Farrar, Straus & Giroux.
Merelman, Richard M. (2003): *Pluralism at Yale*, Madison/London: University of Wisconsin Press.
Milbrath, Lester W. (1955): *Political Participation*, Chicago: Rand McNally.
Mitchell, William C. (1963): "Interest Group Theory and 'Overlapping Memberships': A Critique", unpubl. paper.
Modood, Tariq (1999): "Multiculturalism, Secularism and the State", in: Bellamy/Hollis, eds., op. cit., 79-97.
New York Times (1984): "Project Democracy Takes Wing", No. 56,050, May 29, B 10
Nicholls, David (1974): *Three Varieties of Pluralism*, London: Macmillan.
Nuscheler, Franz (1980): "Sozialistischer Pluralismus", in: Heinrich Oberreuter, ed.: *Pluralismus*, Opladen: Leske & Budrich, 143-162.
Panitch, Leo (1979): "The Development of Corporatism in Liberal Democracies", in: Schmitter/Lehmbruch, eds., op. cit., 119-146.
Phillips, Anne (2004): "Democracy, Recognition and Power", in: Engelstad/Østerup, eds., op. cit., 57-78.
Putzel, James (2005): "Globalization, Liberalization, nd Prospects for the State", *International Political Science Review* 26, 5-16.
Ringen, Stein (2004): "Wealth and Decay. The Norwegian Study of Power and Democracy", *Times Literary Supplement*, February 13, 3-5.
Rogin, Michael Paul (1967): *The Intellectuals and McCarthy: The Radical Specter*, Cambridge/London: M.I.T. Press.
Rokkan, Stein (1966): "Norway: Numerical Democracy and Corporate Pluralism", in: Dahl, Robert A., ed.: *Political Opposition in Western Democracies*, New Haven: Yale University Press, 70-115.
Rothman, Stanley (1960): "Systematic Political Theory: Observations on the Group Approach", *American Political Science Review* LIV, 15-33.
Salisbury, Robert H. (1979): "Why No Corporatism in America?", in: Schmitter/Lehmbruch, op. cit., 213-230.

Sartori, Giovanni (1997): "Understanding Pluralism", *Journal of Democracy* 8, 58-69.

Schlesinger, Arthur M. (1992): *The Disuniting of America*, New York/London: W. W. Norton.

Schmitter, Philip C./Lehmbruch, Gerhard, eds. (1979): *Trends Toward Corporatist Intermediation*, Beverly Hills/London: Sage.

Smith, Adam (1776): *An Inquiry Into the Nature and Causes of the Wealth of Nations*, Vol. II, London: A. Strahan.

Stanovcic, Vojslav (1992): "Problems and Options in Institutionalizing Ethnic Relations", *International Political Science Review* 13, 359-379.

Stears, Marc (2002): *Progressives, Pluralists, and the Problems of the State*, Oxford/New York: Oxford University Press.

Steffani, Winfried (1980): *Pluralistische Demokratie*, Opladen: Leske & Budrich.

Stigler, George J. (1954): "The Economist Plays With Blocs", *American Economic Review*, Papers & Proceedings, XLIV, 7-14.

Streeck, Wolfgang (1983): "Between Pluralism and Corporatism: German Business As-sociations and the State", *Journal of Public Policy* 3, 265-284.

Truman, David B. (1951): *The Governmental Process*, New York: Alfred A. Knopf.

Van Dyke, Vernon (1976/77): "The Individual, the State, and Ethnic Communities in Political Theory", *World Politics* XXIX, 343-369.

Waldron, Jeremy (1997): "Minority Cultures and the Cosmopolitan Alternative", in: Kymlicka, Will, ed., op. cit., 93-119.

Walzer, Michael (1997): "Pluralism: A Political Perspective", in: Kymlicka, Will, ed., op. cit., 139-154.

Williamson, Peter J. (1989): *Corporatism in Perspective*, London: Sage.

In 1981, Praxis International *was launched as a journal first of "Marxist humanist", subsequently of "democratic socialist" orientation. Seyla Benhabib and Svetozar Stojanović, its editors, published the following article in 1986. Adding an international dimension, and including the military institution in the pluralist approach to participatory democracy, I tried to show how and why pluralism and socialism may not only be compatible, but complementary tasks. In addition to numerous other scholars, the editorial board of* Praxis International *included Mihailo Marković and Rudi Supek, along with Stojanović members of the Yugoslav Praxis group which Tito had attempted to silence: The original journal* Praxis, *started in 1965 as a forum for discussing ways of attaining "self-management socialism", was banned nine years later, the legendary summer schools on Korčula island stopped, members of the group who taught at Belgrade University suspended. International protests, however, met with some success. The group was conceded a research institute,* Praxis *was continued as* Praxis International *by Oxford publisher Basil Blackwell until 1991, while the Inter-University Center in Dubrovnik replaced Korčula as a venue for regular international meetings of philosophers and social scientists.*

Pluralism as a Critical Political Theory

I

When elaborated during the first two decades of the twentieth century, the concept of pluralism in its initial stages assailed monist ideas ascribing to the modern state „a unitary and absolute sovereign power" as the sole and direct source of either legal or political authority.[1] On principal and on empirical grounds, pluralists stressed the fundamental independence of social associations – trade unions no less than churches – from the sovereign command of the state. Insofar as alternative institutional arrangements were proposed, however, these were apt to vacillate between transferring sovereignty to the diverse groups, channelling dynamic social interests into permanent corporate arrangements, or even reintroducing, in new clothes, „the monist's overlord".[2]

---

1 Hsiao, Kung Chuan (1927), *Political Pluralism*, London/New York: K. Paul, p. 7.
2 For the last quote, see Coker, Francis W. (1921): „The Techniques of the Pluralist State", *American Political Science Review*, XV, p. 207. The „sovereign group" and corporate fallacies were first critically referred to by Elliott, William Yandall (1925): „Sovereign State or Sovereign Group?" (1925), *American Political Science Review*, XIX, p. 479, and Bonn, Moritz J. (1925): *Die Krisis der europäischen Demokratie*, Munich, p. 115.

Redefining sovereignty so as to represent the „totality of social purposes", and interpreting group organization as part and parcel of the „multicellular democratic organism"[3] provided the way out of the impasse for pluralism: If the social needs of individuals, expressed by their associations, constitute one focal point and governmental interventionism the other, the two are linked by the „constant and complex interactions" of „the individual, the group, the state."[4] The pluralist norm, then, is expressed precisely by that „constructive *social* policy… for the *individual* man" which accounts for the state's attributes as a „public service corporation" promoting men's positive liberties.[5]

In a second step, pluralism was thus constructed as a dynamic theory centring on the fundamentally associative character of society, yet placing the „individual at the centre of things",[6] while stressing the state's task to act as an agency for the political improvement of individual conditions of existence. Rapidly, however, it was discerned that repudiating the state's claim to *formal* sovereignty would not suffice, if the pluralists were to remain true to their effort of forging a political philosophy attempting „to formulate the fundamental content of freedom and democracy".[7] Accepting the pluralist norm of socio-political interaction also meant recognizing that an egalitarian basis for such a process had yet to be created by redistributing *material* advantages between social classes: While „the State has sovereign rights", political power is largely „the handmaid of economic power… The political personality of the average citizen is made ineffective for any serious purpose".[8] The conclusion, at the time, was unambiguous:

"No political democracy can be real that is not as well a reflection of an economic democracy…The present system of property does not in the least involve the present technique of industrial direction."[9]

Pluralism was thus originally formulated as a theory at once positive *and* normative of social (interest) groups and of individual participation (via associations) in the political process – a theory unavoidably critical of capitalist economy and society which, just as unavoidably, it proposed to transcend:

---

3   Cf. Hsiao, op. cit., pp. 141, 144.
4   Follett, Mary P. (1920): *The New State*, New York: Longmans, Green, pp. 10, 61.
5   Ibid., pp. 182, 184; Laski, Harold J. (1968; [1]1919): *Authority in the Modern State*, Hamden: Archon, pp. 31, 55.
6   Cf. Laski, Harold J. (1977; [1]1925): *A Grammar of Politics*, London: George Allen & Unwin, p. 67; also id.: *Studies in the Problem of Sovereignty* (1917), New Haven/London: Yale University Press, p. 19.
7   Magid, Henry Meyer (1941): *English Political Pluralism*, New York: Columbia University Press, p. 65.
8   Laski, *Studies*, p. 15; and id. (1921): *The Foundations of Sovereignty and Other Essays*, London: Harcourt, Brace, p. IX.
9   Laski, *Authority*, p. 38; id., *Grammar*, p. 112.

"The objective of the pluralist must be the classless society...If the main ground of conflict is thus removed, it becomes possible to conceive of a social organization in which the truly federal nature of society receives institutional expression.

In such a social organization, authority can be pluralist both in form and expression."[10]

II

Two generations later, however, it was the very concept of political pluralism that came to be identified, for West European societies, as a major barrier against social and economic reforms meant to redistribute advantages between social classes:[11] While

pluralism's embrace of positive government [had] first put it at an ideological pole opposite capitalism..., the two apparent antitheses [had] ultimately disappeared... Capitalism and pluralism were not actually synthesized, however; in a sense, they absorbed each other.[12]

The reasons for that development were at least threefold. The conceptual approach of „analytical", in contrast to „philosophic" pluralism,[13] offered a status quo-centred alternative: whereas the pluralist conception aimed at reinstating individual man, acting through his freely established associations, as the central political figure capable of influencing a polity at once grown overwhelmingly powerful and largely monopolised by the economically strong, group theory *strictu senso*, turning against individualism and institutionalism at the same time, limited itself to proclaiming the group as the central analytical category:[14]

---

10 Laski, *Grammar,* p. XII. Ernest Barker (who was Laski's tutor at Oxford) had earlier emphasized the „polyarchical" character of a social order constituted by organized groups, but had confined his normative argument to noting that the state would have to gain correspondingly in regulatory power to prevent group despotism. Cf. Barker, Ernest (1915): *Political Thought in England from Herbert Spencer to the Present Day,* London/New York: Williams & Norgate, p. 183; also Adolf M. Birke (1978): *Pluralismus und Gewerkschaftsautonomie in England,* Stuttgart: Klett-Cotta, p. 197. The West-German „neo"-pluralist school (cf. infra), not desirous of going beyond current concepts of the Western European welfare state, has stressed its indebtedness to Barber. Cf. Fraenkel, Ernst (1964): *Der Pluralismus als Strukturelement der freiheitlich-rechtsstaatlichen Demokratie,* München: C. H. Beck, p. 11.

11 Cf. Parkin, Frank (1972): *Class Inequality and Political Order,* St. Albans: Paladin, pp. 181 ss.

12 Lowi, Theodore J. (^{2rev}1979): *The End of Liberalism,* New York/London: W. W. Norton, p. 35.

13 Latham, Earl (1952), *A Group Basis of Politics,* Ithaca: Cornell University Press, p. 9, and Lijphart, Arend (1968), *The Politics of Accommodation,* Berkeley/Los Angeles: University of California Press, p. 2n., argue in these terms.

14 Truman, David B. (1951): *The Governmental Process,* New York: Alfred A. Knopf, p. 48. Even more emphatically, Arthur F. Bentley – whose *Process of Government* (Evanston: Principia) served as the „principal bench mark" for Truman's thinking (cf. Truman, op. cit., p. IX) – had argued in 1908 that every activity can be stated „either on the one side as indi-

55

We do not, in fact, find individuals otherwise than in groups... ,The individual' and ,the group' are at most merely convenient ways of classifying behavior, two ways of approaching the same phenomena, not different things.

Attempting „to reduce human behavior to patterns of group interactions and their disturbances", the group doctrine blinded its protagonists to the importance of changes in the socio-economic structure as well as in the normative dimensions of political action.[15] However, for reasons that will be discussed below, the approach prevailed. Initial pluralist propositions gave way to the behavioral interest „analytical" pluralism displayed in the structure and activity of existing – even more, of dominant – groups. Attempting to pass as value-free, group theory succumbed to the normative temptation by assuming conservative and apologetic traits.[16]

Reflecting the process whereby paradigms tend to emerge in the social sciences, the prevalence of the group approach was favored by the descriptive interest political sociology had begun to display – especially in the United States – in the lobbying activities of „pressure groups". The influences exerted by organized business, labor, farm, and other professional groups – but also by veterans', women's, or temperance organizations – on political parties, legislatures, executives, and administrative bureaucracies were being subjected to increasing scrutiny. As social interests successively began to organize, and „pressure politics" became increasingly topical, the „acceptance of groups as lying at the heart of the process of government" was judged conceptually „unavoidable".[17]

In the political domain, finally, the rise of fascism and communism seemed to suggest „the similarities between the extreme Right and the extreme Left and the dangers of mass movements". Haunted by the twin specters of radicalism and totalitarianism, „modern" pluralism pitted group politics – ultimately, politics of group leadership -, because they produced „sensible and orderly" conflict, against the „irrationality and chaos" of mass politics:

---

vidual, or on the other side as social group activity", but that, in interpreting social processes, the former „is in the main of trifling importance", whereas the latter „is essential, first, last, and all the time" (ibid., p. 215).

15 Cf. Rothman, Stanley (1960): „Systematic Political Theory: Observations on the Group Approach", *American Political Science Review*, LIV, pp. 31, 32.

16 Cf. Hale, Myron Q. (1960): „The Cosmology of Arthur F. Bentley", *American Political Science Review*, LIV, pp. 956, 958 on Bentley; Bluhm, William T. (1965): *Theories of the Political System,* Englewood Cliffs: Prentice Hall, pp. 357-358, on Latham and Truman.

17 In offering this statement, Truman, op. cit., p. 46, on the same page refers to a considerable body of pressure group studies published between World Wars I and II.

Pluralism analyzes efforts by masses to improve their condition as threats to stability. It turns all threats to stability into threats to constitutional democracy. This is a profoundly conservative endeavor.[18]

In its tendency to equate group politics with Western representative democracy, the „vulgarized version"[19] of the pluralist model was considerably strengthened by the advent of the Cold War confrontation between the Atlantic Alliance and the Warsaw Pact. A more or less explicitly normative element was reintroduced into the theory, particularly in the West German version of „neo"-pluralism[20] – substituting, however, „totalitarianism" (successively identified with Stalinism, communism, or even socialism in general) for monism as the principal counterpart to pluralism.

The notion of monism which had pointed to structural defects of capitalist societies – because an economic system that „reserves disposition over productive means to private owners and their authorized agents, the ‚managers'", has justly been labelled not pluralist but monist -,[21] thereby all but disappeared from consideration. The static descriptive and the anti-totalitarian normative dimension blended in a manner to ensure the „astonishing career"[22] of pluralism as the prevailing „public philosophy" which „public men" have grown accustomed tuse rather instinctively both as guideline and justification for their policies.[23] „Modern" pluralism has thus served to legitimize and stabilize existing power structures in the „free world's" postwar societies.

III

Like national pluralism, international pluralism is structurally biased in more than one respect: Interdependence is fundamentally „lopsided" and „asym-

---

18 The quote is taken from Robin, Michael Paul (1967): *Intellectuals and McCarthy: The Radical Specter*, Cambridge/London: M.I.T. Press, p. 282. Cf. also, for the preceding argument, pp. 15, 25, 78-79.

19 Lowi, Theodore J. (1967): „The Public Philosophy: Interest-Group Liberalism", *American Political Science Review*, LXI, p. 12.

20 As developed by Ernst Fraenkel (1964): *Deutschland und die westlichen Demokratien*, Stuttgart: Kohlhammer; id., *Der Pluralismus als Strukturelement*, op. cit.; id. (1969): „Strukturanalyse der modernen Demokratie", *Aus Politik und Zeitgeschichte*, B 49/69; id. (1973): *Reformismus und Pluralismus*, Falk Esch & Frank Grube, eds., Hamburg: Hoffmann & Campe; also Kremendahl, Hans (1977): *Pluralismustheorie in Deutschland*, Leverkusen: Heggen; Steffani, Winfried (1980): *Pluralistische Demokratie*, Opladen: Leske & Budrich. For a critical discussion, cf. Eisfeld, Rainer (1972): *Pluralismus zwischen Liberalismus und Sozialismus*, Stuttgart: Kohlhammer.

21 Pross, Helge (1963): „Zum Begriff der pluralistischen Gesellschaft", in: Max Horkheimer, ed.: *Zeugnisse – Theodor W. Adorno zum 60. Geburtstag*, Frankfurt: Europäische Verlagsanstalt, p. 447.

22 Steffani, *Pluralistische Demokratie*, op. cit., p.

23 Cf. Lowi (1967), op. cit., passim.

metric in power".[24] On the economic, military and political levels, an international hierarchy persists (albeit in varying degrees) between the capitalist „center" and the Third World „periphery", in relations between capitalist countries themselves, and finally within the so-called Socialist system. Today's international relations are very obviously characterized by economic, political, and military threats, pressures, destabilizing acts, direct aggressions („interventions"), and hegemonic control; by the manifest reality of the capacity for thermonuclear „overkill", and by the distinct possibility of ecocide, as much as genocide.

In such a less than pluralist environment, socio-political values, structures and goals „developed in the ‚mother country of liberalism'" (meaning the United States), „or in the fatherland of socialism" (referring to the Soviet Union) „may function as exemplary models because of their place of origin, not by virtue of their substance".[25] By a „total diplomacy", pyramiding „labor, diplomacy, intelligence, and business activities in foreign policy",[26] patterns of ideological interpretation – reinforced by enticements and pressures – are being spread in order to exercise influence on socio-political processes in any one country. At the same time, these values and norms serve to justify precisely the occurring „penetrative" (Rosenau) activities. Among them, the „public philosophy" of pluralism has been of crucial importance. A most recent example is provided by the National Endowment for Democracy (NED) which, set up in the United States during 1984, is destined to promote „American-style *pluralistic* societies" in foreign countries.[27] For its first year, it received from Congress $26.3m in federal money;[28] additional corporate donations were expected to start flowing before long.

Even more instructive is the case of the Portuguese „revolution of carnations" during 1974/75 where the „Atlantic" yardstick of pluralism was unequivocally applied to the granting of economic aid, elucidating the drastic manner in which, both within the Eastern *and* Western spheres of influence, not only foreign, but also domestic policy options have been reduced: After the dictatorial Caetano regime had been overthrown by Portuguese officers in early 1974, and Portuguese administrations had repeatedly asked the EC for

24 Vernon, Raymond (1971): „Multinational Business and National Economic Goals", *International Organization,* XXV, p. 705; Morse, Edward L. (1971): „Transnational Economic Processes", *International Organization,* XXV, p. 393.
25 Galtung, Johan (1981): „Pluralismus und die Zukunft der menschlichen Gesellschaft", in: Dieter Senghaas, ed.: *Kritische Friedensforschung,* Frankfurt: Suhrkamp, p. 57.
26 Cox, Robert W. (1971): „Labor and Transnational Relations", *International Organization,* XXV, p. 555.
27 *New York Times* (1984): „Project Democracy Takes Wing", No. 56,059, May 29, p. B 10.
28 Of which $13,8m went to the AFL/CIO-run American Institute for Free Labor Development, $2,5m to the U.S. Chamber of Commerce's new Center for International Private Enterprise, and $5m each to the Democratic and Republican National Committees' newly created international institutes. Cf. ibid.

financial support, the EC Council of Heads of State and Government, on 17 July 1975, finally declared that „the EC, because of its political and historical tradition, can grant support only to a *pluralist* democracy."[29]

At the time, a social mass movement among the industrial and rural workers of Lisbon and the Portuguese South, as well as a series of political crises mobilizing an ever widening part of the population, had turned the original coup into a social revolution. The leftward trend of the country's internal social and political power struggle was reflected by the composition of successive cabinets and by their socializing measures. From spring to autumn, 1975, Portugal had left-leaning (as distinct from moderate or social-democratic) governments.[30] The North Atlantic Alliance, however, viewed the country not as a developing polity and society in its own right, but solely in terms of a „domino" – NATO's „crumbling Southern flank" – in the East-West power contest.

Because of its deteriorating economic situation, U.S., NATO and EC attitudes came to be particularly important for Portugal – and particularly for the final outcome of the domestic political conflict. A loan was conceded by the EC not before October, 1975, after a new, de facto social-democratic government had been in office for three weeks; disbursements were finally made in April, 1976.

In foreign policy, as well as domestically, the notions of „modern" pluralism have contributed to shape the perception of Western interests. These notions, however, have increasingly met with criticism, leading to a normative initiative implying structural societal changes and accordingly termed „structural" or „socialist" pluralism. Incidentally, hardly four weeks before the EC ultimatum, the group of Portuguese officers that had overthrown the dictatorship had declared that their aim consisted in precisely such a „socialist pluralism".[31]

IV

A more profound critique of „modern" pluralism attempting to arrive at a „structurally" pluralist alternative would start from where early pluralists had left off, namely the rise of business corporations and industrial combines on the one hand, and trade unions on the other hand, in an attempt to define the social obligations of both and to discuss the unequal distribution of power

---

29 Cf. Commission of the European Communities (1976), *Die Beziehungen zwischen der EG und Portugal*, Brussels, p. 8.

30 For more comprehensive analyses, cf. this book's Section V below.

31 For a translation of the entire text (published on June 21, 1975), cf. Appendix J to Fields, Rona M. (1975), *The Portuguese Revolution and the Armed Forces Movement*, New York/London: Praeger.

between capital and labor.[32] In striking contrast, a definite lack in diagnosing and researching economic constraints has persisted in „modern" pluralist thinking. That oligopoly, „the most frequent market form of modern [capitalist] economies",[33] and the resulting monopolistic competition are „group phenomena", has been acknowledged by the group approach.[34] Still, its advocates have failed to draw any systematic consequences from this insight, even though oligopoly capitalism has continued to make ineffective, in Harold Laski's quoted words, „the average citizen's political personality".

In order to update and reformulate in a more systematic manner the early pluralist's analysis, five separate – if interconnected – aspects of socioeconomic development need to be considered:[35]

(1) Pursuing tactics of integration and collusion, oligopolistic corporations have advanced from being „price takers" to being „price makers". Their „administered" prices show a perverse flexibility over the business cycle, preparing the way for stagflation. As means of effective *external* (public) control over these groups' pricing and investment-financing power, the anti-trust, monetary, and fiscal tools of interventionist government have proved inadequate.

(2) With regard to sales, assets, and number of employees, large corporations have developed into social and public (rather than individual and private) institutions. Although every such corporation is, in fact, a „body politic" with an „internal government", it is not subject to effective *internal* (private) control, because the typical small stockholder, for all practical purposes, has become „disenfranchised".

---

32 Cf. Laski, *Foundations of Sovereignty*, pp. 97/98, 272 ss.; Follett, *New State*, p. 170.
33 Sylos-Labini, Paolo (1969): *Oligopoly and Technical Progress*, Cambridge: M.I.T. Press, p. 14; cf. also Rothschild, Kurt W. (1971): „Price Theory and Oligopoly", in: Alex Hunter, ed.: *Monopoly and Competition*, Harmondsworth: Penguin, passim.
34 Cf. Latham, Group Basis, p. 5.
35 For some of the following considerations, see already Eisfeld, *Pluralismus*, esp. chs. XI, XVI, XVII. Among the relevant literature, cf. Berle, Adolf A./Means, Gardiner C. (1967): *The Modern Corporation and Private Property*, New York: Macmillan; Dahl, Robert A. (1959): „Business and Politics: A Critical Appraisal of Political Science", *American Political Science Review*, LIII, 1-34; Galbraith, John Kenneth (1968): *The Affluent Society* (Harmondsworth: Pelican); Hymer, Stephen/Rowthorn, Robert (1970): „Multinational Corporations and International Oligopoly: The Non-American Challenge", in: Charles P. Kindleberger, ed., *The International Corporation*, Cambridge/London: M.I.T. Press, 57-91; Kefauver, Estes (1966*): In a Few Hands*, Harmondsworth: Pelican; Mielke, Siegfried (1973): „Multinationale Konzerne: Zur Deformation pluralistischer Systeme", in: Günther Döker/Winfried Steffani, eds.: *Klassenjustiz und Pluralismus*, Hamburg: Hoffmann & Campe, 362-378; Preiser, Erich (1971): „Property, Power, and the Distribution of Income", in: Kurt W. Rothschild, ed.: *Power in Economics*, Harmondsworth: Penguin, 119-140; Riesman, David (1958): *Die einsame Masse*, Reinbek: Rowohlt; Whyte, William H. (1956): *The Organization Man*, New York: Simon & Schuster.

(3) The privileges of oligopoly are reinforced by those of quasi-monopoly (Preiser): Owning, or controlling, property advances elasticity in a person's conduct of life, while lack of property still forces relative rigidity upon the wage-earner.

(4) While trade unions have, at least within certain limits, added to the independence of wage-earning blue-collar workers, the compliance and docility of salaried white-collar employees (their „other-directedness", in Riesman's famous expression) has increased with the grouping of business firms into ever larger organizational units. White-collar strata, however, have been increasing, in absolute numbers as in proportion, in the course of and due to the implied logic of economic development.

(5) Finally, multinational corporations – in fact, international oligopolies – have come to decree part and parcel of what happens in national economies by transferring production facilities and investment outlays between countries, shifting profits via transfer-pricing, and moving large amounts of liquid assets. In a nutshell, they pursue fiscal and foreign exchange policies without, again, individual governments sufficiently controlling or checking their power.

By taking into account these structures, strategies, performances, and perceptions, pluralist theory is capable of explaining, on a coherent, group-oriented basis, the segmentation of the earlier rigid class structure into blue- and white-collar strata differentiated by vocation and attitude; the continuing inequalities of economic influence and control; central origins of political apathy and alienation; the resulting unequal chances fort he organized representation of interests; finally, the most important sources and limits of state interventionism.

At the same time, the normative challenge posed by pluralist analysis becomes apparent: given the present economic structure, the individual cannot realize his inherent possibilities by means of the multifarious social groups and associations. Pluralism's inherent anti-monist, anti-hierarchical, participatory implications qualify the approach normatively to transcend the participatory barriers structurally embedded in the capitalist socio-political system.

V

The tendency of present pluralism „to function only in certain sectors, whereas others remain highly authoritarian",[36] does not apply, of course, merely to the economic base of society. When it was first suggested to analyse socio-

---

36 Beyme, Klaus von (1980): „The Politics of Limited Pluralism? The Case of West Germany", in: Stanislaw Ehrlich/Graham Wootton, eds.: *Three Faces of Pluralism*, Westmead: Gover, p. 97.

political systems by sectors in order to discover their more or less pluralist or monist character (instead of considering capitalist representative democracies as *a priori* pluralist), three sectors, because of their hierarchical, authoritarian structure were immediately singled out as being „from a pluralist viewpoint, institutions apart": governmental bureaucracy in general; the foreign policy apparatus in particular; finally, the armed forces.[37] Concerning the latter, it was noted even at the time that „a not insignificant part of politics is determined by military considerations in the largest sense", and it was emphasized that it would be „inconsistent" to leave the military domain outside the scope of pluralism.[38] However, once more the (understandable) research myopia of „modern" pluralists prevailed and contributed to the failure of political science to link military developments to the problem of maintaining (not to mention extending) already limited pluralist structures.

The case of the foremost European „axis" country defeated during World War II, (West) Germany, may serve to illustrate the importance which trends in armament and the existence of armed forces are apt to acquire for democracies that are usually referred to as „pluralist".

The Federal Republic of Germany, formally demilitarized – along with the whole of the former „Reich" – at the Potsdam Conference, existed without armed forces (not counting frontier protective troops) for six years – though not, of course, as an entirely sovereign state. A „military constitution" proper was inserted into the West German Basic Law only in 1956, after the latter had been amended two years earlier by assigning legislative competence in defense matters to the federal parliament. In 1955, West Germany joined the North Atlantic Alliance; during the same year, the first regiments were enrolled. Hardly two decades later, these had expanded into the largest conventional force in Europe, disposing of 12 army divisions and altogether 460,000 soldiers. These, plus 180,000 civilian employees working in the armed forces administration (not counting the 120,000 civilians employed by the allied troops stationed in the Federal Republic, by 1973 accounted for 12.5% of all government personnel.[39]

Available data suggest that universal military training contributes to rigidities of perception and conduct (a „militarization of needs") tending to offset the development of less conventional standards that would coincide with pluralist norms. This is especially salient for the West German case, where the „citizen in uniform" concept was introduced during the 1950s as a deliberate break with Germany's military past. Meant to advance, by „intra-

---

37 Narr, Wolf-Dieter (1969): *Pluralistische Gesellschaft*, Hannover: Niedersächsische Landeszentrale für Politische Bildung, pp. 59, 62, 67.
38 Ibid., p. 62.
39 Cf. Schmidt, Manfred G. (1975): „Staatliche Ausgabenentwicklung und Akkumulation im Rüstungssektor der Bundesrepublik", *Gesellschaft*, 5, p. 28.

unit guidance", the draftees' civic education, it was, by degrees, reduced to military „human relations" and „anti-totalitarian indoctrination".[40] Its failure has tended either to reinforce, in draftees, psycho-social deficiencies acquired during their pre-military socialization – those rigidities already referred to -, or has forced upon them a segmentation of attitudes into „conventional" and „post-conventional" patterns, required by conflicting military and civilian roles,[41] but hardly conducive to the development of a profoundly pluralist culture.

West Germany's steady military spending is acting, in budgetary terms, as a constraint on welfare and social security expenditure, thus contributing to thwart – under conditions of persisting mass unemployment – the established pluralist principle of offering a „new" (or even, hopefully, „fair") deal to those social groups whose living conditions are deteriorating. In spite of decreasing public revenues and efforts to reduce the national debt, defense spending is still given highest priority, with labor and social security outlays falling behind, and expenditures for children, family and health decreasing conspicuously,[42] so that the continuing military build-up is at least indirectly financed out of non-defense cuts. In the United States and the United Kingdom, the „warfare-welfare tradeoff" (Peroff)[43] has been even stronger in evidence.

Finally, the West German government has actively encouraged first the build-up, subsequently the concentration of an armament industry.[44] Thus, firms on the one hand have become increasingly dependent on armament contracts for their existence; on the other hand, the defense industry's oligopolistic structure is permitting large corporations to contract out from under more restrictive governmental armament planning by first increasing their capacity and then campaigning for the production and purchase of additional weapons systems, arguing that otherwise their firms „would collapse".[45]

---

40   Cf. Bredow, Wilfried von (1973): *Die unbewältigte Bundeswehr*, Frankfurt: S. Fischer, pp. 101 ss.; Bald, Detlef at al. (1981): „Innere Führung und Sozialisation. Ein Beitrag zur Sozio-Psychologie des Militärs", in: Reiner Steinweg, ed.: *Unsere Bundeswehr? Zum 25jährigen Bestehen einer umstrittenen Institution*, Frankfurt: Suhrkamp, pp. 137 ss.

41   Cf. Bald et al., op. cit., pp. 151 ss.; Wakenhut, Roland (1979): „Effects of Military Service on Political Socialization of Draftees", *Armed Forces & Society*, 5, 626-641.

42   Cf. Krasemann, Peter (1985): „Sozialausgaben und Rüstungsfinanzierung in der Bundesrepublik", in: Reiner Steinweg, ed.: *Rüstung und soziale Sicherheit*, Frankfurt: Suhrkamp, p. 70.

43   Peroff, Kathleen (1977): „The Warfare-Welfare Tradeoff: Health, Public Aid, and Housing", *Journal of Sociology and Social Welfare*, IV, pp. 46-55.

44   For, e.g., the aviation industry, cf. Schlotter, Peter (1975): *Rüstungspolitik in der Bundesrepublik Deutschland. Die Beispiele Starfighter und Phantom*, Frankfurt/New York: Campus, pp. 82 ss. For figures on domestic armament expenditures during the 1960s and 1970s, cf. Schmidt, op. cit., p. 36.

45   Again for West Germany, cf. Schlotter, op. cit., pp. 35 ss. For the U.K. and especially the U.S., where the strategy has been observed on a much larger scale, cf. Prins, Gwyn (1983): *Defended to Death*, Harmondsworth: Penguin, pp. 150 ss.

Thus, not only does the goal of „reconversion", of economic readjustment to civilian production, not enter into corporate considerations,[46] but organized as well as unorganized labor is included in lobbying efforts for self-perpetuation of the defense industry.[47] The build-up of an armament industry has resulted in entrepreneurial *and* labor pressure for the continuing production of new, plus the additional export of existing weapons systems, thereby undermining the support for and democratic legitimacy of defense cuts and more comprehensive disarmament efforts, which would most certainly have to be considered as advantageous to national and international pluralism. This again raises the question of the values and norms of large parts of the population.[48]

The consequences of the internationalization of capital have been the subject of much scholarly debate – although even there contributions from the pluralist camp in political science have been, to say the least, rare. In comparison, the internationalization of militarism seems to have gone largely undiscussed.

To grasp realistically what is going on, the traditional notion of militarism needs to be replaced no less than the more recent concept of an isolated military-industrial complex. Instead, „civil" society itself has to be pictured as moving in the direction of a system in which the distinction between (formerly civilian) policy and (formerly military) strategy is being eroded by the common momentum of political/ideological/military/academic/corporate/ organized labor interaction. The outcome of the process may be considered a continuous technological, manufacturing, and political „warfare overachievement capability", in qualitative as well as in quantitative terms.[49]

---

46 For a survey of the reconversion literature, cf. Albrecht, Ulrich (1979): *Rüstungskonversionsforschung*, Baden-Baden: Nomos. Relevant post-WW II experiences exist for demilitarized West Germany and especially for the United States, where some systematic federal planning was done.

47 For example, in 1975/76 shop committees from West Germany's largest defense contractors clamored for governmental licensing of „stop-gap" (i. e. export) orders from „non-tension regions", because otherwise „colleagues who had carried out their duty to the state" (!) would stand in peril of losing their jobs. By 1980, with unemployment mounting, the employees of the Howaldt shipyard in Kiel struck for several hours, with their management's consent (!), to emphasize their demand fort he production and delivery – which had come under public criticism – of two submarines to the Pinochet dictatorship in Chile. Cf. Mechtersheimer, Alfred (1977): *Rüstung und Politik in der Bundesrepublik: MRCA Tornado*, Bad Honnef: Osang, p. 137; Rodejohann, Jo (1985): „Nicht nur einfach ein Job: Arbeitsplatzrisiken in der westdeutschen Rüstungsindustrie", in: Steinweg, *Rüstung*, p. 133.

48 If much more empirical research would appear necessary to further substantiate preliminary results like these, one of the problems involved is precisely that such research has not been promoted by a common and profound concern to overcome the rather narrow reasoning of „modern" pluralist analysis.

49 This attempt at a more comprehensive formulation has been suggested by the arguments of Senghaas, Dieter (1972): *Rüstung und Militarismus*, Frankfurt: Suhrkamp, pp. 11 ss., and Prins, *Defended*, pp. 136, 148 ss.

Such militarisation is brought about „subtly, noiselessly, hardly contested anywhere".[50] Like a disease, the ideologies and strategies of ever new „compensating armaments" are spreading to through the First and Second and from both to the Third World. Increasingly, moreover, U.S. „vital" interests and the military means to secure them have become globally defined, as indicated by conceptions like „power projection" (signifying the capability to intervene), „forward deployed presence" or „integrated battlefield", the latter referring to development of the ability „to deliver conventional and/or nuclear fires throughout the spectrum of a battle... in all U.S. army units worldwide."[51] The USSR, as far as its resources are apt to permit, can be counted upon (if it has not already done so) to follow this change in strategical emphasis. It should not be a matter of much conjecture that the socio-political structures, the values and norms promoted by an ever more sophisticated global militarization not only pose a medium- or even short-term threat to the survival of the human race, but an immediate challenge to pluralists everywhere.

VI

When – two generations after the socialist implications of pluralist theory had first been spelt out -, the anti-participatory, inherently monist bias of oligopoly capitalism came to be critically assessed again by pluralists, it was also apparent that ‚actually existing' socialism had long been degenerating into monopoly socialism.[52] By Euro-communist parties (particularly the PCI), by dissenters from the ranks of their more orthodox sister organizations, by Yugoslav and Czechoslovakian communists, pluralism was re-discovered as „an inner requirement of socialism".[53] It was acknowledged that pluralist interests would continue to exist in socialist societies, that such societies would entail „neither the disappearance of differences nor the ceasing of strife and dissension", and that, in the relations and contradictions between social interests, „no social power (may) be absolute arbiter...particularly not on the basis of state authority."[54] Accepting organizational autonomy not

50 Senghaas, Dieter (1977): *Weltwirtschaftsordnung und Entwicklungspolitik. Plädoyer für Dissoziation*, Frankfurt: Suhrkamp, p. 223.
51 General Donn R. Starry, now in charge of the U.S. Rapid Deployment Force, quoted by Evangelista, Matthew A. (1983): „Offense or Defense: A Tale of Two Commissions", *World Policy Journal*, I, pp. 53, 57.
52 The expression was coined by Kuron, Jacek and Modzelewski, Karol (1969): *Monopolsozialismus – Offener Brief an die Polnische Vereinigte Arbeiterpartei*, Hamburg: Hoffmann & Campe, esp. pp. 12-13.
53 Lombardo-Radice, Lucio (1965): *Pluralismus in der gesellschaftlichen Praxis*, Salzburg, p. 1. He was then a member of the PCI Central Committee.
54 Cf. ibid., pp. 1, 3; Kardelj, Edvard (1962): *Über die Prinzipien des Vorentwurfs der neuen Verfassung des sozialistischen Jugoslawien*, Belgrade, p. 6.

only for „the judiciary, the economic administration, the system of education, science, etc.", but also for trade unions and, last not least, for „those people and groups who do not support socialist options"[55] followed as the logical next step in the „discovery of socialist pluralism":[56] Existing civil rights might thus be freed from structural limitations because of which „they have dried up in capitalist society", and present „rigid" pluralism might be transformed into a „dialogical" and „dialectical" pluralism.[57]

These positions directly influenced the Czechoslovakian discussion before and during 1968.[58] The necessity not only to „recognize the pluralist structure of socialist society" but to institutionalize „guarantees for the confrontation of interests"[59] was accepted during the short-lived Czechoslovakian experiment: Until the country came under military occupation,[60] „reform communists' projected workers' councils, political, producers' and consumers' associations as „multiple autonomous subjects" of the economic and political process.[61]

The Yugoslav model, having evolved since 1950 through successive stages of extensive discussion and no less continuous constitutional experimentation and change, has so far remained the only attempt to arrive at an institutionalized „pluralism of self-managed interests in society"[62] by applying one structural principle, the delegate system, to the sectors of associated labor, socio-political affairs, and commune/republic/federation. Increasingly rooted in a growing critique of „actually existing" socialism's statist tradition that suffocated the effective representation of workers' rights by independent

55 Lombardo-Radice, ibid.; Ingrao, Pietro (1964): „Ein Ansatz zu einer Diskussion ueber den politischen Pluralismus", in: id.: *Massenbewegung und politische Macht*, Hamburg: VSA, p. 72. Ingrao was then a member of the PCI National Directorate. In 1976, he was elected President of the Italian Chamber of Representatives.

56 Sláma, Jiří (1968): „Die Entdeckung des sozialistischen Pluralismus", in: Josef Skvorecky, ed.: *Nachrichten aus der CSSR*, Frankfurt: Suhrkamp, pp. 191-199..

57 Lombardo-Radice, ibid.; Ingrao, op. cit., p. 75.

58 Cf. Klokocka, Vladimir (1966): „Verfassungsprobleme im sozialistischen Staatssystem", *Der Staat* 5, pp. 74, 78; and id. (1968): *Demokratischer Sozialismus*, Hamburg: Konkret, p. 33.

59 Klokocka, *Demokratischer Sozialismus*, pp. 35, 41.

60 After the Czechoslovakian attempt at fundamentally reforming existing socialism had been put down, „pluralist marxism" was promptly castigated by the orthodox East German SED as leading to the „ideological decomposition of Marxist-Leninist parties and, in consequence, to the unchaining of counter-revolution in the socialist camp". Cf. Klaus, Georg/Buhr, Manfred, eds. (1976): *Philosophisches Wörterbuch*, Leipzig: VEB Bibliographisches Institut, p. 940.

61 Cf. Sláma, op. cit., p. 192, 195; Pelikán, Jirí, ed. (1971): *The Secret Vysocany Congress – Proceedings and Documents*, London: Allen Lane, pp. 202 ss.

62 Kardelj, Edvard (1979): *Die Wege der Demokratie in der sozialistischen Gesellschaft*, Cologne/ Frankfurt: Europäische Verlagsanstalt, p. 107.

organizations,[63] the Yugoslav perspective of „expropriating political authority" after economic property[64] primarily (though by no means exclusively) hurts itself through the „specific position of power" unchangingly conferred, in the Yugoslav political system, on the League of Communists.[65]

No less than the Portuguese „revolution of carnations" referred to earlier, but with more immediately brutal consequences for the country concerned, the Czechoslovakian experiment proved that socialist pluralism is a prospect whose attempted realization endangers material and ideological interests in the Atlantic and actually existing socialist „camps", and therefore touches off internal and external resistance. Much more drastically than the short-lived Portuguese experience of 1974/75, the decade-long Yugoslav effort demonstrates that structural (i. e. socialist) pluralism denotes an aim as well as a drawn-out, difficult process continuously menaced, apart from foreign intervention, by domestic compromises and setbacks, bureaucratic resistance, individual and group egoism.

Yet, at the very least, conceptions of structural pluralism seek to diminish institutional rigidity, socio-economic inequality, and political apathy in a more decisive manner than might be envisaged under foreseeable capitalist and actually existing socialist systemic conditions. Such conceptions have ranged from the Yugoslav and Czechoslovakian experiments briefly described here to the Portuguese constitution of 1976.[66] More recently, they

---

63 Cf., e. g., Marković, Mihailo (1968): *Dialektik der Praxis*, Frankfurt: Suhrkamp, pp. 97 ss.; Stojanović, Svetozar (1972): *Kritik und Zukunft des Sozialismus*, Frankfurt: S. Fischer, pp. 37 ss., 41 ss.

64 Horvat, Branko (1979): *Some Political Preconditions for a Free Society*, unpubl. paper, Moscow: XI IPSA World Congress, p. 5.

65 The problem is admitted by Kardelj, *Wege der Demokratie*, p. 68. The country's ethnic, cultural, and linguistic fragmentation, increased by profound economic inequalities and jealousies between the six republics and two autonomous provinces of Yugoslavia, provides the second most important hurdle. Research conducted in Serbia and Croatia has pointed, moreover, to unsatisfactory connection and coordination on all levels of the delegate system, to marked discrepancies between formal participation and actual influence, finally to insufficient social representativity of the system on higher levels. Cf. Marinković, Radivoje and Tomić, Vinka (1979): *The Functioning and Implementation of the Delegational System in Yugoslavia*, unpubl. paper, Moscow: XI IPSA World Congress; Šiber, Ivan et al. (1979): *The Functioning and Realization of the Delegate System*, unpubl. paper, Moscow: XI IPSA World Congress. For a recent survey (published in Slovania) of a good part of the Yugoslav discussion over the decades, cf. Bibič, Adolf (1981): *Interesi in politika*, Ljubljana: Delavska Enotnost. – The debate over pluralism has also been taken up in Hungary. Cf. the appropriately titled article by Bayer, József (1983): „A pluralizmus mint kényes kérdés" [‚Pluralism as a Delicate Question'], Part I, *Kritika* 83/10, Oct.; Part II, *Kritika* 83/11 (Nov.).

66 The constitution proclaimed as its fundamental principle the „plurality of democratic expression and democratic political organization" in order „to ensure the transition to socialism". The form of industrial and agrarian social property „which shall tend towards preponderance" was to be based on „production managed by local authorities; and on the kooperative sector". The constitutional revision during 1982 abolished the greater part of

have included Robert A. Dahl's proposals (rooted in his analyses of American government) „to achieve the best potentialities of pluralist democracy" by realizing a „radical alternative to the American and Soviet status quo" of concentrated (pseudo-private here, pseudo-public there) economic power in the form of self-managed market socialism, combined with external controls and a decentralization of political authority.[67] And, from an „abstract alternative", they have been brought back to include the „sum of real particular worlds" by Michael Rustin's contention (founded upon his background in the British New Left) that „pluralist socialist politics" should be developed not least by drawing on the experiences of (feminist, cultural, environmental, workers' plans, anti-nuclear) single-issue movements and groupings „within which individuals have found meaning".[68]

These notions cannot be discussed here in detail. Like other, comparable perspectives resulting from critiques, by structural pluralists, of capitalist and actually existing socialist societies, they have merged into a common set of propositions focusing on the self-management of blue- and white-collar employees in corporations and firms, reinforcement of consumer associations and their rights, indicative planning of resources and investments, and a more profound and continuous fusion of everyday „social" with periodical „political" activity through a network of organizational groupings.[69] By insisting that, in terms of social and political justice, more horizontal and vertical mobility, more participatory democracy, less inequality and hegemony (over foreign societies in space as well as, by using up available resources, over future generations in time) should be realized within and between societies,[70] an additional international dimension has been introduced, and the military institution has been included in the normative pluralist approach.

VII

Already domestically, the increasing tendency of governments over the last decade to substitute social policies (designed to ameliorate injustices) by strengthening states' means of violence and by a more pronounced policing

---

this (as judged by Mário Soares, General Secretary of the Partido ‚Socialista') „ideological burden".

67   Cf. Dahl, Robert A. (1975): *Und nach der Revolution?*, Frankfurt/New York: Campus (transl. from id. [1970]: *After the Revolution. Authority in a Good Society*, New Haven/London: Yale University Press), pp. 107, 121, 130; id. (1982*): Dilemmas of Pluralist Democracy*, New Haven/London: Yale University Press), pp. 129, 202 ss.

68   Cf. Rustin, Michael (1985): *For a Pluralist Socialism*, London: Verso, pp. 36, 84, 94, 174.

69   In addition to the literature already referred to, see also Fischer, Ernst (1968): *Auf den Spuren der Wirklichkeit*, Hamburg: Rowohlt; Galtung, Johan (1971): *Pluralismus und die Zukunft der menschlichen Gesellschaft*, Frankfurt: Suhrkamp 1971; Bermbach, Udo/ Nuscheler, Franz, eds. (1973): *Sozialistischer Pluralismus*, Hamburg: Hoffmann & Campe.

70   Cf. Galtung, *Pluralismus und die Zukunft*, esp. pp. 186 ss.

of society, poses a problem of alarming dimensions for pluralists. Still, the vexing problems of what to do about the armed forces, military policies, and the international threat systems have – apart from the substantially isolated efforts of peace research – received scant attention. Yet they need to be addressed alongside the democratization of the economy by any cogent structurally pluralist exposition.

What structural changes would have to be wrought within the armed forces to prevent military, rigid, hierarchical values from „spilling over" into society, and to prevent military influence fusing with other interests into the tangled web of relationships referred to above?

For a brief time, the Portuguese officers – the so-called Armed Forces Movement, or MFA – who overthrew the Caetano dictatorship in 1974 and who, as already noted, expressly advocated a socialist pluralism, attempted to provide an answer. These officers, politicized by the increasingly savage and hopeless colonial wars the regime has been waging in Africa, were very much aware of the dangers a mere „operational" attitude extolling traditional military discipline and professionalism over structural change – if it continued to prevail among the armed forces – would imply for their program of bringing decolonization, democracy and economic development to Portugal. Accordingly, the MFA – initially a mere officers', mainly a captains' movement – intended to change both the hierarchical relations between the upper and lower armed forces echelons and the estranged relations between the military and civil society.

When delegate assemblies were set up for the army, the navy, and the air force – as well as on a comprehensive armed forces level – by March, 1975, officers, non-coms and privates obtained representation in the ratio of 4 : 1 : 1. If officers thus kept their numerical superiority, the move, for military thinking, was certainly revolutionary. A „new" soldier, politically informed and alert, came to be in demand, and a dynamic understanding of command and discipline – calling fort he replacement of simple top-down orders by group participation in decision-making processes – was promoted. „Detachments of dynamization" were added to the staffs and units of the three services, always including non-coms and privates in addition to officers. Apart from the delegate assemblies, the new detachments developed into the most important feature of the reorganized armed forces.

The attempted „democratization of the barracks" – the combination of politicization, participation and pluralism – suggests an important contribution to the theory and practice of socialist pluralism. By allowing for organized group processes and individual participation not merely on the – in itself increasingly important – technical („team") level of handling complex weapons systems, such democratization would be apt to promote, in a comprehensive sense, the soldiers' qualifications, their capability to engage in joint reflection and action. By favoring decentralization – the determination and practice of action in small groups -, it would tend to work against a hierarchy that is proving, to the everyday experience of civil and military life, neither humane *nor* effective. To a much larger degree than presently, the armed forces would be established as part and parcel of civil society.

From group discussion and participation among the military, alternative proposals to prevailing defense strategies – political „inputs" to the public, to parties, parliaments, and governments – might result. The West German „Darmstadt Signal", a group of 150 officers and N.C.O.s which, having emerged during the missile deployment debate of 1983, continues to speak out publicly and in seminars for steps toward disarmament and for alternatives to nuclear deterrence policies, provides an example of such – as yet informal – participation.[71]

The emergence of „participatory armed forces" should be accompanied by gradual „transarmament", the elimination, by stages, of „the more provocative, aggressive, or escalatory aspects of armaments" and the definition of national defense „in the narrowest and strictest sense".[72] Such a process would, of course, imply both institutional *and* value changes occurring „in a gradual, interactive manner"[73]. Step by step, present nuclear deterrence policies would have to be replaced by a „mixed" strategy combining conventional military, paramilitary (guerilla) and non-military (i. e.. social) means.[74]

Such an „inoffensive defense" – which has also been termed „defensive defense" or „defensive deterrence" – is based on recognizing that nuclear defense would equal nuclear aggression in literally annihilating a society's own population. Inoffensive defense is „as much a signal of political resistance as it is of military defense."[75] It implies a fundamental alternative to the present East-West threat system. Its emphasis on small, mobile, highly autonomous units (using precision-guided weapons), combined with civil

---

71 An analysis of the Portuguese attempt may be found in Eisfeld, Rainer (1984): *Sozialistischer Pluralismus in Europa. Ansaetze und Scheitern am Beispiel Portugal*, Cologne: Wissenschaft und Politik, esp. parts III/IV. The Portuguese effort started to run off the rails when the MFA attempted to act, simultaneously, as „motor of the revolutionary process". Ideological cleavages between military factions were prone to appear to the extent that political parties and foreign governments now attempted to impress their political projects upon the MFA. In the end, a revolt of left-wing units was suppressed by carefully prearranged measures of a „centrist coup" that expanded into a general purge and terminated the MFA. As a consequence, delegate assemblies and detachments of dynamization were immediately abolished. Professional officers came to the fore again; during 1976, U.S. and West German military advisers flocked to Portugal.

72 Forsberg, Randall (1984): „The Freeze and Beyond: Confining the Military to Defense as a Route to Disarmament", *World Policy Journal* I, pp. 287, 310.

73 Ibid., p. 309.

74 Cf. Galtung, Johan (1984): „Transarmament: From Offensive to Defensive Defense", *Journal of Peace Research* 21, pp. 127-139.

75 Kaldor, Mary (1983): „Beyond the Blocs: Defending Europe the Political Way", *World Policy Journal* I, p. 14.

disobedience and non-violent action of a country's groups and associations, clearly favors the sort of „participatory" armed forces advocated here.

VIII

Transarmament measures would combine domestic with foreign policy effects: in foreign policy by confidence-building measures and cooperation, hopefully initiating a „virtuous circle of trust";[76] domestically by strengthening participatory structures in military and civil institutions. As a concept centering on the membership of individuals in – more or less (permanently) organized – groups and associations which exert influence on each other and on governments to translate conflicting or complimentary interests into distinctive policies, pluralism, *provided its implications are taken seriously*, is necessarily a participatory concept. By exploring foundations for and alternatives to unequal positions of socio-economic power – implying unequally distributed political resources -, *pluralism becomes structural in its analysis, socialist in its program.* As monist barriers to participation are neither only embedded nationally nor merely in economy and civil society, pluralism must *add an international as well as a military dimension* to its argument.

Thus, in summary, pluralism, if not reduced to a mere ideology, proves a more inclusive and, at the same time, more radical concept than is usually acknowledged – a dynamic theory of the socio-political democratization of capitalist and actually existing socialist societies. To the extent that such a fundamental, if yet tentative alternative to the systems of East and West should gain more ground in European political culture, if might – for a start – work as an antidote to the ideological hegemony which both „modern pluralism" and „democratic centralism" have been enjoying, for obvious reasons and with doubtful results, within the respective „camps".

---

76 Rustin, *Pluralist Socialism*, p. 255.

II.
Political Science
and
State Power

In 2010, Leslie A. Pal (Carleton University, Ottawa) and I co-edited a volume reviewing the development and state of political science throughout Central-East Europe. The book's chapters, written by scholars from the countries under survey, provided the first comprehensive account of the discipline's institutionalization in 19 post-communist countries. In addition to research and teaching, problems of funding – including outside support by foreign governments, foundations and universities – received extensive attention. The work identified Western interventions as powerful external forces pushing Central-East Europe's nascent political science "cultures" toward convergence. But it also depicted another external factor primarily responsible for persisting disciplinary disparities: the rise of "hybrid" political regimes in the region. Where autocratic elements have persisted, the institutionalization and independence of political science have been negatively affected. Recommended by the International Political Science Association (IPSA), the book (published by Barbara Budrich) contained an introductory overview written by the two editors, which appears here. A shorter version was pre-published in the June 2010 issue of European Political Science, *the journal of the European Consortium for Political Research.*

Political Science in Central-East Europe and the Impact of Politics: Factors of Diversity, Forces of Convergence

With Leslie A. Pal

1 Democratization and the Emergence of "Hybrid" Regimes

Political Science has sometimes been portrayed as an inherently "moral" discipline, imbued with democratic ideals, bound to contribute to the "emergence and stabilization of democracy".[1] This is a powerful narrative because it adds ethical legitimacy to the field – something which political scientists may find helpful in cases where the discipline's institutionalisation meets with resistance.

---

1   Huntington, Samuel P. (1988): „One Soul at a Time: Political Science and Political Reform", *AmPolScRev* 82, 3, 7.

History records, however, "that political science has also been practiced under non-democratic regimes".[2] Authoritarian states have demonstrated a use for the discipline – albeit for a truncated version adapted to their purposes. Some have been known to offer material support and official prestige to political scientists, even if distinctions between scholars and ideologues become blurred.

Such "authoritarian temptations" might have been solely an issue of sober reflection about the discipline's past,[3] had not post-1989 political transformation in East-Central Europe refused to follow "a clear and simple trajectory leading from state socialism to Europe and democracy."[4] In many cases, political elites and individual players chose to struggle over institutions and power, rather than "competing over policy alternatives and votes".[5] During the process, initial wide-spread visions of straightforward democratization "grew more and more blurred by...new... uncertainties".[6]

An initial post-Cold War wave of democratization was followed by what has been referred to as "an even larger wave of hybridization" – implying continuing (rather than "transitional") absence or abolition of one or more key attributes of democracy such as free and fair competitive elections, civil liberties, the accountability of governments. The result has been more or less "hybrid" regimes.[7] Recent attempts at assessing the ensuing state of democracy in Central-East-Europe's post-communist countries have ranged from "not fully outgrown 'adolescence' after 13 years" for the Baltic states[8] to "a seemingly endless transition" in the case of Romania.[9] Mirroring the actual variety of both democratic and "hybrid" cases, classifications at present include "consolidated democracies" (such as the Czech Republic, Hungary,

2   Easton, David/Gunnell, John G./Stein, Michael B. (1995): "Introduction", in: id. (eds.): *Regime and Discipline. Democracy and the Development of Political Science*, Ann Arbor: University of Michigan Press, 3.
3   Cf., e. g., Eisfeld, Rainer/Greven, Michael Th./Rupp, Hans Karl (1996): *Political Science and Regime Change in 20th Century Germany*, New York: Nova.
4   Hankiss, Elemér (2002): „Brilliant Ideas or Brilliant Errors? Twelve Years of Social Science Research in Eastern Europe", in: Max Kaase/Vera Sparschuh (eds.): *Three Social Science Disciplines in Central and Eastern Europe*, Berlin/Budapest: GESIS/Collegium Budapest, 21.
5   Christensen, Robert K./Rakhimkulov, Edward R./Wise, Charles, R. (2005): "The Ukrainian Orange Revolu-tion: What Kind of Democracy Will the Institutional Changes Bring?", *Communist and Post-Communist Studies* 38, 228.
6   Hankiss, ibid.
7   Levitsky, Steven/Way, Lucan A.: *Competitive Authoritarianism: The Emergence and Dynamics of Hybrid Regimes in the Post-Cold War Era*, unpubl. manuscript, http://sitemaker.umich.edu/ comparative.speaker.series files/ levitsky_with_bibil.pdf, accessed 11/12/2009, 4, 20.
8   Reetz, Axel (2005): „Die vierten Parlamente in Estland, Lettland und Litauen: Ähnliche Voraussetzungen, verschiedene Pfade", *ZParl* 36, 347, 348.
9   Mungiu-Pippidi, Alina (2001): „The Return of Populism – The 2000 Romanian Elections", *Government & Opposition* 36, 252.

Poland, or Slovenia), "defective democracies" (for instance, Albania, Bulgaria, Moldova, Romania, Ukraine) and "competitive autocracies" (e. g., Armenia, Belarus, Georgia, Russia).[10]

The picture of post-communist countries in some sort of 'gray zone' between open autocracy and liberal democracy"[11] should not be painted too bleakly. While Slovakia could have been labeled as "competitive authoritarian" between 1994 and 1998,[12] the 1998 elections – won by an opposition coalition – returned the country to the path to democratization. The 2002 and 2006 elections consolidated the establishment of – according to the current Freedom House survey – a "pluralistic democracy" with a "vibrant" civil society.[13] Ukraine, during the 2004/2005 'Orange Revolution', emerged from a competitive autocracy at "midpoint" on the way towards a consolidated democracy,[14] even if fierce infighting has since barred further progress. Serbia, impeded by the late fall of the Milosevic regime (2000) and the increasingly dysfunctional union with Montenegro (2003-2006), has made democratic headway under a new (even if so far insufficiently implemented) constitution.[15]

The situation would look much brighter, were it not for the authoritarian turn in Russia and the shadow it casts on the region's democratization process. Between 2000 and 2008, Vladimir Putin and a supporting group of political players established a competitive autocracy with a rubber-stamp parliament, limits to the competitiveness of elections, harassment of independent media and journalists, drastically reduced horizontal separation of powers, an extensively regulated civil society, and impediments to the freedom of expression and assembly.[16]

---

10 Cf. Levitsky/Way, ibid., 1, 2, and Melville, Andrei (2008): *Russia in Today's World: An Experiment in Multidimensional Classifications*, UNISCI Discussion Paper No. 17 (May), 56.

11 Croissant, Aurel/Merkel, Wolfgang (2004): "Introduction", *Democratization* 11 No. 5, Special Issue: Consolidated or Defective Democracy? Problems of Regime Change, 3.

12 For a contrary view, cf. Henderson, Karen (2004): "The Slovak Republic: Explaining Defects in Democracy", *Democratization* 11 No. 5 (n. 11), 148/149 et passim.

13 Cf. Levitsky/Way, 1; Geoffrey Pridham (2003): „The Slovak Parliamentary Election of September 2002: Its Systemic Importance", *Government and Opposition* 38, 334; www.freedomhouse.hu/index.php?   option=242:nati-ons-in-transit-2009&ca,   accessed 11/12/2009, 480, 481.

14 D'Anieri, Paul (2005): „The Last Hurrah: The 2004 Ukrainian Presidential Elections and the Limits of Machine Politics", *Communist and Post-Communist Studies* 38, 248; see also Christensen et al. (n. 4), 228.

15 Cf. Commission of the European Communities (2009): *Serbia 2009 Progress Report*, COM(2009) 533, 6/7.

16 For overviews see Beichelt, Timm (2004): „Autocracy and Democracy in Belarus; Russia and Ukraine", *Democratization* 11 No. 5 (n. 11), esp. 120 ss., 126 ss.; Stykow, Petra (2008): "Die Transformation des russischen Parteiensystems: Regimestabilisierung durch personalisierte Institutionalisierung", *ZParl 39*, particularly 773/774, 784.

A presidential party, "United Russia", founded in 2001 for the purpose of endorsing Putin's policies, won a two-thirds majority of seats in two successive parliamentary elections, benefitting from electoral legislation requiring parties to be registered as "all-Russia" associations, from partisan use of state resources, and from biased media reporting.[17] Regional governors, popularly elected to office until 2005, were reduced to presidential appointees. Nongovernmental associations, dissenting demonstrators, and non-state media have been obstructed and attacked under restrictive legislation, sometimes also unlawfully.[18] The message to civil society has been unmistakable: groups or individuals considered detrimental to state authority will be marginalized.

Putin's policies have been justified by the proclaimed need to strengthen administrative capacity, create political stability, and ensure economic prosperity against the backdrop of the political turmoil and economic deprivation experienced by a majority of Russians during the 1990s. Certainly, the regime "derives legitimacy from citizens' broad endorsement",[19] as evidenced by Putin's high approval ratings among the public.

Divergences in democratic performance have thus become a distinct feature of the region's post-communist states. Twenty years after the collapse of the Soviet Union and the Warsaw Pact regimes, no universal era of democracy has been ushered in throughout Central and Eastern Europe. The variety of transitions from communism, different in ideological and institutional consequences, clearly affected the evolving political studies discipline, generating modifications in concepts, theories, methods and research agendas.

2 "Scientific Communism", Regime Hybridization and Ideological Continuities in Political Science

With Russia's recent political evolution as a first example, it comes as no surprise that "reforms of the political system" in the early 2000s "dramatical-

---

17 Cf. www.osce.org/odihr-elections/14523.html for the OSCE observation mission's report on monitoring the 2003 parliamentary elections (accessed 11/12/2009); see also the OSCE report after observing the 2004 presidential elections (www.osce.org/odihr-elections/14520.html, accessed 11/12/2009). Because of Russian restrictions, the 2007 parliamentary and the 2008 presidential elections were boycotted by OSCE observers. Addressing the 11th "United Russia" congress on Nov. 21, 2009, Putin's successor Medvedev confirmed and criticized administrative manipulation of regional elections.

18 Cf. Amnesty International (2008): Document – Russian Federation: Freedom Limited. The Right to Freedom of Expression in the Russian Federation (www.amnesty.org/en/ library/asset/EUR46/008/2008/en/32ee.118-8f09-4e99-8c47-f7eddbee710f/e, accessed 11/12/2009).

19 Stykov, ibid., 773.

ly changed" the research agenda of Russian political science.[20] The "visible decline of electoral competition" and "reduction of electoral politics" compromised "prospects for study[ing] electoral processes". Curbing regional governments' power "confined the field for regional political studies". Finally, "the non-transparent character of political elites' recruitment and rotation complicates research on these dynamics." The discipline inevitably is constrained, even contorted by the systems within which it operates: political and institutional developments "are critical for the perspectives of political science."[21]

An extreme case is Belarus, where "official" political science – part of a split professional community – has been contributing to the development of an ideology of "Belarusian statehood" promoted by autocratic president Aleksandr Lukashenka. The thrust of that ideology's rhetoric has been to popularize the message that there exists a "peculiar [collectivist] Belarusian mentality" and, consequently, a peculiarly Belarusian – state-centered and anti-Western – "way of [economic, social and political] development".[22] In this official interpretation, the "basic source of the Belarusian tradition is considered to be the Soviet era", and Belarusian ideology should retain a considerable part of that experience.[23]

Such ideological continuity was explicitly promoted not just by the government of Belarus, but also in Romania, where PCR members created the post-1989 National Salvation Front, and where the subsequently formed Social Democratic Party's "reconstructed" communists carried national elections in 1990 and 1992. In academe, instructors in "scientific Communism" concurrently "changed their vocabulary, without unwrapping their understanding of politics from its Leninist core". Successive governments set up the necessary public "institutions of continuity", so that the "members of this network" succeeded in perpetuating an approach to politics "indebted to nationalism and vulgar Marxism".[24] As in Belarus, this is not the entire picture: several university departments and think tanks have assumed roles as agents of conceptual change. But no Romanian political science community worthy of the name has so far emerged.

---

20 For this and the following quotes, cf. Ilyin, Mikhail/Malinova, Olga (2008): "Political Science in Russia: Institutionalization of the Discipline and Development of the Professional Community", *GESIS Newsletter*, Special Issue: Political Science Research and Teaching in the Russian Federation, 11.

21 These developments would of course, in principle, not exclude both comparative and critical studies. For the absence of the latter, see below. Regarding the former, the article paraphrases the opinion of a leading Russian comparativist, who is "rather critical" about the condition of his sub-field.

22 Bekus, Nelly (2008): „European Belarus versus State Ideology: Construction of the Nation in the Belarusian Political Discourses", *Polish Sociological Review* 163, 273, 274, 275/276. 23 Ibid., 276, 277.

24 Barbu, Daniel: „Political Science – Romania" (2002), in: Kaase/Sparschuh (n. 4), 327, 331, 338.

Ideological continuity, involving both conceptual and methodological constraints, may have persisted for a different reason, even without governmental aid and abetment. There was the factor of the "survival" of instructors schooled in "scientific Communism", among them jurists, sociologists, philosophers. In Albania, for example, the 1990s – due to governmental corruption, economic and political turmoil, organizational and functional problems of educational institutions – was essentially a lost decade. A small number of faculty were dispatched to European universities to learn modern approaches, but a true scholarly discipline of political science did not begin until 2000. In Moldova, the persistence of low academic salaries and a lack of aspiring newcomers seem to have been more responsible for such "survival" than the return of a non-reformed Communist Party to power for nearly a decade in the 2001 and 2005 elections. Indeed, these "survivors" have stayed on to the extent that Marxist-Leninist and Western approaches are currently pursued side by side. In Serbia, the persistence of the Milosevic regime, and of instructors close to that regime, likewise worked to impede the discipline's evolution well into the 21st century. The situation has not been that much different in Armenia and in Slovakia – where most "scientific Communism" faculty were able to keep their positions during and after the "velvet" revolution – or in Ukraine, where the training of qualified younger political scientists has been beset with difficulties.

In the Czech Republic, in contrast, a new generation of political scientists, primarily trained in Western methods and approaches, was quickly recruited after 1989. The influence of Marxist-Leninist cadres remained marginal. Generational change also played a decisive role in Bulgaria and Estonia. In Lithuania, a different approach was used: employment contracts required academics to publish, and where professors of "scientific Communism" lacked such publications, contracts were terminated. Nowhere, however, with the single exception of the German Democratic Republic after unification,[25] were instructors in Marxism-Leninism summarily dismissed.

In three instances – Hungary, Poland, and Slovenia – a different kind of continuity left its mark on the evolving discipline, which at first glance might impress the observer as beneficial rather than detrimental. During the 1960s and 1970s, these countries for different reasons experienced a "controlled liberalization of intellectual life, though with some recurrence of tough orthodox policies."[26] Professional contacts with Western scholars and universities were (re)established, and for political scientists, the "IPSA Connection" became particularly important. In Poland, mandatory courses in Marxism-Leninism had been already abolished in 1957, subsequent to the "October Thaw". Obligatory political science classes arrived a decade later. In Slove-

---

25 For details, cf. Eisfeld/Greven/Rupp (n. 3), 151, 161/162.
26 Gebethner, Stanisław/Markowski, Radosław (2002, [rev]2009): *Political Science – Poland, Knowledge Base Social Sciences Eastern Europe*, Berlin: GESIS, 4 (accessed 11/15/2009)

nia, the Yugoslav leadership's abortive experiments in "self-management socialism"[27] led to an institutionalization of political science during the 1960s. Hungary was the latecomer: only in the 1980s, following the 1979 IPSA World Congress in Moscow,[28] did "so-called 'legitimizing' debates" emerge which "set the stage for the institutionalization of political science", and only then was some "research related to political science" carried out.[29] "Scientific socialism" departments in Hungary continued to exist until 1989, even if Western concepts and frameworks were increasingly slipped into mandatory courses.

In each instance, this would prove an ambivalent situation, similar to what has been noted for the Russian discipline concerning the "groundwork" supposedly laid in the USSR by political studies "on a limited range of issues (mostly chronologically or geographically distant)... under the guise of other disciplines." Ideological notions intruded into research and persisted: these studies shaped "terminological conventions" that continue "to interfere with the development of more advanced research approaches... in post-Soviet Russia".[30]

On the one hand, early research, publishing and teaching activities contributed to "reinforcing the status" of political science even before 1989. Once the process of political transformation got under way, some intellectual and institutional resources were already available, on the basis of which the discipline could evolve further. Nevertheless, the final result in the Slovenian case has been judged "a relatively weak" discipline – "even in relation to other social sciences in the country." Resources came to work as constraints: an "excessively normative stand" often prevailed; empirical research was rare; important sub-fields of the discipline were neglected; qualified instructors were lacking.[31] In the case of Polish political science, it has been argued that "this particular legacy is very likely the main factor" why the discipline "did not flourish after 1990 as visibly" as in those instances where "its development started from scratch."[32]

---

27 Cf. Sekelj, Laslo (1992): „'Real-Existing Selfmanagement' and the Disintegration of Yugoslavia", *Südosteuropa* 41, esp. 326, 329, 330.
28 An exercise in „peaceful coexistence", held at Lomonosov University, whose students were not permitted to attend the sessions' often spirited debates.
29 Szabó, Maté: „Political Science – Hungary" (2002), in: Kaase/Sparschuh (n. 4), 258, 260.
30 The article quoted here refers to political studies of ethnicity as an example, but adds that difficulties deriving from stereotypes introduced by Soviet social studies "might be found also in the other sub-fields of political science": Ilyin/Malinova, ibid. (n. 20), 10.
31 Cf. Bibič, Adolf (1996): „The Development of Political Science in Slovenia: Democratisation and Transformation of the Discipline", *European Journal of Political Research* 29, 426/427, 428, 444. A section in Danica Fink-Hafner (2002): "Political Science – Slovenia", in: Kaase/Sparschuh (n. 4), 362, was captioned: "Redefinition of the discipline since 1990: from one periphery to another?"
32 Gebethner/Markowski, ibid. (n. 32), 5.

3 Prevalence of Functionalism, Absence of Critical Theories

Two characteristics provided the background to the discipline's beginnings in practically every Central-East European country. They were, first, the excessively normative stand (owing to dogmas about the presumed merits of "actually existing socialism") just referred to, and second, a paucity of empirical research (to avoid revealing the gap between official statements and deviant reality). But, of course, these characteristics fail to explain the conceptual and methodological consequences during and after transformation. An unpublished assessment of dominant trends in Lithuanian political science prepared by Dovile Jakniunaite and Inga Vinogradnaite may help to arrive at some general conclusions about the region under survey:

"The research agenda is to a considerable degree shaped by national political concerns... [and] present-day problems of the political process... There is a... reluctance to engage in broader cross-national comparisons... and a general orientation towards applied research... Methodological and meta-theoretical debate is virtually absent."

From this vantage point, we derive three hypotheses for the discipline's development in European post-communist countries:[33]

1. Functionalist, institutionalist and neo-institutionalist approaches predominate in Central-Eastern European political science. Political studies are largely focused on the "management" of existing systems of government.
2. Critical theories are almost totally absent.
3. Theses (1) and (2) hold equally well for consolidated democracies, defective democracies, and competitive autocracies. Therefore, the above assumption of a linkage between different regimes and different political science approaches should be modified in part.

Belarus again provides a convenient starting-point. As summarized by Svetlana Naumova: "There is not a single governmental research unit concerning itself with any issue save state-building. Etatist schemes and a narrow institutional approach continue to dominate the agenda."[34] In Hungary, since publications during the early 1990s emphasized political institutions, the "institutional approach has prevailed ever since" (Arató/Tóth). Or take Bulgaria ("...democratic consolidation, institution-building, powers, activities, relationships of the centers of government" as "'hot topics'...considered from an institutionalist approach", with studies of elites and their strategies providing an additional focus – Kostova/Avramov); single out Czech political science with, according to Holzer/Pšeja, its "current focus on institutions and political behavior"; pinpoint Estonia where institutionalism has been dominant in

---

33 For the first two, cf. already Hankiss, ibid. (n. 4), 20, 22.
34 This and the following assessments may be found in chapters of the book edited by Eisfeld and Pal, to which the present article served as an introduction.

studies of policy-making and the party system (Pettai); choose Moldova (...based on institutional and functional methods, the majority of publications continue to display a descriptive character" – Mosneaga); Serbia ("overproduction of party studies... focus on institution-building...mostly of a descriptive nature" – Pavlović), or Slovakia (emphasis, once again, on institutions – Rybar). The same pattern keeps re-surfacing.

In a way, that is hardly surprising. Establishing a new political system – a parliamentary or presidential democracy, with (either embedded or defective) checks and balances, popular majority, rule of law, political parties and interest groups – means that political science, once institutionalized, will rather automatically turn to explaining the workings of that system. This holds as well for autocracies, which – as mentioned at the outset – also have use for such information. To a certain extent, political science in any country with new political institutions will be descriptive and institutionalist. The problem, obviously, is to what extent, and how can it grow beyond that focus?

In a number of countries (Armenia, Croatia, Lithuania, Moldova, Romania, Serbia), analyses of domestic government and politics have not or have only rarely proceeded to a comparative level. In others, such as Bulgaria, Estonia, Georgia, Hungary, Latvia, Slovakia, Ukraine, comparative work – particularly in the form of area studies, including other post-communist countries and transformation processes – acquired early importance. In Russia, an ambitious comparative project resulted in the recent publication of an index-based *Political Atlas of the Modern World*, whose variables range from resources of state capacity and potential for international influence to quality of life, the institutional basis of democracy and, finally, external and internal threats[35].

The protracted impact of Marxism-Leninist ideology (or, in the former Yugoslavian states, of a more original "Marxian" approach) produced two initially different consequences, which came to coincide in today's virtual absence of any critical theory of politics and society. In a few instances, the Soviet period's anti-empirical normativism proved habit-forming, with the result that, at least for a time, this (again) "excessively normative stand" persisted after transition – as in Romania, Serbia or the Czech Republic. In a majority of cases, the discredit wrought upon Marxist or Marxist-inspired approaches extended to normative conceptions as such. "The community of

---

35 Cf. Melville, ibid. (n. 10), p. 56/57 et passim, and id. (ed., 2009): *Political Atlas of the Modern World*, Moscow: MGIMO University Press. Among 192 countries, Russia comes off 7th in international influence and 27th on the state capacity index, but ranks only 73rd in quality of life, 93rd as to institutional democratic potential, and 81st on the index of threats (including AIDS, demographic decline, and undiversified exports). From the "institutional basis of democracy" rating, Melville and his collaborators conclude that Russia is "leaning" neither "toward manifest autocracies" nor "mature democracies" (*Political Atlas*, 200).

'normativists' is small" – a statement about Lithuanian political science [36] that might be made about most Central-East European countries. Two exceptions may be noted. One is Ljubljana University's Institute for Social Sciences which, since 2006, includes a Research Center for Critical Politology. That Center's work "is based on a critical theory of society, comparable to that developed by the 'Frankfurt School'" (Zajc).[37] The second is Zagreb University's Faculty of Political Science, where Croatian academics have been including "diminished" subtypes of democracy in their research on East-European transformation processes, investigating long-, medium- and short-term "reasons for democratic deficits".[38]

Generally, the influence of scholars, university departments and foundations from Western Europe, Scandinavia and the United States, of the European Union, U.S., British and French government programs has encouraged the merging of Central and Eastern Europe's nascent political science "cultures" into an empirically oriented political science "mainstream" focusing on national political systems, comparative politics, European studies and international relations. Across the region, the discipline's emphasis is on current politics and policy-making (monitoring, polling, offering expertise) and on applied research. This tendency has been favored by the emergence of numerous non-governmental research institutes and analytical centers ("think tanks"), often financed by Western foundations, with the professed mission of contributing to the evolution of civil society and the consolidation of democracy. Bulgaria and Georgia are particularly conspicuous instances; in the latter case, these institutions have been judged "an effective basis for disseminating social sciences and a specific feature of Georgian social science development."[39] A closer look at Western advice and funding seems warranted.

4   The Role of International Donors and Partners

The collapse of the Soviet Union and the concomitant rise of sovereign states, the majority of which wanted to "modernize," created an unprecedented opportunity for the West, the "winner" in the Cold War. Modernization, of course, meant to certain extent "westernization" and at least initially even a degree of Americanization. Consultants from the World Bank, the UNDP, the OECD, bilateral donor agencies, foundations and NGOs swarmed over the region, acting as transmission belts of so-called "best practices" in economic policy (creating market economies through legal reforms, privatization, and

---

36   Cf. the assessment by Jakniunaite and Vinogradnaite referred to above.
37   As in n. 34.
38   As in n. 34.
39   As in n. 34.

de-regulation), infrastructure, governance, and core institutions (e.g., health and education institutions).

To a large extent, the exercise depended on winning "hearts and minds," especially minds, and to literally convert the way that people thought about government, management, law, or human rights. In addition, the successful transition from communism to post-communism (initially optimistically assumed to result in stable democratic, market societies) meant converting old elites to new ideas, and raising a new generation of elites better suited to a post-communist world.

The higher education system was the obvious target for these efforts. Ironically, whereas under communism the social sciences, and particularly political science, public policy, and public administration, had been smothered if not eradicated by "scientific socialism" and the varieties of Marxism-Leninism, western organizations and governments aimed precisely at these disciplines in order to engender democracy in the political system, and democratic administration and public policy-making within the state. While there was of course some sensitivity to local circumstances and pride, the agenda was basically to encourage reforms that would align these disciplines with western standards. It must be said as well that in most countries, academics within these disciplines were starved for knowledge of western methods, theories, approaches, and methods. They willing embraced and participated in this "know-ledge transfer", in part because in many cases enormous resources (by eastern European standards) flowed with the reform process.

On the bilateral front, the Germans were very active in the early days of transition, but afterwards as well. In Slovakia, the Friedrich Ebert Stiftung and Konrad Adenauer Stiftung supported the purchase of computers and development of libraries; in Ukraine, by funding conferences, round tables, seminars, they provided important venues for communication, and also supported applied research. The Konrad Adenauer Stiftung was particularly important in the Czech case, where the discipline, even after some years, remained inward looking and thus disadvantaged in applying for EU funding. In Serbia, after 2000, the Friedrich Ebert Stiftung in Belgrade supported research on political parties, party competition, party identification, electoral behavior, political participation, public opinion, and democratization. The foundation also sponsored publications on various topics in Romania and Georgia.

As would be expected, the United States played an active role as well. With respect to Albania and Armenia, during the 1990s, pedagogical support for modernizing higher education began to flow into the country – both by IREX, the International Research and Exchanges Board under the auspices of the US Agency for International Development (USAID), and the US State Department. Summer schools and international conferences were held, inaugurating – as far as Albania was concerned – the institutionalization of the discipline at Tirana University. Of course, the American influence was much broader than USAID. It came from several sources. First, the simple fact that American political science is the largest concentration of scholars, departments and institutions in the world gives it a gravitational pull in terms of publications, pedagogy, and research. Second, American universities, as institutions, were engaged in partnerships with sister institutions in the region to develop courses and train teachers and researchers. For example, American institutions were active in Moldova, Bulgaria, and Lithuania. Third, as noted earlier, there were numerous instances of young scholars from the newly emergent states winning scholarships and financial support to study at American institutions, learn about American political science, and bring it back to their home countries.

Finally, and obviously, the Europeans and the EU took a hand in what was happening as well, initially through the TEMPUS (Trans-European Mobility Program for University Studies). This was launched in 1990 with a direct focus on countries from the former Soviet Union, as well as the Middle East. If we exclude the Middle East for a moment, the target regions were Eastern Europe (Armenia, Azerbaijan, Belarus, Georgia, Moldova, Russian Federation, Ukraine), Central Asia (Kazakhstan, Kyrgyzstan, Tajikistan, Turkmenistan and Uzbekistan), and the Western Balkans (Albania, Bosnia and Herzegovina, Croatia, the former Yugoslavian Republic of Macedonia and the Federal Republic of Yugoslavia). The intent was robustly transparent: "to establish new courses or reform former ones in the list of national priorities; to help higher education institution to restructure and to reform their management; to encourage institutions to work together and set up networks, for instance in a particular discipline; to help higher education institutions to assist in the transition process in the social, economic and political fields by organising retraining courses for professionals outside the academic world; to provide limited material so that institutions are equipped with basic logistics at least."[40]

Not every report in this volume highlights TEMPUS, but it obviously became involved in all the countries reviewed here. The chapters on Belarus, Latvia, Albania, Lithuania, and Estonia make specific mention of the contribution of TEMPUS in developing their disciplines. Coupled with TEMPUS was a successor program, TACIS (Technical Aid to the Commonwealth of Independent States), which was originally aimed at a dozen countries in eastern Europe and central Asia (Armenia, Azerbaijan, Belarus, Georgia, Kazakhstan, Kyrgyzstan, Moldova, Russia, Tajikistan, Turkmenistan, Ukraine and Uzbekistan. Chapters on Belarus, Moldova, and Georgia refer to TACIS as an important support mechanism for the evolution of political science.

---

40   http://www.tempus.am/tempus%20program/prog.html

In recent years the converging effects of the EU have been felt most powerfully in the rapid spread of the Bologna process, an effort to create a European Higher Education Area (EHEA). The Bologna Declaration was signed in 1999 by representatives of 29 European nations. The reform process has since expanded to 46 countries – obviously, participants do not have to be members of the EU. The broad aim is standardization of the overall structure of bachelor, master, and doctoral programs in terms of both credits and years spent in each cycle, with an aim to facilitate quality assurance, standards, and mobility by mutual recognition through the European Credit Transfer and Accumulation System (ECTS). A sign of the impact of Bologna is that practically every chapter mentions the process. This is a powerful converging force that is creating structural symmetries in all 46 countries, increasingly also in terms of competencies and quality assurance, as well as mobility among students and faculty, and the facilitation of joint research. Later in this chapter we will review some of the enduring specificities of the discipline in different countries in central and eastern Europe, but in ten or twenty years these may be eclipsed by a more uniform EHEA.

An extraordinarily important and influential catalyst to the development of political science in the region was not an international government organization, or a major national, but in fact a private donor: virtually every country report highlights the role of the Soros Foundation in supporting the early development of institutions, teaching and training in political science. George Soros,[41] the billionaire financier, listed by *Forbes* as the 29th richest person in the world, is both a philanthropist and activist. Galvanized as a student by the teachings of Karl Popper, he became an implacable foe of communism as well as a defender of the "open society." He was actively engaged in supporting dissidents in Poland and Hungary, privately financed the Central European University, and more recently was reputed to have been engaged in supporting the "Rose Revolution" in Georgia.

A key pillar of an "open society" is a transparent and accountable political system, and Soros (someone with strong academic inclinations and a writer on financial systems as well as global capitalism)[42] understood the special role of the social sciences in building the foundation of an open society. He also recognized the institutional brickwork necessary for that foundation: universities, NGOs, think tanks, networks of scholars, researchers and activists. His activities in central and eastern Europe in the 1990s – through

---

41   Cf. Kaufman, Michael T.: Soros: *The Life and Times of a Messianic Billionaire*, New York: Alfred A. Knopf 2002; also the earlier study by Slater, Robert: *Soros: The Unauthorized Biography, the Life, Times and Trading Secrets of the World's Greatest Investor*, New York: McGraw-Hill 1997.

42   E. g., *The Alchemy of Finance* (1988), New York: Simon and Schuster; *The Crisis of Global Capitalism: Open Society Endangered* (1998), New York: Little, Brown; *George Soros on Globalization* (2002), New York: Public Affairs; *The New Paradigm for Financial Markets* (2008), New York: Public Affairs.

the Open Society Institute and sometimes nationally based Soros Foundations – were extraordinary. It is no exaggeration to say that political science in the region would be considerably less developed without Soros's interventions. Examples of this early work abound: in Albania, the sponsoring of research projects; in Armenia, pedagogical training programs; in Moldova, support for the training of political science instructors in France and the U.S., for operating the "think tank" IDIS Viitorul (established in 1993), for founding, in 1999, of the Institute of Public Policy; in Romania, financial aid through the Open Society Foundation to another "think tank", the Romanian Academic Society; in Georgia, the financing by the Open Society Institute of projects contributing to the transformation of social science university curricula; in Ukraine, financial assistance for political science research through the Renaissance Foundation (but also abandonment at an early stage, for unspecified reasons, of that foundation's "Megaproject HELP – Higher Education: Leadership for Progress" to create two political science/European studies quality centers); in Lithuania, being one of the most generous sponsors for the re-education of political scientists in foreign institutions; in Latvia, similar funding to seek credentials and training abroad.

In Bulgaria, the Soros Foundation (with the United States Agency for International Development) provided initial funding of the American University in Blagoevgrad. Through its International Higher Education Support Program, the Open Society Institute continues to assist the European Humanities University, originally founded in Minsk, since 2004 located in Vilnius (Lithuania) as a Belarusian university-in-exile. The role of Budapest's Central European University (CEU), established by Soros in 1991, has remained particularly important as a sort of social science Mecca for students in the region. Teaching in English, with a large complement of foreign scholars, and located in the heart of Europe, CEU has been a perfect instrument for the inculcation of western standards of social science education, particularly in political science. According to its mission statement, the university continues to work "hand-in-hand with the Open Society Institute, providing academic and professional backing for OSI's global agenda of democratic governance, human rights, and economic, legal and social reform".[43]

The Soros Foundation also created the Local Government and Public Service Initiative (LGI), which targeted research and training at the local government level and the public sector more broadly, as well as PASOS (Policy Association for an Open Society, established in 2003), linking think tanks throughout the region. It was further instrumental in the original and continued funding for NISPAcee (Network of Institutes and Schools of Public Administration in central and eastern Europe), which embraces both academic institutions as well as ministries throughout the region, attracting

43   www.ceu.hu/about/organization/missionhistory

scholars as well as practitioners, and sponsoring research and conferences. Its original objective was to build anew the foundations of public management scholarship and practice in central and eastern Europe, as well as build bridges to western scholarship and best practices.

Surveying these efforts in international support and funding and – it must be frankly stated – intervention and proselytizing,[44] it is easier to both understand and appreciate the development of political science in the region. As a thought experiment, imagine that the hundreds of millions of dollars spent in this effort over twenty years had not happened. Given the distinct origins and experiences mentioned in this overview, it is clear that the disciplines in our survey would have spun out into their own widely distant orbits, or conceivably even imploded, becoming black holes in a galaxy of separately burning stars.

5 Problems of Fragmentation and Deficient Research

And yet, the disciplines that travel in these now more proximal orbits are considerably different as regards their composition. Some resemble more or less compact planets. Others recall the image of numerous minuscule asteroids: individual and institutional cooperation are deficient, research networks underdeveloped, professional interests insufficiently represented. Fragmentation of the discipline will subsequently be a recurrent theme.

In Georgia – where the political science community is "deeply segmented in terms of theoretical and methodological approaches"[45] – and Moldova, repeated attempts to establish national political science associations have gone awry for lack of human and financial resources. In Belarus, several such organizations exist which play no public role and have failed to unite the political science community. Bulgaria has had a political science association since 1974, whose journal *Political Research* had to be discontinued after 1993, because "Bulgarian political scientists are still too fragmented to guarantee the journal's financial support". The Czech Republic's Political Science Association "lacks resources, influence and organizational capacity". Divi-

---

44 To illustrate that foreign financial donors need not just good intentions, but also tact, former Romanian Minister of Culture Andrei Pleşu commented, in his own particular way, on a certain apocryphal story. Both the story and the comment bear repeating: "Ava Gardner decided to leave one of her husbands and submitted 'mental cruelty' as grounds for divorce. Asked to explain this in greater detail, she said Thomas Mann's Magic Mountain was the cause. 'He forced me to read this damned book.'" Adds Pleşu: "Mutatis mutandis, Eastern Europe's intellectuals sometimes feel like Ava Gardners terrorized by 'civilizing' spouses. And in this case, it's not even Thomas Mann..." (Pleşu, Andrei [2002]: "Financing Difference: Fostering the Social Sciences in the Field of Tension Between Homogenization and Differentiation", in: Kaase/Sparschuh, ibid. (n. 4), 14.

45 Cf. above, n. 34. These and the subsequent quotes – including those following the table - have also been taken from the book's respective country reports.

sion is present here, too – between one group that sets the discipline's research agenda, and a second group which, due to its members' media presence, determines the discipline's public perception. The Romanian Political Science Association has sunk into obscurity, its political science community "split into factions viciously fighting each other". And in Ukraine, the discipline is also "plagued by low quality research and fragmentation".

The subsequent, more detailed table highlights the persisting considerable differences between the region's political science communities:

Country	
Albania	Severe communist experience; 1990s the "lost decade" of a tumultuous transition. Political science is taught at Tirana University only since 2000 and at several private universities (licensed from 2003). The Bologna system has been introduced. Private research institutes ("think tanks") were set up with foreign support over the last decade.
Armenia	Armed conflict over the Karabakh region with Azerbaijan, pre-dating Armenian independence, was followed by political instability, violence and corruption. The first political science courses, developed during 1990/91, aimed at replacing "scientific communism" by the civic education of a new generation of citizens. However, "scientific communism" faculty remained in place. Development of the discipline proceeded hesitantly. The Bologna system has been introduced. Non-governmental research centers play a considerable role.
Belarus	Little pressure for reform during the Gorbachev period. Formation of political science began in 1992/93 (Belarusian State University, European Humanities University [EHU], both in Minsk, the latter now in exile [Lithuania]). The Bologna system, while introduced in theory, is not practiced; the two-tier postgraduate system (candidate/doctor) has been retained. Re-emergence of an authoritarian state after 1996, which from 2003 mobilized political science in "state-directed institutions" to support an ideology of Belarusian statehood. A parallel, independent sector of research and study institutes, likewise dating from 1992/93 and in part also registered in Lithuania, continues to operate, as does EHU from Vilnius. The discipline is deeply divided: "two sciences, two professional communities, two systems of communication".
Bulgaria	Pragmatic, nationalist and nepotistic communist regime. Early beginnings of the discipline: BCP Academy for Social Sciences and Public Policy, 1970-1989; Research Institutes of Contemporary Social Theories and International Relations (Bulgarian Academy of Sciences), 1975-1989. Establishment of Political Science Department (at the time "History and Theory of Politics") at Sofia University in 1986, at University of National and World Economy in 1990, at the private New Bulgarian and American in Bulgaria Universities in 1991. The Bologna system has been introduced. Low academic salaries require second jobs. Disuniting effect of intense rivalry for research funds. No national political science journal. Private research and study centers were founded with foreign support after 1989.
Croatia	Civil war 1991-1995 ("Krajina"); defective democracy in the 1990s.

Early beginnings of the discipline in 1962 at the University of Zagreb's Faculty of Political Sciences: amalgamated ("science_s"), ideologized, insufficiently professionalized. A single discipline with sub-fields evolved during the 1990s; the Bologna system has been introduced. The Faculty remains the only political science teaching institution and the only significant research center in the country, though new ones are projected for 2009/10.

Czech Republic   Early beginnings of the discipline were twice abolished by the communist regime (1945-52 School of Political and Social Sciences, Prague; 1967-70 ["Prague Spring"] Charles University Prague, Comenius University Bratislava). Re-establishment occurred after 1989 at the country's most prestigious universities and was only marginally influenced either by communist instructors, by returning émigrés, or from abroad. The Bologna system has been introduced. At present, 9 peer-reviewed political science journals are published. The scholarly community remains bifurcated – researchers with international reputations hardly contribute to building Czech political science; researchers preoccupied with the discipline's domestic development do not publish internationally.

Estonia   Minimal communist legacy. Formative influences from the United States, Great Britain and the Scandinavian countries. Small political science community that started from scratch, but rapidly inter-nationalized. The Bologna system has been introduced. Exemplary efforts at public research funding. Considerable impact of the discipline on public debates (societal stratification, minority policies, electoral reform).

Georgia   Civil wars 1991-95 (including the secessionist territories of Abkhazia and South Ossetia), Rose Revolution 2003, defective democracy and Georgian-Russian military conflict 2008 have resulted in a political science "community" not united by common professional standards and deeply segmented in terms of theoretical and methodological options, reflecting profound political cleavages in Georgian society. Two major trends are a reformist approach that idealizes western methods and models, and a traditionalist approach that aims at rediscovering the Georgian past. Georgian-language teaching materials are rare, and there is little research.

Hungary   Well-developed political science community, with roots in the mid-1980s and even earlier in the late 1970s as a commission in the Academy of Sciences under Kadar's "goulash communism". There remains a strong tradition of public intellectuals, and the distinction between them and professional political scientists is sometimes blurred. The Bologna system has been introduced. Hungary also has a unique institution, the English-language, Soros-financed Central European University (CEU), with degrees accredited both in the United States and Hungary), as well as a growing number of think tanks such as Századvég and Demos.

Latvia   "Re-educated" faculty from philosophy, history and law played a major role, aided by formative assistance from Scandinavian countries. Weak research tradition, reinforced by extremely low public funding, better developed at private institutes (limited, however, to applied policy research). Against the backdrop of a large Slavic minority, the role of ethnicity in politics, models of societal integration, and minority rights have figured prominently in the discipline. The Bologna system has been introduced.

Lithuania

Comparable to Latvia, "re-educated" faculty played a certain role, while the discipline was built on western, primarily Scandinavian models (with some American influence). There is a general orientation toward applied research, driven by current political concerns (weak civil society, corruption, ineffective civil service, unstable party system) and generat-ing policy recommendations. The tendency is reinforced by close links between academics and government agencies (e. g., consulting), and by the existence of numerous private "think tanks". The Bologna system has been introduced.

Moldova

The initial (1991-1994) Popular Front Government's nationalist orienta-tion, subsequently the election (twice) of an unreformed Communist administration (2001-2009) led to pressures on political science educa-tion, even an exodus of scholars from the country. The discipline's evolution was further impeded by a continuing pre-ponderance of "scien-tific communism" faculty, who continue to pursue Marxist-Leninist approaches, even if the Bologna system has been introduced. Low aca-demic salaries, lack of coordination on every level of education and research policies contribute to profound fragmentation and a deep-seated malaise of the political science "community". There is no national politi-cal science journal.

Poland

Periods of "thaw" under communist rule permitted the early emergence of an active political science community. A national association was founded in 1956, teaching institutions were established in 1967 (Warsaw) and 1970 (Cracow), a Political Science Committee set up at the Polish Academy of Sciences in 1972. International contacts through IPSA played a major role in the discipline's evolution. 82 public and private higher education institutions currently offer study programs in political science. The Bologna system has been introduced.

Romania

Former communists won the first two elections during transition (1990, 1992); party school and universities retained their communist staff. The small political science "community" is highly factionalized; university corruption further impedes the implementation of professsional stand-ards. A largely Soros-financed "think tank", the Romanian Academic Society, promotes academic excellence. The Bologna system has been introduced.

Russia

"Political and state studies" existed even under communist rule; a corre-sponding Soviet association was formed in 1960, and the 1979 IPSA World Congress was held in Moscow. But this was not an academic discipline. After the collapse of communism, there was rapid growth in institutions and personnel. Since 2007, slow moves toward a higher education reform in line with the Bologna system have been made; the two-tier Soviet system of conferring post-graduate degrees (candi-date/doctor) has been retained. Public funds in support of research and further development of university centers remain short and unevenly distributed between the country's center and periphery.

Serbia

Development was retarded by a decade since many faculty kept ties with the "transformed communists" retaining power until 2000. Political science is taught at only one institution, the Faculty of Political Science in Belgrade (established as a party school for the teaching of Yugoslavian "self-governing socialism" in 1960, transformed into a university faculty in 1968). The Bologna system has been adopted, but not fully implemented. The political science community is small and poorly integrated internationally. Several governmental and private research institutes have been set up, the latter with foreign support.

Slovakia	Due to the „velvet" character of the Czechoslovakian revolution, communist faculty were largely kept on, seriously impeding the modernization of the discipline. The Slovak government established a number of new universities during 1997/98, all of which offered political science programs. Private universities and independent research institutes were added; funding from abroad played a major role. The Bologna system has been introduced. Research tradition, however, is weak. Journals are published by departments or institutes, contributing to the profession's fragmentation. The discipline remains poorly connected to international research.
Slovenia	Among the states of former Yugoslavia, Slovenia for extended periods had the most flexible communist regime, and Slovenian social sciences remained open towards Western ideas. Early developments of the discipline were analogous to those in Serbia (establishment of a teaching school for "self-government socialism" in 1960, transformation into a Faculty of the University of Ljubljana by 1968). The discipline participated in the debates preceding Slovenian independence and democratization and, with support from abroad, quickly modernized after 1989. The political science community is small, but strongly integrated internationally. As in Croatia and Serbia, a single department of political science (at the Ljubljana Faculty of Social Sciences) remains the sole teaching institution for the discipline. The Bologna system has been introduced. Public research funding is available as part of national research programs.
Ukraine	Competitive authoritarian, corrupt regime under Kuchma 1994-2004. The discipline's development in terms of quality and professional standards was impeded by the continued influence of instructors from "scientific communism". The community grew rapidly after 1993 (when political science was recognized as a separate academic field), but remained fragmented. The Bologna system has been introduced, the two-tier postgraduate system (candidate/doctor) retained. With a strong tradition in the humanities, empirical research is weak and overshadowed by abstract theorizing. Public funding of research is limited, selective and arbitrary.

The quote immediately preceding the table and data in the table itself point to low quality research as a further deficiency. This shortcoming has been linked to fragmentation not just in Ukraine, but also in Slovakia – both disciplines burdened, as noted above, by strong personal continuities -, where political science "still suffers from elementary problems", and remains "on the whole, amateurish and largely a-theoretical." For Belarus, "a deficit of institutionalization, curbs on research themes, a shortage of qualified personnel" have been identified as identical problems in the state-directed and the independent research sectors. In Bulgaria, quality research remains an unrealized ambition because of inadequate funding and low academic salaries, obliging professors to "regularly have a second job". In Moldova, things are much the same. In deeply polarized Georgia, "hidden ideologization and teleology" continue to intrude into research; "professional standards are not well established". In Romania, these standards are "acknowledged by a minority only". Serbia, like Albania, is another case where the 1990s was a lost decade: lacking analytical tools and theoretical paradigms, and insufficiently distanced from the regime, Serbian political scientists "played a poor role in analyzing and explaining transition processes and post-communist politics." Research only began to evolve after 2000. And as regards Latvian political science, research "has traditionally been weak," because "there was no real pressure on faculty to publish." Accordingly, both "the quantity and quality of research offer room for growth."

In other words, cohesion of the discipline and a high quality of research are lacking in almost half of the countries included here.

6 Diversity, Convergence, and Some Horizons for Central/East European Political Science

For the purposes of this concluding assessment, the surveyed states may be grouped as follows:

1. Six present or former CIS (Commonwealth of Independent States) members: Armenia, Belarus, Georgia (withdrew in 2008), Moldova, Russia, Ukraine (de facto participation until 2005).
2. Three Balkan states: Albania, Bulgaria, Romania.
3. Three further Balkan states emanating from the former Yugoslavia. Croatia; Serbia, Slovenia.
4. Three Baltic states: Estonia, Latvia, Lithuania.
5. Two former "reform communist" states: Hungary, Poland.
6. Two states emanating from former Czechoslovakia: Czech Republic, Slovakia.

Regime hybridization has been pervasive in both the first and second group, with competitive autocracies concentrated in the first. The two groups form a geographical cluster, which may play a role in the consolidation of authoritarian features. "The less a young democracy is surrounded by stable democratic countries", according to a recent hypothesis, "the lower are the costs of semi-democratic rulers to violate constituent rules of liberal democracy. This is especially true for countries at the eastern fringe of eastern Europe."[46]

---

46 Merkel, Wolfgang/Croissant, Aurel (2004): „Conclusion: Good and Defective Democracies", Democratization 11 No. 5 (n. 11), 207.

Excepting Russia and, partly, Bulgaria, these are also the countries where political science is weakly embedded, fragmented, and poorly connected internationally. In addition to the above depiction, this may largely be recognized from the extent to which (and, if at all, at what point in time) professional – let alone peer-reviewed – journals have appeared:

Political Science Journals or General Outlets

Country	
Albania	*Albanian Journal of Politics* (since 2005; peer-reviewed, in English)
	Polis (since 2006; in Albanian)
	Politika & Shoqëria [Politics & Society] (since 2000; in Albanian)
Armenia	*21st Century* (since 2003; Armenian, Russian and English editions)
	Globus National Security (in Armenian)
Belarus	*Vestnik Belorusskogo Gosudarstvennogo Universiteta* [Bulletin of the Belarusian State University] (government-controlled; in Belarusian)
	Belorusskaya Dumka [Belarusian Thought] (since 1996, government-controlled; in Belarusian)
	Politicheskaya Sfera [Political Sphere] (since 2001; in Belarusian)
Bulgaria	*Razum* [Reason – Journal for Politics and Culture] (since 2002; in Bulgarian)
Croatia	*Politička misao* [Political Thought] (since 1962, with four issues a year in Croatian and one in English as *Croatian Political Science Review*)
	Anali [Annals] (since 2004; in Croatian)
	Međunarodne studije [International Studies] (since 2000; in Croatian)
	Političko obrazovanje [Political Education] (e-journal, since 2006; in Croatian)
Czech Republic	*Politologický časopis* [Czech Journal of Political Science] (since 1993; peer-reviewed, in Czech)
	Mezinárodní vztahy [Journal of International Relations] (since 1966; peer-reviewed, in Czech)
	Politologická revue [Political Science Review] (since 1995; in Czech)
	Revue Politika [Politics Review] (since 2003; in Czech)
	Politics in Central Europe (since 2005, peer-reviewed; in English)
	Perspectives. Central European Review of International Affairs (since 1993, peer-reviewed, in English)
	Středoevropské politické studie [Central European Political Studies Review] (e-journal, since 1999; in Czech)
	Evropská volební studia [European Electoral Studies] (since 2006; in Czech)

Global Politics (e-journal, since 2001, in Czech)

Estonia *Trames Journal of the Humanities and Social Sciences* (since 1997, peer-reviewed; in English)

Georgia None

Hungary *Politikatudományi Szemle* [Hungarian Political Science Review] (since 1992; in Hungarian)

Külpolitika [Foreign Policy] (since 1974; in Hungarian)

Southeast European Politics (since 2000, peer-reviewed; in English)

Századvég [End of Century] (since 1985, re-launched in 1996; in Hungarian)

Kommentár [Comment] (since 2006; in Hungarian)

Latvia *Humanities and Social Sciences* (since 1993; in English) *Latvijas zinātņu Akadēmijas Vēstis* [Proceedings of the Academy of Sciences, Section A: Human and Social Sciences] (since 1946; in Latvian, English, German and Russian)

Lithuania *Politologija* (since 1989; in Lithuanian)

Lithuanian Political Science Yearbook (since 2000; in English)

Viešoji politika ir administravimas [Public Policy and Administration] (since 2002; in Lithuanian)

Lithuanian Foreign Policy Review (since 1998; in English)

Lietuvos metinė strateginė apžvalga [Lithuanian Annual Strategic Review] (since 2003; in Lithuanian and English)

Tiltai: humanitariniai ir socialiniai mokslai [Bridges: Humanities and Social Sciences] (since 1997; in Lithuanian, English and German)

Sociologija: mintis ir veiksmas [Sociology: Thought and Action] (since 1997; in Lithuanian and English)

Moldova *Revista de Filozofie, Sociologie si Stiinte Politice* [Journal of Philosophy, Sociology and Political Science] (since 1991; in Moldavian)

Administrarea publica [Public Administration] (since 1993; in Mol-davian)

MOLDOSCOPIE – Probleme de analiză politică [Problems of Political Analysis] (since 1992; in Moldavian)

Revista de Relatii Internationale [Journal of International Relations] (since 2006; in Moldavian)

Poland *Studia Polityczne* [Political Studies] (since 1991; in Polish)

Przeglad Politologiczny [Political Science Review] (since 1966; in Polish)

Civitas. Studie z Filozofii Polityki [Studies on the Philosophy of Politics] (since 1997; in Polish)

Politeja [Political Letters] (since 2004; in Polish)

Europa Środkowo-Wschodnia [Central-Eastern Europe] (since 1991; in Polish)

Sprawy Miedzynarodowe [International Affairs] (since 1948; in Polish)

Stosunki Miedzynarodowe – International Relations (since 1982/2000; in

	Polish and other languages)
Romania	*PolSci – The Romanian Journal of Political Science* (since 2001; peer-reviewed, in English)
	Romanian Journal of Society and Politics (since 2001; in English)
	Studia Politica – Romanian Political Science Review (since 2001; in Romanian, English, French, German, Italian
	Sfera Politicii [Sphere of Politics] (since 1992; in Romanian and English)
	Idei în dialog [Ideas in Dialogue] (since 2004; in Romanian)
	Transylvanian Review of Administrative Sciences (since 1998, peer-reviewed; in English)
Russia	*Polis – Political Studies* (since 1991; in Russian)
	Politicheskaia nauka [Political Science] (since 2000; in Russian)
	Politex – Politicheskaia expertisa [Politex – Political Expertise] (e-journal, since 2005; in Russian)
Serbia	*Nova srpska politička misao* [New Serbian Political Thought] (since 1998; in Serbian)
	Godisnjak [Yearbook], Serbian Political Science Association (since 2007; in Serbian)
Slovakia	*Politické vedy* [Political Sciences] (since 1998, in Slovak)
	Slovenská Politologická Revue [Slovak Review of Political Science] (e-journal, since 2001; in Slovak)
	Studia Politica Slovaca (since 2008; in Slovak)
	International Issues and Slovak Foreign Policy Affairs (since 1992; in English)
Slovenia	*Teorija in Praksa* [Theory and Practice] (since 1963; in Slovenian)
	Družboslovne razprave [Social Science Debates] (since 1984, in Slovenian)
	Journal of International Relations and Development (since 1998, peer-reviewed; in English)
	Lex Localis – Journal of Local Self-Government (since 2003, peer-reviewed; in English)
Ukraine	*Lyudyna i Polityka* [Man and Politics] (since 1999; in Ukrainian)
	Natsional'na bezpeka i oborona [National Security and Defense] (since 2000; in Ukrainian and English)
	Politychnyi Menejment [Political Management] (since 2003; in Ukrainian)

In the third group of states, which resulted from the disintegration of Yugoslavia, Serbian political science was considerably disadvantaged vis-à-vis Croatia and Slovenia, because the country's eventual transition to democracy only occurred in 2000. At present, the discipline has no professional research journal at its disposal, and (as may gleaned from this chapter's concluding table below) the Serbian Political Science Association's membership amounts to just one tenth of its Slovenian and a mere twenty-fifth of its Croatian counterparts. Lack of competition among academic centers remains a conspicuous feature in Serbia as in Croatia and Slovenia, with the discipline's teaching (and, by and large, also research) restricted to a single university.

As noted earlier, Croatian political science has generated analytical efforts at explaining reasons for the country's democratic deficits, focusing on long-established belief patterns and behavioral traditions, on institutional arrangements and the personality structures of leading political figures. Slovenian political scientists, for their part, have been working on a critical theory of advanced societies inspired by the Frankfurt School of socio-philosophical inquiry. These efforts may eventually contribute to what Dovile Jakniūnaite and Inga Vinogradnaite, in our book's chapter on the Lithuanian discipline, identify as a tendency "to challenge the 'mechanical' application" of Western concepts by looking for "a more elaborate conceptualization" of the "experienced 'realities'" in the region's post-communist countries.

One of the perennial issues in Central and Eastern European countries since the Habsburg and Czarist empires, it should be recalled, has been policies shaping the position of ethno-cultural minorities. As recently as 1993, Czechoslovakia split over the question how to satisfy the demands of the Slovaks as the largest minority group, with Hungarians (10%) and Roma figuring as sizable minorities in newly independent Slovakia. Armenia, Georgia, Moldova, Ukraine experienced ethnically driven struggles – not to mention the atrocities of "ethnic cleansing" during the civil wars in Serbia and Croatia. In the Ukrainian case, these were settled by establishment of the Autonomous Republic of Crimea (60% Russians, 25% Ukrainians, 12% Crimean Tatars) within Ukraine, while conflicts in the other instances continue to linger. High on the agenda of a regionally inspired discipline would be major contributions to the debate on how to make the most of migration and the increasing ethno-cultural diversity of societies. A political science of "recognizing" minorities, in other words, which, by blending political, psychological, cultural and economic approaches, would seek to advance integration and cultural cross-fertilization, in contrast to discrimination, segmentation and ensuing socio-political cleavages.[47]

With Russian minorities accounting for 28% of the Latvian and 25% of the Estonian population, political science disciplines in these two Baltic States have been setting examples regarding comparative, policy-oriented studies on ethno-cultural conflict and accommodation. In Ukraine, too, with a Russian population of some 17% concentrated in the Eastern region, the

---

47 Cf. also Rechel, Bernd (ed., 2009): *Minority Rights in Central and Eastern Europe*, London: Routledge, with country reports on Bulgaria (Bernd Rechel), the Czech Republic (Eva Sobotka), Estonia (Vello Pettai/Kristina Kallas), Hungary (Balazc Visi), Latvia (David Galbreath/Nils Muiznieks), Lithuania (Dovile Budryte/Vilana Pilinskaite-Sotirovi), Poland (Peter Vermeersch), Romania (Melanie H. Ram), Slovakia (Stefan Auer) and Slovenia (Jelka Zorn).

discipline's evolution has included a focus on ethno-politics. A comparable thrust has not evolved in Bulgaria with its Turkish (nearly 10%) and Roma (5%) populations, or in Romania and Slovakia with their ethnic Hungarian minorities of 6.5% and 10%.

In 2008, *Politics and Central Europe*, the journal of the Central European Political Science Association to be discussed below, dedicated a thematic issue to "Values and Diversity in Contemporary Europe", focusing on religious symbols in the public space as a salient expression of cultural pluralisation. In general, however, pushing the elaboration of well-reasoned responses to such pluralisation closer to the discipline's center of attention provides one more conspicuous instance where, in Krisztina Arató's and Csaba Tóth's concluding words on Hungarian political science, "regional cooperation in Central and Eastern Europe waits to be strengthened."[48] The determined transfer of resources, information and conceptual approaches from the West to the East, discussed earlier in this chapter, has produced its drawbacks – among them the fact that, at present, international links established by Central and East European political scientists are typically West European. In the Czech case, even two largely separate groups of academics have emerged, needing to be integrated: Scholars "building the domestic discipline", who are "hardly present" internationally; and those who do not "significantly" contribute to research and teaching in the Czech language, but "have achieved success in the international" – meaning the Western – "arena".[49] As the subsequent country chapters will show, fragmentation more often than not also implies a divide between a minority of internationally connected and a majority of inward-looking academics.

Such absence of internal cohesion has its analogy in a lack of sustained regional interaction between the disciplines considered here.[50] Professional associations could play a considerable role in promoting scholarly cooperation and the creation of networks. However, organizations as different in membership and scope of activities as the Czech, Lithuanian, Romanian and Slovenian Political Science Associations have uniformly attested to a lack of human and financial resources as a constraining factor for such services.[51]

The disparities are displayed in this chapter's final table. Disadvantages due to regime hybridisation or late transition to democracy once again become apparent:

---

48 Quoted from the book's chapter on Hungary (see also above, n. 129).
49 Quoted from the book's chapter on the Czech Republic.
50 That conclusion may be drawn from McGrath, Conor (2008): „ Increasing cooperation among political science associations in Europe", *European Political Science* 7, 360, 365. The same result emerged from an October 2009 workshop organized by Irmina Matonyte for the Vilnius University's Institute of International Relations and Political Science and the Lithuanian Political Science Association, attended by participants from 7 Central-East European countries (Belarus, Latvia, Lithuania, Moldova, Poland, Russia, Ukraine).
51 Cf. McGrath (2008), 358.

Political Science Associations

Country	Est.	Active/Reduced/ Inactive	Comments
Albania	2000	Active	Founded in 2000. Not an IPSA member. Since 2005 publishes the *Albanian Journal of Political Science* and co-sponsors the CEU online journal *Southeast European Politics*.
Armenia	2003	Inactive	Not an IPSA member.
Belarus	1993	Reduced	1. Belarusian Association of Political Science. "Governmental"; about 100 members. Conferences limited to other CIS countries. Not an IPSA member.
	1998		2. Belarusian Academy of Political Science. "Governmental". Not an IPSA member.
	1997-2006	Inactive	3. Belarusian Association of Think Tanks (BATT). "Non-Governmental". 18 members.
			First steps have been taken by the Belarusian Institute of Strategic Studies toward setting up a new organization.
Bulgaria	1974	Active	50-60 members. Established to join IPSA for the 1979 Congress in Moscow. The Sofia University for National and World Economy's Department of Political Science is a member of the European Consortium for Political Research (ECPR).
Croatia	1966	Active	The association has 500 members. It includes political scientists serving as educators, civil servants, and in the media, and belongs to IPSA, the Central European Political Science Association (CEPSA) founded in 1994, and the recently (2007) established European Confederation of Political Science Associations (ECPSA). The Zagreb Faculty is an ECPR member.
Czech Republic	1990	Active	With some 380 members, the CPSA belongs to IPSA, CEPSA and ECPSA. Five departments/institutes – the Institute of Sociology of the Academy of Science, the Institute of International Relations, the Faculty of Social Sciences at Charles University, the Faculty of Social Sciences at Masaryk University, and the Department of Political Science at Palacký University – are institutional members of ECPR.
Estonia		Inactive	Attempt at establishing an association failed in

			the 1990s. Departments at Tallinn and Tartu Universities are members of ECPR.
Georgia	1998	Inactive	Two founding attempts during the 1990s had to be discontinued for lack of human and financial resources.
Hungary	1982	Active	Currently it has some 500 members, including many students. It operates in thematic sections that organize discussions and other events. HPSA joined IPSA in 1985, is also a member of CEPSA and ECPSA. Departments at CEU, ELTE and Miskolc University are ECPR members.
Latvia	2003	Active	With approximately 35 members, the association is a member of ECPSA, but not of IPSA. Departments at Latvia, Riga Stradiņš and Vidzeme Universities are institutional members of ECPR.
Lithuania	1991	Active	The association has about 70 members. It joined IPSA in 1994. Since 2001, it has also been a member of CEPSA (and more recently, of ECPSA). The Institute of International Relations and Political Science at Vilnius University is an ECPR member.
Moldova		Inactive	Attempts in 1994 and 2004 to form an association failed.
Poland	1956	Active	Joined IPSA in 1956, CEPSA in 1994. Departments at the universities of Krakow, Lodz and Lublin are members of ECPR.
Romania	1999	Reduced	The first association was formed in 1994, but failed. Another attempt was made in 1999. It publishes the *Romanian Journal of Society and Politics*, but otherwise is hardly active. Member of IPSA and ECPSA.
Russia	1991	Active	The Russian Political Science Association is a successor of the Soviet Association of Political Science (set up in 1960, former Soviet Association for Political and State Studies), a member of IPSA and of ECPSA. During the last years its membership has stabilized around 550-600 who represent more then 50 regions. In 2006 the Youth Branch of RPSA was reconstituted (it combines more than 400 young political scientists from 27 regions). PRSA is an initiator and organizer of the All-Russia Political Science Congresses that – since 1998 – are held every 3 years.
Serbia	2006	Active	The Serbian Political Science Association was

			only re-established in 2006, after having first been founded in the early 1950s as a part of the Yugoslav Association of Political Science (dissolved in the 1990s). It joined IPSA in 2008, and presently counts about 20 members.
Slovakia	1990	Active	The SPSA joined both IPSA and CEPSA in 1994, and also belongs to ECPSA. It has about 90 members. The department at Comenius University Bratislava is an ECPR member.
Slovenia	1968	Active	The Slovenian Political Science Association has 234 members and holds annual conferences. The organization is a member of IPSA, CEPSA and ECPSA. The Ljubljana University's Faculty of Social Sciences became an ECPR member in 1992.
Ukraine	1992	Active / Reduced	The association has 220 members and is a member of IPSA. So far, it has not addressed problems of research quality, professional ethos, educational standards, and linking Ukrainian political science inter-nationally.

As also evidenced by the table, there have been two attempts since 1989 to create region- or even continent-wide opportunities for deliberation and knowledge exchange by setting up more continuous working relationships between national associations.

The first such attempt was the 1994 establishment of the Central European Political Science Association (CEPSA) by the Austrian, Czech, Hungarian, Polish, Slovak and Slovenian national organizations, later joined by their Croatian and Lithuanian counterparts. Jerzy Wiatr (Poland) was CEPSA's first president for a decade, followed by Attila Ágh (Hungary) in 2003. Since 2006, a new generation has assumed the mantle, represented by Silvia Mihalikova (holder of the Jean Monnet Chair at Bratislava's Comenius University) and her 2009 successor Karin Liebhart (teaching European studies at Innsbruck and Vienna).

The second venture consisted in the more recent (2007) founding of the European Confederation of Political Science Associations (ECPSA), eight of whose presently 22 members stem from post-communist Central-Eastern Europe (Croatia, Czech Republic, Hungary, Lithuania, Romania, Russia, Slovakia and Slovenia). Suzanne Schuettemeyer, former Chair of the German Political Science Association, was elected ECPSA's first president. The ECPSA Executive Committee mirrors the numerical preponderance of Western and Northern European groups, with just one of its five members coming from East-Central Europe (more precisely, Hungary). The association's mission statement emphasizes issues of teaching, curricula, qualification, and mobility in the European Higher Education Area created by the Bologna process. In a survey preceding the ECPSA launch, national associations had suggested a number of practical measures that would particularly benefit smaller, modestly endowed groups, such as reciprocal offers of reduced conference and membership fees, organization of joint conferences and workshops both at associational and sub-section levels, compilation of a register of research interests to facilitate networking.[52] While ECPSA's mission statement does not, of course, exclude such activities (fee reduction has, in fact, been tackled on a bilateral basis), it also does not grant them priority.

CEPSA, in contrast, lists annual conferences as its "main activity", supplemented since 2005 by the publication of *Politics in Central Europe*, a peer-reviewed journal brought out in Pilsen by the West Bohemian University's Department of Politics and International Relations. Consecutive conferences were held in Austria, Croatia, the Czech Republic, Hungary, Lithuania, Slovakia and Slovenia, with sessions organized by post-doctoral students "an important part" of such meetings.[53] The most recent (September 2009) conference, however, did not take place as a separate event, but as a mere workshop within the annual conference of the Polish Political Science Association. *Politics in Central Europe*, on the other hand, has continued to flourish. So far, eight thematic issues have focused on, e. g., the international role of small European states, the Europeanisation of Central European parties, European energy security and – as mentioned above – public policies vis-à-vis religious diversity.

CEPSA's conferences and journal certainly provide a measure of support to the emergence of a political science with a more distinctly "regional" stamp. The central problem remains, of course, that in those countries where the discipline is deeply fragmented, either no political science association has formed, or existing associations are largely inactive – with the consequence that engagement in CEPSA continues to be restricted to a core group of organizations. In the end, CEPSA does not seem to work as a very strong catalyst of Central/East European convergence.

From this chapter's final table, we can deduce that the ECPR (European Consortium for Political Research), whose activities date back to 1970, acquired new institutional members throughout Central-East Europe after 1990. Their total number in the countries surveyed here amounts to 31. Albania, Croatia, Lithuania, Slovakia and Slovenia each have one single member institution, while Armenia, Belarus, Georgia, Moldova, Serbia and Ukraine are lacking any. To put these numbers in perspective, it should be added that the United Kingdom alone has 53, Germany 46, Spain 18, Italy 17, and the United States – somewhat paradoxically, but attesting to ECPR's international standing – 30.[54]

With its joint workshop sessions, general and graduate conferences, summer schools and journals in mind, ECPR has been characterized as "for

---

52 Cf. McGrath (2008), 60.
53 www.cepsa.cz/index.php?page=about, 1, accessed 12/28/2009.
54 http://ecprnet.eu/membership/member_countries.asp, accessed 12/28/2009.

most practical purposes...*the* European Political Science Association".[55] Regarding Central-East Europe, it may well become again "the major force" to socialize political scientists "into a broad, but nevertheless diverse 'mainstream' of shared standards of excellence and relevance"[56] – provided that a significant external factor does not interfere with the process:

The Soros Foundation, the European Union, American, German and Scandinavian agencies, foundations and university departments, and the Bologna process were earlier identified as external factors pushing the region's nascent political science disciplines toward a measure of convergence. However, the rise of "hybrid" political regimes has been operating as a countervailing force, tending to limit such convergence. Should the process of "hybridization" persist or even intensify, it will not cause political studies to disappear, because – as noted at the outset – authoritarian regimes, too, need their trained "eyes and ears" to understand and deal with competing political systems. But any proliferation of defectively democratic or competitively autocratic regimes will bode ill for the existence of independent political science in Central and Eastern Europe.

---

55 Berg-Schlosser, Dirk (2007): „European Political Science – The Role of the European Consortium for Political Research (ECPR), in: Hans-Dieter Klingemann (ed.): *The State of Political Science in Western Europe*, Opladen/Farmington Hills: Barbara Budrich, 414.
56 Berg-Schlosser, ibid., 412.

In the previous chapter, the extent became apparent to which external factors – in the broadest sense, social and political events – may impinge on the evolution of an academic discipline. If we look around for a country where such events, during the 20th century, have repeatedly produced drastic changes in social structure, ideological orientation, political behavior, and governmental set-up, Germany emerges as a sure-fire candidate. Consequently, attempts were launched after World Wars I and II to politically educate the various classes in German society: Widespread "unpolitical" attitudes – or so the diagnosis ran – were ultimately responsible for the repeated catastrophic upheavals. The establishment of a German Political Studies Institute – a Deutsche Hochschule für Politik -, located in Berlin, was intended after 1918 to provide an extramural solution to the problem. In 1933, however, the new regime found collaborators among the institute's staff, as it did elsewhere, who were prepared to help bring into line political science. The following chapter explores the reasons for such lack of immunity to the authoritarian temptation and reconstructs the subsequent reduction of the discipline to an instrument of the Nazi regime. It appeared first in 1999 as part of a jointly compiled volume by Michael Th. Greven, Hans Karl Rupp and this author: Political Science and Regime Change in 20th Century Germany *(Nova Science Publishers).*

German Political Science at the Crossroads: The Ambivalent Response to the 1933 Nazi Seizure of Power

I

Compelled by the National Socialists to leave their home country for political and/or "racial" reasons, German intellectuals investigating problems of government and society – historians, sociologists, psychologists, political scientists – were forced into exile in large numbers between 1933 and 1938. Most of these expelled scholars, sometimes after arduous detours through various European countries, eventually wound up in the United States.

The experience of exile became significant for both the emigrants and the social sciences in America. The exiles contributed to the development of new and to the sophistication of existing approaches. In such areas as political theory, comparative government, and international relations, for instance, exiled German scholars exerted a considerable influence on American political science. Hannah Arendt, Hans J. Morgenthau, Karl Löwenstein, Franz L. Neumann, John H. Herz, Karl W. Deutsch are among the names that instantly spring to mind.

The exiled political scientists, whether advocating structural reforms or supporting the socio-political status quo they found, shared a commitment to democratic values and politics – liberty and human dignity, equal rights and opportunities, government by majority rule. In many cases, it was this commitment that, in the first place, had led to their dismissal. Not a few cooperated with American government agencies during the war, later continuing to advise United States occupation authorities in Germany. Several, too, became involved in efforts to introduce the discipline into German university studies as part of an attempt at renewing Germany's traditional educational system.

The emigrants' attachment to democratic ideals, the mere circumstance of their exile seemed to suggest that the – still largely extramural – beginnings of German political science during the Weimar Republic, too, had been democratically inspired. This, in fact, became the accepted version in writings about the evolution of political science in Weimar Germany. The emerging discipline was presented as a "thoroughly republican-democratic enterprise" that, having supported the Weimar Republic "against challenges from the Left and Right", consequently refused "to offer its services in 1933 to National-Socialism" (Fijalkowski 1981: 3; Kastendiek 1977: 139/140). Portraying the science of politics, of all sciences, as having avoided being caught up in the political miscarriages of Germany's past – "the only discipline uniformly rejecting any cooperation with the Nazis" (Beckmann 1987: 3) – provided a powerful narrative. Not least because it added legitimacy to a field whose institutionalization met with initial resistance from many universities, the portrayal was gratefully accepted among the political science community.

Closer inspection has proved such alleged homogeneity a fiction. Heterorather than homogeneity marked German political science before and during the Nazi seizure of power. As the discipline started to evolve in Weimar Germany, three different schools – a national, a functional and a democratic approach – emerged. When the curtain came down in 1933, these were to differ considerably in their degree of immunity to the antidemocratic temptation. The reasons that were responsible for such heterogeneity will be explored next.

II

A German Political Studies Institute (*Deutsche Hochschule für Politik*) – an extramural facility, free of the rigid constraints of Germany's traditional system of higher education – was twice, in the course of 20th century German history, considered the adequate institutional response to the perceived need of politically educating the German people. In 1920 as in 1949, it would be located in Berlin, and would originally resemble an adult education establishment offering evening classes. So far, the two projects bore a striking resemblance. In other respects, however, there were important differences.

After 1945, the task of political education appeared to consist "in helping to provide the informational and behavioral underpinnings required by a 'democratic fresh start'" (Blanke/Jürgens/Kastendiek 1975: 54). Not so after 1918. In the words of Theodor Heuss, first Director of Studies at the *Deutsche Hochschule für Politik* (much later, of course, also the German Federal Republic's first President), German politics, "forced into a system of humiliations by external force and through its own fault, [knew] but *one* issue: the struggle for national liberation" (Heuss 1921: 33/34). To that aim, the DHfP had to contribute by instruction and example.

The necessary money was initially provided, first and foremost, by Prussia and the *Reich*, supplemented by grants from industry (Bosch, Siemens). The Prussian Minister of Education, Carl Heinrich Becker, echoed Heuss: Fostering political understanding should be "deliberately" employed "to strengthen Germany domestically and to contest other peoples externally" (Becker 1919: 13).

Nor did Ernst Jäckh, the *Hochschule*'s first and only president, mince words when he pronounced himself in favor of an institute that would provide "a focal point around which to crystallize a new Germany and, thereby, a new Europe possessed by a new spirit (albeit not the pointless, brutal 'spirit' of Versailles)" (Jäckh 1921: 31). Thirteen years later, after Hitler's appointment as Chancellor, Jäckh was no less unequivocal. In letters to the new Prussian Minister of Education, Bernhard Rust, and to Hitler's aide Hans Heinrich Lammers, Chief of the *Reich* Chancellery, he emphasized the *Hochschule*'s "unique opportunity to speak out abroad in favor of German revision politics" (Jäckh 1933d: 411) – 'revision' again referring, of course, to a removal of the constraints imposed on Germany by the Versailles Peace Treaty.

Those letters were never mentioned by Jäckh after 1945, who also omitted the part about "the pointless, brutal 'spirit' of Versailles" from post-World War II reprints of his earlier speech (cf. Jäckh 1952: 14; id. 1960: 77/78). At the time, however, the revisionist impulse was unmistakable when the DHfP came to be established. For the Institute's sponsors, the purpose of political science consisted in aiding German aspirations to recapture the country's prewar position of power on the continent, refusing to acknowledge the defeat of 1918. Even where Jäckh ostensibly invoked the "new" spirit of a "new" Europe, he merely took into account the fundamentally *changed* European environment affecting Germany's *traditional* aim of continental hegemony – as evidenced by his (and Heuss') rejection not only of the Versailles settlement, but also of French Foreign Minister Aristide Briand's later Pan-European proposals (cf. Heuss 1929: 117; Jäckh 1932a: 46).

Intent on "displacing the existing continental power structure to the advantage of the *Reich*", revisionism pervaded Weimar Germany's society during the twenties (cf. Salewski 1980; for the quote, see Hillgruber 1984: 84). In theory as in practice, it reinforced a functional, instrumentalist approach to both domestic and foreign policy. If democratic government, if the League of Nations proved unable to achieve revision, both might be expendable.

Functional interpretations of democracy did not appear with amazing suddenness. During the war, Jäckh (who in 1916 was awarded a chair for his efforts at the Institute of Oriental Languages – *Orientalisches Seminar* –, established by Bismarck as a facility for training recruits to the Foreign Service) and Heuss had collaborated with Friedrich Naumann as political journalists in promoting German war aims. Naumann, a publicist and politician who became famous when, in 1915, he circulated his ideas on a "fourth world empire" *Mitteleuropa* to be shaped by Germany, had earlier supported a "democratic imperialism" promoting social reform at home, thereby securing a solid foundation for national expansion overseas (cf. Naumann 1900). He, in turn, had been thoroughly influenced by Max Weber, for whom "all questions of government were vastly eclipsed by Germany's interest in its power as a nation". Consequently, parliamentarization and democratization to Weber "first and foremost offered a means to achieve domestic prerequisites for an effective world policy" (Mommsen 1959: 394).

Naumann died in 1919, Weber in 1920. It was the former who had first suggested establishing a center for political education, even starting a "Civics School" for the liberal Progressive People's Party (FVP) which, after the revolution of November 1918, was reorganized and became the German Democratic Party (DDP). When Jäckh took over from Naumann, he endeavored to put the venture on a broader basis, including among its tasks training for the Civil Service and the education of future "leaders".

Selecting and training political leaders had been another common theme running through the works of Weber and Naumann, which was now adopted by the DHfP's functionalists: "If a problem exists for modern democracy that deserves the most impassioned consideration, it is the problem of leadership" (Heuss 1921: 35). Grounded on liberal elitist thinking no less than on past acquiescence in Germany's authoritarian political system (including the Bismarck myth), the leadership ideal was tied to "great-man doctrines" and came to acquire "metaphysical significance" during the twenties (Struve 1973: 9; Döring 1975: 231). More often than not, even self-styled republicans were wont to link an overemphasis on leadership to the eventual destinies of Weimar Germany "in a manner that did not exclude an antiparliamentary and antidemocratic backlash" (Faulenbach 1980: 310).

III

During the Great War, Ernst Jäckh had not contented himself with supporting Friedrich Naumann's design of *Mitteleuropa* "unified under German leadership, politically and economically consolidated against England and America on one, against Russia on the other side" (Fischer 1969: 746). Driven by inflated war-time expectations, he had proclaimed a Greater Central Europe (Germany, Austria-Hungary, Turkey, Bulgaria, Romania and Greece) to be led "organically", "without despotism", by the German Empire, complementing Germany's "seaward orientation, especially toward a future 'Middle Africa'" (Jäckh 1916: 6, 11, 17). The extent to which such conceptual pathology was rampant at the time is indicated by the fact that programs like Jäckh's were considered "moderate", because they renounced formal annexations, focused on Eastern rather than Western Europe, and lacked a repressive domestic element.

After Germany's defeat in 1918, the *völkische* – radical nationalist – version of revisionism immediately commenced to crystallize around the country's alleged *Mitteleuropa* "mission". The self-styled "national opposition's" concept remained vague in detail, yet concrete in its rejection of the political settlement the Versailles and St. Germain treaties had introduced into Central Europe. Essential targets of nationalist ire: the "inflated multi-ethnic Polish state" and the "Czechoslovakian motley conglomeration" (Boehm 1923: 15). Against these, German "leadership of Central Europe" would have "to be earned, perhaps asserted in combat" (Brauweiler 1925: 249). As Martin Spahn, Reichstag delegate for the German National People's Party (DNVP), summed up the radical revisionist approach: "If we succeed in shaping Central Europe, we shall rise again to the position of Europe's leading people" (Spahn 1925: 40).

A conservative Catholic historian, Spahn had received his first chair at the University of Strasbourg in 1901, his second (after the return of Alsace to France) in 1920 at the University of Cologne. A year later, he left the catholic Center Party, joining the DNVP where he sided with newspaper tycoon Alfred Hugenberg's rabidly antidemocratic position. By 1933, explaining that "we need a single leader, and that is Hitler", he switched his political allegiance again, going over to the National Socialist parliamentary party.

In 1919, Spahn was recruited into the "revolutionary-conservative" circle that had been gathering around the literary and art historian Arthur Moeller van den Bruck, author of the notorious pamphlet *The Third Reich*, who would commit suicide by 1925. Lihe his principal associates, Heinrich von Gleichen and Max Hildebert Boehm, Moeller van den Bruck had been involved in the war-time propaganda efforts of the Supreme Army Command run by Hindenburg and Ludendorff. Experiencing the Great War as a "formative process" of the first magnitude, the group responded to the November Revolution by proclaiming the "politicization of the nation" under mass-based authoritarian – rather than monarchical – leadership (cf. Moeller van den Bruck [3]1931: XI, 280). When the Versailles Treaty was signed in June 1919, the circle, to emphasize its protest, assumed the name June Club.

Fundamentally, "politicizing the nation" was not too different from what Jäckh and his more moderate faction had in mind. In the case of the June club, however, the aim was equal to "converting the people to nationalism" (Moeller van den Bruck), "militantly opposing a state that intends to force republican persuasions on us", "expelling by revolutionary methods the liberalism which had invaded Germany" (Spahn 1928: 2; id. 1933: 1). Like Naumann, Jäckh and their collaborators, Gleichen and Spahn began planning for a school of politics to "educate leaders". Gleichen and Jäckh were in touch during 1919, and initially it seemed that agreement on a common project might be reached. However, Jäckh was not willing to forego, in addition to funding provided by industrialists Robert Bosch and Carl Friedrich von Siemens, subsidies from the Prussian and *Reich* governments. When that option proved unacceptable to the June Club, Jäckh went ahead single-handedly. On October 24, 1920, the DHfP was inaugurated. German Foreign Minister Walter Simons and Wilhelm (Bill) Drews, soon to be appointed President of the Prussian Administrative Court, were among the speakers.

A mere week later, on November 1, the revolutionary-conservative group followed suit by establishing a *Politisches Kolleg* (Political College, PK), also located in Berlin, under the direction of Martin Spahn. The institute's program for "scholarly political analysis" appealed to a "militant and manly community" of students "unwilling to let the fatherland perish by the hands of inadequate leaders and external enemies" (Politisches Kolleg 1922/23: 3). Financial support, during the subsequent seven years, would be provided by heavy industry – or, more precisely, by Alfred Hugenberg's *Wirtschaftsvereinigung zur Förderung der geistigen Wiederaufbaukräfte* (Economic Association for the Promotion of Spiritual Reconstruction), to whose coffers coal and steel corporations such as Vereinigte Stahlwerke (Albert Vögler), Gutehoffnungshütte (Paul Reusch) and others regularly contributed (see Leopold 1977: 12, 18, 180 n. 67). By 1927, the DNVP would temporarily join a governmental coalition (before its final, fatal radicalization under Hugenberg's leadership allied the party with the Nazis), and public funds would become available.

The role of the Political College has been downplayed by successive studies. A University of Chicago dissertaion is exemplary in asserting that "the *Politisches Kolleg* never developed an identity or a program" and that, consequently, its competition with the DHfP "from the very beginning...degenerated into parody" (Korenblat 1977: 63; see, however, Korenblat 2006 for a more nuanced assessment). Both contentions are rash, to say the least. The individuals recruited for the College staff forged an approach focusing on a set of ideas that included conceptions of "nation", "state", "leadership", "pan-Germanism", and "Mitteleuropa". Precisely because it was higly ideological, the approach implied a program. When the *Hochschule* and the PK concluded a formal cooperation agreement (*Arbeitsgemeinschaft*) in 1927, continuing – even extending – the arrangement on an informal basis from 1930, that program increasingly took hold at the DHfP. The influence it exerted on the School's teaching and research would prove far more important than the PK's institutional demise.

IV

"The revision of Versailles must commence by revising Weimar" (Mariaux 1932: 83): Writ large, that was the momentum at the back of the "New Front" slogan coined by the June Club (cf. Moeller van den Bruck/Gleichen/Boehm 1922). Domestically no less than externally, by defeating 1789 and 1989 – "inner" and "exterior" France -, every essential outcome of the Great War was to be undone. Political science would have to contribute: On the one hand, "occupied with politics", it was charged with reasoning out "the heritage of the political Romantics and of every 19th century conservative approach". On the other hand, "rooted" as it was "in politics", it supposedly had to reflect "our people's distinctive political disposition, inclined neither towards Western nor towards Eastern Europe" (Spahn 1931: 1/2; Politisches Kolleg 1922/23: 4).

'Science' thus was to build on the ideology of a distinctively German "peculiar course" which
• had virtually pervaded the political culture of Imperial Germany (see, e. g., Mommsen 1995: 208),
• had found its most "graphic expression" (Mommsen: ibid.) in the "ideas of 1914" – order, duty, community – which were meant to counter the ideals of 1789, liberty, equality and fraternity (see, e. g., Kjellén 1915; Plenge 1916; Troeltsch 1925), and
• after 1918 would continue to serve, with marginal modifications, as a basis for the "national opposition's" campaign against the Weimar Republic.

The conception of political science, as it was published at the *Kolleg* and taught not least in extension courses for student fraternities, drew on several essential components of such presumed distinctiveness:
First and foremost, a notion of the *homogeneous nation*, a "community originally rooted in blood and soil" (Spahn 1931: 2/3; cf. also Boehm 1923: 315), distinct from "atomistic" capitalist society.

Second, rejecting "mechanistic" Western conceptions of parliamentarism, the idea of a *corporatist, "organic"* state, conquering "decay", reinforcing leadership by "preparing thr ground for a new upper stratum" (Brauweiler 1925: 248).

Third, a firm belief in the paramount role of *strong political leadership*, entitled to "devotion and allegiance" (ibid.: 246; Boehm [3]1933: 50), as opposed to democratic "leveling".

Fourth, derived from a refusal to come to terms with the demarcation lines drawn in 1918, an *emphasis on irredentism*, perceiving the ethnically German population of border regions as the "genuine object of German foreign policy" (Hoetzsch 1925: 4/5).

Finally, the perspective (already discussed above) of *Mitteleuropa*, implying German hegemony in that area as "the German people's historical duty" (Brauweiler 1925: 249), a "continuing German mission" (Boehm 1925: 252).

The approach pursued at the Political College amounted to *politicized*, rather than political, science. Inevitably, it paved the way for the Nazi dogma that *no* science could escape being political science, serving purposes laid down by political, viz. National-Socialist, authorities. It could hardly come as a surprise that, among the *Kolleg*'s principal figures, none remained immune to the Third Reich's ideology after 1933.

How immune, however, to the conceptions put forward by the national approach did the *DHfP's* founders prove in the first place? As indicated earlier, both Jäckh and Heuss – and, it should be added, another close associate of Friedrich Naumann, DDP Reichstag delegate Gertrud Bäumer who also became involved with the *Hochschule* – shared a commitment to revisionism no less than to the notion of strong leadership. Did terminological affinity involve affinity in content?

The answer can only be ambiguous. If the DHfP founding circle "stood on the ground of bourgeois liberalism" (Gay 1974: 42), such liberalism meant the principles espoused by the German Democratic Party which, significantly, would change its name to State Party in 1930. While the DDP has been labeled the Weimar Republic's "constitutional party *par excellence*", it also subscribed to a "democratic nationalism" instrumental in preventing "the development of a pragmatic sense of political realities" (Hess 1978: 367). The party insisted on the *relative* merits of democracy as a form of government "appropriate" to the present (cf. Heuss 1920: 43/44; id. 1926: 38). It emphasized the significance of community – the "national corpus mysticum" (Bäumer 1928: 5) – and leadership ("a truly authoritative democracy leads": Jäckh 1931a: 1). And the "vigorous" foreign policy that was endorsed to regain Germany's "proper place in the world" included irredentism, justified as a principle "forced on Germany" (Heuss 1926: 282; id. 1927: 15). On top of that, the impact of the Great Depression and the challenge of the French government's 1930 proposal to negotiate a Pan-European confederation (implying acceptance of the territorial status quo) combined in triggering a revival of Naumann's *Mitteleuropa* design by the DDP. "Natural economic laws", or so Jäckh predicted, would "take their course", reinforcing Germany's position in Central Europe (Jäckh 1931b: 18).

Any reference to corporatist traditions is conspicuously absent from the list. Parliamentary democracy was accepted, *provided* it ensured strong government. Revisionist aims remained limited to foreign affairs, revisionist methods to a strategy of "pacifist imperialism" – economic penetration, political pressure, diplomatic negotiations – which, as diagnosed by Jäckh, was at the heart of America's international successes (id. 1929: 105) and should be copied.

However, the perceptions of democracy as merely a (more or less) adequate *method* of government; of community and leadership as essential elements of democracy; of international conciliation as, again, primarily a *tool* for achieving revision – these would serve as a first step helping to bridge, at the *Hochschule*, part of the gap between the camps of radical and democratic nationalism. During the Weimar Republic's final stages, they would provide an opening for the endorsement auf authoritarian schemes as "solutions" to Germany's political crisis. And even in 1933, Ernst Jäckh would not be alone among DHfP "liberals" in misjudging Nazism, after it had come to power, as merely a "more vigorous" revisionism, a "more determined" variety of national community-building.

V

Who, actually, were the DHfP students, asked the author of a confidential report to the Rockefeller Foundation in early 1926 – "are they indeed the prospective political leaders of the country?" His answer was immediate and unequivocal: The practical value of the institute's diploma had to be considered "extremely small" (Fehling 1926: 2).

Even at the DHfP proper, however, "education of leaders", in spite of Heuss' initial strong emphasis, was no longer a fashionable subject. Rather, a posture "above party" and spirit of "civic loyalty" (*Staatsgesinnung*) were advertised as the institute's virtues with increasing success. Domestically no less than internationally, the *Hochschule* gained in reputation during the period of the Weimar Republic's "relative stability" between the curbing of hyperinflation and the onset of the Great Depression. Subsequent to its cooperation agreement with the Political College, however, it also split up along conceptual lines. Henceforth, DHfP lectures and publications would be open not to a reassuringly "moderate" right, as has been contended (Lehnert 1989:

454/455), but to the intransigent enemies of a republic which they despised as "an interim of dishonor and bondage" (Brauweiler 1933).

In 1924, Jäckh managed to set up a Board of Trustees, chaired by Supreme Court President Walter Simons. Close to the DDP at the time, Simons would resign from the Court five years later over a face-off with the SPD-led Grand Coalition. By early 1933, he and Jäckh would be offering the new regime a "reorganization" of the DHfP Board. Continuing to be attracted to the "ideas of 1914", Simons would go on to defend, in 1935, the anti-Semitic Nuremberg laws, admonishing American critics that the United States, for want of comparable racist ordinances, would degenerate into a "state of mulattos and mestizoes" (see Gründer 1978: 258, 276/277, 284).

For the present, however, Simons' presence on the Board added to the DHfP's prestige. So did the membership of other public figures, such as Hjalmar Schacht (Federal Reserve Bank) and Otto Meissner (*Reich* Chancellery) – both, again, DDP members -, Carl Duisberg and Ludwig Kastl (*Reich* Association of German Industry), Chancellor Wilhelm Marx (Center Party), and Otto Braun, Prussia's Social-Democratic head of state government. By 1927, the Board's roster read like an excerpt from the German "Who is Who".

During 1926/27, the Rockefeller Foundation and the Carnegie Endowment for International Peace became involved in subsidizing the *Hochschule* – its archives, its library, not least its publications. A first Carnegie Chair in International Relations was established in 1927, to be filled by successive German and foreign scholars on a yearly basis, or to be used for the payment of visiting lecturers. Rockefeller funds made possible "most of the major publication ventures sponsored by the *Hochschule*" (Korenblat 1978: 217) and permitted the institute to set up, in 1932, its short-lived research division.

The involvement of the foundations reflected the growth of American interest in Germany – and vice versa. After the Dawes Plan had been signed and the role of reparations agent devolved on the United States, American capital commenced to flow to Germany. As the Depression would prove, the loans were a two-edged sword even if, in the short run, they helped to pay German reparations. American economic involvement also inspired political hopes in German private and government circles smarting under French preponderance. They were reflected by Jäckh's suggestion that American influence in Europe should be based on Germany and that Germany's role, in turn, would depend on an alliance with the United States (Jäckh 1929: 17, 105).

Jäckh's renewed application for Rockefeller funds in 1927 furnished another proof of his advertising talents. He credited a development to the DHfP which had rather resulted from political pressure on the institute, with considerations of self-interest playing a supplementary role. According to Jäckh, the Political College had "now become part of our work", the "central quality" of the *Hochschule* thus being "acknowledged officially again" (Jäckh 1927: 1/2). Actually, the *Reich* Department of the Interior had gone to the DNVP, after the "national opposition" had agreed to join a governmental coalition. The party was, consequently, in a position to press for its demands of integrating the College, threatened by a reduction of its industrial funds, into the Hochschule, and of providing additional governmental subsidies for the enlarged institute. Planning to supplement its main by an advanced level course (*Akademische Abteilung*), the DHfP was not adverse to such a prospect.

Negotiations between *Kolleg* and *Hochschule* resulted in an agreement which gave the DNVP two seats on the Board of Trustees. Martin Spahn and Otto Hoetzsch (the latter a professor of East European history at the University of Berlin and, like Spahn, a DNVP Reichstag delegate) were included in the permanent faculty, Max Hildebert Boehm and Karl Hoffmann (a foreign policy specialist at the College) taken on as instructors. The DHfP expressed its hope that, henceforth, the PK's own courses would also be taught "in the spirit of a strict stance above party".

That stipulation would prove the stumbling block after the DNVP, having suffered a severe elctoral setback in 1928, opted tor an adamantly anti-republican course under the chairmanship of Alfred Hugenberg. Any further increase in public subsidies was, moreover, precluded by the Depression. In March, 1930, a large Board of Trustees' majoriuty voted to terminate the agreement with the College.

Rather than having their influence cut back during the subsequent months, however, Spahn and his nationalist circle managed to negotiate a subsequent enlargement. They were aided by two two developments that occurred between March and June, 1930.

At the national level, Heinrich Brüning's appointment as chancellor of a Presidential cabinet by Hindenburg was meant and publicly perceived as a first decisive step toward authoritarian rule. At DHfP level, a scholar was appointed Director under Jäckh (following the promotion of his Social Democratic predecessor, Hans Simons, to Prussian government official) who had very rapidly turned from a religious socialist into a "self-styled 'Tory-Liberal'" (Winks 1987: 40): Arnold Wolfers, who would soon denounce "an extreme form of democratic constitution" (Wolfers 1932: 758) as the "inherent weakness" of the Weimar Republic. It was Wolfers who "energetically and successfully" (Brauweiler 1932: 1) pressed for an arrangement that favord the revolutionary-conservative cause.

Under the terms of that agreement, Spahn and Hoetzsch remained on the DHfP faculty (to be joined in 1932 by Max Hildebert Boehm and Heinz Brauweiler, the College's leading propagandist of the corporatist state). Beyond retaining Hoffmann, two more PK teaching staff were hired as instructors – one, Kleo Pleyer, a rabid anti-Semite. Expelled from Bavaria after the

1923 Hitler putsch, Pleyer had been indicted again two years later for participating in nationalist student riots against Emil Julius Gumbel, a Jewish pacifist scholar (who would be deprived of his academic position at the University of Heidelberg even before the National-Socialist advent to power). Lately,
Pleyer had worked as an assistant to Boehm – who has no less reason to be
satisfied with the settlement worked out by Wolfers and approved by the
Board: He was appointed to set up a Center for Problems of Expatriate Germans in Post-War Europe (*Deutschtumsseminar*), one among five DHfP
Centers, two of which (the Eurasian and the Geopolitical Center) were already run by individuals of, or close to, revolutionary-conservative persuasion.

As explained by Wolfers, the new Center would prove the *Hochschule*'s
"determination to provide valuable support, by academic teaching and scholarly research, to every effort having to do with ethnic policies (*Volks-
tumspolitik*), the national question, and the problems of Germans living on
and beyond the country's frontiers" (Wolfers 1930/31: 116). The Swiss-born
Wolfers, later a luminary at Yale advising OSS, the War and State Departments, consistently misread the authoritarian and racist threat to the Weimar
Republic. Up to the autumn of 1932, he would insist that constitutional "reforms" contemplated by Hindenburg ("a pillar of German democracy") and
the Papen government were "moderate"; that the danger of "dictatorship by
one party (had) been taken from Germany"; that, finally, the Nazi Party as a
mass movement provided "a safeguard against social reaction", even "a force
making for democracy" ever more "likely to come to the fore" (Wolfers
1932:769, 771).

Subsequent to January 30, 1933, Wolfers undauntedly went on to inform
American audiences that "Hitler (had) the very highest esteem for what he
calls 'European culture' to defend against the threat of 'Asiatic bolshevism'"
(Wolfers 1933a: 180), and that it might "become the greatest ambition of the
European dictatorships to prove that they (were) better able, with their independence from parliamentary pressure, to give peace to Europe and the world
than their democratic predecessors" (Wolfers 1933b). A supporter of the
functional approach to political science in his own right, Wolfers persisted in
the same sort of self-deception about Nazism that would be exhibited by
Jäckh.

VI

When, after 1945, *the Hochschule* was re-established, the original institute
was in retrospect idealized as a bulwark of democracy – not least, as has been
indicated and will be explained in more detail below, by Jäckh himself. That
could make convincing reading because, compared to the "structural and

philosophical rigidities" exhibited by Germany's universities, the DHfP "did maintain an openness to...alternative conceptions of politics and democracy" (Korenblat 1978: 7, 357). In addition to the national and functional varieties, a democratic approach to political science came to exist at the institute. Domestically, it focused on equality, social justice, political participation; in foreign relations, on renunciation of hegemony, an abandonment of territorial demands, and peaceful conflict settlement. The impact of that approach on the political orientation of the *Hochschule* would be overplayed later.

Otto Suhr who, as Social Democratic mayor of Berlin, would give his name to the re-established institute after World War II, taught as a DHfP instructor from 1928-30; Eckart Kehr, whose monograph on domestic and social forces at the back of Wilhelminian "world policy" would come to rank as a pioneering study in German historiography, from 1929-32; Franz L. Neumann (he would publish his classical work *Behemoth – Structure and Practice of National Socialism* in American exile) for the same period; Hans Speier, whose analysis of salaried employees responding to National Socialism would finally appear four decades later, during 1932 for just under a year.

Among scholars of democratic persuasion, only three, however, were included among permanent faculty (as distinct from teaching staff): Hermann Heller, appointed professor at the University of Frankfurt in 1931, who – like Kehr – would die in his first year of exile; Hajo Holborn, who held the second DHfP Carnegie Chair, also established in 1931; finally, Sigmund Neumann, lecturer at the *Hochschule* since 1929 and a faculty member in 1932. These scholars concurred in their analyses of the Bismarckian system's weaknesses which had "broken the back of German liberalism", feudalized the middle class, "depoliticized" the electorate and the parties (Heller 1926: 40; id. 1971b: 631/632; Holborn 1933a: 20ss.; Neumann 1930: 166; id. 1933: 59). *By interpreting such features in terms of a distinct deficit in Germany's political culture, they transformed the ideological notion of the country's "peculiar course" into an explanatory model.*

Heller, Holborn and Neumann also focused, in their approach, on the disparity between changes in political institutions and the survival of Imperial Germany's social structures after the Great War. They were unanimous in arguing that the conspicuous lack in social homgeneity posed a "serious threat" to political democracy, including the risks of dictatorship and civil war (Heller 1928: 40; Holborn 1930: 28; Neumann 1933: 60, 65, 76).

Differences between the functional and the democratic approaches emerged most visibly in their analyses of fascism and National Socialism. While not mincing words about the "browbeating" of the press and the opposition parties in Italy, Theodor Heuss maintained that Mussolini's "personality" made him a "leader" (Heuss 1926: 97). Adolf Grabowsky who ran the DHfP's Geopolitical Center and, with Richard Schmidt, edited the *Zeitschrift*

117

für Politik (Journal of Politics), acknowledged that "platitudes" and "parade-ground drill" governed Italian public life. Yet he praised Mussolini for "having made giant strides in eliminating brutal class conflict" (Grabowsky 1928: 410, 416/417; id. 1932a: 315, 316). In contrast, Hermann Heller in a much more perceptive study argued that Mussolini was a dictator aiming at absolute rule, rather than a "leader" interested in basing his actions on widely held values; that, consequently, the "normless dictatorship" of fascism in no way resembled a "national community of purpose"; and that class conflict might be eliminated by enlarged economic, social and political participation but hardly by resorting to "aestheticized violence" and "forced depoliticization" (Heller 1931: 43 ss., 56, 65, 157/158).

When Heuss published an inquiry into the German Nazi leader's political development, entitled *Hitlers Weg*, a reviewer was struck by "a lack of flatly repudiating National Socialism's most ruthless attributes" (see Jäckel 1968: XXIV). Such lack may hardly be explained by "contemporary uncertainties" (ibid.: XXXVI). Rather, it revealed an *analytical* uncertainty typical of the functionalist approach. The democratic school, in contrast, predicted that a National Socialist regime would bring "the end of the rule of law in a centralized police state" (Neumann 1973: 109), even forcseeing that the Nazi party", "forced to let down" many supporters after its advent to power, would "have to resort to force not just against adversaries, but against a good many followers" (Holborn 1933b: 25).

To pass the acid test, political science at the DHfP between 1930 and 1933 would have had to focus
* first, on the gradual infringement, by established conservative elites, of the Weimar Constitution and
* second, on the aggressive reactionary populism of the National Socialist mass movement.

The writings of Heller, Holborn, and Sigmund Neumann indicate the achievements of which a homogeneous discipline, in ths sense of a general commitment to democratic values, might conceivably have been capable.

As matters stood, no adequate analytical assessment of National Socialism emerged. By 1933, that failure would make it easier, at the DHfP and elsewhere, to harbor illusions about Germany's new regime.

VII

Looking back, from the distance of a decade, on the destruction of the Weimar Republic and the liquidation of the *Hochschule für Politik*, Ernst Jäckh would present himself, in his memoirs titled *The War for Man's Soul*, as a cool, calm adversary of the Nazis, a shrewd, unfazed judge of men and events. Hindenburg, Meissner, Schacht, above all Papen were dubbed "pathetically deceived deceivers", "short-sighted nationalists", "narrow-minded reactionaries", Goebbels the "devil" whom he, Jäckh, had been able to "dupe" by deciding to "fight" over the *Hochschule*: "For once, this Machiavelli, nay, Mephistopheles, of the Hitlerites was not to have his way by threats and brute force. I wanted him to acknowledge rights and laws" (Jäckh 1943: 66ss., 72, 107/108).

Reality, in several ways, had been different from Jäckh's assertions. Since 1927, the institute's publications had been open to writers enlarging on both "democratic and antidemocratic options" (Wolfers 1928: VII). While including essays by Heller, Neumann, and Carl J. Friedrich, two volumes on *Problems of Democracy* (I: 1928; II: 1931), followed by the DHfP's only published *Political Research Annual* (1933), had printed Carl Schmitt's infamous "friend-foe" argument about the presumed essence of politics; Max Hildebert Boehm's diatribes on the irreconcilability of irredentist policies and democratic government; Otto Koellreutter's avidly illiberal polemics.

By October, 1932, two National Socialists – Hans Heinrich Lammers, future chief of the *Reich* Chancellery, and economist Carl August Fischer, soon to fill a chair at the University of Hamburg – had been added to the roster of instructors. Rather than resisting right-wing barrages against republic and democracy, the *Hochschule* had lent them respectability. As a Rockefeller Foundation official would sum up the DHfP strategy by early 1933: "Jäckh ha(d) been clever in adjusting the School to (the) changing political situation by going further and further to the Right in selecting his lecturers, without sacrificing the old Left element in his permanent staff" (Sickle 1933a: 2).

During 1931/32 and as late as February, 1933, Jäckh had continued to defend, in response to skeptical British and American interrogators, the increasingly authoritarian policies pursued by Hindenburg and his entourage, by Brüning's and Papen's Presidential administrations:

Hindenburg was sized up by Jäckh as "the German Washington: 'first in war, first in peace'"; Brüning as "the synthesis of thinking-action known only in the old Greek philosophers"; Papen as "*le chevalier sans peur et sans reproche*" – "reactionary? No – if 'reactionary' means essaying an unconstitutional policy or trying to turn backward the wheel of evolution" (Jäckh 1933a: 10, 11, 20; id. 1932b: 2; id. 1931c). Only "very unwillingly" had Hindenburg signed a series of emergencey decrees – aiming, as he did according to Jäckh, at the "consolidation and stabilization...of the democratic Republic". The President and his State Secretary, Otto Meissner, "equally experienced and trustworthy", would continue "safeguarding the constitution". Hitler, as judged by Jäckh, found himself "controlled" and a political "prisoner" – "chancellor only in name". Whatever "the result of the experiment", it would "transform National Socialism" (Jäckh 1933a: 16, 18, 19, 21, 24).

Seriously flawed assumptions and effusive personal praise had added up to gross political misjudgments. Attempting to reach an accommodation even with Nazism could, as a result, seem merely one more small step.
By 1943, Jäckh would contend that, after the rigged elections of March 5, 1933, he had decided to "leave Germany for good", as now "terror and lawlessness would deluge the country" (id. 1943: 107). When addressing, on March 27, the participants of a DHfP course for Prussian civil servants, he had sounded very different (Jäckh 1933b: 401):

Three major, even historically decisive dates have intervened between the pre sent and the last course: January 30, March 5, March 21. In turn, they signify: the legal transition of governmental power to a revolutionary movement; the seizure of that power by the national revolution; the legitimization of that revolution by the nation as embodied in the Reichstag.

Jäckh then proceeded to name Lammers and a few other Nazi figures (such as educationalist Ernst Krieck, who had meanwhile also been recruited as instructor) to document a National Socialist presence at the Hochschule. He concluded his address by referring to "an idea of his former student" and associate professor at the University of Hamburg, Adolf Rein, that from now on "the 'political' (would) replace the 'philosophical' university of the 18th and 19th centuries, just as the latter (had) outstripped the 'theological university' which (had) dominated" earlier.

Displaying an "extraordinary capacity of adaptation" (Sickle 1933e: 2), Jäckh was attempting to convince the regime that it might profit from the institute if it would only forego complete Nazification, viz. putting Goebbels' Propaganda Ministry in charge. The DHfP could be used, as he wrote Bernhard Rust, the Prussian Minister of Education, as a "unique" instrument "to speak out abroad in favor of German revision politics" (Jäckh 1933d: 411). During March, Jäckh and Walter Simons offered Rust and Wilhelm Frick, *Reich* Minister of the Interior, to "reorganize" the *Hochschule*'s Board of Trustees. Jäckh impressed on Hitler's aide Lammers that he had "access to the whole British press, actually to any kind of conference in London, Oxford, or Cambridge". Keeping in mind "the absolutely misinformed American public, another lecture tour to the United States" might also be appropriate, where he had, time and again, performed "most effectively" (id. 1933c: 37).

Lammers arranged a meeting between Hitler and Jäckh on April 1, 1933. Later, Jäckh would melodramatically embellish his report on the encounter, from disarmingly greeting "with a Swabian 'Grüß Gott!'" the guards hollering 'Heil Hitler!', to his early prediction of the *Führer*'s "inevitable doom" (id. 1943: 97). What he desribed in his memoirs as an "exchange (of) views on problems of German and international politics" (ibid.: 93), was more prosaically referred to in the minutesof the meeting as "confidentially informing Prof. Jäckh about the objectives of German policy with regard to his lecture tours abroad... and his answers to inquiries by foreign visitors" (*Nieder-*

schrift 1933: 456). Otherwise, the meeting was inconclusive. Hitler simply referred Jäckh to Goebbels for further discussing the issue of the *Hochschule*'s intended transfer to the auspices of the Propaganda Ministry.

That transfer, however, was already definite. Goebbels had carried the day against Rust and Frick. On April 16, Jäckh advised Lammers of his resignation from the office of President of the German Political Studies Institute.

Later, Jäckh would publish two versions of his resignation letter – one in the United States (1943), another in West Germany (1952). *Both were distorted, calculated to persuade the reader of Jäckh's ostensibly unbending opposition to National Socialism.*

However, Jäckh also claimed to write history – the history of the DHfP. *In juggling with the facts of his biography, he was whitewashing a discipline. An apparent 'document', Jäckh's letter seemed 'proof' that the study of politics and government in Germany had withstood the totalitarian temptation.* As I have argued earlier (Eisfeld 1991: 99/100), it played a pivotal role in promoting the myth that, unlike German society, German political science did not need to come to terms with the past.

The letter's first printed version (Jäckh 1943: 290/291) was terse and to the point. It consisted of six sentences – a single paragraph, beginning and concluding thus:

I have informed the commissar entrusted with the negotiations by Reich Minister Dr. Goebbels that in view of the proposed reorganization of the Hochschule für Politik, I resign from the office of president of the School. You will understand my attitude all the more easily when you know that I have always refused to be tied down by a governmental office, in Imperial as well as in Repuiblican Germany I have always been anxious to stick to my own political line – that democratic outlook of which Friedrich Naumann was the greatest representative.
I expressed my determination also to Chancellor Hitler at our recent meeting.

Those lines read impressive, because they omitted *four fifths* of the original text. The second published version (Jäckh 1952: 20/21) was even more questionable, *adding* a further paragraph that had never been included in the resignation letter. Part – just part – stemmed from an address which Jäckh had given *six weeks later* – not in Germany, but *in London* (Jäckh 1933f: 3):

That the Hochschule is now taken over by the state has meant (among other things) the application of the new regulations for civil servants, including the 'Arian Paragraphs'(,) to my Hochschule. In other words, it would have meant dismissing those of my tried and valued friends and fellow(-)workers who came under those regulations. I could not bring myself to do that, and therefore resigned.

The remaining sentences, as published in 1952, had been *completely fabricated* by Jäckh:

You know yourself that and how I have made no secret of my view that the present persecution of Jews, which I condemn, is an injustice as un-German as it is inhuman. All my life, I have sided with those who were unjustly oppressed and persecuted. To me, that is a must.

On April 1, 1933, when Jäckh was received by Hitler, the regime had organized the first public boycott against Jewish stores. To have, supposedly, protested that ominous act with a noble, at the time already exceptional, statement must have seemed an attractive idea to Jäckh.

His actual letter to Lammers (Jäckh 1933e: 90/91) cannot be reproduced here in full (for the complete text, see Eisfeld 1991: 101/102). The final reason for Jäckh's later distortions was that it certainly did not reveal the writer's decision "to leave Germany for good". Jäckh was merely laying out new activities for himself. After informing Lammers about his resignation from the position of DHfP President, he continued:

Regardless whether Germany may be termed a First, Second, or Third Reich, remain resolved to serve our common mother country and the German nation ... I hope I may go on counting on your approving and favorable support, whether heading the Rockefeller Institute of Political Research, in my informal activities abroad, or in some other connection.

Even if his strategy of accommodation had failed, Jäckh, undaunted, would embark on a new course – the establishment of a Research Institute of International Relations, financed by the Rockefeller Foundation, its trustees and staff carefully parceled out between figures of "liberal" and "national(-socialist)" affiliation. Only when those efforts, too, came to nothing, Jäckh would liquidate the DHfP and go into exile.

VIII

Since early 1933, Jäckh and Wolfers had been negotiating a renewal of the Rockefeller Foundation grant. Continued Rockefeller support was of considerable importance to the DHfP – economically (governmental and private contributions had been cut back as a result of the depression), but also politically (to impress the significance of the *Hochschule*'s international ties on the new regime). The Foundation's directors approved renewal on March 17; however, they would reverse themselves three weeks later (Korenblat 1978: 326, 329).

At least in principle, Jäckh could initially feel confirmed in his strategy by the Rockefeller Foundation. "Some further concessions will have to be made, but they need not destroy the validity of the School", John Van Sickle, Assistant Director of the Foundation's Social Science Division, noted at the end of February (Sickle 1933a: 2). Four weeks later, he still seemed prepared to tolerate such consequences: "Jäckh will doubtless have to sacrifice some of his Jewish and Left teachers and considerable teaching freedom. Wolfers believes, however, that freedom of research will be maintained. Bergstraesser, of Heidelberg" – about whom more below – "takes the same attitude" (Sickle 1933b: 1).

Funding by the Rockefeller Foundation had permitted the DHfP to set up a Research Division and publish the first *Political Research Annual*. When Jäckh realized that, concerning the transformation of the institute into an establishment supervised by the Propaganda Ministry, he might have to bow to the inevitable, he came up with the idea of separating the teaching from the research part. He suggested that, while the former (including the name Deutsche Hochschule für Politik) would be turned over to Goebbels, the latter should be expanded into "a privately financed research institute, independent of state control, and to be known as *Forschungsinstitut für Weltpolitik*" (Sickle 1933c: 1; for the following, 2/3).

Jäckh had Papen, Meissner, Lammers, Simons, himself, Wolfers, Fritz Berber (Secretary General of the DHfP Research Division), and Erich von Prittwitz und Gaffron (representing the Carnegie Foundation) slated for the Board of Trustees. As permanent staff, he had in mind again Wolfers and himself, Boehm and Brauweiler, Berber, Heuss, and Sigmund Neumann. Finally, Jäckh was envisaging five study groups to focus on problems of Northeast Europe, Southeast Europe, corporatist conceptions of the state, statute labor, finally state and higher education – perceptible concessions to Nazi priorities at home and abroad.

One June 1, Jäckh terminated his address at the London Conference of Institutions for the Study of International Relations by a "farewell" in his capacity as DHfP President and a "welcome" as Head of the "Research Center of International Relations in its present form" (Jäckh 1933f: 5). But he had missed the proverbial boat. Three weeks earlier, reacting to the deteriorating situation in Germany, the Rockefeller Foundation's Executive Committee had voted against a transfer of the DHfP appropriation to the new Research Institute, merely agreeing to contribute to the expenses of liquidating the DHfP.

The formal liquidation of the *Hochschule* would not be completed until early 1934, when Jäckh had already emigrated to Great Britain. During that period, he "held his ground" with the regime, insuring that negotiated government funds were fully disbursed and that deposed scholars received "fair compensation" (Korenblat 1978: 335; also Jäckh 1934: 2). His persistence particularly benefited those who, in difficult circumstances, either remained in Germany, like Theodor Heuss, or went into exile, like Sigmund Neumann.

Jäckh had been willing to collaborate with "the Hitlerites", as he was later wont to call them, up to a point where his international standing was involved – which, had he come under Goebbels' Propaganda Ministry, would have been irreparably damaged. When he emigrated, he followed Wolfers who, because of a Jewish strain in his family, had been put on the list of undesirables, yet had continued to strongly support Jäckh's strategies (Sickle

1933d: 1). As professor of international relations at Yale, Wolfers would unaccountably maintain his attitude of qualified benevolence toward Nazi Germany – as late as 1940 arguing for an "agreement" between Britain, France, Germany and Italy "on the extent of their respective power and position in the East and West... and in the Mediterranean" (Wolfers 1940: 390).

John Wheeler-Bennett, a member of the Royal Institute of International Affairs who would later write *The Nemesis of Power*, a highly acclaimed study on the German army's role in the Weimar Republic, noted during 1933 that Jäckh seemed "to be maneuvering, or being maneuvered, into the post of an intellectual ambassador of the new regime" (Sickle 1933e: 2). Even such adaptability, however, might prove insufficient. Rapidly becoming entrenched, the Nazi regime could afford accepting or refusing liberal-conservative overtures on its own terms, including its racist ideology. As will be detailed below, Adolf Grabowsky and Arnold Bergstraesser were two more political scientists who did not decide on emigrating as staunch opponents of Nazism. They were forced into exile because the regime ostracized them as "Jews" or, in the same vein, "Jewish half-breeds".

The susceptibility to collaboration displayed by these scholars contrasted with the uncompromising stand taken by Hermann Heller, Hajo Holborn, and Sigmund Neumann. The latter who, in 1932, had attested National Socialism an "unsurpassed level of demagogy" (Neumann 1973: 86), initially emigrated to Britain. Winding up in the United States, he became affiliated with Wesleyan University – for nearly a decade in the hardly attractive position of visiting lecturer.

Hajo Holborn who had "moved close to the Social-Democratic Party" during the Weimar Republic's final years (Krieger/Stern 1968: XII), was bluntly confronted with the implications of Nazism when, soon after Hitler's accession to power, the brother of his Jewish wife committed suicide – "a young man of strong democratic convictions viewing what was to come in Germany as shameful and disastrous" (Vagts 1976). The Berlin Carnegie Chair held by Holborn was not abolished until early 1934, and while no longer permitted to teach, Holborn was able to continue publishing, under the serial title *Fundamental Problems of International Relations*, a succession of lectures by individual speakers.

He made no concessions. "'Politicization' of the sciences" would be deliberately defined by him, by mid-1933, as "not implying political bias" but "a methodical investigation of political phenomena" (Holborn 1933c: 1). For the final volume, published in 1934, he picked the essay *Germany and the United States Since the Great War* by Friedrich Wilhelm von Prittwitz und Gaffron who had resigned as German ambassador after January 30, 1933. At Yale University, until 1938 in the shaky position of visiting professor, Holborn would again emerge as a brilliant political historian.

By the time Holborn came to the United States, Hermann Heller had already died in Spanish exile from a heart attack. When Prussia's Social Democratic parliamentary party had appealed to the Supreme Court in 1932, after the state government's ouster by Chancellor Papen, Heller had acted as legal Counsel. The ruling by the court which largely upheld Papen's unconstitutional action could only have strengthened Heller's resolve to emigrate after Hitler had been appointed Chancellor.

Harold Laski invited him to lecture at the London School of Economics and Political Science. When Heller discovered that he was being spied upon in London, he accepted an appointment at the University of Madrid, rather than returning to Germany. Some of his most important work was published posthumously, including an article where Heller argued that, as long as political and economic power drastically diverged, the latter might be tempted to "directly" control the former (Heller 1971a: 41) – an argument which has retained its saliency for present-day debates on democratizing the large industrial corporation.

IX

On October 19, 1933 – five days after Nazi Germany had left the League of Nations -, Arnold Bergstraesser, Professor of Political Science (or, as the German metaphor would have it, *Staatswissenschaft*) and Foreign Studies at the University of Heidelberg, asserted in an address given at the Royal Institute of International Affairs (Bergstraesser 1934a: 26ss., 29, 31) that "with the exception of the Socialist parties, the whole population of Germany [had] felt the need of increasing the authority of the State." Bergstraesser continued:

The abuses of democratic institutions in Germany led to this lack of action which became a genuine danger to national life...In comparison with the days of the 'pluralist' party system... the work of officials... has become free from considerations which are not essential for the problem itself...Purely tactical considerations of party policy will not obtrude as war formerly the case.

The organization of the professional groups and the new adjustment of the relations between capital and labor have been arranged by the assistance of the Party organization... The government in its eceonomic policy is consequently not bound to consider plans of demagogic origin whose execution would be to the disadvantage of the whole... Thus despair is destroyed and confidence created among those who had previously too many reasons to suppose that some few individuals were utilizing the common ill to their own advantage.

Bergstraesser delivered that talk although, five months before, he had been given compulsory leave pursuant to the "non-Aryan" section of the so-called Act to Restore a Professional Civil Service – in fact a law to purge the administration of Social Democrats and Jews. Only under the provisions of another, the "veterans", clause of the same act his removal had been first suspended, then revoked.

In 1930, Bergstraesser had applied for the DHfP Carnegie Chair, but had lost to Hajo Holborn. Appointed professor by 1932, he also joined the *Hochschule*'s faculty, teaching both in Berlin and in Heidelberg. During the same year, he became involved in expelling from that latter university the statician Emil Julius Gumbel who was accused of having "vilified", in a lecture, "the memory of the dead of the Great War", and whose books, furnishing evidence of the incredible leniency wich the Weimar Republic's justice had exhibited in punishing right-wing assassinations, would be burned on the bonfires of May 10, 1933. Appointed referee by the department, Bergstraesser – though bound to confine his account to the details of the case – described Gumbel as a "demagogue", obfuscating rather than clarifying the facts in his account (see Eisfeld 1991: 81/82).

Both Gumbel and Bergstraesser had volunteered in 1914, but had drawn very different conclusions from their war-time experiences. Bergstraesser remained attached to the – in his own words – "towering heights of the unifying experience of 1914" (id. 1929: 147), that deeeply felt "sense of national awakening" (Mommsen 1995: 208) that had gripped Germany at the outbreak of hostilities. When reviewing Erich Maria Remarque's pacifist novel *All Quiet on the Western Front*, he was able to perceive merely that the author had "violated his responsibilities to past and future", because "campaigning for peace...blinds to the true situation of our country" (Bergstraesser 1929: 146/147).

Accordingly, Bergstraesser rejected "acceptance of the notion of rapprochement as an indispensable principle of politics" (id. 1930: 89):

To come to an agreement with respect to these questions..., e. g. the question of disarmament, the Eastern frontier and the union with Austria, would mean today making the will of the enemy one's own, i. e. in practice giving up the right to determine for ourselves our national policies.

In his 1933 address, Bergstraesser stated that he had "felt for many years that nothing but dictatorship would restore order and confidence in Germany" (id. 1934a: 44). A year before, he had told German exchange students on the eve of their departure that "as to government, the appropriate form remains to be found" (id. 1932: 8). Bergstraesser had kept echoing Max Weber's premise that "for internal as well as external reasons", Germany had the "duty" to be a world power (id. 1930: 89). The longer parliamentary democracy seemed incapable of achieving that status for the country, the more Bergstzraesser would adopt the 'national opposition's" emphasis on "will" and "determination".

Adolf Grabowsky and Richard Schmidt, editors of the *Zeitschrift für Politik*, concurred with Arnold Bergstraesser's conviction that the Weimar Republic lacked a "decisive", "courageous", "positive" foreign policy, "particularly in the East"; that it had "not produced a leading elite" and had, therefore, "historically failed" (Grabowsky 1931: 442, 445; id. 1932b: 189/190). Schmidt, who held a chair in public law at the University of Leipzig, reproached the republic for "sacrificing even the minimum in instruments of state power indispensable for prevailing internationally" (id. 1924: 189/190). Frustrated with parliamentary democracy, these sometimes 'republicans by force of reason' (*Vernunftrepublikaner*) would wax ever more unreasonable: a "national awakening, even if it led to more oppression", was to be "preferred over crippling passivity", "an injustice over disarray" (Grabowsky 1932c: 370; Schmidt 1933: 91).

Like so many scholars who had harbored social darwinist values to the detriment of humanist norms, and whose resentful discontent lent itself to political irresponsibility, Grabowsky and Schmidt merely had to continue in the 'Third Reich' where they had left off in the republic. When the Geneva Disarmament Conference commenced in 1932, the *Zeitschrift für Politik* had published a special issue on the problem which had been translated into English and French. After Nazi Germany withdrew from both Disarmament Conference and the League of Nations, another such issue entitled *Disarmament and Equal Rights* was compiled, to be used for propaganda purposes by the Foreign Ministry. In a joint foreword, Grabowsky and Schmidt, after justifying the German exodus, noted that solving the disarmament problem on the regime's conditions "undoubtedly [would] involve the question of peace or war" (Schmidt/Grabowsky 1934: 2, 4).

When that same regime in November, 1933, held a referendum on Germany's withdrawal from its international commitments, 950 academics – even after the autodafé of May 10 – would sign a *Declaration in Favor of Adolf Hitler and the National Socialist State* which read, in part (NS-Lehrerbund 1933):

All science is indissolubly linked to the intellectual nature of the nation from which it has grown… German science appeals to the educated of the world to view with the same sympathy they expect for their own nations the struggle of the German nation united behind Adolf Hitler for freedom, honor, justice and peace.

The *Zeitschrift für Politik*'s next issue, edited by Grabowsky and addressing *Fundamental Aspects of the Saar Struggle*, was again, as disclosed by Vice Chancellor von Papen who contributed the introduction, "meant for a wide audience" (Papen 1934: VII). The issue was prompted by the imminent plebiscite which would permit the inhabitants of the Saarland – placed under League of Nations administration by the Versailles Treaty – to decide on affiliation with France or Germany. According to Grabowsky, the former country's aim consisted in keeping the Saar "brutally chained to France" (Grabowsky 1934: 73).

Two months later, the 'Night of Long Knives' stunned Nazi Germany. In addition to the SA (Storm Trooper) leadership, General Kurt von Schleicher

(Hitler's precursor as Chancellor) and his wife, Bavarian politician Gustav von Kahr and other conservatives were murdered on June 30, 1934. Grabowsky, who was of Jewish ancestry, saw the writing on the wall. Without delay, he emigrated to Switzerland.

Richard Schmidt would stay, until his retirement, on the editors's roster of the *Zeitschrift für Politik* (even if nominally) for another two years. In 1934, the dean of the University of Leipzig's Law Department lauded him for the "versatility of his talents" which had allowed Schmidt to "live up to" this century's "enormous change in legal views, including the latest revision" (*Festschrift* 1936: V).

Schmidt emerged as a central figure in the attempt to justify, on the basis of scholarly reasoning, the emasculation of political science in Nazi Germany. Like Heuss or Jäckh, he had earlier been reluctant to consider any political system an "ideal", insisting on "comparative government" as the "essential subject of political science" (Schmidt 1924: 24/25). He had, in 1924, established a Center for Foreign Studies (*Auslandskunde*) at the University of Leipzig. After "a strong hand" had come to "liquidate the disastrous interlude in the evolution of our country's laws" (id. 1934: V), Schmidt brusquely dismissed the quest for general constitutional principles which were "impossible to discover". In the last instance, Schmidt argued, reverting to familiar ground, a nation's "distinctiveness", its "tradition", would determine the "adequacy" of any constitution. Consequently, "the focus and method of political science" had "to be thoroughly recast" (id. 1938: 12, 14/15):

Because, in modern states, government and law are shaped by political parties – or, possibly, by a single privileged party, to the exclusion of other organizations -, Scientific Politics has essentially evolved into 'Foreign Studies' (*Auslandskunde*) with a focus on 'Comparative Party Studies'.

Schmidt's approach, of course, had its roots in widely accepted traditions presuming a 'primacy of foreign policy'. The emphasis on international factors also met the regime's tangible interests. Not least, it permitted the discipline to shift to grounds where – initially – ideological restrictions applied less severely.

If Richard Schmidt assisted the process of *gleichschalten* political science, imposing conformity on the discipline, Arnold Bergstraesser, until expelled from the University of Heidelberg in 1936 (after the Nuremberg Race Laws had abolished the "veterans" clause), contributed to academic Nazification by replacing scholarly with political performance criteria. During 1934/35, he approved the doctoral theses of many students who, in several cases, had joined the Nazi party years before Hitler's accession to power. They had, as Bergstraesser would write in two opinions, "interestingly examined the subject in the spirit of National-Socialist politics", "based on sympathy with the present conception of the state" (Bergstraesser 1935a: 66; id. 1935b: 402/403).

These doctorates would serve as cornerstones for many a career, as in the case of Fritz Hippler, expelled for rioting from the University of Berlin in 1932, who would rise to the position of National Film Administrator in the Ministry of Propaganda. In his thesis, he valued German philosopher Paul de Lagarde's "severe struggle against Jewry", asserting that Karl Marx' "permanent opposition against his non-Jewish environment" could only be understood "in terms of racial disposition" (Hippler 1934: 20/21, 230). Bergstraesser applauded these chapters as a "fortunate combination of scholarly talent and vivid political perception" (Bergstraesser 1934b: 234/235).

A second case was even more flagrant and would considerably afflict the development of the politicized discipline until 1945. Franz Alfred Six, soon to emerge as an influential "Nazi for all seasons" (Herzstein 1982: 1987), had joined the party in 1930. He had written a tract which he characterized himself as "nothing more but a resumé of the findings of National Socialist propaganda." A few examples (Six 1936a: 20/21, 33/34, 60):

The East Galician, the fat greasy Jew, the big-shot, the social democrat's cloth cap and the grin of the subhuman communist were, thanks to determined enlightenment by the National Socialist movement, soon engraved on the memory of the masses...
In the Weimar Republic..., Marxism, having seized power, developed the recourse to terrorist methods into police terror and, by terrorist rule over schools and universities, into subjugation of the spirit...
Successfully asserting the National Socialist creed among the German people may consequently be considered the victory of the racially superior, more valuable elements over the racially inferior, base elements of Germandom.

That malignant harangue was acclaimed by Bergstraesser as "a gain, both in content and methodological approach, for the scholarly literature on the dynamics of the modern state" (Bergstraesser 1934c: 502/503). Already a *Sturmführer* (Lieutenant) in the SA, Six would in 1935, after the Storm Troopers' fall from power, join the SS, obtain his postdoctoral qualification – again at the University of Heidelberg – with another pamphlet (The Press of National Minorities in the German Reich) in 1936, and be promoted to SS-*Standartenführer* (Colonel) by 1938. When the moment came for establishing a Department of Foreign Studies (*Auslandswissenschaftliche Fakultät*) at the University of Berlin, Six would be available.

X

Paul Meier from the provincial town of Benneckenstein, whom Goebbels appointed President of the DHfP, and who henceforth would grandly call himself Meier-Benneckenstein, was a dismissed teacher, a Nazi campaign speaker, and recently a senior civil servant in the Propaganda Ministry. He symbolized the ideological conformity imposed on the *Hochschule*. So did the individual who, on May 29, 1933 spoke at the opening ceremony of an instiute that, according to the notices which had been posted, would "no longer be a place for liberal and marxist debates". He was Dietrich Klagges, a former teacher like Meier, who had joined the "movement" in 1925. As a minister in the tiny state of Braunschweig, he had made Hitler a civil servant in 1932, thereby naturalizing him.

Students were screened for "Aryan" descent until, by 1936, membership in the Nazi Party or in one of its mass organizations would be required for admission. Regular indoctrination courses were offered for Storm Trooper and Hitler Youth leaders, the Labor Front, the Women's and Teachers' Leagues. "Racial Studies" was included in the curriculum as a required subject. Additional Centers for Antimarxist Research, Statute Labor, Colonial Policy sprang up or were abolished according to political "demand".

By 1936, the Research Division was reestablished, to be run again by Fritz Berber who had become future Foreign Minister Joachim von Ribbentrop's trusted adviser. Hardly a year later, Berber, having joined the Nazi Party, was awarded a chair at the University of Berlin. The Research Division would publish sober analyses in fields where "political topography" was required "in the interests of the *Reich*" (Six 1941: 736) – on French armaments, the American conception of neutrality, the German minority in Canada. Ideological pamphlets, however, prevailed.

In 1937, the DHfP was upgraded and reconstituted as a *Reichsanstalt*, a facility with *Reich* immediacy. Now called *Hochschule für Politik*, it continued to be run, however, by the Propaganda Ministry. The diploma it conferred was, as before, not equivalent to a university degree. Nor did the training it offered qualify for an administrative career – even if, by 1939, not quite half of the Hochschule's graduates were being employed by government or prty agencies (*Bericht* 1939: 90/91). Pressured by the National Socialist Lecturers' and Students' Leagues, and "not too much impressed" by the HfP (*Reichsministerium* 1938: 202), Goebbels agreed to turn the institute over to Rust's *Reich* Education Ministry, set up for the purpose of bringing the universities under central control.

These developments coincided with a debate on the future of the erstwhile Institute of Oriental Languages where Ernst Jäckh, during World War I, had obtained his professor's title. Earmarked for further expansion to provide the regime with internationally knowledgeable personnel, the institute had been christened Foreign Studies School (*Auslandshochschule*) in 1935. After his appointment to the Foreign Ministry, Ribbentrop lost much of the enthusiasm he had originally professed for the project. By 1938/39, however, another, more powerful player indicated his "profound" interest in the school (Scurla 1938a: 402): *Reichsführer* SS Heinrich Himmler.

Between 1933 and 1936, Himmler's deputy Reinhard Heydrich had recruited a group of academically educated ardent Nazis: Reinhard Höhn, Otto Ohlendorf, Walter Schellenberg, finally Franz Alfred Six. The *Sicher-*

heitsdienst (SD), nucleus of the later Main Security Office (*Reichssicherheit-shauptamt*), evolved into an "ensemble of the most intelligent individuals ever engaged by National Socialism" (Höhne 1967: 196). Insisting on the "scientific standard" of their operations, these men were resolved to transform ideological myths into "bureaucratically applicable knowledge" (Aronson 1967: 276). The elitist SS self-image additionally spurred a determined academic policy which Heydrich was able to pursue the more easily as the SS had, among the senior civil servants of the Education Ministry, recruited a considerable number of members (Kater 1974: 132; Heiber 1966: 124).

Himmler's organisation had, by mid-1938, already succeeded in installing a secret collaborator, Michael Achmeteli, who had built up an extensive collection of records on the Soviet Union, at the Foreign Studies School as professor and director of the Russian Center (Simpson 1988: 73; Scurla 1938b: 23, 36, 41/42). Next, Heydrich pushed for integration of the School into the University of Berlin nd its enlargement into a Foreign Studies Department. He also suggested the individual to serve as State Commissioner in charge of setting up the new department: Franz Alfred Six, only recently promoted to head SD Department II: "Enemy Investigation" (after establishment of the RSHA, he would be put in charge of Department VII: "Ideological Research and Evaluation"), even more recently appointed associate professor of journalism at the University of Königsberg.

After consulting with the Foreign Ministry and the Party Chancellery, the Education Ministry accepted Heydrich's proposal, and Six was transferred to the University of Berlin. When the issue of the HfP's future came up for discussion, the ministry's experts rapidly concurred that the *Hochschule* should be merged with the new department. Six was accordingly instructed in September, 1939 – not quite two weeks after Nazi Germany had invaded Poland. The end of the *Hochschule für Politik* came unceremoniously: Cancellation of the winter semester 1939/40 and a hastly arranged leaving examination, based on reduced requirements.

Meier (-Benneckenstein) faded from the scene. Franz Alfred Six, by contrast, would rise ever higher in the hierarchy of the 'Third Reich'. Holding a chair of foreign policy and foreign studies from 1940, he was appointed, at his request, dean of the new department by the Minister of Education, remaining directly responsible to Rust – not, as was customary, to the rector of the university. Six further succeeded in obtaining for himself (and the SS) an additional Foreign Studies Center (Deutsches Auslandswissenschaftliches Institut, DAWI) in order "to forge links between the department's research and teaching and the pursuit of cultural policies", including "own initiatives in the essential fields of cultural policies" (*Erlassentwurf* 1939). By 1942, the Center would be granted autonomy – permitting Six to change his title from "Director" to "President" -, and Ribbentrop would confer on Six the direction of the Foreign Ministry's Cultural Division, "allowing for exceptional influence by the SS" (*Vermerk* 1942).

Six would terminate his career as SS-*Brigadeführer*, equivalent in rank to a Major General in the German army. He was promoted to *Oberführer* (Colonel) by the end of 1941 after a two months' stint with an *Einsatzgruppe* (Task Force), one of the mobile extermination units which started the systematic massacres of Jews in occupied Soviet Russia. Six had been in temporary command of *Einsatzgruppe B*'s Advance Detail Moscow whose participation in 2457 murders was meticulously recorded – including, during the time Six commanded the detachment, 144 killings near the city of Smolensk (*Trials* n. d.: 174, 524). After the war, an American Military Tribunal would sentence Six to 20 years' imprisonment. Like many other convicted war criminals, he would be released in 1952, subsequent to the shift in American policy triggered by the Cold War. He would first join a publishing house (C. W. Leske) and later be employed by the Porsche Automobile Company as an advertising executive.

Several rapid academic careers would also be started by the establishment of the Foreign Studies Department and continued after World War II – not in political science, but in international and public law (Wilhelm Grewe, appointed West German ambassador to the United States, subsequently to NATO), in sociology (Karl Heinz Pfeffer), in history (Egmont Zechlin). These individuals would be offered chairs after 1945, though they had attributed an "intrinsic value" to "eliminating bolshevism [as the] source of corrupting international law" (Grewe 1941, quoted by Weber 1986: 365), had called for "purging the German people's body of any influence exerted by Jewry" (Pfeffer [38]1935: 171), had participated in plundering the libraries of occupied France (Zechlin 1941; see Eisfeld 1991: 162, 202 n. 107).

An exception to this opportunistic pattern was Albrecht Haushofer who had succeeded Adolf Grabowsky as head of the DHfP's Geopolitical Center in 1933. "Quarter Jewish", according to Nazi jargon, he was protected by 'Deputy Leader' Rudolf Hess, a former assistant of his father, Karl Haushofer, at the University of Munich. Fiercely critical of universal suffrage, parliamentary democracy, and the Versailles Peace Settlement, Haushofer continued to pursue the aim of German hegemony in Central Europe. But he also came to judge the Nazi dictatorship a regime of "fools and criminals" (Haushofer 1939, quoted by Laack-Michel 1974: 346). When, by late 1940, he was appointed professor of geography and geopolitics at the Foreign Studies Department, he had already established contacts with the German resistance. Briefly imprisoned after Hess' flight to Britain, Haushofer was once more arrested subsequent to the July 20, 1944 coup attempt, to be murdered by an SS commando in April, 1945, during the battle for Berlin.

By early 1941, ten among the *Auslandshochschule*'s professors had been transferred to the new Foreign Studies Department, and an equal number of new chairs had been established. The department offered instruction in the form either of a main or a supplementary course – foreign studies degree after 6, interpreter's degree after 4 semesters. SD/RSHA members held the most diverse positions in both department and DAWI, from tutor to professor of state and cultural philosophy. Dossiers of students who either professed interest in intelligence work or seemed "suitable", were passed on to SD and RSHA. The last DAWI progress report of March 1945, addressed to Six, to the university rector, and to the Education Ministry, would state that "the Center's personnel have been increasing their contribution to the duties of the Main Security Office" (*Bericht* 1945: 63).

Publications, like those issued earlier by the (D)HfP, continued to focus on "political topography" and ideology. The former dealt with problems of political economy, foreign policy, and international law: Germany's economic interests in South-East Europe, the structure of the U.S. war economy, Anglo-Saxon plans for a revamped League of Nations. Occasional historical analyses, whether articles or monographic studies – on the evolution of elites in France, on Imperial Germany's acquisition of foreign outposts – were also considered acceptable. In the ideological area, the thrust of propagandist rhetoric was directed toward a message emerging as a major "ideological weapon in the Nazi struggle to win the war" (Herzstein 1982: 3): the image of a European 'New Order' which German hegemony would build throughout the occupied continent.

A decade earlier, Brüning's and Papen's Presidential governments had initiated a shift of German foreign trade to South-East Europe. Their policies prefigured the economic dependence of the region's countries which Nazi Germany's foreign trade strategies had attained by 1941. Small wonder that the regime's protagonists approvingly referred to relations with southeastern Central Europe as the prime example of that "greater regional economy" which was to prove a mere euphemism for the spoliation of occupied Europe (cf. Kluke 1955: 251/252; and this book's chapter on *Mitteleuropa*). In that regard, the motto equaled the 'New Order' slogan which increasingly gained currency after the invasion of the Soviet Union.

The Nazi leaders refused to consider any limits to their ruthless exploitation of manpower, plants, raw materials in conquered Europe. Nor were they prepared to bind themselves with regard to the future destiny of the peoples which they ruled. Precisely because nothing but exploitation was "the common denominator of all economic, political, and social measures" (Neumann 1966: 183), the promise of a European 'New Order' could not but lack substance. It had to remain "grandiose, but vague" (Herzstein 1982: 103).

The Europeanist ideology was disseminated by department and DAWI alike between 1941 and 1944 through publications, courses, conferences. Six led the offensive, publishing the tracts *Europe's Civil Wars and the Present War of Unification* in 1942, *Europe: Tradition and Future* two years later.

When Nazi Germany's military situation became ever more desparate, European brotherhood-in-arms, basis for the continent's alleged "crusade against bolshevism", was increasingly eulogized by the 'New Order' propaganda (Eisfeld 1991: 154/155). In the end, the *Zeitschrift für Politik* was reduced to a pamphlet attempting to work up last-minute enthusiasm by a flow of pathetic verbiage (Pfeffer 1944: 378):

From Narvik to Athens and from Bordeaux to Reval, German soldiers have carried a message that will not die. Europe has come to realize that it belongs together. Neither invasion by foreign enemies not civil war with reactionaries can destroy that knowledge…Today's labor, struggle and death in the European community will tomorrow cause all those men in Europe to finally join our ranks who cherish their own peoples and wish to build the new future.

To the final hour of the Nazi regime, Foreign Studies remained a politically manipulated discipline. The last sentence of the German Foreign Studies Institute's last report dealt with its surrender to the demands of a political agency. In his final statement before the Military Tribunal, Franz Alfred Six, one of that agency's powerful figures, insisted on his scholarly respectability: "I was always a scientist" (*Trials* n. d.: 396).

Jekyll and Hyde: Sebastian Haffner's verdict on Germany, pronounced from exile, fit like a glove the "politicized" science of the 'Third Reich'.

References

Aronson, Shlomo (1967): *Heydrich und die Anfänge des SD und der Gestapo (1931-1935)*, Diss. Berlin.
Bäumer, Gertrud (1928): *Grundlagen demokratischer Politik*, Karlsruhe.
Becker, Carl Heinrich (1919): *Kulturpolitische Aufgaben des Reiches*, Leipzig.
Beckmann, Andreas (1987): "Zerfällt die 'Demokratiewissenschaft'? Geschichte und Perspektive der deutschen Politologie", Deutschlandfunk, September 16, Manuscript.
Bergstraesser, Arnold (1929): "Erinnerung des deutschen Krieges", *Europäische Revue*, 5, 145-150.
Bergstraesser, Arnold (1930): *Sinn und Grenzen der Verständigung zwischen Nationen*, München/Leipzig.
Bergstraesser, Arnold (1932): *Geistige Grundlagen des deutschen Nationalbewußtseins in der gegenwärtigen Krise*, Stuttgart/Berlin.
Bergstraesser, Arnold (1934a): "The Economic Policy of the German Government", *International Affairs*, 13, 26-46.
Bergstraesser, Arnold (1934b): *Dissertationsgutachten Fritz Hippler*, University Archives (UA) Heidelberg, H IV 757/33, Reg.-No. 37, 234/235.
Bergstraesser, Arnold (1934c): *Dissertationsgutachten Franz Alfred Six*, UA Heidelberg, H IV 757/34, Reg.-No. 77, 502/503.

Bergstraesser, Arnold (1935a): *Dissertationsgutachten Hans Brune*, UA Heidelberg, H IV 757/ 33, Reg.-No. 11, 66.

Bergstraesser, Arnold (1935b): *Dissertationsgutachten Kurt Walz*, UA Heidelberg, H IV 757/ 36b, Reg.-No. 62, 250/251.

Bericht (1939): *Bericht über die Entwicklung der Hochschule für Politik seit 1933*, March, typ-ed MS., Bundesarchiv (BA) Koblenz, R 55, Vol. 413, 90/91.

Bericht (1945): Report DAWI on "Continuing Work Under Difficult Conditions of Present War Situation", Humboldt-Universität Berlin, Archiv, No. 233.

Blanke, Bernhard/Jürgens, Ulrich/Kastendiek, Hans (1975): *Kritik der Politischen Wissenschaft*, Vol. 1, Frankfurt/New York.

Boehm, Max Hildebert (1923): *Europa Irredenta*, Berlin.

Boehm, Max Hildebert (1925): *Die deutschen Grenzlande*, Berlin.

Boehm, Max Hildebert (31933): *Ruf der Jungen*, Freiburg.

Brauweiler, Heinz (1925): *Berufsstand und Staat*, Berlin.

Brauweiler, Heinz (1932): *Denkschrift*, April 29, Stadtarchiv Mönchen-Gladbach, Bestand 13/ 15 (Nachlaß Brauweiler), No. 192.

Brauweiler, Heinz (1933): "Der machtvolle Staat", *Der Stahlhelm*, No. 39, September 24, copy, Stadtarchiv Mönchen-Gladbach, Bestand 13/15, No. 107.

Döring, Herbert (1975): *Der Weimarer Kreis*, Meisenheim.

Eisfeld, Rainer (1991): *Ausgebürgert und doch angebräunt. Deutsche Politikwissenschaft 1920-1945*, Baden-Baden.

Erlassentwurf (1939): *Errichtung der Auslandswissenschaftlichen Fakultät an der UniversitätBerlin und des Deutschen Auslandswissenschaftlichen Instituts*, Dec. 18, BA Koblenz, R 2, Vol. 12557.

Faulenbach, Bernd (1980): *Ideologie des deutschen Weges*, Munich.

Fehling, J. A. (1926): Letter to Beardsley Ruml, January 31, Rockefeller Archive Center (RAC) North Tarrytown, Laura Spelman Rockefeller Memorial Collection, Series 3.6, Folder 537.

Festschrift für Richard Schmidt (1936), Leipziger Rechtswissenschaftliche Studien, Heft 91, Leipzig.

Fijalkowski, Jürgen (1981): *Das Otto-Suhr-Institut, Fachbereich Politische Wissenschaft derFreien Universität Berlin*, Part *2: Entwicklung und wissenschaftliche Arbeit*, Berlin.

Fischer, Fritz (1969): *Krieg der Illusionen*, Düsseldorf.

Gay, Peter (1974): *Weimar Culture*, Harmondsworth.

Grabowsky, Adolf (1928): "Die Zukunft des Faschismus", *Zeitschrift für Politik*, 17, 409-435.

Grabowsky, Adolf (1931): "Deutschland nach den Wahlen", *Zeitschrift für Politik*, 20, 435-445.

Grabowsky, Adolf (1932a): "Nachwort" zu: Hagemann, Walter: "Faschismus als europäischesProblem", *Zeitschrift für Politik*, 21, 315-318.

Grabowsky, Adolf (1932b): *Politik*, Berlin/Wien.

Grabowsky, Adolf (1932c): "Vorbemerkung" zu Berkes, Theodor: "Bataille um Südosteuropa", *Zeitschrift für Politik*, 21, 369-371.

Grabowsky, Adolf (1934): "Frankreichs Große Politik und der status quo im Saargebiet", in: id./Sante, G. W. (eds.): *Die Grundlagen des Saarkampfes*, Berlin, 62-73.

Gründer, Horst (1975): *Walter Simons, der Staatsmann, Jurist und Kirchenpolitiker,* Neustadt.

Heller, Hermann (1926): *Die politischen Ideenkreise der Gegenwart,* Breslau.

Heiber, Helmut (1966): *Walter Frank und sein Reichsinstitut für Geschichte des neuenDeutschlands,* Stuttgart.

Heller, Hermann (1928): "Politische Demokratie und soziale Homogenität", in: *Probleme der Demokratie I,* Berlin, 35-47.

Heller, Hermann (2rev1931): *Europa und der Fascismus,* Berlin.

Heller, Hermann (1971a): "Political Power" (1934), in id.: *Gesammelte Schriften,* Vol. 3, Leiden, 35-44.

Heller, Hermann (1971b): "Bürger und Bourgeois" (1932), in: id.: Gesammelte Schriften, Vol. 2, Leiden, 625-641.

Herzstein, Robert Edwin (1982): *When Nazi Dreams Come True. The Third Reich's Internal Struggle Over the Future of Europe After a German Victory,* London.

Heß, Jürgen C. (1978): *'Das ganze Deutschland soll es sein.' Demokratischer Nationalismus in der Weimarer Republik am Beispiel der DDP,* Stuttgart.

Heuss, Theodor (1920): *Die neue Demokratie,* Berlin.

Heuss, Theodor (1921): "Denkschrift zur Errichtung einer Deutschen Hochschule für Politik", in: *Politische Bildung. Wille/Wesen/Ziel/Weg,* Berlin, 33-37.

Heuss, Theodor (1926): *Staat und Volk,* Berlin.

Heuss, Theodor (1927): *Politik,* Halberstadt.

Heuss, Theodor (1929): "Die Deutsche Demokratische Partei", in: Harms, Bernhard (ed.): *Volk und Reich der Deutschen,* Vol. 2, Berlin, 104-121.

Hillgruber, Andreas (1984): "'Revisionismus' – Kontinuität und Wandel in der Außenpolitik der Weimarer Republik", in: id.: *Die Last der Nation,* Düsseldorf, 59-85.

Hippler, Fritz (1934): *Staat und Gesellschaft bei Mill, Marx, Lagarde,* Berlin.

Höhne, Heinz (1967): *Der Orden unter dem Totenkopf,* Munich.

Hoetzsch, Otto (1925): *Deutschland als Grenzland, Deutschland als Reich,* Deutsch-Akademische Schriften, Vol. 7, Marburg.

Holborn, Hajo (1930): *Die Entstehung der Weimarer Verfassung als nationalpolitisches Problem,* Lecture (DHfP), typed MS., Yale University, Sterling Memorial Library, Manuscripts & Archives, Group 579: Hajo Holborn Papers, Folder 11.

Holborn, Hajo (1933a): "Die geschichtlichen Grundlagen der deutschen Verfassungspolitik und Reichsreform", *Deutsche Juristenzeitung,* No. 1, Proofs (Yale University, Sterling Memorial Library, Manuscripts & Archives, Group 579: Hajo Holborn Papers, Folder 32).

Holborn, Hajo (1933b): *Weimarer Reichsverfassung und Freiheit der Wissenschaft,* Leipzig.

Holborn, Hajo (1933c): "Vorwort", in: Zimmern, Alfred: *Internationale Politik als Wissenschaft,* Leipzig/Berlin, I-III.

Jäckel, Eberhard (1968): "Einleitung", in: Heuss, Theodor: *Hitlers Weg,* new ed., Tübingen, XI-XLIV.

Jäckh, Ernst (1916): *Das größere Mitteleuropa,* Weimar.

Jäckh, Ernst (1921): "Rede", in: *Politische Bildung. Wille/Wesen/Ziel/Weg,* Berlin, 31.

Jäckh, Ernst (1927): Letter to Beardsley Ruml, November 29, RAC, Laura Spelman Rockefeller Memorial Collection, Folder 537.

Jäckh, Ernst (1929): *Amerika und wir. Amerikanisch-deutsches Ideen-Bündnis*, Berlin/Leipzig.

Jäckh, Ernst (1931a): *German Leadership*, typed MS., Columbia University, Rare Books & Manuscripts Library, Ernst Jäckh Collection, Box 15.

Jäckh, Ernst (1931b): *A United States of Europe – Is It Possible?*, typed MS., Columbia Univer-sity, Rare Books & Manuscripts Library, Ernst Jäckh Collection, Box 15.

Jäckh, Ernst (1931c): "Sees Sign of New World Teamwork", *Cleveland Plain Dealer*, November 15, Columbia University, Ernst Jäckh Collection, Box 24.

Jäckh, Ernst (1932a): Chapter I/II, in: id./Schwarz, Wolfgang: *Die Politik Deutschlands im Völkerbund,* Geneva, 7-51.

Jäckh, Ernst (1932b): "Germany Riding Out the Storm", *New York Times*, June 25, RAC, Re-cord Group 1.1, Series 717 S, Folder 177.

Jäckh, Ernst (1933a): *The Political Situation of Germany*, Address, Royal Institute of International Affairs, London, February 6, xeroxed MS., RAC, Record Group 1.1, Series 717 S, Folder 177.

Jäckh, Ernst (1933c): Letter to Hans-Heinrich Lammers, March 24, ZstA Potsdam, RK No. 19 850, 37.

Jäckh, Ernst (1933d): Letter to Reichskommissar Dr. Rust, Encl., April 1, ZStA Potsdam, REM No. 1445, 411.

Jäckh, Ernst (1933e): Letter to Hans-Heinrich Lammers, April 16, ZStA Potsdam, RK No. 19850, 90/91.

Jäckh, Ernst (1933f): *Address*, 6th Conference of Institutions for the Scientific Study of International Relations, London, June 1, RAC, Record Group 1.1, Series 717 S, Folder 178.

Jäckh, Ernst (1934): Letter to John Van Sickle, April 4, RAC, Record Group 1.1, Series 717 S, Folder 177.

Jäckh, Ernst (1943): *The War for Man's Soul*, New York/Toronto.

Jäckh, Ernst (1952): "Die 'alte' Hochschule für Politik", in: id./Suhr, Otto: *Geschichte der Deutschen Hochschule für Politik*, Berlin, 5-32.

Jäckh, Ernst (1960): *Weltsaat*, Stuttgart.

Kastendiek, Hans (1977): *Die Entwicklung der westdeutschen Politikwissenschaft*, Frankfurt/ New York.

Kater, Michael H. (1974): *Das 'Ahnenerbe' der SS 1935-1945*, Stuttgart.

Kjellén, Rudolf (1915): *Die Ideen von 1914*, Leipzig.

Kluke, Paul (1955): "Nationalsozialistische Europaideologie", *Vierteljahreshefte für Zeitgeschichte* 3, 240-275.

Korenblat, Steven D. (1978): *The Deutsche Hochschule für Politik. Public Affairs Institute for a New Germany*, Diss. Chicago.

Korenblat, Steven D. (2006): "A School for the Republic? Cosmopolitans and Their Enemies at The Deutsche Hochschule für Politik, 1920-1933", *Central European History*, 39, 394-430.

Krieger, Leonard/Stern, Fritz (1968): "Introduction", in: Krieger/Stern, eds.: *The Responsibility of Power. Historical Essays in Honor of Hajo Holborn*, New York.

Leopold, John A. (1977): *Alfred Hugenberg*, New Haven/London.

Lehnert, Detlef (1989): "'Politik als Wissenschaft'. Beiträge zur Institutionalisierung einer Disziplin in Forschung und Lehre an der DHfP 1920-1933", *Politische Vierteljahresschrift*, 30, 443-465.

Mariaux, Franz (1932): *Nationale Außenpolitik*, Oldenburg.

Moeller van den Bruck, Arthur (31931): *Das dritte Reich*, prepared by Hans Schwarz, Hamburg.

Moeller van den Bruck, Arthur/Gleichen, Heinrich von/Boehm, Max Hildebert (1922), eds.: *Die neue Front*, Berlin.

Mommsen, Wolfgang J. (1959): *Max Weber und die deutsche Politik*, Tübingen.

Mommsen, Wolfgang J. (1995): *Imperial Germany 1867-1918*, London/New York.

Naumann, Friedrich (1900): *Demokratie und Kaisertum*, Berlin.

Neumann, Franz Leopold (1966; 11942, 21944): *Behemoth. The Structure and Practice of Natio nal Socialism 1933-1944*, New York.

Neumann, Sigmund (1930): *Die Stufen des preußischen Konservatismus*, Berlin.

Neumann, Sigmund (1933): "Die Bedeutung des gesellschaftlichen Aufbaus für die Verfassungsstruktur in Deutschland", *Jahrbuch für politische Forschung I: Zum Neubau der Verfassung*, Fritz Berber, ed., Berlin, 56-78.

Neumann, Sigmund (1973, 11932): *Die Parteien der Weimarer Republik*, Stuttgart.

Niederschrift (1933): Minutes of Meeting between Hitler and Jäckh, April 4, ZstA Potsdam, REM Nr. 1445, 456.

NS-Lehrerbund Deutschland/Sachsen (ed.) (1933): *Bekenntnis der Professoren an den deut-schen Universitäten und Hochschulen zu Adolf Hitler und dem nationalsozialistischen Staat*, Dresden.

Papen, Franz von (1934): "Vorwort", in: Grabowsky, Adolf/Sante, G. W. (eds.): *Die Grundlagen des Saarkampfes*, Berlin, VI-VIII.

Pfeffer, Karl Heinz (381935): "Das Judentum in der Politik", in: Fritsch, Theodor: *Handbuch der Judenfrage*, Leipzig, 171-173.

Plenge, Johann (1916): *1789 und 1914. Die symbolischen Jahre in der Geschichte des deutschen Geistes,* Berlin.

Politisches Kolleg (1922/23): *Vorlesungsverzeichnis*, Hochschule für Nationale Politik, Berlin.

Reichsministerium (1938): Reichsministerium für Volksaufklärung und Propaganda, Vermerk, May 5, 1938, BA Koblenz, R 55, Voo. 1046, 202.

Salewski, Michael (1980): "Das Weimarer Revisionssyndrom", *Aus Politik und Zeitgeschichte* B 2/80 (January 12, 1980), 14-25.

Schmidt, Richard (1924): *Wesen und Entwicklung des Staates*, Leipzig/Berlin.

Schmidt, Richard (1933): "Der politische Lehrgehalt in Goethes Lebenswerk", *Zeitschrift für Politik*, 22, 73-91.

Schmidt, Richard (1934): *Einführung in die Rechtswissenschaft auf der Grundlage der neuen Rechtsordnung*, Stuttgart.

Schmidt, Richard (1938): *Grundriß der Allgemeinen Staatslehre oder Politik*, Stuttgart.

Schmidt, Richard/Grabowsky, Adolf (1934): "Foreword", in: id. (eds.): *Disarmament and Equal Rights*, Berlin, 1-4.

Scurla, Herbert (1938a): Aufzeichnungen, Dec. 1, Zentrales Staatsarchiv (ZStA) Potsdam, REM No. 1249.

Scurla, Herbert (1938b): Vermerke, ZStA Potsdam, REM No. 1498.

Sickle, John Van (1933a): Letter to Edmund E. Day, Director Social Sciences, Rockefeller Foundation, February 22, RAC, Record Group 1.1, Series 717 S, Folder 177.

Sickle, John Van (1933b): Memorandum, March 30, RAC, Record Group 1.1, Series 717 S, Folder 177.

Sickle, John Van (1933c): Letter to Edmund E. Day, April 29, RAC, Record Group 1.1, Series 717 S, Folder 178.

Sickle, John Van (1933d): Letter to Edmund E. Day, May 12, RAC, Record Group 1.1, Series 717 S, Folder 178.

Sickle, John Van (1933e): Memorandum, July 18, RAC, Record Group 1.1, Series 717 S, Folder 178.

Simpson, Christopher (1988): *Der amerianische Bumerang. NS-Kriegsverbrecher im Sold der USA*, Vienna.

Six, Franz Alfred (1936a): *Die politische Propaganda der NSDAP im Kampf um die Macht*, Diss. Heidelberg.

Six, Franz Alfred (1936b): *Die Presse der nationalen Minderheiten im Deutschen Reich*, Habilitationsschrift Univ. Heidelberg, typed MS.

Six, Franz Alred (1941): "Das Deutsche Auslandswissenschaftliche Institut im Jahre 1941", *Zeitschrift für Politik*, 31, 733-739.

Spahn, Martin (1925): *Mitteleuropa und das deutsche Volk*, Neuburg.

Spahn, Martin (1928): "Staat gegen Volk! Volk gegen Staat", *Der Student*, 4, No. 12, 2.

Spahn, Martin (1931): "Zielhafte politische Bildung. Aus Anlass des 10jährigen Bestehens des Politischen Kollegs", *Der Student*, 12, reprinted in: Spahn, Martin (1936): *Für den Reichsgedanken*, Berlin/Bonn, 104-108.

Spahn, Martin (1933): Statement, March 24, Bundesarchiv (BA) Koblenz, NS 46/2.

Struve, Walter (1973): *Elites Against Democracy. Leadership Ideals in Bourgeois Political Thought in Germany, 1890-1933*, Princeton.

Trials (n. d.): *Trials of War Criminals before the Nuremberg Military Tribunals under Control Council Law No. 10, Vol. IV: The Einsatzgruppen Case*, Washington D. C.

Troeltsch, Ernst (1925): *Deutscher Geist und Westeuropa*, Hans Baron, ed., Tübingen.

Vagts, Alfred (1976): Memoir, Yale University, Sterling Memorial Library, Manuscripts & Archives, Group 579 (Hajo Holborn Papers), Series I, Box 1, Folder 5.

Vermerk (1942): Vermerk des Persönlichen Stabes Reichsführer SS, Feldkommandostelle des RFSS, Sept. 9, in: Berlin Document Center: Unterlagen Six (Akte "Ahnenerbe").

Weber, Hermann (1986): "Rechtswissenschaft im Dienst der NS-Propaganda", in: Klaus-Jürgen Gantzel (ed.): *Wissenschaftliche Verantwortung und politische Macht*, Berlin/Hamburg, 185-425.

Winks, Robin (1987): *Cloak and Gown. Scholars in America's Secret War*, London.

Wolfers, Arnold (1928): "Vorwort", in: *Probleme der Demokratie I*, Berlin, V-IX.

Wolfers, Arnold (1930/31): "Akademische Feier des 10jährigen Bestehens der DHfP, Arbeits-bericht", in: *Berichte der Deutschen Hochschule für Politik*, Vol. VIII, 115-117.

Wolfers, Arnold (1932): "The Crisis of the Democratic Regime in Germany", *International Affairs*, 11, 757-783.

Wolfers, Arnold (1940): *Britain and France Between Two Wars*, New York.

III.
Political Science and Ideology (1)
Germany's "Peculiar Course":
Coming to Grips with Patterns
of Anti-Democratic Thinking

Neo-pluralism, according to Ernst Fraenkel who introduced the concept into (West-) German political science during the 1960s, "battles – let alone Hitler – the shadow of Stalin." The subsequent chapter attempts to demonstrate that he might as well have written "let alone Hegel": Hegel's conception of the state as superior to civil society – guardianship by a "qualified" elite, not subject to control by the governed – strongly imprinted itself on Germany's political tradition until well into the 20th century, serving to set the country off from the West. Focusing on the decision-making processes of Western-type democracies, particularly on political parties and interest groups, and on the contrast between Western and "totalitarian" political systems, neo-pluralism worked at establishing a fundamentally different paradigm. The article was written as part of a Monographic Section on the elusive and controversial notion of public, as opposed to private, interest, which I edited for the International Review of Sociology *in 1998.*

From Hegelianism to Neo-pluralism: The Uneasy Relationship between Private and Public Interest in Germany

Introduction

In 19th century Germany, the idea of 'the State' as an objectified metaphysical entity came to prevail over the more mundane concept of 'government' derived from the consent of the governed. By preferring '"totalities" over their constituent individuals, by exalting the national body politic as the highest expression of reason and morality (*Sittlichkeit*) (cf Barker, 1915, p. 27; Krieger, 1972, p. 131}, Georg Wilhelm Friedrich Hegel's philosophy provided the doctrine underlying such "sanctification" (Gunnell, 1993, p. 40) of the state.

In developing his conception, Hegel was inspired less by abstract ideals than by the existing, contemporary Prussian state, as it had evolved in response to the French Revolution and the Napoleonic conquests (cf., e.g., Topitsch, 1970, p. 340}. Hegel did acknowledge civil society and private interests as indispensable, but substantial unity had to be achieved by a state grounded in transcendental, not in human authority. The state did not emerge out of civil society, reflecting back on it. Rather, Hegel's thinking revolved around monarchical sovereignty, 'impartial' bureaucratic administration, and corporate representation, qualifying the interests of "the Many" in civil society as "elementary, irrational, violent, and frightful" (Hegel, 1982, Section

143

303). His ideas caught on because Prussia, under the guise of monarchical autocracy, had already come to be largely governed by a caste of professional bureaucrats; because that country's people, "divided into myriads of unconnected social and regional groups", still remained, in political terms, "an amorphous, inarticulate mass" (Rosenberg, 1966, pp. 201, 204); and because German 19th-century history would continue to favor a strong monarchy, underpinned by an extensive bureaucracy, over a weak civil society.

By the standards of the epoch, Prussia after the Stein-Hardenberg era was a *modern* state. So was Bismarckian/Wilhelmine Germany in many ways. But again, its ruling class was not prepared to accept popular control. Modernization, in the case of the 'delayed nation', invariably meant modernization *from above*. Belated German unification was achieved by Prussian arms under Junker command, rather than by an ascending liberal middle class establishing governmental responsibility.

After 1871, the *Rechtsstaat* ideal – concerned "more with the redefinition than with the limitation of the state", less with individual rights apart from the state than with a state whose measures "conformed to general rules' (Krieger, 1972, pp. 253, 460) – came to be definitely substituted for parliamentary democracy. Bureaucratic administration of law, supposedly regulating private and guarding public interest, was largely equated with government. In this respect, too, Hegel's political ideas, as definitely elaborated by 1821 in his *Philosophy of Right*, would reflect "with surprising accuracy the Germany of the Second Empire" (Sabine, 1950, p. 665).

The present essay will first discuss in more detail the confrontation of state and civil society, of common good and private interests, in Hegel's theory, as well as some relationships of that conception to what has been termed Germany's 'peculiar course' in the 19th century. The influence exerted by Hegel's philosophy continued, of course, beyond 1918. After Imperial Germany had been defeated, the founding of the Weimar Republic was regarded by many intellectuals as the advent of merely that "external, necessary and rational state" which Hegel had discerned in the workings of civil society, and whose "system of mutual dependence" was grounded not on metaphysical splendor, but on "selfish purposes" (Hegel, 1982, Section 183). Hegel's traces were no less noticeable in a post-1918 German debate more often than not pervaded by a "hunger for" – social and political – "wholeness' (Gay, 1974, Chapter 4) and, consequently, by disdain for the "pluralism of the competing political groups' ultimately anarchical coexistence' (Smend, 1993, p. 17).

This chapter will, however, not address the complexities of the Weimar situation, where Carl Schmitt's decisionist 'friend-foe' argument about the supposed essence of politics and Rudolf Smend's integrationalist philosophy, influenced by Hegel's thinking, were united in opposing any 'forces which might impede or divide the state' (Schmitt, 1933, p. 186). Rather, focusing on the period after 1945, the article will look at two opposing lines of West German political thought.

The first, arguing in the Hegelian tradition, reproached the West German Federal Republic with its alleged lack of '*Staatlichkeit*', insisting on the supremacy of the state over society which had to be guaranteed by, again, 'impartial' professional civil servants. Ernst Forsthoff, Joseph Kaiser, and Werner Weber were the leading advocates of that school.

The second approach, termed 'neo-pluralist' by its initial proponent, Ernst Fraenkel, finally removed the Hegelian stigma from civil society. Rejecting the conception of a public interest that might be *ex ante* defined and subsequently imposed by 'enlightened' state servants, the neo-pluralist school argued that only the conflict of private interests, limited by constitutional 'rules of the game', could *ex post* determine the common good. In the last instance, the public interest would result, according to Fraenkel, from the "parallelogram of social forces".

Hegel's "monistic solution", offering the "political ideal of a completely integral organic totality" (Krieger, 1972, p. 125), met with recurrent response in Germany because it promised a new and powerful political order to a nation either aspiring after belated unification, as during the 19th century, or deeply frustrated in its ambitions, as after 1918. A pluralist conception of state and society finally gained ground after its proponents, under Cold War conditions, introduced a specific variety of monism, Communist 'totalitarianism', as the principal counterpart to pluralism and as the new *bête noire* of political theory.

"Elementary, Irrational, Violent, and Frightful": Hegel's View of Civil Society's Special Interests

When Herbert Marcuse wrote his study on *Reason and Revolution*, he shrewdly observed that "fear and anxiety', not reactionary beliefs, had prompted Hegel to reject the 1832 English Reform Bill (Marcuse, 1941, p. 248). Emotions such as these had earlier caused Hobbes to denounce associations, condemning them as "worms in the entrails of a natural man" (Hobbes, 1965, Chapter XXIX). And fear and anxiety presumably governed Hegel's thinking when, commenting on the conflict of particular interests, he wished to see such "dangerous convulsions" alleviated by "superior, deliberate regulation", rather than leaving them to "blind necessity"(Hegel, 1982, Section 236).

Hegel conceived civil society quite literally as a 'battleground' for the bellum *omnium contra omnes*, the "warring of every private interest against every other private interest" (Hegel, 1982, Section 289; see also Marx, 1968, p. 243). Even if, following Adam Smith, he argued that "subjective egoism", considering the "interdependence of labor", would inevitably contribute to "satisfying everybody's needs" (Hegel, 1982, Sections 189, 199), Hegel saw the conflict of particular interests as irreconcilable: no *inherent* mechanism existed by which a common interest might be arrived at (cf . Marcuse, 1941, pp. 173-174). Lacking a state – in fact, as Hegel hastened to add, lacking a monarch – the "people" merely impressed him as a "formless", a "chaotic" concept – a very Hobbesian notion indeed (Hegel, 1982, Section 279; c£ Fetscher, 1986, p. 218).

Hegel was the anti-contractual philosopher *par excellence*. He abhorred the idea of the contract at the origin of the body politic, because – as will be shown below – he was deeply convinced that the terror of the French Revolution had invalidated the idea of rational political contract between individuals. Not surprisingly, therefore, state and civil society were not simply separated and contrasted by Hegel. Their relationship was one "of superiority and inferiority" (Sabine, 1950, p. 659): civil society, "the realm of blind inclination and causal necessity", *depended* upon the state

for intelligent supervision and moral significance. Considered by itself, society would be governed only by the mechanical laws resulting from the interaction of of acquisitive and self-centered... individuals.

Conscious action could only emanate from the state, "the power of reason actualizing itself as will", "the sole prerequisite for the attainment of particular ends" (Hegel, 1982, Sections 258, 261). As no preordained harmony existed between private interest and common good, the state's task consisted in stabilizing civil society, "realizing freedom" (Hegel, 1982, Section 258), so that, in the end, the "system of wants" might become "a conscious scheme of life controlled by man's autonomous decisions in the common interest" (Marcuse, 1941, pp, 213-214).

Regulating Private, Guarding Public Interest: 'Neutral' Bureaucracy and Corporate Representation in Hegel's Concept of the State

Why should citizens be incapable of rationally, reasonably controlling their own lives? Why should their autonomous decisions not include the constitutional form of the body politic? Because, to Hegel, history had already answered that question in the negative, proving his fear and anxiety only too justified. Unleashing, after 1793/1794, *la grande terreur* on the republicans themselves, the French Revolution had demonstrated in a "most glaring and frightful" manner (Hegel, 1982, Section 258) the fallacy of the principle of individual will. Basing the state on that "merely apparently reasonable" principle (Hegel, 1982, Section 258) would, by necessity, result in the perversion of freedom.

Hegel's dismissal of the 'atomistic' notion that the individual citizen should, directly or indirectly (by expressing his suffrage), participate in legislative matters, implied a pointed rejection of representative parliamentarism in favor of a corporatist system (Hegel, 1982, Section, 303). From his point of view (Sabine, 1950, p. 660),

the individual (had to be) 'mediated' through a long series of corporations and associations before he arrive(d) at the final dignity of citizenship in the state... The guilds and corporations, the estates and classes, the associations and local communities that made up the structure of the German society... [were regarded] by Hegel as humanly indispensable.

Marcuse, in another felicitous observation, remarked that, according to Hegel, "the unruliness of civil society" had "to be bridled" by the corporations as economic and political institutions (Marcuse, 1941, p. 212). The corporate assembly at the pinnacle oft the system, however, was precisely "*not* designed to deliberate and decide on matters of state' (Hegel, 1982, Section 314). Rather, its public sessions were meant to serve as a 'theater' where officialdom might demonstrate its "efficiency, talents, and virtues' (Hegel, 1982, Section 315). Regarding matters of public policy, the corporate element manifestly remained a mere "illusion": professional administrators, due to their "necessarily more profound and more comprehen-sive judgment", were perfectly "capable of doing their best without the assembled estates" (Marx, 1968, p. 265; Hegel, 1982, Section 301).

These bureaucrats were assigned in Hegel's political philosophy the position of "universal estate" (Hegel, 1982, Section 303). Mainly to be recruited from the middle class, which Hegel considered 'the principal support of the state regarding uprightness and intelligence' (Hegel, 1982, Section 297), they were trained to rule not arbitrarily, but by orderly procedure. Representing "the 'reason' of society", detached from 'acquisitive special interests' (Sabine, 1950, p. 662), supposed to possess moral and instrumental competence, bureaucracy was singled out by Hegel for effectively guarding the public interest.

The Relationship of Hegel's Theory to the Realities of Germany's 19th Century 'Peculiar Course'

Hegel's ideas

gave a special meaning to the concept of the state and invested that concept with connotations, for which there was no analogue in the political thought of France and England, but which made it throughout the 19th century the central principle of German political and juristic philosophy. (Sabine, 1950, p. 664)

Guardianship by a selected and trained minority, not subject to control by the governed – in fact, hierarchical rule under an authoritarian system – continued to work as a powerful vision in Germany well into the 20th century. The notion had such an intellectual impact because it reflected many realities of a profoundly formative process – the process by which Germany achieved national unification, including a decisive 'Prussification' of many of its policies.

In Prussia, the General Legal Code (*Allgemeines Landrecht*) of 1794 had introduced what came to be labeled 'well-earned rights' (remuneration, tenure, and pension) for the members of a bureaucracy who henceforth would refer to themselves as 'servants of the state' rather than 'royal servants' (for the following observations, cf. Rosenberg [1966, pp. 190-191, 199-200, 202, 211, 218]). By 1806, when Prussia was conquered by Napoleon's armies, the "operators of the powerful state machine" (Rosenberg, 1966), evolving into a self-recruiting and self-governing corporation, had largely won emancipation from monarchical authority. Prussia's defeat by French arms triggered the first of several Prusso-German "revolutions from above'. The remaking of the Prussian system by Stein and Hardenberg, involving the abolition of hereditary social estates and the abrogation of the nobility's exclusive legal privileges, further strengthened the position of an already well-entrenched civil bureaucracy which now had every reason to consider itself, in Hegel's familiar words, 'the universal estate".

Gradual German unification resulted in Prussian hegemony within the North German Confederation after 1867, within the Empire from 1871. During the Wilhelmine Era, Prussian state tradition played a "crucial role" in "causing the system of authority to degenerate steadily into a form of mere rule by officialdom" which largely lacked "the breadth of vision and political leadership" earlier demonstrated by Prussia's administrators (Mommsen, 1995, p. 50). Nevertheless, advocates of the authoritarian *Rechtsstaat* were referring to Prusso-German bureaucracy, even two generations later, "in the same breath with England's parliamentary government" – extolling its supposedly just and "equal" personnel policies' which were suggested "to have stolen democracy's thunder" (Morstein Marx, 1935, pp. 163, 197).

Such a concept of 'democratic' personnel selection, rather than democratic decision-making, could persist because it served to set the country off from Western democracies, supposedly in a 'positive' sense (cf. Struve, 1973, pp. 462-463). The ideology of German 'distinctiveness' culminated at the outset of World War I when liberty, equality, and fraternity, the 'French' ideals of 1789, were countered by the German "ideas of 1914" – order, duty, community (cf. Kjellén, 1915, Plenge; 1916; Troeltsch, 1925). Hegel's 'organic', corporatist conception of the state had contributed its share to those notions.

The German Federal Republic's Alleged 'Lack of Staatlichkeit': Hegelianism After 1945

When the West German Federal Republic was founded after World War II, its governmental institutions were consciously modeled after Western parliamentary democracies. West Germany's political system included an array of parties and interest groups which had existed, albeit with considerable structural modifications, since the 19th century, but whose eminent position was now, for the first time, constitutionally acknowledged.

Unavoidably, the Hegelian conception of the state and the common good which had so strongly imprinted itself on Germany's political tradition, did not disappear overnight. Continuing to emphasize that "the pluralism of interests (could) not legitimize political authority', Joseph H. Kaiser, one of its persistent advocates, instead singled out for praise a constitutional solution "of high formal beauty", the "work of a genius" that, allegedly, had brought "peace and prosperity" to another country – the corporatist system of Salazar's Portugal (Kaiser, 1956, pp. 329, 360). Having managed, in contrast with Spain, to keep an internationally low profile as a 'decent' semi-fascist regime, Portugal was, in fact, a repressive dictatorship whose terrorist secret police had been modeled after the Gestapo.

Kaiser made no bones about his reasons for preferring corporatism over pluralism: while the latter had "the power to destroy the state", estates and corporations had "never challenged the state as such, nor denied its supremacy" (Kaiser, 1956, pp. 321, 323). In his insistence on the state's "neutrality vis-a-vis the struggle of social interests", its unique "capability for objective decisions" (Forsthoff, 1968, p. 159), Kaiser was seconded by Ernst Forsthoff and Werner Weber: after "pluralistic oligarchies" had invaded the body politic, the Federal Republic's constitution had "neglected to integrate these groups into a totality resulting in an obligatory common will" (Weber, 1970, pp. 54, 56). Ever in danger, according to Weber, of "dissolution", West Germany "lacked a state with generally accepted authority", which only "a professional civil service with a universal ethos" (Forsthoff, 1968), "committed to serve the common good" (Weber, 1970), could guarantee.

While Werner Weber diagnosed an "extraordinary instability" of the body politic "in domestic and foreign policy matters" – "frayed" as it was by partial interests (Weber, 1970, p. 132; see also Forsthoff, 1964, p. 77) -, Forsthoff came to contradict that remarkably apocalyp-tic analysis, reversing his judgment. He now conceded that "stabilizing forces" were at work in modern

149

pluralist societies, including West Germany. Pluralism "no longer endangered a state' which, admittedly, had suffered a "loss of authority", for pluralist interests, in turn, had lost their earlier divisive, "ideologically explosive quality" (Forsthoff 1959, p. 16). From a post-Hegelian point of view, society itself had become 'rational'.

The 'Parallelogram of Social Forces', Rules of the Game, and the Public Interest: Anti-Hegelian Elements in Ernst Fraenkel's Neo-pluralist Approach

With the establishment of political science as an academic discipline in West Germany, a paradigm gradually emerged that differed fundamentally from the Hegelian tradition of political philosophy. Largely derived from the experiences which scholars expelled by the Nazis had gained in New Deal America, that paradigm focused, first, on the decision-making processes of Western-type democracies, including political parties and pressure groups; second, on the development of liberal thought – in a broader sense – from its early to its more recent forms; third (and probably most apt to ensure the rapid career of the concept), on the contrast between Western and 'totalitarian' political systems.

The approach was typified by Ernst Fraenkel, one of the discipline's dominant 'mentors" during the early post-war period. He introduced the notion of pluralism – or, as labeled by himself 'neo-pluralism' – including a strong normative element, into West German political science. Having initially argued that the concept, as elaborated by Barker, Cole, and Laski during the first two decades of the 20th century, was mainly of historical interest (Fraenkel, 1957, pp. 235-236), Fraenkel rapidly came to conclude that the irrevocable historical development of "monist communities" into "pluralist societies" demanded a pluralist democracy within which the public interest would be reduced to a "regulative idea" (Fraenkel, 1968, p. 42).

Corporatist ideals and the supremacy of a civil bureaucracy that had "barred the political parties from governing" were included by Fraenkel among the "historical burdens on German parliamentarism" (Fraenkel, 1968, pp, 25, 40). A pluralist conception of society and state precluded "the existence of any definitely determinable public interest" that might be "*a priori* defined" and subsequently realized by authoritarian methods. While politically indispensable as a normative principle, the public interest could actually only result "*a posteriori*" from the "delicate" (Fraenkel, 1968) process of reconciling 'the diverging ideas and interests of groups and political parties' (Fraenkel, 1968, p. 168). That process would have to observe "generally accepted rules of the game". Not touching on "broad areas of basic agreement", it would, in fact, be limited to the smaller "controversial sector" of the body politic, permitting public opinion "to choose between competing solutions" (Fraenkel, 1968, pp. 154, 161, 168). In the last instance, the common good would result "from the parallelogram of economic, social, political, and ideological forces", provided that, on balance, the outcome would "correspond to the minimal requirements of a just social order on the objective side and not be regarded as unacceptable by any important group on the subjective side" (Fraenkel, 1968, p. 21).

The similarity of Fraenkel's approach to group theories of politics, as developed in the USA, is evident. E. Pendleton Herring had held already by 1933 that the common good, far from being definable according to "some abstract ideal", may only be conceived "in terms of the parties at conflict *and in relation to the law*" (Herring, 1933, pp. 916-917, emphasis added):

Hence the public interest cannot be given concrete expression except through the compromise of special claims and demands finally effected... They are the parts that make the whole.

In his *Governmental Process*, David Truman (1951) explained that the political system "is not accounted for by the "'um' of organized interest groups in society". Truman included constitutionalism, civil liberties, representative techniques among the "rules of the game", according to which organized groups had to operate. Otherwise, they risked bringing those "wide potential groups" into action which adhered to the values and norms of the "habit background" (Truman, 1951, pp. 51, 159, 524).

The criteria indicated by Truman and by Fraenkel were sufficiently vague to draw repeated criticism. What, in the case of Fraenkel, are we to understand by 'objective' minimal requirements? Exactly which interest groups should be defined as 'important'? And by what process, taking into account the rigid qualification on the 'subjective' side, may attainment of the former be ensured (cf. Eisfeld, 1972, p. 85; Kremendahl, 1977, p. 34)?

These questions, however, need not concern us here in detail. Fraenkel's approach, as compared with the Hegelian tradition, stood for the step from the status quo-oriented, 'peculiarly German' conception of the state to a "reformist" (Fraenkel, 1969, p, 23) theory merging into the larger context of Western political thinking. While remaining problematical, the idea of the common good acquired fundamentally consensual qualities, losing most of its coercive Hegelian implications in the process.

References

Barker, Ernest (1915): *Political Thought in England from Herbert Spencer to the Present Day*, New York, Henry Holt.

Eisfeld, Rainer (1972): *Pluralismus zwischen Liberalismus und Sozialismus*, Stuttgart, W. Kohlhammer.

Fetscher, Iring (1986): 'Georg Wilhelm Friedrich Hegel', in: Fetscher, Iring/Münkler, Herfried (eds.), *Pipers Handbuch der politischen Ideen*, Vol. 4, Munich, pp. 199-226.

Forsthoff, Ernst (1959): *Rechtsfragen der leistenden Verwaltung*, Stuttgart, W. Kohlhammer.

Forsthoff, Ernst (1964): *Rechtsstaat im Wandel. Essays 1950-1964*, Stuttgart, W. Kohlhammer.

Forsthoff, Ernst, ed. (1968): *Rechtsstaatlichkeit und Sozialstaatlichkeit*, Darmstadt, Wissen-schaftliche Buchgesellschaft.

Fraenkel, Ernst (1957): 'Pluralismus', in: Fraenkel, Ernst /Bracher, Karl Dietrich (eds.), *Fischer Lexikon Staat und Politik*, Frankfurt, S. Fischer, pp. 234-236.

Fraenkel, Ernst (1968): *Deutschland und die westlichen Demokratien*, Stuttgart, W. Kohlhammer.

Fraenkel, Ernst (1969): „Strukturanalyse der modernen Demokratie", *Aus Politik und Zeit-geschichte*, No. 49/69, pp. 3-27.

Gay, Peter (1974): *Weimar Culture*, Harmondsworth, Penguin Books.

Gunnell, John G. (1993): *The Descent of Political Theory*, Chicago, University of Chicago Press.

Hegel, Georg Friedrich Wilhelm (1982): *Grundlinien der Philosophie des Rechts*, Works, Vol. 7, Frankfurt, Suhrkamp,

Herring, E Pendleton (1933): "Special interests and the interstate commerce commission", *American Political Science Review*, Vol. 27, pp. 899-917.

Hobbes, Thomas (1965): *Leviathan*, Reinbek, Rowohlt.

Kaiser, Joseph H. (1956): *Die Repräsentation organisierter Interessen*, Berlin, Duncker & Humblot.

Kjellén, Rudolf (1915): *Die Ideen von 1914*, Leipzig, Hirzel.

Kremendahl, Hans (1977): *Pluralismustheorie in Deutschland*, Leverkusen, Heggen.

Krieger, Leonard (1972): *The German Idea of Freedom*, Chicago, University of Chicago Press.

Marcuse, Herbert (1941): *Reason and Revolution. Hegel and the Rise of Social Thought*, London, Oxford University Press.

Marx, Karl (1968): „Zur Kritik der Hegelschen Rechtsphilosophie", in: Marx, Karl and Engels, Friedrich (eds.), *Works*, Vol. 1, Berlin, pp. 201-283.

Mommsen, Wolfgang J. (1995): *Imperial Germany 1867-1918*, London, Arnold.

Morstein Marx, Fritz (1935): "Civil Service in Germany', in: White, L. D. et al. (eds.), *Civil Service Abroad*, New York, pp. 159-275.

Plenge, Johann (1916): *1789 und 1914. Die symbolischen Jahre in der Geschichte des deutschen Geistes*, Berlin, Julius Springer.

Rosenberg, Hans (1966): *Bureaucracy, Aristocracy and Autocracy. The Prussian Experience 1660-1815,* Boston, Beacon, Press.

Sabine, George H. (1950): *A History of Political Theory*, New York, Henry Holt.

Schmitt, Carl (1933): „Weiterentwicklung des totalen Staats in Deutschland", in id. (1940): *Positionen and Begriffe*, Hamburg, Hanseatische Verlagsanstalt, pp. 185-190.

Smend, Rudolf (1933): *Bürger and Bourgeois im deutschen Staatsrecht*, Berlin, Duncker & Humblot.

Struve, Walter (1973): *Elites Against Democracy. Leadership Ideals in Bourgeois Political Thought in Germany, 1890-1933*, Princeton, Princeton University Press.

Topitsch, Ernst (1970): „Kritik der Hegel-Apologeten", in Kaltenbrunner, Gerd-Klaus (ed.): *Hegel und die Folgen*, Freiburg, Rombach, pp. 329-360.

Troeltsch, Ernst (1925): *Deutscher Geist und Westeuropa*, ed. Hans Baron, Tübingen, C. B. Mohr.

Truman, David B. (1951): *The Governmental Process*, New York. Alfred A. Knopf.

Weber, Werner (1970): *Spannungen und Kräfte im westdeutschen Verfassungssystem*, Berlin, Duncker & Humblot.

In a preceding (the next-to-last) chapter, Central Europe – or Mitteleuropa – already surfaced as a region on which German foreign trade strategists had set their sight since the early 1930s: precursor of that "greater regional economy" which the Nazis' "Greater German Reich" would later construct for the purposes of exploitation. Since early World War I, however, and again during the 1920s, Mitteleuropa also served as an acronym for Germany's desired hegemony over territories from Poland to the Black Sea. After World War II, such aspirations seemed a matter of mere historical interest. But from 1990, the Mitteleuropa notion regained unexpected saliency: After Germany had achieved reunification, skeptical voices queried whether both the former Reich and Mitteleuropa might not be "coming back". In 1993, the journal German Politics and Society *published an issue on the subject, to which I contributed the following thoughts.*

Mitteleuropa in Historical and Contemporary Perspective[1]

When the upheaval of 1989 occurred behind what had been the iron curtain, analysts noted that West Germany was indeed using "its economic power to accomplish its political aims", particularly with regard to reunification. Change was sweeping Central Europe "in a nexus of Soviet weakness and West German strength". After German reunification, and due to Soviet '"economic, political, military, and moral" weakness, they claimed, "Germany's relative weight in European affairs is increasing in all of these spheres" (Hoagland 1990: 34, 39; Mead 1990: 594). The Germans, analysts asserted, "are clearly getting the version of 'Europe' they want – with unity and with space for economic and cultural expansion into East-Central Europe" (Weaver 1990: 477). From there it was but a small step to the claim that "the once and future Reich" loomed large – "a return to German hegemony in this part of the world". Conclusion: "Mitteleuropa is coming back" (Mead 1990; 603, passim).

Mitteleuropa? Has not the notion, for decades, remained marginal to intellectual and political discourse in Germany (and elsewhere)? Why would the concept, nevertheless, have remained imprinted upon the consciousness of observers, to surface again the moment Germany's division came to an end? And even if Germany is ranked among the issues that "have returned to haunt the region" – i.e. Central Europe – (Bunce 1990: 427), does Mitteleuropa in fact emerge as a possible, or even a probable scenario?

---

1   For support in obtaining trade and investment data, I am indebted to Dr. Klaus-Dieter Schmidt (Institut für Weltwirtschaft, Kiel).

155

II

Mitteleuropa – as a concept and a strategy – first gained currency during
World War I. Friedrich Naumann argued in 1915 that Germany's lack of
population and territory ("the strongest among small peoples", but still small
compared to the United States, Britain or Russia) meant that it had to fashion
"the fourth world state" through the economic "affiliation of the other Central
European states and nations" (Naumann 1915: 167, 177}. Naumann's argument coincided almost to the letter with the war aims memoranda submitted
to the German government hardly a year earlier by Arthur von Gwinner, first
director of the Deutsche Bank, and Walther Rathenau, member of the board
of directors of the electrical corporation AEG. They also advocated Mitteleuropa, "unified under German leadership, politically and economically
consolidated against England and America on one, against Russia on the
other side" (cf. Fischer 1969: 746). War-time expectations inflated the concept to the point where Naumann's collaborator and later the president of the
Berlin School of Politics, Ernst Jäckh, proclaimed a Greater Central Europe
including Germany, Austria-Hungary, Turkey, Bulgaria, Romania, and
Greece, to be led "organically," "without despotism", by Germany, and
"complementing our seaward orientation, especially toward a future 'Middle
Africa'" (Jäckh 1916: 6, 11, 17). The extent to which such conceptual pathology was rampant is indicated by the fact that programs like these were considered "moderate," because they renounced formal annexations, concentrated on Eastern instead of Western Europe, and lacked a repressive domestic
element.

If Naumann's design was less grandiose, it was also more explicit than
Jäckh's: The "supra-national, cartelized state" of Central Europe would arrive
politically "formless, featureless, and democratically inadequate", even if
Naumann did not exclude a possible future economic parliament (Naumann
1915: 166, 252). He argued that, for economic reasons, Central Europe's
small states had no choice but to accept either "German, Russian, or British
leadership", as they could not afford to remain isolated for more than another
generation. History decreed that economic *Anschluß* was "imperative, cate-
gorically neces-sary" (Naumann 1915: 178). Neumann suggested that the new
economic area's central administrative body should base its legislation on
agreements reached by economic associations and interest groups (ibid.: 133-
134, 242, 25). Fundamentally however, discipline and organization, the
"German economic creed", were expected to shape the "character of Central
Europe." Even if Naumann, as pointed out by Henry Cord Mayer in his 1955
book *Mitteleuropa in German Thought and Action*, called for a spirit of compromise and flexibility, he left no doubt that Mitteleuropa's "core" would be
German (ibid.: 101, 104, 108-109, 114).

III

After Germany's defeat in 1918, a radical revisionism almost immediately started to crystallize around the alleged German Mitteleuropa "mission." Insisting on "displacing the existing power structure to the advantage of the German Reich", revisionism aimed at a restoration of German continental hegemony under changed conditions. During the twenties, it pervaded Weimar society, reinforcing, in theory as in practice, a "functional," instrumentalist approach in domestic and foreign policy. If democratic government and the League of Nations proved unable to bring about revision, both institutions might be expendable (cf. Salewski 1980; for the quote, see Hillgruber 1984: 84).

The *völkisch* – racially nationalist – Mitteleuropa concept remained vague in its details, yet concrete in its rejection of the political settlement the Versailles and St. Germain treaties had introduced into Central Europe. The "inflated multi-ethnic Polish state" and "the Czechoslovakian motley conglomeration, questionably structured politically no less than nationally" (Boehm 1923: 315), were particularly denounced. German "leadership of Central Europe" would have "to be earned, perhaps obtained with a fight" (Brauweiler 1925: 249). As Martin Spahn, Reichstag delegate for the German National People's Party (DNVP), summed up the 'national opposition's' approach: "If we succeed in shaping Central Europe, we shall rise again to the position of Europe's leading people" (Spahn 1925: 40).

The economic impact of the Great Depression and the political challenge of the French government's 1930 proposal to negotiate a Pan-European confederation, with its implied acceptance of the existing territorial status quo, combined to influence the German foreign relations debate and strategy. Both worked towards bridging part of the conceptual gap between the camps of radical and "democratic" nationalism (for the latter, cf. Hess 1978); Naumann's economic Mitteleuropa design was revived by the German Democratic Party (now, significantly German State Party). Economically and politically, Mitteleuropa came to be perceived, by an increasing number of players, as a definite opportunity to restore German hegemony during the final phase of the Weimar Republic. Brüning's presidential cabinet embarked on the 'positive', 'vigorous' foreign policy consistently demanded by the 'national opposition'. Preferential agreements concluded with Hungary and Romania initiated a shift of German foreign trade to southeastern Central Europe (cf. Gessner 1977: 92 ss., 97 s s.), prefiguring the economic dependence of that region's agricultural countries on Germany which was actually attained by the 'Third Reich's' foreign trade policy.

German exports

Country	Year	% of German exports	% of recipient country's imports
	1928	1.0	13,6
Yugoslavia	1933	0.7	13.2
	1938	2.6	32.5
	1928	1.3	19.1
Hungary	1933	0.8	19,6
	1938	2.7	30.3
	1928	1.4	23.7
Romania	1933	0.9	18.5
	1938	3.0	28.0

Source: O. N. Haberl, "Südosteuropa und das Deutsche Reich vor dem Zweiten Weltkrieg", *Südosteuropa*, Vol. 39 (1990), pp. 515-516.

By 1941, German exports to the countries listed had jumped to between one-half and three-fourths of imports on the part of the recipients. Small wonder that the Nazi regime approvingly referred to relations between southeastern Central Europe and Germany as the prime example of that "greater regional economy" which, like the 'New Order' ideology, was to prove a mere euphemism for the spoliation of Europe (cf. Kluke 1955: 251-52). The renewal of plans for Central Europe by the Weimar presidential cabinets had laid the foundation for these policies.

IV

The renaissance of concepts of Mitteleuropa that took place in the 1980s expressed another refusal to accept the international status quo – though quite dissimilar in character from Weimar Germany's revisionism. Emerging from discussions among East-Central European exiles and dissidents, this renaissance primarily aimed at creating a regional cultural identity in opposition to Soviet-induced uniforrnization and ideological "brainwashing" (Kundera 1984: 33). It was conducive to common policies of "détente and reform", economic cooperation, and cultural linkages {cf. Waever 1990: 480; Glotz l986: 585). These concepts were evidently based on the assumptions that both Germany and Europe would remain divided `between blocs; that 'actually existing' socialism would not crumble, because the USSR, as a last resort, would continue to keep regimes in place by force, or by threat of force; and that at most, one could hope for a larger measure of "Europeanization," meaning an all-European security perspective based on détente and confidence-building – Central Europe as "an emergency partnership" (Bender 1987: 30).

Only rarely did this debate recall the "negative, dark traits" of the region's interwar political culture, including harsh authoritarianism, aggressive nationalism and militant anti-Semitism, that might continue to haunt Central Europe (cf. Hanák 1988: 34 ss.; Grupinski l988: 63-64). Rather it amounted to an often wistful appeal to value Central Europe's "imaginary existence", in cultural terms, "over the facts of Realpolitik" (Hanák 1988: 36), even if this meant willingness "to be hamstrung with regard to direct political activity" (Grupinski 1988: 56).

In view of the consequences of the Mitteleuropa-"mission" which Germans had claimed for themselves, the question of Germany's inclusion into Central Europe was heatedly debated by East European scholars and writers. Meanwhile, arguments favoring a "cultural" Central Europe were picked up and disseminated in West Germany. They were seized upon not least by Social Democrats like Peter Glotz who envisioned an "enlightened," "co-reformist" East-West policy of "decreasing the divisive effect of borders" – a means of "squaring the circle" with regard to the supposed permanence of the European, and therefore of the German, split (cf. Waever 1990: 480; Glotz 1986: 585).

Normally, after the revolution in East-Central Europe, ideas about a "cultural" Central Europe might be assumed to have lost much of their significance, since "ordinary politics" (Waever) have begun to reemerge in the former Warsaw Pact countries. However, a shrewd observer like the Hungarian philosopher Mihály Vajda was quick to discern

that the idea of Central Europe's cultural identity today is backed by rather strong economic impulses and interests... The fact that the concept has recently gained such strength is plainly due to...economic elements...The Federal Republic of Germany is Central Europe's strongest country, able to get the other Central European countries out of their misery. (Vajda l989: 56).

Subsequent events in southeastern Central Europe have lent a saliency to this argument that could not have been expected at the time Vajda made his observation.

V

Czechoslovakia, Poland, and Hungary would again "be at the center of German policy in the future", prophesied one writer in 1990. His reason: Even today German investment there "is substantially greater than investment from any other country" (Mead 1990: 6l2). This assertion deserves a closer look.

Percentages of Foreign Direct Investment (1990)

	Poland	Romania	Czechoslovakia
FRG	41.1	19.9	28.3
Austria	6.6	6.6	29.8
France	4.7	14.0	2.3
UK	4.9	3,7	3.0

Source: J. R Agarwal, "Ausländische Direktinvestitionen...", Die Weltwirtschaft (1990), No. 2, p. 133

The table indicates that Germany is indeed very substantially ahead in Poland. Germany leads the field in Romania, with France (and Italy, omitted here) close behind, and is at Austria's heels in Czechoslovakia. (In Hungary; in contrast, the latter two countries' direct investment ratio is reversed: Austria follows Germany as a close second [for details, see Biró 1992: 198, 112].)

While this evidence somewhat qualifies the above-quoted assertion, a further fact needs to be considered. The capital actually involved is still pathetically small, peanuts by American standards:

Foreign Direct Investment in Selected Comecon Countries
Increase in East-West Joint Ventures 1989-91 (Millions of US dollars)

Country	Jan. l, 1989	Oct. 1, 1990	Dec. 31, 1991
Poland	13	190	630
Hungary	289	700	1,200

Source: Agarwal, p.131 (1989-90); calculation by Klaus-Dieter Schmidt (1991)

With liberalization continuing in East-Central Europe, larger investments may be expected. Nevertheless, for the near future the data should be helpful for keeping the proverbial sense of proportion.

Regarding Germanys share in the region's foreign trade, the pattern changed rather noticeably during 1990 in the wake of the drastic shift of trade away from the former Comecon area.

West German Exports

Country	Year	% of West German Exports	% of Recipient Country's Imports
	1970	1.8	22.1

160

Yugoslavia	1980	1.4	17.3
	1988	1.1	17.3
	1970	0.4	5.7
Hungary	1980	0.6	13.0
	1988	0.5	13.9
	1970	0.6	10.0
Romania	1980	0.5	6.7
	1988	0.1	2.7

West German Exports
(FRG territory according to the boundaries valid before Oct. 3, 1990)

Country	Year	% of West German Exports	% of Recipient Country's Imports
Yugoslavia	1990	1.3	18,1
Hungary	1990	0.5	17.1
Romania	1990	0.2	11.4

Source: Institut für Weltwirtschaft Kiel (FRG Statistical Yearbooks)

* Including Bosnia-Herzegovina, Croatia, Slovenia

In the cases of Poland and Czechoslovakia, the proportional rise in imports; from Germany has been even more spectacular: 26.5% of Poland's and very nearly 22% of Czechoslovakia's 1990 imports originated in the Federal Republic (as defined by its pre-October borders), while in 1988 the corresponding shares had amounted to a mere 11.4 and 9,5 percent. Export percentages on the part of the FRG remained at their previous 0.7/0.5 levels.

On the German side, these changes have not resulted from any purposeful shift in trade flows, comparable to the one that occurred during the thirties. Nevertheless, the emerging state of affairs is remarkably similar to the interwar pattern. Is the contraction of intra-Comecon trade generating the structural prerequisites for reducing the region, once again, to its supposedly "historical role as "German foreign policy turf"" (Livingston 1992: 168)?

VI

There can be little doubt that, henceforth, Germany will indeed be "more" of a "Central" European state than it was in the past, given the FRG's previously unqualified orientation toward the West. If tentative answers to questions regarding the implementation of a Central European role arc sought, two contradictory tendencies may be discerned at present. On one hand, the "model" which Germany was supposed to offer to East-Central European countries has become badly tarnished. On the other, "Euro-stalling" (Goldstein 1991/92: 129) by the members of the European Community may provide Germany with a more internationally free hand than envisioned in most scenarios a year ago.

As quoted above, "economic, political, military and moral" weight were German assets vis-á-vis Central Europe widely referred to during and after 1989-90. One particularly unequivocal assessment (Markovits/Reich 1992: 62} summed up:

Germany's European neighbors, whether Eastern or Western, consider intensive economic contacts with the Germans to be essential for them to prosper... In the East, this belief includes the political sphere, because it is chiefly the Federal Republic's democratic institutions and arrangements which East European countries regard as exemplary in their transition to liberal-democratic polities ... East Europeans believe proximity to the Germans to equal the mystical touch of a bearer of blessings.

Economically, however, the German integration process is proving "more disruptive and costly than widely thought at the outset" (OECD 1992: 10). This is at least partly attributable to two of the government's decisions: first, to apply the "shock therapy" of monetary union to the East German economy and, second, to finance the huge transfers to the new states largely by massive deficit spending and consequently heavy public borrowing. For eastern Germany, these policies may result either "in speedy transformation" or "in a Mezzogiorno-type economy... whereby a permanently disadvantaged region is created, requiring massive resource transfers for many years" (Owen 1991: 171; also Collier/Siebert 1991: 200). In any case, unemployment and underemployment (part-time work and early retirement) have soared to over 30% in the new Lander, demonstrating to Eastern Europe that the sacrifices required by transition "fall disproportionately on blue·-collar workers" (Kramer 1992: 147). The ex- perience is justifiably throwing doubt upon the one element which had lent, "in the eyes of so many East Europeans, a particularly high degree of legitimacy to the 'German model'" (Markovits/ Reich 1992: 56) – its "social dimension".

Politically, constitutional changes in Poland or Romania, let alone the "divorce" of the Czech and Slovak republics, have hardly tended to observe the "example" set by Germany. Nor have several recent German initiatives with regard to East-Central Europe proved particularly inspiring. Germany pressured the European Community into diplomatically recognizing Croatia and Slovenia, thereby setting a precedent which precipitated the recognition of ethnically mixed Bosnia-Herzegovina – an act that may well have triggered the savage civil war there. "Intensive" negotiations with Romania resulted in an agreement permitting Germany to deport a majority of would-be Gypsy refugees hack to that country, notwithstanding persistent reports of attacks on Gypsies there. And the accord between German coalition and opposition parties to tighten the constitutional provisions on asylum by turning back asylum-seekers arriving from surrounding "safe countries", creating a "cordon sanitaire" around Germany, is bound to put a heavy burden, in human and financial terms, on Poland and Czechoslovakia.

These latter issues touch on the final, moral, dimension, where the recent German record, to say the minimum, has been unimpressive. Racist attacks on refugees and other foreigners, including homicide, murder, and relentless fire-bombings of shelters for asylum-seekers, left seventeen people dead and more than 500 wounded during 1992. Responses to the wave of right-wing violence by state and federal governments, police, and courts were shockingly slow to develop and initially far from adequate. These initial deficiencies contributed to the impression that under the double strain of reunification-induced financial burdens and refugee influx, one of the winners of the cold war was at least partly blaming the victims of violence in lieu of the criminals. This probably – and with good reason – did more to blemish the image of Germany as a "model" democracy than any other single circumstance.

Across Europe, economic anxieties, ideological disorientation, and the anger resulting from perplexed insecurity have fueled re-nationalization. In the German case, revived nationalism has functioned as a sounding board for governmental officials and political parties intent on curbing immigration. However; the political elite has resisted it to the extent that it adhered to the perspective of European Political Union embodied in the Maastricht Treaty.

A year ago, further "deepening" of the European Community seemed to be inevitable. The 1986 Single European Act had extended qualified majority voting to most economic policy areas – though the instrument was less frequently used than permitted by existing provisions, which had also lowered the threshold for resorting to the procedure. EPC (European Political Cooperation), accorded legal status in 1986, had since been institutionally streamlined. The Council of Ministers, not the national foreign ministries, handles the agenda and works toward solutions. The Single European Market, to be progressively established until December 1992, could be expected to cut even deeper into national autonomy in economic policy. The Maastricht Treaty, finally, proclaimed as its aim the politicization of the process of integrating the Twelve; its provisions for arriving at monetary union, and at common foreign and security policies, seemed to chart a course toward what Iohan Galtung had early, if critically; proclaimed "a superpower in the making."

Instead, the Danish and French referenda, while (barely) different in their outcome, reflected widespread uncertainty about EC aims and, particularly, policies. The recent EC presidency term, occupied by a Britain almost "viscerally" ambivalent about the Community (Davidson 1992: 2), came to symbolize the sort of political "Euro-stalling" that, against the background of a slowdown in the European economy, culminated in the Edinburgh summit. The "deepening" process was weakened by exempting Denmark from the monetary union and common defense aims of the Maastricht Treaty, with the feasibility of the former remaining fundamentally in doubt, not least because of disequilibria caused by Germany's financial management of reunification. On the other hand, it was decided to open another "widening" round by commencing negotiations with Austria, Finland, and Sweden early in 1993, even before Denmark and the United Kingdom have had time to ratify the Maastricht Treaty.

VII

Progressively "deepening" the European Community in the sense of integrating it "more" along federal lines and eventually "widening" it to include Central Europe had been perceived solutions to the problems confronting the whole post-cold war continent, Even where the number of players involved substantially surpassed that of the Community' s members, western economic diplomacy vis-à-vis East-Central Europe came to be largely EC-based. The OECD countries' PHARE economic support program, rapidly extended to cover Czechoslovakia, Bulgaria, Romania and, initially, Yugoslavia in addition to Poland and Hungary (hence the acronym PHARE: "Poland/ Hungary: Assistance to Restructuring the Economies") was organized and administered by the EC commission. EC association agreements with Hungary, Czechoslovakia, and Poland were concluded in December, 1991. Progressively establishing a free trade zone is their explicit goal.

This has not meant, however, that a Community increasingly determined to act in unison has successfully moved to fill the vacuum left by the economic, political, and ideological collapse of "actually existing" socialism Nor has the CSCE managed to do so, despite what seemed promising beginnings. The rock on which attempts at a "European" foreign policy have primarily foundered has, of course, been the civil war in former Yugoslavia. The results of what attempts were made to arrive at common and more decisive steps in this matter have, by turns, been labeled "schizophrenic" or "derisory" in the international press. A sturdier EC has emerged from neither the economic, nor the foreign, policy challenges of 1992.

The essay must, therefore, end on an inconclusive note. In contrast to the Weimar era, no influential political players have emerged in Germany indicating that they would, oven in a rudimentary way, desire to pursue once more the Mitteleuropa concept. No broad ideological background for such a venture seems to exist. Economically however, the writing is on the wall. The separation of Czechoslovakia into two economically and politically weaker states is bound to strengthen Germany's position in the region. If the European Community fails to coalesce in matters of political and security integration, disillusionment about the EC may favor additional bilateral arrangements in East-Central Europe. Finally, if the permission given to Denmark to opt out of the main tenets of the Political Union Treaty should come to mean that other EC members do not feel bound by those tenets, largely feeling free to act unilaterally in a politically fragmented Community, then Mitteleuropa might evolve from an unlikely outcome into a conceivable possibility.

References

Agarwal, Jamuna P.: "Ausländische Direktinvestitionen in Osteuropa", *Die Weltwirtschaft* 2 (1990), 126-137.

Bender, Peter: "Mitteleuropa – Mode, Modell oder Motiv?", *Die Neue Gesellschaft/Frankfurter Hefte* 34 (1987), 297-304.

Biró, Gerd: "Die Präsenz Deutschlands und Österreichs in der Wirtschaft Ungarns", *Südosteu-ropa* 41 (1992), 106-115.

Boehm, Max Hildebert: *Europa Irredenta*, Berlin 1923.

Brauweiler, Heinz: *Berufsstand und Staat*, Berlin 1925.

Bunce, Valerie: "The Struggle for Liberal Democracy in Eastern Europe", *World Policy Jour nal* 7 (1990), 395-424.

Collier, Jr., Irwin L./Siebert, Horst: "The Economic Integration of Post-Wall Germany", *Ameri-can Economic Review* (AEA Papers & Proceedings) 81 (1991), 195-201.

Fischer, Fritz: *Krieg der Illusionen*, Dusseldorf 1969.

Gessner, Dieter: *Agrardepression und Präsidialregierungen in Deutschland 1930-33*, Düssel-dorf 1977.

Glotz, Peter: "Deutsch-böhmische Kleinigkeiten oder: Abgerissene Gedanken über Mitteleuro-pa", *Die Neue Gesellschaft/Frankfurter Hefte* 33 (1986): 584-585.

Goldstein, Walter: "EC: Euro-Stalling," *Foreign Policy* 85 (Winter 1991-92), 129-147.

Grupinski, Rafal: „Schwierigkeiten mit der Mitte Europas", in: Hans-Peter Burmeister et al., eds., *Mitteleuropa – Traum oder Trauma?*, Bremen 1988, 51-64.

Haberl, Othmar Nikola: "Südosteuropa und das Deutsche Reich vor dem Zweiten Weltkrieg," *Südosteuropa* 39 (1990), 501-526.

Hanék, Péter: "Schöpferische Kraft und Pluralität in der mitteleuropäischen Kultur", in: Bur-meister et al., *Mitteleuropa*, op. cit., 28-50.

Hess, Jürgen C.: *"Das ganze Deutschland soll es sein." Demokratischer Nationalismus in der Weimarer Republik am Beispiel der DDP*, Stuttgart 1978.

Hillgruber, Andreas: „'Revisionismus' – Kontinuität und Wandel in der Außenpolitik der Wei-marer Republik", in id., *Die Last der Nation*, Düsseldorf 1984, 59-85.

Hoagland, Jim: "Europe's Destiny", *Foreign Affairs* 69 (1990), 33-50.

Jäckh, Ernst: *Das größere Mitteleuropa*, Weimar 1916.

Kluke, Paul: "Nationalsozialistische Europaideologie", *Vierteljahreshefte für Zeitgeschichte* 3 (1955), 240-275.

Kramer, Mark: "Eastern Europe Goes to Market," *Foreign Policy* 85 (Spring 1992), 134-157.

Kundera, Milan: "The Tragedy of Central Europe", *New York Review of Books* 31, 26 April 1984, 33-38.

Livingston, Robert Gerald: "United Germany: Bigger and Better?", Foreign Policy 87 (Summer 1992), S. 157-174.

Markovits, Andrei S./Reich, Simon: "Deutschlands neues Gesicht: Über deutsche Hegemonie in Europa", *Leviathan* 20 (1992), 17-63.

Mead, Walter Russell: "The Once and Future Reich", *World Policy Journal* 7 (1990), 593-638.

Meyer, Henry Cord: *Mitteleuropa in German Thought and Action 1815-1945*, Den Haag 1955.

Naumann, Friedrich: *Mitteleuropa*, Berlin 1915.

OECD: *Economic Survey: Germany*, Paris 1992.

Owen, Robert F.: "The Challenges of German Unification to   EC Policymaking and Perform-ance", *American Economic Review* (AEA Papers & Proceedings) 81 (1991): 171-75.

Salewski, Michael: "Das Weimarer Revionssyndrom," *Aus Politik und Zeitgeschichte*, 12 Ja-nuary 1980, 11-25.

Spahn, Martin: *Mitteleuropa und das deutsche Volk*, Neuburg 1925

Vajda, Mihály: "Mitteleuropa: Nostalgie oder Projekt?," OstEuropaForum 77 (1989), 49-57.

Waever, Ole: "Three Competing Europes: German, French, Russian", *International Affairs* 66 1990), 477-493.

IV.
Political Science and Ideology (2)
Another Peculiar Course:
American 'Gun-Mindedness' –
Some Origins and Consequences

America's frontier experience shaped the country's "distinctiveness" – promoting a leveling spirit and a rapacious instinct for acquisition, bequeathing to succeeding generations an armed society sustained by an ideology of "progress through violence". Drawing on both the myth and the factual life of an archetypical gunfighter, the following chapter discusses that ideology. The analysis demonstrates that the myth, by constructing an epic narrative, attaches historical "sense" to an otherwise disjointed biography. In the process, violence is legitimized by linking that narrative to the stages through which, and the means by which, the American nation is supposed to have progressed. The article was first published in the Journal of Criminal Justice and Popular Culture *(1995), then included in a volume of JCJPC papers entitled* Interrogating Popular Culture *(1998). Subsequently, Western history enthusiasts chanced upon it, reprinting it twice: in the National Association for Outlaw and Lawman History's* Quarterly *(2000) and in the Western Outlaw-Lawman History Association's* Journal *(2007). For that most recent publication, I prepared an updated version of the text, which is included here.*

Myths and Realities of Frontier Violence:
A Look at the Gunfighter Saga[1]

I

In the third volume of his monumental trilogy on the enduring myth of the frontier in American popular and political culture, Richard Slotkin coined the term "Gunfighter Nation" for 20th century America. The term was not merely meant to denote, like Richard Hofstadter's expression "gun culture", an emotional involvement with guns as a peculiar American characteristic, resulting in a heavily armed populace and a lack of satisfactory gun controls.[2] Rather, Slotkin concerned himself with the myth of the violent frontier as the site of the clash between savagery and civilization – and with the development of that myth into what he called "a set of symbols" capable of "shaping the thought and politics" even of the industrial world power that the present

---

1   This is the revised version of a paper presented in 1994 at the 24th (Chicago) Annual Meeting of the Popular Culture Association. For a 2007 reprint in the *Western Outlaw-Lawman History Association Journal* (Vol. XVI No. 2, 22-32), the text – including the notes – has been substantially enlarged.

2   Richard Hofstadter: "America as a Gun Culture", *American Heritage*, Vol. 21, October 1970, 4–10, 82–85.

United States is, "by transcending the limitations of a specific temporality".[3] Reducing and abstracting from reality, Slotkin tells us, the myth creates a historical cliché. Such a cliché may serve to interpret new experiences as mere recurrences of familiar happenings. To project from the past into the present or even the future helps in creating a "moral landscape", providing the terms for responses to reality that may insofar be classed as pathological, as they reflect a refusal to learn.

Briefly stated, the term "gunfighter nation" summarizes Slotkin's hypothesis that the violent frontier has continued to provide patterns of identification and legitimization for American society up to the present day.

Despite the pivotal function which he ascribed to the cult of the gunfighter, Slotkin judged that figure a comparatively recent addition to the pantheon of frontier mythology. He spoke of a "subject ... distinctly marginal" until the Cold War years (principally, the Fifties), claiming that[4]

"'gunfighting' (as) a kind of art or profession ... is the invention of movies like *The Gunfighter*[5] ... the reflection of Cold-War era ideas about professionalism ... exaggerat(ing) this aspect of (the protagonists') lives."

A source that, in contrast, had earlier portrayed a "gallery of gunfighters" – Eugene Cunningham's *Triggernometry*, published in 1934, reprinted in 1941, 1967, 1978 and 1996 – was dismissed by Slotkin as, again, marginal.

However, the "evolution" of dime and nickel novels had already proceeded during the 1880's and 1890's from portraying "Revolutionary patriots" and frontier scouts to "two-gun men", "pistol dead shots", even "Wild West duelists".[6] Three more instances should suffice to demonstrate that, shortly after the turn of the 20th century, and definitely before the height of the Great Depression, the gunfighter of fact *and* fiction had come into his own:

- William Barclay "Bat" Masterson, himself no stranger to gunfire, produced a series of articles for *Human Life* magazine in 1907, headed "Famous Gunfighters of the Western Frontier", dealing with, for example, Ben Thompson, John Henry "Doc" Holliday, and Wyatt Earp.[7]
- When paying tribute to Earp and Masterson in a 1921 article, actor William S. Hart referred to them and their likes, mentioning James Butler "Wild Bill" Hickok, Holliday and Thompson, as "gunfighters".[8]

3 Richard Slotkin: *Gunfighter Nation. The Myth of the Frontier in Twentieth-Century America*, New York 1992, 4/5, 6/7, 14, 24.
4 Slotkin, 383/384.
5 Released in 1950, starring Gregory Peck.
6 See lists compiled by Albert Johannsen: *The House of Beadle and Adams*, Vol. 1, Norman 1950, and also Dixon Wecter: *The Hero in America*, New York 21963 (11941), 345.
7 Robert K. DeArment: *Bat Masterson. The Man and the Legend*, Norman/London [3]1989 ([1]1979), 380.
8 Ibid., 396.

- Finally, and crucially important for the way the concept would gain acceptance, the *Saturday Evening Post* – with, at the time, a weekly circulation of 2.5 mio. copies – during October/November 1930 printed a four-part advance publication of Stuart N. Lake's inflated Wyatt Earp 'biography'. The second installment was captioned 'Guns and Gunfighters', with Lake once again emphasizing, in addition to Earp's supposed skills, Hickok's and Masterson's deftness at what he termed 'gun play'.

Eugene Cunningham did not tread new ground when he, among many others, contributed to further establishing the image in the public mind, claiming "the gunman's story (to be) the story of the frontier."[9] On that score, Slotkin was wrong.

Paradoxically, he may be the more right in asserting that (1) the myth of the violent frontier – in fact, the saga of the gunfighter –[10] has evolved into a "venerable tradition", and (2) for this reason continues to guide the American society's collective perceptions of present and future courses of action.

Locating the origins of the gunfighter mystique in the 19th and the first decades of the 20th century should provide an opportunity for testing Slotkin's hypothesis by examining the factual *and* the legendary career of a sufficiently "prominent" case. We propose to look at the ways the myth has swerved from reality in such a specific case, attempting to diagnose if and how it provides those patterns of identification and legitimization central to Slotkin's argument.

---

9   Eugene Cunningham: *Triggernometry*, Vol. 1, London 41978 (11934), 13. In his critical study of *The Western Hero in History and Legend* (Norman 1965), Kent Ladd Steckmesser consequently ranked the gunfighter, along with the mountain-man, the outlaw and the soldier, as "another classic in our great Western myth" (105).

10   Into which that of the cowboy has, of course, blended. To indicate the popularity of the myth, a single instance, Jack Schaefer's novel *Shane*, must suffice here. Shane is portrayed as the quintessential gunfighter: black trousers, black coat and hat, ivory plates set into the grip of his gun (black again), the hammer filed to a point. The gun is kept in Shane's saddle roll until the time arrives when the protagonist, cool and competent, has to face a room full of men – when "the impact of the menace that marks him" takes effect "like a physical blow". The book's hardcover edition (first published in 1949), after three printings was followed by a juvenile edition that went through another four printings. In 1953, the film, starring Alan Ladd, was released. The novel's pocket book edition saw 65 printings until 1983. Two years later, an unacknowledged remake – different in detail, but identical in basic plot –, *Pale Rider*, was produced and directed by Clint Eastwood. The number of individuals gunned down on the screen had by now increased tenfold. – The prototype of the fictitious gunfighter, to which Jack Schaefer's portrait of *Shane* remained indebted, had much earlier been introduced by Zane Grey in his 1912 novel (another instant success) *Riders of the Purple Sage*: Jim Lassiter, black-garbed, roaming the West, always ready to place his dexterity with firearms into the service of a good cause.

II

The obvious choice as the subject of such a case study is James Butler "Wild Bill" Hickok (1837–1876), with an entry in the *Encyclopedia Britannica*, a memorial in Illinois, at least seven major biographies, and more than a dozen films to his credit. Prentiss Ingraham's dime novel "life" of Hickok (written in 1881, reprinted in 1884 and 1891) had already referred to him as "the Pistol Prince". Forty-five years later, Frank Wilstach's Hickok biography, a curious mixture of legend-building and determined research, had been titled "Wild Bill Hickok, Prince of Pistoleers".[11]

Sponsored by the Kansas State Department of Education, even a 1939 "guide to the Sunflower State" – one of a series compiled, during the Great Depression, by the WPA Federal Writers' Project – had referred to Hickok as "the best-known gunman in the old West."[12]

One supposed reason for Hickok's fame is mentioned in the entry written by biographer Richard O'Connor for *Collier's Encyclopedia*:[13]

Hickok's reputation as one of the greatest of the peace officers of the post-Civil War West was built in the years from 1868 to 1871, when he was sheriff at Hays City and city marshal at Abilene, during the wildest days of their history. Unaided, he kept the cowtowns under control, walking the streets with .44 revolvers on his hips ... establish(ing) himself as the prototype of the iron-handed marshal who held the line until civilization caught up with the frontier ...

Now consider the facts:
The entry suggests several years of uninterrupted and unaided service. Hickok's *actual* peace-keeping activities, however, were limited to four and a half months during 1869 in Hays City and eight months during 1871 in Abilene. During 1868 and 1870, he did not serve at all in any such function (excepting a stint as Deputy U. S. Marshal to which, however, O'Connor does not refer). Rather – and even while he held his offices –, he pursued a gambling career.

---

11 New York 1926. – A note on sources seems appropriate here. As in several other instances – e.g., Wyatt Earp, John Wesley Hardin, John H. "Doc" Holliday, or Henry "Billy the Kid" McCarty –, "a fearful amount of fabricating" (Wilstach) has been going on for decades about Hickok's alleged exploits. Among authors subsequently quoted, Nichols and Buel (by their distorted and false accounts) contributed to creating the Hickok legend, Wilstach, Connelley, and O'Connor (by largely, though not wholly, uncritical repetition) to perpetuating the saga. The contrasting strand of research into primary sources, such as contemporary (city, state, and federal, including court and army) records and newspaper accounts, letters and diaries, is represented by Cunningham, Dawson, Dykstra, Drago, Hansen, Miller/Snell, Steckmesser, and – most thoroughly – Rosa. For a methodical correction of untruths in the extensive literature about frontier gunfighters, cf. Ramon F. Adams: Burs Under the Saddle, Norman 1964.
12 *Kansas. A Guide to the Sunflower State*, American Guide Series, New York [2]1949 ([1]1939), 355.
13 Richard O'Connor: "Hickok, Wild Bill", *Collier's Encyclopedia*, Vol. 12, New York 1966, 99.

He had one deputy in Hays City. The Abilene City Council appointed three deputies to assist him. They did most of the patrolling. Hickok "stayed ... at his games ... If wanted, (he) had to be looked up."[14]

O'Connor was aware of these facts. In his own earlier biography of Hickok, he had even quoted the deputies' names.[15] And he had painted a much more realistic picture of his protagonist when commenting on Hickok's murder by Jack McCall, remarking that "a slightly different shift in circumstances" might have made a McCall of Hickok: "The revolver was their common denominator."[16]

Yet O'Connor preferred to construct for *Collier's* an image of Hickok as a lone, dedicated agent of law and order, in stark contrast to the judgment passed on the gunfighter by Stuart Henry, brother of Abilene's first mayor, the later Kansas "wheat king" T. C. Henry:[17]

"He acted only too ready to shoot down, to kill out-right, instead of avoiding assassination when possible as the higher duty of a marshal. Such a policy of taking justice into his own hands exemplified, of course, but a form of lawlessness."

Doubtlessly, O'Connor was aware that a tradition idolizing Hickok as the peace officer incarnate had already been fashioned by a succession of magazine articles, dime novels, books, and movies.[18] A particularly influential piece of myth-making had originated, a generation earlier, from William E. Connelley, secretary of the Kansas State Historical Society. It was Connelley who had eulogized Hickok as a plainsman beating "the dark forces of savagery and crime" (he would not be the last Hickok researcher to become fascinated by his subject).[19] And he had carried the argument to Homeric heights:[20]

14 Stuart Henry: *Conquering Our Great American Plains*, New York 1930, 274/275 (for the quote); Joseph G. Rosa: *They Called Him Wild Bill*, Norman [2]1974 ([1]1964), chs. 8, 10.

15 Richard O'Connor: *Wild Bill Hickok*, New York 1959, 129, 148.

16 ibid., 255.

17 Henry, 274/275.

18 Among the latter, especially William S. Hart's Wild Bill Hickok (1923) and Cecil B. de Mille's The Plainsman (1937).

19 William E. Connelley: *Wild Bill and his Era*, New York 1933, 7. – Joseph G. Rosa, in concluding his original archive-based study *They Called Him Wild Bill*, offered this observation: "Peacemaker or killer, hero or villain, there was a man" (Rosa, 311). In the same vein, he chose to terminate his subsequent account *Wild Bill Hickok. The Man and His Myth* (Lawrence 1996) with the following quote from an article in American Rifleman: "Whatever else we may say of him, this much is true: He shot straight, and asked few favors ... and he walked like a man in the presence of his enemies." Such fascination, however, may not always serve as the best yardstick when evaluating historical documents. While discussing, in *They Called Him Wild Bill*, the killing of ruffian Samuel Strawhun by Hickok during his brief tenure as sheriff of Ellis County, Rosa had included an eyewitness report printed in a contemporary (1869) newspaper which proved that Strawhun had not raised a gun, but a beer glass against Hickok (cf. Rosa, 147/148). In two subsequent books, Rosa made the unsubstantiated assertion that Strawhun had "smashed" a glass, threatening

"(Hickok) contributed *more than any other man* to making the West a place for decent men and women to live in."

Yet in Hays City, Hickok was defeated after his brief time as sheriff in the November 1869 election by his deputy. Two years later in Abilene, the City Council dismissed him without a word of thanks. He had worked for Russell, Majors and Waddell before the Civil War, driving wagons, stagecoaches, tending stock; had been employed as an army wagon master and government scout; had, after 1865, gambled for a living, worked as a Deputy U.S. Marshal, scouted for the U.S. Cavalry. After his discharge in Abilene, his uncertain income for the remaining five years of his life again came from gambling, interrupted by a brief attachment to the "Buffalo Bill Combination", playing to audiences in the East. His services as a lawman, consequently, were mere biographical episodes.

A first device by the use of which the gunfighter myth operates should now have become apparent. It attaches historical "sense" to an otherwise disjointed biography, permitting individual identification with acts supposedly committed in the fulfilment of a "mission".

That mission – and, consequently, the purported sense of Hickok's life on the frontier – consists in "taming" the West in order to permit *progress by violence*. Without the Hickoks, the Earps, the Mastersons, bringing "order out of chaos",[21] no pioneers like those evoked by Walt Whitman –

the rivers stemming, vexing, piercing deep the mines within, the surface broad surveying, the virgin soil upheaving, Pioneers! O pioneers!

This interpretation transforms the gunfighter into a true pioneer himself. Stimulated by "that onward-thrusting, high-flaming spirit of the Pioneer" – Connelley writing about Hickok[22] –, he emerges as a *necessary* element of

Hickok with a "jagged" glas (Joseph G. Rosa: *Wild Bill Hickok. The Man and His Myth*, Lawrence 1996, 125), further dramatizing the situation in *Wild Bill Hickok, Gunfighter*, College Park 2001, 112: "A pacifist once... blanched when I described to him the terrible injuries which could be sustained by having a broken and jagged beer bottle or glass jabbed into one's face". The original newspaper report quoted by Rosa simply reads: "Wild Bill set the glasses on the counter, Stra[whu]n took hold of one and took it up in a threatening manner. He had no time to execute his design for a shot fired by Mr. Hickok killed him." The source given by Rosa for his allegation in *Wild Bill Hickok: The Man and His Myth* (251, n. 37) is Rev. Blaine Burkey: *Wild Bill Hickok the Law in Hays City*, Hays ²1975, 10–12. However, not the slightest reference to a "broken" or "jagged" glas may be found in Burkey's text (who quotes an additional eye witness account published in 1876, confirming that Strawhun "picked up a glass to strike"). Rather, Burkey (11) raised the question: "Since when is it justifiable to shoot to kill a man who is raising a beer glas in a threatening manner?" Concerning his recent depictions of the Strawhun killing, the conclusion seems to suggest itself that Rosa has joined the ranks of Hickok myth makers. Cf. also below, n. 29.
20   William E. Connelley: *Wild Bill – James Butler Hickok*, Reprint from Collections of the Kansas State Historical Society, n. p., n. d. (1928), 27 (emphasis mine).
21   Wilstach, 159.
22   Connelley (as in n. 19), 7.

westward expansion. In the last instance, it is none other than the gunfighter who guarantees "that civilization may be free to take another step forward on her march of progress".[23] Such a combination of devotion and boldness certainly invites identification.

Subsequently, three violent incidents in the career of Hickok – again, the facts as well as the legend – will be reviewed, demonstrating that the *overall* mechanism just diagnosed works no less conspicuously *in detail*, each level reinforcing the other. Moreover, a second modus operandi adding to the myth's persuasiveness will be identified as the analysis proceeds.

The incidents to be discussed below are the so-called "Rock Creek Massacre" – the quarrel, in fact, that ended with Hickok killing his first man –; a fight with troopers from the Seventh Cavalry in Hays City; and, finally, the last shooting in which Hickok was involved, with two men dying under his bullets. The factual events will be outlined first. In a second step, the idealizations will be contrasted with the actual outcomes and prevalent motives.

III

That James Butler Hickok's career in the public imagination was started by a "terrible tale" in the February 1867 issue of *Harper's Magazine* hardly bears repeating. Recounting how Hickok had slain a certain "M'Kandlas" and nine other border ruffians – some found "killed with bullets, others hacked and slashed to death with a knife" –,[24] George Ward Nichols provided a hero's name to which subsequent authors might attach further imaginary exploits.

The more because *Harper's New Monthly Magazine* was, of course, anything but another *National Police Gazette*. Founded in 1850 as a literary, popular science, and travel digest, it rapidly attained the largest circulation among periodicals published in the East – not least because its concept also appealed to a large readership in the *West*: According to a contemporary report, it could be found even "in the humblest (western) cabins".[25] Unavoidably, more and more texts were published by *Harper's* that dealt with the – albeit largely romanticized – frontier. During the second half of the sixties, the magazine rapidly regained its pre-Civil War circulation of close to 200,000 copies.[26] (The American population at the time numbered just under 40 million.) A 12-page article, profusely illustrated, including a full-page engraving of Hickok, could be quite literally expected to attract attention across the whole country.

23   As in n. 20.
24   George W. Nichols: "Wild Bill", *Harper's New Monthly Magazine* Vol. 34, No. 201, 282.
25   Frank Luther Mott: *A History of American Magazines*, Vol. 2: 1850–1865, Cambridge 41970 (11938), 121.
26   Mott, 384, 391, 393; cf. also James Playsted Wood: *Magazines in the United States*, New York 31971 (11949), 73 ss.

The truth about the incident was brought to light by Charles Dawson and George Hansen in 1912 and 1927, respectively. As stock tender for Russell, Majors and Waddell at Rock Creek Station, Jefferson County, Nebr., Hickok in July 1861 shot and killed David C. McCanles, the station's erstwhile owner. Two of McCanles' employees whom he wounded were subsequently dispatched by other agents of the stage line.[27]

McCanles had come resolved to either collect an outstanding debt from the (unknown to him, already bankrupt) company or to reclaim his property, evicting the occupants by physical force. Trusting in his strength, McCanles was very probably unarmed. At the most, he may have had a shotgun strapped to his horse's saddle[28] which, however, he did not attempt to seize before being shot by Hickok.

A personal feud already existed between McCanles and Hickok, who had become enamored of the former's mistress. McCanles is also supposed to have acted tyrannically toward the much younger and physically inferior Hickok. When matters came to a head, Hickok killed him from behind a curtain.[29] One of McCanles' wounded companions (James Woods) was hacked to death, the other (James Gordon) riddled with buckshot. Neither Hickok nor his accomplices received even a scratch.[30] While they were ar-

27 Charles Dawson: *Pioneer Tales of the Oregon Trail and of Jefferson County*, Topeka 1912, 218 ss.; George W. Hansen: "True Story of Wild Bill-McCanles Affray in Jefferson County, Nebraska, July 12, 1861", *Nebraska Historical Magazine* 10 (1927), 71–112.

28 As contended by Dawson, 216 (who also wrote that McCanles' two employees, "as was customary in that day, … had pistols in their holsters, strapped around their bodies"). In his 1927 article, Hansen reported (a) that the bodies of McCanles, Woods and Gordon had been buried the following morning by Frank, Thomas and Jasper Helvey from the neighboring Helvey ranch; (b) that Frank Helvey had told him "at various times, since my first acquaintance with him in 1870, particularly in 1912 when we were both associated on the committee to mark and dedicate monuments on the Oregon Trail, and again in my office a few weeks before his death" [in July 1918] that, when he and his brothers gathered up the bodies, they found "no guns near any of them". Cf. Hansen, 86; for photo of Helvey and data on him, cf. ibid., 124.

29 In a footnote to the 1974 edition of *They Called Him Wild Bill*, Rosa wrote that Horace Wellman, the station superintendent, "too, had access" to the weapons which Hickok had placed behind a curtain "in preparation for trouble" (Rosa, 47 n. 21). Twenty years later, he claimed that "opinion remain[ed] sharply divided" on the question: "Did Hickok shoot McCanles, or was it Wellman?" (Joseph B. Rosa: *Wild Bill Hickok: The Man and His Myth*, Lawrence 1996, 116). However, he failed to offer any evidence for the alleged controversy.

30 McCanles had brought his 12 year old son Monroe along, who escaped the slaughter. In a 1927 interview, Monroe McCanles stated: "Now to bear me out that those men were not armed, – when Woods and Gordon ran up to the door, if either or both had been armed they sure would have had their revolvers in their hands, and while Jim was shooting Woods, one or the other would have done some shooting, or if Woods had been armed, he would not have let Wellman knock him in the head without trying to defend himself. Now more evidence that Gordon was unarmed; … After Gordon made his getaway, being wounded, the Station outfit put [a blood hound] on his trail; the dog trailed him down the creek 80 rods when they caught up with him while warding the dog off with a stick. If he had been armed, is it not reasonable to suppose he would have defended himself?" (M. I. McCreight: "The

raigned in court on a charge of murder, the preliminary examination did not, for various reasons, result in a trial. Hickok left the region, enlisting in the Union Army as a civilian scout.

Nine years and three killings later ("not counting Confederates and Indians", as the saying went), Hickok returned to Hays City, which he had departed after failing to be re-elected for sheriff. In a saloon, he was attacked by two drunken soldiers, one of whom pulled him down, the other placing a pistol against his head that, however, misfired.[31] The assailants ended up on the barroom floor, seriously wounded by Hickok's bullets. One trooper died, later receiving a passing mention in Custer's *My Life on the Plains*;[32] the other recovered.

If Hickok and his opponent had been rivals for the same woman in the circumstances that resulted in his first killing, and liquor generating heedless courage had played a prominent part in the Hays City affray, both ingredients were involved in Hickok's last shooting scrape that occurred in Abilene. This was at the height of the Texas cattle trade, when Southern drovers or gamblers and Yankee marshals heartily despised each other, colliding in the Kansas cowtowns more often than not. A particular enmity concerning a prostitute named Jessie Hazel seems to have evolved between Texas gambler Phil Coe and Marshal Hickok. At the end of the 1871 cattle season, the Texas cow hands went on a final drunken spree. When Coe defied the firearms ordinance by shooting his gun, Hickok and he came to a confrontation. "Wild Bill" killed not only the Texan, but also a special policeman, Mike Williams, who accidentally rushed into the line of fire.[33]

The personal feud – the drunken brawl – the services of a prostitute: these were the motives that provided the principal reasons in every shooting. Such encounters were as stupid and meaningless, as they were common on a frontier where, "like firearms, whiskey was always within reach and more or less constantly imbibed".[34] Violence, when it erupted, was usually devoid of any higher purpose. It fell to the myth to invent such a purpose by first distorting the actual events and then, in a second step, interpreting not a real, but a fictitious conflict.

'McCandless' Gang", *Forest & Stream* XCVII (1927), 740–742, 762–763; for the quote, cf. 742).

31 W. E. Webb: *Buffalo Land*, Philadelphia/New York 1874, 146; Rosa, 158.

32 Norman 1962 (New York 11874), 45.

33 Harry Sinclair Drago: *The Legend Makers*, New York 1975, 32/33; Nyle H. Miller/Joseph W. Snell: *Great Gunfighters of the Kansas Cowtowns 1867–1886*, Norman ²1967 (Topeka ¹1963), 131 ss.

34 Robert M. Utley: *High Noon in Lincoln. Violence on the Western Frontier*, Albuquerque 1987, 21.

IV

When J. W. Buel, in his 1880 "biography" *Life and Wonderful Adventures of Wild Bill, the Scout* depicted the fight at Rock Creek as an encounter "without a parallel", he had Hickok's opponents inflict terrible wounds on his hero: a fractured skull, seven balls in his legs and body, three gashes on the breast, a cut to the bone on the left forearm. Such dedicated sacrifice on Hickok's part called for an ethical imperative of the highest kind, and for a reward in moral, immaterial terms. Buel did not fail to provide both:[35]

This murderous gang had killed more than a score of innocent men and women for the purpose of robbery, and yet their power was such that no civil officer dared undertake their arrest ... After this dreadful encounter, ... the people of that section worshiped Bill as no other man. He had civilized the neighborhood.

Hickok's clash with two drunken troopers that occurred in Hays City had to wait two generations longer for an analogous "explanation". Buel sensationally magnified the incident. He not only blew it up into "a fight with fifteen (!) soldiers", but had Hickok literally wading in his own blood that "filled ... his boots" from the multiple injuries he had suffered while allegedly killing four of his intoxicated opponents.[36] Frank Wilstach, in his 1926 life of the "Prince of Pistoleers", adhered to Buel's version, even if toning it down considerably.[37] However, it could not but impress the reader as a vulgar brawl, meaningless except that it displayed the hero's prowess under the most adverse circumstances.

It fell to Connelley to discover a "mission" behind Hickok's resort to his guns by distorting the actual proceedings, shifting them back in time to Hickok's last (!) night in office as Sheriff of Ellis County, and having him foil a plot engineered by Captain Tom Custer, George Armstrong Custer's troublesome brother. An arrogant officer, the younger Custer – or so Connelley would have his readers believe – "thought his military connection made him immune from arrest by civil authority".[38] When Hickok nevertheless took him into custody for some offense, Tom Custer swore revenge:

He selected three reckless and desperate ruffians and accompanied them into town with the understanding that they would kill Wild Bill. It was planned that one soldier would leap upon his back and force him over, while another was to pinion his arms. The third man was then to kill him.

Vestiges of what actually took place may be recognized in the presentation. Of course, Hickok prevented the trio from executing their conspiracy in,

35   Buel (as in n. 15), 13, 19.
36   Buel, 51.
37   Frank J. Wilstach: *Wild Bill Hickok, the Prince of Pistoleers*, New York 1926, 172/173
38   William E. Connelley (as in n. 17), 131 (also for the following).

according to Connelley, "probably the most famous incident of coolness, nerve and shooting the world has known".[39]

Comparing his rendering of the incident with the earlier version offered by Elizabeth B. Custer in her book *Following the Guidon*, published in 1890, provides an additional idea of the methods by which Connelley proceeded. Custer's narrative is subsequently reproduced first, followed by Connelley's:[40]

Three desperate characters [from the Seventh Cavalry decided] to kill Bill... It was planned that one soldier should leap upon his back, and hold down his head and chest, while another should pinion his arms. It is impossible in the crowded little dens, imperfectly lighted, and with air dense with smoke, always to face a foe. Wild Bill was attacked from behind, as had been planned. His broad back was borne down by a powerful soldier, and his arms seized, but only one was held in the clinching grasp of the assailant. With the free hand the scout drew his pistol from the belt, fired backward without seeing, and his shot, even under these circumstances, was a fatal one. The soldier dropped dead, the citizens rallied round Wild Bill, [and] the troops were driven out of the town (*Custer*).

It was planned that one soldier would leap upon his back and force him over, while another was to pinion his arms. The third man was then to kill him. Bill was found in a small saloon so imperfectly lighted that it was almost impossible to distinguish one person from another. This enabled them to approach him. One] powerful soldier leaped upon him, bearing him over, and the second clasped him round to pinion his arms. Bill wrested one arm free. With *his left hand* Bill drew his pistol and fired backward over his shoulder at the man forcing him down. The soldier fell from Bill's back a dead man. *In a minute Bill was erect. He shot the soldier who was waiting in front of him with drawn pistol. Then he fired over his shoulder and killed the man who had pinioned his arms and who had his pistol drawn... A number of soldiers [brought] to aid these select three if they should fail...* were driven from the town... [by] the citizens (*Connelley*).

Connelley's version was also preferred by O'Connor two and a half decades later, tallying – as it did – with Hickok's now accepted social function: Acting once again as the advancing civilization's deadly instrument, he punished the infringements of, according to O'Connor, "desperadoes in uniform", whom "the civilians unfortunate enough to live in their vicinity found ... not much preferable to the savages they were being protected from."[41] Equally important, in Connelley's and O'Connor's fictionalized account Hickok's real foe, other than the nameless rowdy troopers, acquired an identity: Captain Custer with his brazen claim to immunity personified *licence*, where Hickok stood for *order*.

After Hickok had subsequently shot and killed Phil Coe in Abilene, Buel interpreted the latter's death, paralleling his depiction of the Rock Creek event, as "a most fortunate event for the better class of citizens of Abilene,

---

39   ibid., 132.
40   As in n. 39 (emphasis mine); Elizabeth B. Custer: *Following the Guidon*, Norman 1966, 163/164.
41   O'Connor (as in n. 13), 130.

because it at once improved the morals of the place."[42] Wilstach, in similar terms, narrated a purported conspiracy by Texas cowboys planning "Bill's destruction", because they resented the new marshal's intent to, once again, bring "order out of chaos": When they "drew lots as to who was to have the honor of taking Bill's scalp", a "particularly desperate person named Phil Coe drew the short straw."[43] Connelley in his turn, before he arrived at describing the Coe incident, had already vastly aggrandized Hickok's performance in Abilene, maintaining that "it was a situation which never before existed in any town in America. It was the iron will of one man holding at bay the malice, crime and recklessness of the wickedest town on the frontier." Subsequently, with regard to the Coe – and Williams! – killings, he claimed that "a hundred pistols were drawn and cocked as Wild Bill fired his first shot. By the time he fired the second time, ... Coe's friends were gone". Subsequently, Connelley had Hickok – ever the civilizer – seek "a clergyman and le[a]d him to Coe's bedside".[44]

In the same vein, Connelley managed to cope with the problem presented to Hickok glorifiers after Dawson's book had reduced the Rock Creek "massacre" to its true dimensions of another squalid frontier brawl. Dawson had also pointed out that, although David McCanles, Hickok's victim, was apt to act tyrannically and overbearing, and had embezzled money before establishing himself at Rock Creek, he was a rugged pioneer rather than a rascal. He had never committed either homicide or murder. Undaunted, Connelley maintained that McCanles' life "had been one of progressive degeneracy". To leave not the slightest room for doubt, he added that "if ever a man deserved killing, it was McCanles at Rock Creek Station".[45] Although Nichols' and Buel's tall tales about Rock Creek had finally been deflated, a killing "for which almost any fair jury would have given (Hickok), at the least, a long penitentiary sentence",[46] and which very probably sprang from both hate and

---

42   Buel (as in n. 15), 54.
43   Wilstach (as in n. 38), 175, 176, 177.
44   Connelley (as in n. 19), 154, 159/160. Summing up his research into surviving municipal records, Robert Dykstra wrote: "The traditional Wild Bill seems to be in a sort of free-agent status as marshal, completely divorced from the prosaic duties of the modern police officer or the discipline and direction of a municipal employer. Modification of the traditional image seems in order on this perhaps subtle but important point" ("Wild Bill Hickok in Abilene", *Journal of the Central Mississippi American Studies Association*, Kansas Centennial Issue 1961, 20–48; for the quote, 42). The evidence, in addition, is that "Hickok relegated much of the police work to [his deputies]" (Larry D. Underwood: *Abilene Lawmen. The Smith-Hickok Years, 1870–1871*, Lincoln 1999, 140; see also above, n. 14, 15), and that "Texas Street" – the section of Abilene bounded by the railroad, ending in the stock yards –, because of Hickok's merely sporadic enforcement of the firearms ordinance, "simmered or more or less boiled in a kind of truce" (Henry – as in n. 14 –, 275).
45   Connelley (as in n. 20), 9, 21.
46   Cunningham (as in n. 9), Vol. 2, 41.

panic, continued to be presented in terms of an act by a man of "intrepidity" who "killed when he was compelled to kill in the line of duty".[47]

V

If this was the first method of legitimizing and idealizing gunfighter violence, a second way emerged early in Hickok's mythical career – in fact, with Nichols' *Harper's Magazine* article. It reinforces the mechanism so far portrayed. And where the first mode permits individual identification, the second legitimizes collective attitudes and behavior by depicting successive stages in American history as conflicts between civilization and savagery.

Such black-and-white stereotypes encourage a restricted understanding of social – past no less than present or future – realities. Against this simplified background, violence comes to be perceived not merely as indispensable, but as *morally* adequate. When savagery challenges civilization, there need be no hesitation, no complicated, drawn-out negotiating process. The quick bullet is the legitimate – *and* easy – response.[48]

Writing about the killing of "M'Kandlas" by Hickok, Nichols did not even mention the name "Rock Creek". In fact, the prelude to events proper was quite different from Buel's account, with Hickok allegedly relating how "it was in '61, when I guided a detachment of cavalry ... in South Nebraska", continuing to recount that he had earlier known "M'Kandlas and his desperadoes ... in the mountains":[49]

This was just before the war broke out, and we were already takin(g) sides in the mountains, either for the South or the Union. M'Kandlas and his gang were border-ruffians in the Kansas row, and of course they went with the rebs.

There is a significant shift of emphasis in the way lines are drawn here: Wild Bill, "Yankee" *and* scout for the Union, confronts McCanles, gang leader *and* rebel combined. Again, it was Connelley who took up the thread, asserting that[50]

... the Southern confederacy ... exerted a powerful influence on (McCanles') life ... His associates were the southern or border-ruffian element ... The fight ... in which he was killed prevented McCanles from becoming a Confederate soldier.

After the tone had thus been set, Connelley pursued the Civil War subject further:[51]

---

47 Connelley, 19, 27.
48 Cf. also John G. Cawelti: *The Six-Gun Mystique*, Bowling Green 1975, 36, 46.
49 Nichols, 282/283.
50 Connelley (as in n. 20), 9, 11.
51 ibid., 26.

In scouting ... for the military ..., Wild Bill put his life in jeopardy daily for more than four years ... to preserve the Union in the Civil War. He became a spy, and put his life in forfeit time after time by entering Confederate camps.

Connelley then proceeded to Hickok's role in the next phase of American history – the Indian Wars:

As valuable as were his services ... in saving the Union, they were fully equalled by his work on the frontier ... No other scout rode through such dangers ... He rode by night and watched by day for years ... from fort to fort, from post to post.

And finally, on to the cowtown frontier: Here Hickok "ruled with an iron hand, presenting the unique spectacle of one man, by his courage and skill, holding at bay all the lawless element".[52]

The archetypal gunfighter myth thus constructs, in the form of an epic, allegedly biographical narrative, a comprehensive pattern of the *stages* through which, and the indispensable *means* by which, the American nation is supposed to have progressed:

- the violent conquest of the morally inferior Southern "rebels" during the Civil War;
- the equally violent defeat of the culturally inferior "savages" during the Indian wars;
- the no less violent elimination of the "outlaws" posing a threat to stability during the final phase of frontier settlement.

To sum up: The case study of a particular and prominent gunfighter legend illustrates those clichés that are central to the American mythology of the frontier as a place with moral significance, where civilization and savagery clashed, and of national progress by violence through a succession of frontiers. Allegedly representative of this civilizing process, the mythical Hickok personifies the force of American patriotism in the fight against Confederate secession, of advancing white settlement against the roving Plains Indians, and of law in the unruly frontier towns. In exemplary fashion, Hickok's mythical career demonstrates how a moral and civilizing purpose has been projected onto a violent past and, by constant repetition, has been carried forward into the present day.

Such fatal continuity indeed permits, as suggested by Richard Slotkin, to speak of a "gunfighter nation" with regard to patterns of attitude and behavior unchangingly extolled by books, films, even encyclopediae[53] – a *popular*

---

52   William E. Connelley: "Hickok, James Butler", *Dictionary of American Biography*, Vol. V, New York 1932, 4.
53   In 1992, a book on Hickok "for young people" was published, whose authors ("with over sixty years of teaching experience"), after claiming that "the events described all c(a)me from first-hand reports", proceeded to dish up every disproved fabrication on record: Mac-Canles allegedly "stepped forward, his hand moving toward his gun"; "a jury said he [Hickok] fired in self-defense" when killing McCanles; Tom Custer's vow "to get even"

culture blending into *political* culture when, for instance, an American president (Dwight D. Eisenhower, in this case) – during 1953 publicly referred to the *leitmotif* of his life:[54]

I was raised in a little town ... called Abilene, Kansas. We had as our Marshal a man named Wild Bill Hickok. Now that town had a code, and I was raised as a boy to prize that code. It was: Meet anyone face to face with whom you disagree ... If you met him face to face and took the same risks, you could get away with almost anything, as long as the bullet was in front.

That you can get away with almost anything, as long as the bullet is in front: A more fitting eulogy to Hickok and a more revealing invocation by a president of the United States – more revealing, in fact, than John F. Kennedy's reference to the "New Frontier" which Slotkin cites – are hardly imaginable.

---

was the reason for Hickok's clash with several soldiers in Hays; after accidentally gunning down a special policeman in Abilene, Hickok – overcome by remorse – "that same night turned in his badge"; and so forth (Carl R. Green/William R. Sanford: *Wild Bill Hickok*, Berkeley Heights 1992, 4, 15, 30, 33). In addition, one might list recent novels such as *The Memoirs of Wild Bill Hickok* by Richard Matheson (New York 1996), or *And Not to Yield. A Novel of the Life and Times of Wild Bill Hickok* by Randy Lee Eickhoff (New York 2004, Winner of the Western Heritage Award 2005).

54 Steckmesser (as in n. 7), 158, n. 16.

From the frontier on to the Red Planet: "One moment, I stood in the starlight on the Arizona hills. The next instant, I opened my eyes upon a strange and weird landscape. I knew that I was on Mars." An obvious literary figment, originating from the fertile pen of Edgar Rice Burroughs. Not so when it comes to the following sentences: "The next century will see pioneering men and women working and living throughout the inner Solar System. Through vigorous leadership on the space frontier, America can make this happen." They were set down by none other than President Reagan's National Commission on Space under the chairmanship of former NASA Administrator Thomas Paine. The frontier metaphor had early on permeated discourses on America's space effort – testimony to the power of a cultural cliché which has conditioned America's popular and political culture through its promises of further expansion. Serving to interpret new experiences as recurrences of familiar happenings, the frontier myth may reflect a deep-seated refusal to learn. The following article was written as a contribution to the multidisciplinary volume Imagining Outer Space, *published by Palgrave Macmillan in 2012.*

Projecting Landscapes of the Human Mind onto Another World: Changing Faces of an Imaginary Mars[1]

Reporter: 'Is there life on Mars?'
Returning Astronaut: 'Well, you know, it's pretty dead most of the week, but it really swings on Saturday night.'
(Popular NASA joke)

1 Deceptive World

For centuries, the planet Mars continued to deceive terrestrial observers like no other celestial body in our solar system. Believing to discern ever more distinct features on Mars through Earth-bound telescopes, astronomers designated these as continents, oceans, even canals, to which they gave names. With exceedingly rare exceptions, however, the markings did not correspond

---

1 This chapter's argument is partly based on Rainer Eisfeld and Wolfgang Jeschke, *Marsfieber*, Munich: Droemer, 2003. Much like Robert Markley's subsequent *Dying Planet. Mars in Science and the Imagination*, Durham: Duke University Press 2005, the book discussed both the imagined Red Planet and the actual Mars progressively unveiled by robotic missions.

to geomorphological, or rather areomorphological, structures. Actually, they originated from the different reflectivity of bright and dark surface regions changed in its turn by wind activity which has continued to transport and deposit fine dust across the planet. Space probes, rather than telescopes, were needed to explain these processes and to shed light on the Red Planet's true characteristics[1].

Until robotic explorers arrived, no other planet seemed to offer such clues for educated guessing – first to the conjectural astronomy of the 19th century, subsequently to the science fiction of the latter part of that period and the 20th century. Conjectural astronomy was the term used, in the wake of Bernard de Fontenelle's 1686 *Conversations on the Plurality of Worlds* and Christiaan Huyghens' 1698 *The Celestial Worlds Discover'd, or Conjectures Concerning the Habitants, Plants and Productions of the Worlds in the Planets*, to denote that branch of the discipline which engaged in hypothesizing on 'the living conditions and natural environments of other celestial bodies'[2]. While expected to be not directly contradicting astronomical observations, such suppositions were, to a high degree, matters of interpretation, often based on 'few definitely established and unambiguous data'[3].

In contrast to the discipline's mathematical branch, conjectural astronomy was intended to bridge the widening rift of mutual incomprehension between the humanities and the sciences. From the 17th to the 19th century, the encyclopaedic outlook on learning, so central to the Enlightenment, included both the spiritual and the material world. Inexorably, however, the progress of scientific research fostered specialization. Conjectural astronomy, in contrast, increasingly resorted to manifest speculation, relegating stellar and planetary astronomy to the role of ancillary sciences in the service of a preconceived, stoutly held idea, based on philosophical considerations: that intelligent life existed throughout the universe, including the solar system's planets.

German astronomers' Wilhelm Beer and Johann Heinrich Maedler's mid-19th century assumption that it would 'not be too audacious to consider Mars, also in its physical aspects, as a world very akin to our earth'[4], went unchallenged in its time. By 1906, however, when American astronomer Percival Lowell published his spectacular – and highly speculative – interpretation *Mars and its Canals*, scientists debated issues such as the composition of the Martian atmosphere or the planet's climate controversially and much more sceptically. Within a year, a devastating rebuttal by British biologist Alfred Russel Wallace appeared under the title *Is Mars Habitable?* Wallace answered the question in the negative: Realistic temperature estimates pre-

---

2   Wilhelm Beer and Johann Heinrich Maedler, *Beiträge zur physischen Kenntniss der himm-lischen Koerper im Sonnensysteme*, Weimar: Bernhard Friedrich Voigt, 1841, VII.
3   Beer and Maedler, Beiträge, ibid.
4   Beer and Maedler, Beiträge, 124, 125.

cluded animal life; low atmospheric pressure would make liquid water – let alone Lowell's supposed irrigation works – impossible. Science and fiction were irrevocably parting ways.

A mere decade after Beer and Maedler had published their treatise on the solar planets' physical properties, the term 'Science-Fiction' was introduced in 1851 by British essayist William Wilson in his work *A Little Earnest Book upon a Great Old Subject*. When coining the expression, Wilson referred to a 'pleasant story', 'interwoven with... the revealed truths of Science', itself 'poetical and true'. By the 1890s, the emerging genre included not merely pleasant, but definitely unedifying tales putting mankind at the mercy of technically superior beings from other celestial bodies. The planetary novel was coming into its own: No longer were planets conceived as self-contained distant places. Rather, their inhabitants might seek out other worlds with either benevolent or inimical intent[5].

Mars, supposedly older than the Earth (according to what was then believed about the formation of the solar system), particularly fired the imagination. Intersecting around the turn of the century, conjectural astronomy and science fiction served as vehicles for succeeding generations to 'project [their] earthly hopes and fears' onto Mars[6]. These pipe dreams and nightmares came to vary not least according to the economic, social, and political upheavals that would figure uppermost in men's minds during successive periods. Two examples illustrate the remarkable length to which some authors were prepared to go in offering their allegories:

In the wake of the October Revolution, Soviet writer Alexei Tolstoi and movie director Yakov Protazanov imagined during the early 1920s that it would take the arrival by spaceship of a terrestrial revolutionary, Gusev, to whip the exploited workers of Mars into a proletarian uprising (*Aelita*). The 'world' to be revolutionized by the 'vanguard of the proletariat' did not need to be identical with Earth...

By the mid-1950s, with female emancipation considered a dire threat in many quarters, a British flick portrayed Nyah, *Devil Girl from Mars*, as landing her flying saucer by a country tavern, explaining to the male customers that the birth rate had fallen alarmingly after the introduction of matriarchy. For breeding purposes, her planet needed men! Rather than, in post-Victorian resignation, 'closing their eyes and thinking of Mars', however, the British males put up embittered resistance[7].

---

5   Brian Aldiss and David Wingrove, *Trillion Year Spree. The History of Science Fiction*, London: Paladin, 1988, 603 n. 47; Martin Schwonke, *Vom Staatsroman zur Science Fiction*, Stuttgart: Enke, 1957, 43.

6   Carl Sagan, *Cosmos*, New York/London: Random House, 1980, 106.

7   This brief reference to the British film goes back to *Marsfieber*, 163. *Devil Girl on Mars* was subsequently discussed by Robert Markley, *Dying Planet*, 227-9.

Looking at the 'mainstream' (there were always mavericks, of course) of the ways in which the treatises, the novels and short stories, the movie scripts by successive generations of astronomers and science fiction writers depicted an imaginary Mars, we may discern a sequence of 'faces' attributed to the planet on which this chapter's subsequent sections will focus:

An *Arcadian Mars* (1865 ff.) exhibiting 'all the various kinds of scenery which make our earth so beautiful'; a highly civilized *Advanced Mars* (1895 ff.) crisscrossed by immense canals; a forbidding *Frontier Mars* (1912 ff.) where the rugged adventurer and the toiling pioneer might again come into their own; a *Cold War Mars* (1950 ff.), source of an assault on the Earth, or haven for refugees after our planet would have perished from nuclear war; finally, a *Terraformed Mars* (1973 ff.), again with strong frontier undertones, lending itself to human colonization and exploitation. While these 'types' would often overlap – with the frontier metaphor, in particular, persisting into the present -, each type set the tone for a generation.

2 Arcadian Mars

'Life, youth, love shine on every world... This divine fire glows on Mars, it glows on Venus'[8]. With unmatched fervor and elegance of style, Camille Flammarion (1842-1925) argued the case for intelligent extraterrestrial life during the second half of the 19th century, bolstered by the authority of the renowned astronomer who, in 1887, founded the Société Astronomique de France. His description of the Martian environment, in his very first work *La pluralité des mondes habités*, which would be reprinted 30 times until the century's end, informed the astronomical and popular discourse on the Red Planet for nearly a generation:

The atmospheres of Earth and Mars, the snowfields seasonally expanding and shrinking on both planets, the clouds intermittently floating over their surfaces, the similar apportionment of continents and oceans, the conformities in seasonal variations: all this makes us believe that both worlds are inhabited by beings who physically resemble each other... In our mind's eye, we behold, here and there, intelligent beings, united into nations, vigorously striving for enlightenment and moral betterment[9].

In 1840, Beer and Maedler had drawn the first chart of Mars. Capital letters denoted observed 'regions' – darker spots on bright ground. (Before the Mariner 9 space probe permitted production of the first '*reliable* map'[10], more

---

8   Camille Flammarion, *Les Terres du Ciel*, Paris: Marpon & Flammarion, 1884, 208.
9   Camille Flammarion, *Die Mehrheit Bewohnter Welten*, Leipzig: J. J. Weber, 1865, 51-2, 71. Flammarion published the book as a 20 year old.
10   Oliver Morton, *Mapping Mars*, New York: Fourth Estate, 2002, 37-8.

than 130 years would elapse). The letters used by Beer and Maedler remained in use for two and a half decades, until Richard Proctor replaced them by the names of Mars observers on the map which he composed in 1867. Proctor also 'improved' on the way his compatriot John Phillips had, three years earlier, designated darker parts as 'seas' and brighter, reddish tracts as 'lands'. Proctor's chart showed continents and islands, oceans and seas, inlets and straits. These features had a suggestive effect. They seemed to portray a second – albeit smaller – Earth, with just a different division into zones of land and water.

The suggestion was deliberate. Proctor depicted Mars as a 'miniature of our Earth', waxing hardly less rhapsodically than Flammarion about the prettiness of the place:

The mere existence of continents and oceans on Mars proves the action of... volcanic eruptions and earthquakes, modelling and remodelling the crust of Mars. Thus there must be mountains and hills, valleys and ravines, water-sheds and water-courses... And from the mountain recesses burst forth the refreshing springs which are to feed the Martia[n] brooklets...

And in a brilliant phrase, which Percival Lowell would later reclaim for entitling his final book, Proctor called Mars 'the abode of life', without whose existence 'all these things would be wasted'[11].

Proctor (1837-1888) was Honorary Secretary of the Royal Astronomical Society. Like Flammarion's work, his study of our solar system's planets subtitled 'under the light of recent scientific researches' continued to be reprinted until the advent of the 20th century. Public fascination was spurred further when the Mars opposition of 1877 led to the discovery of two small moons by Asaph Hall – and to the observation, by Giovanni Schiaparelli, of markings that the Italian astronomer took for *canali*, channels furrowing the planet's surface, some of which he compared to 'the Strait of Malacca, the very oblong lakes of Tanganyika and Nyassa, and the Gulf of California'[12]. After Schiaparelli reported that some of the lines he had sighted between 1877 and 1882 ran for 4800 kilometers, attaining a width of 120 kilometers, it came as no surprise that Flammarion was among the first to comment:

One may resist the idea, but the longer one gazes at [Schiaparelli's] drawing, the more the interpretation suggests itself... [that] we are dealing with a technological achievement of the planet's inhabitants.[13]

11 Richard A. Proctor, *Other Worlds than Ours*, London: Longmans, Green, 31872 [11870] 85, 109-0.

12 Giovanni Schiaparelli, *Astronomical and Physical Observations of the Axis of Rotation and the Topography of the Planet Mars: First Memoir, 1877-1878*, translated by William Sheehan, MS, Flagstaff: Lowell Observatory Flagstaff (Archives), 1994, 124.

13 Giovanni Schiaparelli, 'Découvertes nouvelles sur la planète Mars', *Révue d'Astronomie populaire* 1.7 (July 1882), 218 ; Camille Flammarion, 'La planète Mars', *Révue d'Astronomie populaire* 1.7 (July 1882), 216.

In the minds of some of the period's foremost astronomers, the image of a lush and youthful Arcadian Mars would soon begin to give way to that of a much more ancient world possessing no natural water-courses, but artificial waterways surpassing anything so far constructed on Earth.

3   Advanced Mars

As judged by a present-day astronomer, after Giovanni Virginio Schiaparelli (1835-1910) had taught a whole generation of observers how to see Mars, it became eventually 'impossible to see it any other way. Expectation created illusion'[14]. If channels discernibly divided Mars to the extent of making its topography 'resemble that of a chessboard', if several such *canali* even 'form[ed] a complete girdle around the globe of Mars' – could they any longer be interpreted as natural attributes, 'like the rilles of the Moon'[15]? Might they not more convincingly be explained as non-natural features, as *canals* serving a purpose which had to be derived from the planet's characteristics?

The landscape of Advanced Mars which was construed by Percival Lowell from 1895 in response to Schiaparelli's revelations differed dramatically from that of Arcadian Mars. No more stately oceans, no impetuous rivers. A much grimmer environment predominated on Earth's neighbor world: 'The rose-ochre enchantment is but a mind mirage... Beautiful as the opaline tints of the planet look, ...they represent a terrible reality... [a] vast expanse of arid ground..., girdling the planet completely in circumference, and stretching in places almost from pole to pole'[16].

Erudite descendant of a wealthy Boston family, excelling in mathematics and literature, composing Latin hexameters at 11 and using his first telescope at 15, Percival Lowell (1855-1916) became enthusiastic about Flammarion's impressive compilation *La Planète Mars* (1892) and his views on the habitability of the planet. In 1894 he founded his own observatory near Flagstaff, Arizona Territory, with the express purpose of studying the conditions of life on other worlds, particularly on Mars. From his first twelve months of observations, Lowell drew conclusions which he immediately published in a book that 'influence[d] and shape[d] the imagination of writers' such as Wells and Lasswitz[17]. The darker regions of Mars he took to be "not water, but seasonal

---

14   William Sheehan, *The Planet Mars*, Tucson: University of Arizona Press, 1996. 85.
15   Schiaparelli, *Astronomical and Physical Observations*, 123, 124.
16   Percival Lowell, *Mars as the Abode of Life*, New York/London: Macmillan, 1908, 134
17   Mark R. Hillegas, 'Martians and Mythmakers: 1877-1938', in *Challenges in American Culture*, eds. Ray B. Browne et al., Bowling Green: Bowling Green University Popular Press, 1970, 156.

areas of vegetation", with the planet depending, for its water supply, "on the melting of its polar snows". Then came the clincher:

If, therefore, the planet possess inhabitants,... irrigation, upon as vast a scale as possible,... must be the chief material concern of their lives... paramount to all the local labor, women's suffrage, and [Balkan] questions put together[18].

After the ironic aside, Lowell turned his attention to the canals which, he held, were dug precisely for such "irrigation purposes":

What we see is not the canal proper, but the line of land it irrigates, dispos[ing] incidentally of the difficulty of conceiving a canal several miles wide... What we see hints at the existence... [of] a highly intelligent mind... of beings who are in advance of, not behind us, in the journey of life[19].

Much later, Carl Sagan would famously quip that, most certainly, intelligence was responsible for the straightness of the lines observed by Lowell. The problem was just "which side of the telescope the intelligence is on'[20].

While the 19th was turning into the 20th century, canals – like automobiles, dirigibles and airplanes – had come to symbolize progress, the triumph of technology over nature. In 1869, the Suez Canal had reduced the sea route to India by 10,000 kilometers, permitting Phileas Fogg and Passepartout to accomplish their imaginary journey around the world in 80 days. Work on the Panama Canal had begun in 1880, and even if the first French effort had foundered, a second American construction attempt was under way. Canals, whether on Earth or (supposedly) on another world, continued to make for headlines: On 27 August 1911, the *New York Times* captioned a one-page article. 'Martians Build Two Immense Canals in Two Years', its headline read. 'Vast Engineering Works Accomplished in an Incredibly Short Time.'

And Lowell's arid, aging Mars offered a further fascinating perspective: A community that had forsworn armed conflict[21], unified by a common endeavor, valiantly fighting its imminent doom, demonstrated to war-torn Earth what a civilization might achieve once it had overcome strife and hate.

Sunlight might be converted into electricity on Mars' high plateaus, even stones into bread by extracting protein and carbohydrates from rocks, soil, air and water. And material advancement might release additional energies needed for moral improvement. Such was the vision offered by Kurd Lasswitz in his 1897 novel *Auf zwei Planeten*. While an abridged English translation would only appear by 1971, the book was immediately translated into a number of other European languages and a popular German edition, which

18   Percival Lowell, *Mars*, Boston/NewYork: Houghton, Mifflin, 1895: 122, 128-9
19   Lowell, *Mars*, 165, 208-9.
20   Carl Sagan, 'Hypotheses', in: *Mars and the Mind of Man*, New York: Harper & Row, 1973, 13.
21   Percival Lowell, *Mars and its Canals*, New York/London: Macmillan, 1906, 377

continued to be reprinted, was published in 1913. Until the Nazis branded the book as 'un-German', the novel sold 70,000 copies in Germany[22].

Lasswitz portrayed a Mars on which the 'colossal effort' required by irrigation had united the original 154 states into a single league. Thanks to the canal system – and here Lasswitz sounded like pure Lowell -, 'the desert region was traversed by fertile strips of vegetation nearly 100 kilometers wide which included an unbroken string of thriving Martian settlements'[23]. A one-year mandatory labor service for both sexes helped maintain the network of canals. The discovery of anti-gravity had made Martians 'the masters of the solar system', permitting them to construct a wheel-shaped space station 6,356 kilometers above Earth's North Pole. Due to terrestrial arrogance, the first contact between men and 'Nume' ended in the occupation of Europe by the league of Martian states and the establishment of a protectorate aimed at 're-educating' mankind.

Wielding power over the Earth, however, worked to morally corrupt the Martian conquerors. When they threatened to extend their protectorate to the United States, American engineers secretly succeeded in copying Martian arms and taking over their space station. Faced with a choice of violating their highest values by resorting to a war of extinction, or leaving the Earth, the Martians chose to depart. Terrestrial nations not just concluded an alliance, but went on to adopt new constitutions in a Kantian 'spirit of peace, liberty and human dignity'[24]. A peace treaty with Mars ensured co-existence on the basis of equality.

However, an alternative scenario might be imagined, derived from the hypothesis that Martians had failed 'in attempting to safeguard the habitability of their planet'. In that case, might not beings with minds 'vast and cool and unsympathetic' feel tempted to resort to aggression, pitilessly exterminating mankind in search of 'living space'? Rather than Lasswitz' pacifist vision, the result would be the social-Darwinist *War of the Worlds* that Herbert George Wells envisioned in the same year. Skilfully, Wells gave the debate about the significance of the surface features on Mars a new twist. 'Men like Schiaparelli', he wrote, 'failed to interpret the fluctuating appearances of the markings they mapped so well. All that time the Martians must have been getting ready'[25].

Contrary to what a cursory reading of his tale might suggest, Wells did not depict the inhabitants of Mars – a Mars, it should be repeated, much older than the Earth, according to prevailing opinion – as alien monstrosities. Ra-

22   Franz Rottensteiner, 'Kurd Lasswitz: A German Pioneer of Science Fiction', in *SF: The Other Side of Realism*, ed. Thomas D. Clareson, Bowling Green: Bowling Green University Popular Press, 1971, 289.
23   Kurd Lasswitz, *Auf zwei Planeten*, Frankfurt: Zweitausendeins, 1979 [11897], 98.
24   Lasswitz, *Planeten*, 875.
25   H. G. Wells, *The War of the Worlds*, New York: Pocket Books, 1953, 2.

ther, regarding their appearance, he projected on them those 'characters of the Man of the remote future' which he had predicted as the final stage of human evolution in an earlier essay[26]: An expanding brain and head, diminishing bodies and legs, unemotional intelligence, nourishment by absorption of nutritive fluids – blood in the case of the Martian invaders -, atrophy of ears, nose, and mouth, the latter 'a small, perfectly round aperture, toothless, gumless, jawless'. Wells' Martians were not so much invaders from space as invaders from time, 'ourselves, mutated beyond sympathy, though not beyond recognition'[27].

Lasswitz, in a Kantian vein, had intended to confront Europe's imperialist powers with the alternative notion of a world governed by reason and peace. Wells' *War of the Worlds* remorselessly held the mirror up to contemporary colonialism. During 1897/98, Imperial Germany occupied the Chinese port of Kiautschou; China had to cede a further part of Hongkong to Great Britain; France consolidated its position in West Africa; the United States annexed the Hawaiian Islands. In Asia, in Africa, in the Pacific, native populations were being subjugated or pushed back. 'Are we such apostles of mercy', Wells asked rhetorically, 'as to complain if the Martians warred in the same spirit?'[28].

Finally, Wells could not only count on an audience turned receptive, by a spate of recent novels – such as George Chesney's *The Battle of Dorking* (1871), William Butler's *The Invasion of England* (1882), William Le Queux's *The Great War in England* (1894) –, to the notion of French and (more frequently) German raids on England. Moreover, these authors had already begun to explore a theme on which Wells focused his attention in *The War of the Worlds*: The disappearance of any distinction between battle fronts and zones where civilians might feel reasonably safe, the expansion of mechanized 'total' warfare to engulf entire populations[29].

Such total war was raging in China forty years later, after Japanese armies had invaded the country in 1937. For a brief moment, it had been avoided in Europe after Czechoslovakia had yielded, under British and French pressure, to the Munich Agreement. The war scare was still fresh in many Americans' minds when CBS, on 30 October 1938, aired *The War of the Worlds* as a 60-minute radioplay, directed by Orson Welles, with the action transferred to New Jersey. Presented as a series of increasingly ominous news bulletins, the first half of the broadcast produced mass hysteria: All over the United States, people 'were praying, crying, fleeing frantically... Some ran to

26   H. G. Wells, H. G. (1893): 'The Man of the Year Million', in *A Critical Edition of the War of the Worlds*, eds. David Y. Hughes and Harry M. Geduld, Bloomington: Indiana University Press, 1993, Appendix III, 291-2, 293.
27   Frank McConnell, *The Science Fiction of H. G. Wells*, New York/Oxford: Oxford University Press, 1981, 128, 130.
28   McConell, *Science Fiction*, ibid.
29   McConnell, *Science Fiction*, 132-3

rescue loved ones. Others... sought information from newspapers or radio stations, summoned ambulances and police cars'[30].

An estimated 250,000 people believed the United States to be under attack by either Germany, Japan – or indeed from Mars. In a bewildering world troubled by prolonged economic depression, wars and political crises, many Americans thought anything might happen.

By the time, H. G. Wells had turned social reformer, slowly despairing of men's folly. His last ideas about an invasion from Earth's 'wizened elder brother' Mars, published under the title *Star Begotten* shortly before Orson Welles' broadcast, differed considerably from his first – though not without a self-deprecating glance back[31]:

Some of you may have read a book called *The War of the Worlds* – I forget who wrote it – Jules Verne, Conan Doyle, one of those fellows. But it told how the Martians invaded the world, wanted to colonize it and exterminate mankind. Hopeless attempt! They couldn't stand the different atmospheric pressure, they couldn't stand the difference in gravitation... To imagine that the Martians would be fools enough to try anything of the sort. But –

But if they resorted to cosmic rays instead? Modifying the genetic structure of unborn children, creating new beings that were, in fact, *their* spiritual children? That was the obsessive idea with which the tale's protagonist wrestled, until he discovered that his wife, their son – that he himself was star begotten, a changeling. The change, however, was benevolent, meant to salvage mankind – 'a lunatic asylum crowded with patients prevented from knowledge and afraid to go sane' [32]- from stupidity and immaturity by making humans more flexible, more open-minded, more innovative.

Mature Martian civilization emerged as a deus ex machina for solving, by imperceptible intervention from outside, those pressing problems which mankind found itself unable to surmount.

4 Frontier Mars

Implying, as it did, that the Red Planet's inhabitants would beat humans to accomplishing space flight, the idea of Advanced Mars ran counter to deeply engrained expansionist impulses of the imperialist age. Small wonder the tabloid journalist Garrett Putnam Serviss immediately responded to Wells' tale with a serial in the sensationalist *New York Evening Journal*. Entitled *Edison's Conquest of Mars* and published in 1898, it depicted the 'wizard of

---

30   Hadley Cantril, *The Invasion from Mars. A Study in the Psychology of Panic*, Princeton: Princeton University Press, 1940: 47.
31   H. G. Wells, *Star Begotten*, London: Chatto & Windus, 1937: 50-51.
32   Wells, *Star Begotten*, 167-8.

Menlo Park', aided by Lord Kelvin and Konrad Roentgen, as devising both a disintegrator ray and an electric spaceship (admittedly based on the operating principles of the Martian machines). Financed by the great powers, 100 spaceships – armed with 3,000 disintegrators – were built and flew to Mars, where they wrecked havoc by forcibly opening the 'floodgates of Syrtis Major', thereby deluging the planet's equatorial regions.

Lasswitz had already attributed the defeat of his Martian conquerors to American engineering talent and 'daring'. By presenting an entire arsenal of innovative weapons, Serviss left no doubt about America's claim to global leadership: Technologically superior, the 'new world' had outrivaled the 'old' as the torchbearer of progress.

Yet, Serviss' tale did not set a new trend in wishful thinking about the Red Planet. Lowell's arid Mars was taking hold in the public mind, and Serviss' vast oceans and floodgates were just too wildly off that mark. For a significant change in perspective to occur, American cowboy, gold miner, salesman and – finally – novelist Edgar Rice Burroughs (1875-1950) had to write *A Princess of Mars* in 1912. He rechristened Mars, gave it the name Barsoom – and henceforth Mars exploration would be 'as much a re-creation of the past as a vision of the future'[33].

American rather than European science fiction authors now took the lead in projecting their fantasies onto the Red Planet, building on a 'forceful...cultural tradition' that would eventually inspire the U. S. space program no less than it initially spurred 'romantic vision[s]' of exploring, even colonizing Mars: the myth of America's western frontier[34]. Rather than 'highbrow' European-style literature, the 'entertainment industry'[35] of 'lowbrow' American pulp fiction with its international outlets provided the medium for two generations of writers including, subsequent to Burroughs, most prominently Leigh Brackett (1915-1978). Burroughs and his heirs retained Lowell's deserts and canals, but discarded the idea of a sophisticated Martian civilization. Instead, they depicted towns, ancient beyond imagination, lying in the southern hemisphere of Mars, their outskirts touching the shores of the dried-up Low Canals that once discharged their waters into the now dust-blown bed of a long-vanished ocean. The towns, once ruled by pirate kings, bore names such as Jekkara, or Valkis, or Barrakesh. Their women – partly resembling Indians, partly Mexicans – wore tiny golden bells chiming temptingly. Barbarian tribes came to these places from distant deserts, such as Kesh and Shun. Santa Fe on Mars...

---

33 Howard E. McCurdy, *Space and the American Imagination*, Washington/London: Smithsonian Institution Press, 1997, 2.

34 McCurdy, *Space*, Washington/London: Smithsonian Institution Press, 1997: 2, 233-4.

35 Benjamin S. Lawson, 'The Time and Place of Edgar Rice Burroughs's Early Martian Trilogy', *Extrapolation* 27.3 (March 1986), 209.

A Terran spaceport did exist at Kahora, not far from Olympus Mons. But only hard-boiled adventurers dared approach the Low Canals, after having galloped across the Drylands on half-wild saurians. They had 'the rawhide look of the planetary frontiers' about them[36] and wore their ray-guns low in their holsters. For Barrakesh, Jekkara, Valkis were towns outside the law.

The scenario was Leigh Brackett's, dreamt up during the 1940s. Like its American counterpart, the 'planetary frontier' signified no demarcation line, as the term was understood by Europeans, but rather the advancing rim of settlement, site of the violent clash between savagery and civilization. After the U. S. government had announced, in 1890, the 'closing' of the frontier in its statistical meaning of less than six inhabitants per square mile, the frontier – 'by transcending the limitations of a specific temporality' – came to be projected from the past into the present and even the future. Creating a specific 'moral landscape' by depicting the course of American history as progress through violence (or, as Burroughs would have it in *A Princess of Mars*, Ch. XXVI, 'through carnage to joy'), the myth of the frontier continues to provide patterns of identification and legitimization for individual and collective attitudes and behavior to the present day[37]. The rugged individualist – the onward-thrusting pioneer – the hardy adventurer, all armed *and morally justified* to shoot or to slash in a stereotyped black-and-white situation of good versus evil: These are the vivid images evoked by the frontier metaphor. They re-emerged in 'the "space opera" (as opposed to "horse opera")' with the 'typical structures and plots of westerns', but the 'settings and trappings of science fiction'[38].

Burroughs virtually defined the sub-genre, creating the quintessential space opera character: Captain John Carter, a 'gentleman of the highest type' and former plantation owner from Virginia, who had proved his prowess in the Civil War, and who was magically teleported from Arizona – where he had been battling Apaches – to Mars[39]. He made no effort to conceal that John Carter was modeled on Captain John Smith, a 17th century Virginian colonist who figured prominently in another American legend – the narrative of Pocahontas, Indian 'princess' of the Powhatan tribe. Supposedly, Pocahontas (at the tender age of 12 or 13) had become enamored of Smith and had rescued him from torture by her tribe. After arriving on a Mars peopled by warlike black, red, green and yellow races, Burroughs' John Carter met and married the 'incomparable princess' Dejah Thoris, daughter of the Jed (ruler) of Helium, chief of a red-skinned people that exhibited 'a startling resem-

36   Leigh Brackett, *The Secret of Sinharat*, New York: Ace Books, 1964, 8.
37   Richard Slotkin, *Gunfighter Nation. The Myth of the Frontier in Twentieth-Century America*, New York: Atheneum, 1992: 4-5, 6-7, 14, 24.
38   Lawson, 'Time and Place' , 213.
39   Edgar Rice Burroughs, *A Princess of Mars*, New York: Random House, 2003 [11912]: XXIII-IV, 14-5.

blance... to... the red Indians of...Earth'[40]. In *The Princess of Mars* and Burroughs' subsequent Mars novels, it was Carter's task to repeatedly save Dejah Thoris, with the extraordinary physical powers lent to him by Mars' lesser gravity, from a fate 'worse than death'. To leave not the slightest doubt about the tradition he was embracing, Burroughs chose this context to revive another stereotype of frontier melodrama: With 'a cold sweat', his main protagonist reflected that if he should fail, it would be 'far better' for Dejah to 'save friendly bullets...at the last moment, as did those brave frontier women of my lost land, who took their own lives rather than fall into the hands of the Indian braves'[41].

Frontier Mars became a place where only-too familiar characters lounged in the doorways of Earth's latest colony – Northwest Smith for one, created in 1933 by writer Catherine L. Moore (1911-1987), 'tall and leather-brown, hand on his heat-gun'; where everybody understood the 'old gesture' when that gun was drawn with a swift motion, sweeping 'in a practised half-circle'[42]; where John Carter, Northwest Smith and their likes fought human or half-human tribes; where conflicts were invariably 'resolved' by resorting to weapons. An 'extension of our original America', with 'Martians await[ing] us' whom 'we [could] assimilate to our old myths of the Indian', Frontier Mars was destined to remain a very 'parochial' planet[43], familiar rather than alien.

5   Cold War Mars

'Watch the skies!' moviegoers were counseled in 1951 at the end of the science fiction film *The Thing from Another World*. The Cold War had turned hot in Korea. Who knew what the Communists, 'masters of deceit' (FBI Director J. Edgar Hoover), aggressively pushing from outside, subversively boring from within, threatening 'the continuance of every home and fireside'[44], might have up their sleeve?

Two years later, the 10 year-old stargazing protagonist of *Invaders from Mars* did watch the skies at night, only to observe a flying saucer landing and burrowing in the sandy ground across from his home. Everyone who investi-

---

40   Burroughs, *Princess*, 152.
41   Burroughs, Princess, 75.
42   Catherine L. Moore, 'Shambleau', in idem, *Northwest Smith*, New York: Ace Books, 1981 [1933], 2, 3.
43   Leslie A. Fiedler, *The Return of the Vanishing American*, London: Paladin, 1972, 25; Lawson, 'Time and Place', 208.
44   J. Edgar Hoover, *Masters of Deceit. The Story of Communism in America and How to Fight it*, New York: Pocket Books, 1958, VI.

gated next morning – the child's father, his mother, a neighbor girl, two po-
licemen, finally the local chief of police – was 'transformed' in succession,
displaying an implant in the neck and behaving robot-like.

Invaders from Mars recounted not just an invasion, but a 'conspiracy', an
emerging 'fifth column' of concealed infiltrators. Neither parents nor friends
could be trusted anymore – a patent allusion (including the unfeeling attitudes displayed by affected adults) to rampant paranoia about the supposed
subversion of American life by Communists. The invaders themselves were
depicted as puppets, telepathically controlled by a 'supreme intelligence'. As
might be expected, the military – alerted by the boy's school psychologist
and her friend, an astrophysicist – arrived in time to save the day and blow up
the Martian saucer.

'By the beginning of the decade, movies were America's most popular
entertainment'; only from the mid-fifties would they be outranked by television. *Destination Moon* (1950) 'made the idea of space travel not only plau-
sible but fascinating'. *The Thing from Another World* (1951) 'brought the
idea of creatures from other planets coming here to vivid life'[45]. From 1950,
too, the screen added Martian landscapes to those portrayed in the printed
media. *Rocketship X(pedition) M(oon)*, Kurt Neumann's bleak movie of
humans arriving on a Mars destroyed by nuclear war, and *The Martian
Chronicles*, Ray Bradbury's seminal novel of the Red Planet's colonization
against the backdrop of atomic war eventually engulfing Earth, both came out
during that year.

In *Rocketship XM*, the first manned spaceflight to Earth's satellite was
thrown off course by a swarm of meteors and forced to land on Mars. The
crew found themselves in a post-nuclear wasteland, deducing 'from artefacts
and ruins so radioactive they can't approach them that there had once been a
high civilization on Mars, but that atomic warfare reduced the Martians to
savagery'[46]. Mutated Martians attacked the expedition, killing two and
wounding a third crew member. The rest of the crew escaped, but the rocket
ran out of fuel on its return flight and crashed. A year before, the Soviet Union had detonated its first nuclear device. President Truman had ordered
development of the hydrogen bomb in early 1950. 'The idea that we now had
the potential to wipe out civilization entirely was beginning to permeate mass
culture' – and was projected onto Mars by 'the first film to expound such a
grim warning about our possible future'[47].

The Soviet explosion and Truman's announcement drew an immediate
response from a 30 year-old writer, Ray Bradbury, who felt that man might
'still destroy himself before reaching for the stars. I see man's self-

---

45   Bill Warren, *Keep Watching the Skies. American Science Fiction Movies of the Fifties,* Vol.
      1, Jefferson/London: McFarland, IX, 2.
46   Warren, *Keep Watching,* 11.
47   Warren, *Keep Watching,* ibid.

destructive half, the blind spider fiddling in the venomous dark, dreaming mushroom-cloud dreams. Death solves it all, it whispers, shaking a handful of atoms like a necklace of dark beads'[48].

On May 6, 1950, *Collier's* published one of Bradbury's most powerful stories, *There Will Come Soft Rains*. It had no human protagonists. Rather, it focused on the final 'death' of an electronically programmed house, left standing empty among glowing radioactive ruins, after its occupants had perished, their images – as had happened in Hiroshima – 'burnt on the wood in one titanic instant'[49]. The story was included by Bradbury as a chapter in his loosely-knit classic of the same year, *The Martian Chronicles*, intended by the author to 'provide a mirror for humanity, its faults, foibles, and failures... an allegory transplanted to another world'[50].

Before being killed off by chicken pox which American colonists had introduced to Mars, the planet's golden-eyed 'natives' had inhabited crystal houses at the edge of the canals that – attuned to nature – 'turned and followed the sun, flower-like'. The settlers not only brought chicken pox. They also brought gas stations, and luggage stores, and hot-dog stands. With their hammers, they 'beat the strange world into a shape that was familiar', they 'bludgeon[ed] away all the strangeness... In all, some ninety thousand people came to Mars'. But the majority left again when flashing light-radio messages from Earth reported that there was war, that everybody should come home. To those who had remained on Mars, the night sky soon offered a horrible sight[51]:

Earth changed... It caught fire. Part of it seemed to come apart in a million pieces... It burned with an unholy dripping glare for a minute, three times normal size, then dwindled.

Humans had turned two worlds, Mars and Earth, into 'tomb planet[s]'[52].

However, Bradbury – influenced by both Burroughs and Brackett – had also decided 'that there would be certain elements of similarity between the invasion of Mars and the invasion of the Wild West'[53]. The frontier myth held that America and its democracy would be reborn at every new frontier between Atlantic and Pacific – and beyond. One family, more fortunate than the folks annihilated in *There Will Come Soft Rains*, had escaped the inferno on Earth (with rumours maintaining that a second one had also made it to Mars). The father had promised the children that they would set out for a picnic and would see Martians. Now they were gazing at their reflections in a canal – and the Martians stared back at them.

---

48   Ray Bradbury, quoted in William F. Nolan, 'Bradbury: Prose Poet in the Age of Space', *Magazine of Fantasy & Science Fiction* 24.5 (May 1963), 8.
49   Ray Bradbury, *The Martian Chronicles*, New York: Bantam Books, 1951, 185.
50   Sam Weller, *The Bradbury Chronicles*, New York: William Morrow, 2005, 156, 159.
51   Bradbury, *Martian Chronicles*, 2, 86, 158.
52   Bradbury, *Martian Chronicles*, 172.
53   Ray Bradbury, as quoted in Weller, *Bradbury Chronicles*, 155.

The implication was evident. Bradbury's 'intensely critical examination' of the frontier myth – of 'the shallow and mercurial properties of America's predominant cultural construct'[54] – notwithstanding, Mars emerged as another 'virgin land' (Henry Nash Smith) where America might both survive and regenerate. The Frontier Mars image, in other words, had proved its adaptability to the hydrogen bomb age, reducing Cold War Mars to a mere variation of an already familiar theme. And, as would soon become evident, the frontier metaphor had not exhausted its usefulness.

6 Terraformed Mars

For American engineer Robert Zubrin, the writing presently 'is on the wall': He holds that 'without a frontier from which to breathe life, the spirit that gave rise to the progressive humanistic culture that America for the past several centuries has offered to the world is fading.' Zubrin is convinced that "the creation of a new frontier presents itself as America's and humanity's greatest need'. And he 'believe[s] that humanity's new frontier can only be Mars'[55].

Zubrin, and the Mars Society formed in 1998 on his initiative, consider privately funded Mars flights and the establishment of a permanent Mars base as just initial steps. To fulfil the planet's mission of reinvigorating terrestrial civilization, its atmospheric and surface conditions need to be dramatically changed by a long-term project. Mars must be 'terraformed'.

According to the *Shorter Oxford English Dictionary*, terraforming implies a process of planetary engineering, aimed at creating an extraterrestrial environment that would be habitable for humans. First use of the term has been credited to science fiction writer John Stewart ('Jack') Williamson in a 1942 novella. The concept started to gain a certain scientific acceptability after Carl Sagan had published an article in 1961 on introducing algae into the atmosphere of Venus to slowly change that planet's extremely hostile conditions. In 1973, Sagan followed with a brief piece 'Planetary Engineering on Mars'[56], kicking off the debate with regard to the Red Planet.

To terraform Mars, both atmospheric pressure and surface temperature would have to be raised. The 'global warming' process – basically comparable to that which Earth is presently experiencing – would require an increase

54 Gregory M. Pfitzer, 'The Only Good Alien is a Dead Alien: Science Fiction and the Metaphysics of Indian-Hating on the High Frontier', *Journal of American Culture* 18.1 (Spring 1995), 58.

55 Robert Zubrin, *The Significance of the Martian* Frontier, www.javanet.com/-campr.2/New Mars/Pages/Frontier 1.html, 1998.

56 Carl Sagan, 'Planetary Engineering on Mars', *Icar us* 20 (1973), 513-514.

in 'greenhouse gasses', such as carbon dioxide or more powerful fluorocarbons, for which several ways have been proposed, and the subsequent build-up of a hydrosphere providing the water necessary to sustain life[57].

The idea was, of course, picked up by science fiction – most elaborately by Kim Stanley Robinson in his trilogy *Red Mars/Green Mars/Blue Mars* (1992-96). The work focused on the century-long conflict between 'Greens', whose sense of mission prompted them to contaminate the Red Planet with robust mosses and lichens at every opportunity, and the 'Red' environmentalists who were finally driven underground.

As before, such imaginary landscapes have revealed more about the desires, the hopes, the anxieties of those who designed them, than about any future 'green' or 'blue' Mars. While Zubrin took care to link the emergence of a terraformed Martian frontier to the promotion of values such as individualism, creativity and belief in the idea of progress, his basic approach was far more hard-nosed[58]:

If the idea is accepted that the world's resources are fixed, then each person is ultimately the enemy of every other person, and each race or nation is the enemy of every other race or nation. The inevitable result is tyranny, war and genocide. Only in a universe of unlimited resources can all men be brothers.

Put differently: Either a new frontier will be opened up – or containment, rather than self-containment, will become the 'natural' order of things...

Objections against such reasoning were the exception. In terms reminiscent of Bradbury, but more starkly, historian Patricia Limerick in her contribution to the 1992 volume *Space Policy Alternatives* emphasized the social-Darwinist consequences of 'rugged individualism' that had shaped the 'conquest' of the American West, including greed and corruption, violence against 'aliens' (Indians and Mexicans), environmental destruction. She rejected the simplified picture, again extolled by Zubrin, of equating westward expansion with democracy and progress, for that picture had 'denied consequences and evaded failure'[59].

Because of 'America's pioneer heritage, technological pre-eminence, and economic strength, it is fitting that we should lead the people of this planet into space', the Paine Commission had stated in 1986. Chaired by an earlier NASA Administrator, it included UN Ambassador Jeane Kirckpatrick, former test pilot Charles Yeager and retired Air Force General Bernard Schriev-

57 Christopher P. McKay, Owen B. Toon and James F. Kasting, 'Making Mars Habitable", *Nature* 352 (8 August 1991), 489-96; Christopher P. McKay, 'Restoring Mars to Habitable Conditions: Can We? Should We? Will We?', *Journal of the Irish Colleges of Physicians and Surgeons* 22.1 (January 1993), 17-9.

58 Zubrin, *Significance*.

59 Patricia Nelson Limerick, 'Imagined Frontiers: Westward Expansion and the Future of the Space Program', in *Space Policy Alternatives*, ed. Radford Byerly, Jr., Boulder: Westview Press, 1992, 249-262.

er (who had directed IRBM Thor and ICBM Atlas development). In their report, tellingly entitled *Pioneering the Space Frontier*, the members had proposed to 'stimulate individual initiative and free enterprise in space', and had resolved that 'from the highlands of the Moon to the plains of Mars', America should 'make accessible vast new resources and support human settlements beyond Earth orbit'[60].

This was no space opera. This was a National Commission on Space, appointed by the President of the United States, issuing a declaration that, with its 'fervent optimism and cheeriness', was 'vintage 1890's... a picture of harmony and progress where historical reality shows us something closer to a muddle'[61].

Abstracting and reducing from reality, the frontier myth has created a historical cliché. Clichés, as Richard Slotkin – among others – has reminded us, may serve to interpret new experiences as mere recurrences of past happenings, reflecting a refusal to learn. Identifying Mars as merely another 'frontier', projecting a moral purpose on the adaption of that so-called planetary frontier to human settlers' needs, tops a tradition of invoking a highly problematic cultural stereotype.

References

Brian Aldiss and David Wingrove, *Trillion Year Spree. The History of Science Fiction*, Lon-don: Paladin, 1988.

Victor R. Baker, *The Channels of Mars*, Austin: University of Texas Press, 1982.

Wilhelm Beer and Johann Heinrich Maedler, *Beitraege zur physischen Kenntniss der himm-lischen Koerper im Sonnensysteme*, Weimar: Bernhard Friedrich Voigt, 1841.

Leigh Brackett, *The Secret of Sinharat*, New York: Ace Books, 1964.

Ray Bradbury, *The Martian Chronicles*, New York: Bantam Books, 1951.

Edgar Rice Burroughs, *A Princess of Mars*, New York: Random House, 2003 [¹1912].

Hadley Cantril, *The Invasion from Mars. A Study in the Psychology of Panic*, Prince-ton: Prince-ton University Press, 1940.

Rainer Eisfeld and Wolfgang Jeschke, *Marsfieber*, Munich: Droemer, 2003.

Leslie A. Fiedler, *The Return of the Vanishing American*, London: Paladin, 1972.

Camille Flammarion, *Die Mehrheit Bewohnter Welten*, Leipzig: J. J. Weber, 1865.

Camille Flammarion, *Les Terres du Ciel*, Paris: Marpon & Flammarion, 1884.

Camille Flammarion, 'La planète Mars', *Révue d'Astronomie populaire* 1.7 (July 1882), 206-216.

---

60   Paine Commission, http://history.nasa.gov/painerep/parta.html, 1986.
61   Limerick, 'Imagined Frontiers', 253-4, 256-7.

Mark R. Hillegas, 'Martians and Mythmakers: 1877-1938', in *Challenges in American Culture*, eds. Ray B. Browne et al., Bowling Green: Bowling Green University Popular Press, 1970, 150-177.

J. Edgar Hoover, *Masters of Deceit. The Story of Communism in America and How to Fight it*, New York: Pocket Books, 1958.

Kurd Lasswitz, *Auf zwei Planeten*, Frankfurt: Zweitausendeins, 1979 [[1]1897].

Benjamin S. Lawson, 'The Time and Place of Edgar Rice Burroughs's Early Martian Trilogy', *Extrapolation* 27.3 (March 1986), 208-220.

Patricia Nelson Limerick, 'Imagined Frontiers: Westward Expansion and the Future of the Space Program", in *Space Policy Alternatives*, ed. Radford Byerly, Jr., Boulder: Westview Press, 1992, 249-262.

Percival Lowell, *Mars*, Boston/New York: Houghton, Mifflin, 1895.

Percival Lowell, *Mars and its Canals*, New York/London: Macmillan, 1906.

Percival Lowell, *Mars as the Abode of Life*, New York/London: Macmillan, 1908.

Robert Markley, *Dying Planet. Mars in Science and the Imagination*, Durham: Duke University Press, 2005.

Frank McConnell, *The Science Fiction of H. G. Wells*, New York/Oxford: Oxford University Press, 1981.

Howard E. McCurdy, *Space and the American Imagination*, Washington/London: Smithsonian Institution Press, 1997.

Christopher P. McKay, Owen B. Toon and James F. Kasting, 'Making Mars Habitable", *Nature* 352 (8 August 1991), 489-496.

Christopher P. McKay, 'Restoring Mars to Habitable Conditions: Can We? Should We? Will We?', *Journal of the Irish Colleges of Physicians and Surgeons* 22.1 (January 1993), 17-19.

Catherine L. Moore, 'Shambleau', in id., *Northwest Smith*, New York: Ace Books, 1981 [1933], 1-33.

Oliver Morton, *Mapping Mars*, New York: Fourth Estate, 2002.

William F. Nolan, 'Bradbury: Prose Poet in the Age of Space', *Magazine of Fantasy & Science Fiction* 24.5 (May 1963), 7-22.

Paine Commission, http://history.nasa.gov/painerep/parta.html, 1986.

Gregory M. Pfitzer, 'The Only Good Alien is a Dead Alien: Science Fiction and the Metaphys ics of Indian-Hating on the High Frontier', *Journal of American Culture* 18.1 (Spring 1995), 51-67.

Richard A. Proctor, *Other Worlds than Ours*, London: Longmans, Green, [3]1872 [[1]1870].

Kim Stanley Robinson, *Mars Trilogy*, New York: HarperCollins, 1992-1996.

Franz Rottensteiner, 'Kurd Lasswitz: A German Pioneer of Science Fiction', in *SF: The Other Side of Realism*, ed. Thomas D. Clareson (Bowling Green: Bowling Green University Popular Press, 1971, 289-306.

Alfred Russel Wallace, *Is Mars Habitable?*, London: Macmillan, 1907.

Carl Sagan, 'Hypotheses', in: *Mars and the Mind of Man*, New York: Harper & Row, 1973, 9–16.

Carl Sagan, *Cosmos*, New York/London: Random House, 1980.

Giovanni Schiaparelli, 'Découvertes nouvelles sur la planète Mars', *Révue d'Astronomie popu-laire* 1.7 (July 1882), 216-221.

Giovanni Schiaparelli, *Astronomical and Physical Observations of the Axis of Rotation and the Topography of the Planet Mars: First Memoir, 1877-1878*, translated by William Sheehan, MS, Flagstaff: Lowell Observatory Flagstaff (Archives), 1994.

Martin Schwonke, *Vom Staatsroman zur Science Fiction*, Stuttgart: Enke, 1957.

Garrett P. Serviss, *Edison's Conquest of Mars*, Los Angeles: Carcosa House, 1947 [¹1898].

William Sheehan, *The Planet Mars*, Tucson: University of Arizona Press, 1996.

Richard Slotkin, *Gunfighter Nation. The Myth of the Frontier in Twentieth-Century America*, New York: Atheneum, 1992.

Bill Warren, *Keep Watching the Skies. American Science Fiction Movies of the Fifties*, Vol. 1, Jefferson/London: McFarland, 1982.

Sam Weller, *The Bradbury Chronicles*, New York: William Morrow, 2005.

H. G. Wells, *Star Begotten*, London: Chatto & Windus, 1937.

H. G. Wells, *The War of the Worlds*, New York: Pocket Books, 1953 [¹1898]

H. G. Wells, 'The Man of the Year Million' (1893), in *A Critical Edition of the War of the Worlds*, eds. David Y. Hughes and Harry M. Geduld, Bloomington: Indiana University Press, 1993, Appendix III, 290-294.

Robert Zubrin, *The Significance of the Martian Frontier, www.javanet.com/-campr.2/New Mars/Pages/Frontier 1.html*, 1998.

V.
Political Science and Policy Transfer
Foreign Pressures and Domestic Politics
During Portugal's Transition to Democracy

The following chapter was written for the book Portugal in the 1980's: Dilemmas of Democratic Consolidation, *edited by Kenneth Maxwell and published in 1986 by Greenwood Press. The text examines the structural problems involved in Portugal's relationship with Western Europe; almost in passing, it also reconstructs an important phase in the European Union's history. It argues that the constraints of Portugal's persisting political and economic imbalances might overwhelm the advantages of EC entry. Politically, at least, the chronic instabilities generated by the rapid turnover of successive governments have since abated. Economically, however, the vicious circle of accumulating current account deficits and harsh austerity programs has persevered, culminating in the present financial crisis. Factors identified in the subsequent chapter continue to afflict Portugal: low industrial and agricultural productivity, inferior vocational training and education standards, weak competitiveness, severe unemployment, high public debt, inefficient bureaucracy. With regard to GDP per capita, Portugal continues to rank third lowest in the euro area.*

Portugal and Western Europe: Shifting Involvements

A Hesitant Relationship's Politics and Economics

The year was 1970, and the occasion was Portugal's opening bid for the negotiations about to begin in Brussels, finally resulting in the Portuguese-EC Free Trade Agreement of 1972. The year 1972 had also been fixed as the date when the United Kingdom's accession to the Common Market would become effective. Great Britain was Portugal's most important foreign market; seven years later, it would still absorb one-third of Portuguese exports. The United Kingdom and Portugal had been among the states establishing the European Free Trade Association in 1960. Portugal, at the time, had been the sole country to be conceded substantial non-reciprocal advantages by Annex G to the EFTA Convention: Portuguese elimination of import duties on industrial products was allowed to proceed much more slowly than was reduction by the other Six – zero duties only by 1980, instead of 1966. Moreover, Portugal was permitted to introduce new duties for protecting "infant industries".Between 1960 and 1970, Portuguese exports to EFTA countries increased by 15 percent, while exports to EC member states declined by 3.5

percent.[1] Obviously, the EC common tariff hurt Portugal's trade, and when the United Kingdom joined the Common Market, Portugal was "virtually forced" to come to terms with the European Community.[2] Portugal at the time was (and had progressively become since 1961) a "warfare state",[3] allotting over 40 percent of `its annual budget to military expenditures that financed the increasingly savage colonial wars in Guinea-Bissau, Angola, and Mozambique. The trade agreement's political implications, therefore, were severely criticized by the exiled Portuguese socialists, the European Confederation of Free Trade Unions, and by the Dutch opposition parties. The treaty not only diplomatically strengthened the Caetano dictatorship, it also enabled Portugal "to continue and increase her military expenditures," thereby contributing to continued armed repression of the African independence movements.

The Dutch government, however – and its attitude may be taken as exemplary for the EC – officially kept to the view that "purely commercial" arrangements were at issue. The Portuguese minister of foreign affairs followed suit. "You keep asking political questions," he told the journalists interviewing him in Brussels, after he had presented his country's opening statement to the EC Council. "I am concerned simply with the economics of the situation."[4]

On April 25, 1974, the Portuguese Armed Forces Movement (Movimento das Forças Armadas, MFA), reacting to the deteriorating military situation in Africa, overthrew the Salazar-Caetano "Estado Novo." On June 27, a mere two months after the coup, the First Provisional Government asked the European Community for economic support. On November 25/26, the Third Provisional Government presented urgent proposals for new special trade terms (under the two-year-old free trade agreement) and for a comprehensive arrangement protecting Portuguese emigrant workers in EC member countries: there were 850,000 Portuguese in France alone by 1974.

These proposals, however, were submitted after General António de Spinola had gone on television for his dramatic farewell address to the country. The MFA had picked Spinola, former military governor of Guinea-Bissau (then Guiné Portuguesa), as Portugal's new president. While evolutionary rather than revolutionary change – movement toward "a representative democratic regime similar to others in Western Europe... in which the interests of

---

1   Data provided by Klaus Esser, et al.: *Portugal: Industrie und Industriepolitik vor dem Beitritt zur Europäischen Gemeinschaft*, Berlin 1977, p. 221
2   Peter Guinee: *Portugal and the EEC*, Amsterdam 1973, p. 66.
3   Douglas Porch: *The Portuguese Armed Forces and the Revolution*, London/Stanford 1977, p. 12.
4   Cf. Guinee, *Portugal and the EEC*, pp. 73 ss.; the quotes are on pp. 74, 88.

the propertied would be defended"[5] – seemed at first guaranteed after the April coup, its immediate chances were destroyed by Spinola's gamble, supported by conservative groups, to extend or regain his personal powers during successive crises in July and September 1974 (and, finally, by an abortive military coup on March 11, 1975). These crises radicalized a part of the MFA and mobilized an ever widening segment of the population. The industrial workers of Lisbon and Setubal and the rural proletariat of the southern Alentejo contributed to the accelerating mass movement that, during the summer of 1975, began to bear the traits of a social revolution.

Following Spinola's resignation from the presidency, "the Community leadership lacked the will... to give rapid satisfaction to the demands put forward by the Portuguese".[6] EC attitudes were particularly important for Portugal because of its rapidly deteriorating economic situation: While merchandise exports rose only from $1.8 billion (1973) to $2.3 billion (even declining in 1975 and 1976), merchandise imports shot up from $2.8 billion to $4.3 billion in 1974. Because of climbing international prices, by far the most marked increases were not in amounts but in value of cereal and, especially enormous, of crude oil imports. Income from tourism and emigrant remittances fell drastically; clandestine capital outflow through the undervoicing of exports alone has been estimated at $108 million for 1975. Labor migration from Portugal decreased by 45 percent (barely 45,000 persons as against nearly 80,000 in 1973) after France, West Germany, and other countries had reacted to the 1973-75 world recession by unilaterally suspending the import of labor. Meanwhile, due to returnees from Angola and Mozambique, and to the demobilization of military personnel, Continental Portugal's population swelled from 8.43 million in 1973 to 8.68 million in 1974 and 9.09 million in 1975, unemployment and underemployment rising stiffly with it.[7] Judged against the background of worsening terms of trade and international recession, Portuguese revolution and decolonization could hardly have happened in a more unfavorable situation.

The EC Foreign Ministers' Council, however, during Portugal's "hot summer" of 1975, on May 26 and again on June 24, hedged on economic aid,

5 Lawrence S. Graham: "The Military in Politics: The Politicization of the Portuguese Armed Forces," in Lawrence S. Graham and Harry M. Makler, eds.: *Contemporary Portugal*, Austin/London 1979, p. 234.

6 Council of Europe, Parliamentary Assembly: *Report on the Situation in Portugal*, Doc. 3609, Strasbourg, April 21, 1975, p. 18.

7 For the data, cf. Robert N. McCauley: "A Compendium of IMF Troubles: Turkey, Portugal, Peru, Egypt", in Lawrence G. Frank and Marilyn J. Seiber, eds., *Developing Country Debt*, New York 1979, p. 151; World Bank, ed.: *Portugal: Current and Prospective Economic Trends*, Washington D.C., 1978, p. 73; Manuel Barboza and Luis Miguel P. Beleza: "External Disequilibrium in Portugal 1975-78", in Fundaçao Calouste Gulbenkian, ed.: *II International Conference on the Portuguese Economy*, Vol. 2, Lisbon 1980, pp. 57, 62; information supplied by the Ministry of Social Communication in Lisbon.

voicing its concern with "political stability" and "democratic development" in Portugal. Finally, on July 17, France's president "vetoed a Community loan... for fear of subsidizing a socialist-communist alliance".[8] The EC Council of Heads of State and Government, instead, presented Portugal with what amounted to a "virtual ultimatum":[9] "The EC, because of its political and historical tradition, can grant support only to a pluralist democracy."[10] By "pluralist," the Council was, of course, referring to the North American-Western European public philosophy[11] – and not to the creed professed by the MFA: Four weeks earlier, the group of Portuguese officers that had overthrown the Caetano regime had declared that their aim consisted in a "socialist pluralism" repudiating "the implantation of socialism by violent or dictatorial means" and implying "recognition of the existence of various political parties, even though they do not necessarily defend socialist options".[12]

Conducive to the Western European attitude was the concern of political and military strategists over what they termed "NATO's crumbling Southern flank": Soviet naval buildup and Communist Party strength around the Mediterranean were perceived as two blades of a scissor fragmenting NATO political cohesion and endangering NATO military communications; the revolutionary process in Portugal seemed to pose an immediate threat to both.[13] Accordingly, the threshold was quickly reached after which any real change in the status quo became "intolerable"[14] to NATO: Portugal was not viewed as a developing policy and society in its own right; the country's situation, on the contrary, was put squarely into the context of the East-West conflict.

Contrary to the EC Council, the Commission had, in a memorandum of June 11, 1975, pleaded for "immediate" and "spectacular" economic aid to "strengthen Portuguese democracy".[15] As Hans Beck, deputy chief of cabinet to the EC Commission's vice president Wilhelm Haferkamp (a West German Social Democrat), asserted in the periodical *Neue Gesellschaft* (published by the SPD-affiliated Friedrich Ebert Foundation), the Commission's motivation can be taken to have stemmed "not from political altruism" but rather from

---

8   Jonathan Story: "Portugal's Revolution of Carnations: Patterns of Change and Continuity," *International Affairs* 52 (1976), 431.
9   Tad Szulc: "Hope for Portugal," *New Republic*, August 30, 1975, p. 9.
10 Cf. Commission of the European Communities: *Die Beziehungen zwischen der EG und Portugal*, Brussels 1976, p. 8
11 The role of the concept of pluralism as a guideline and justification of Western European (and U.S.) foreign policy has been explored in the author's *Sozialistischer Pluralismus in Europa: Ansätze und Scheitern am Beispiel Portugal*, Cologne 1984
12 For a translation of the entire MFA Program text, cf. Appendix IV to Porch, *Portuguese Armed Forces*, pp. 248 ss.
13 Cf. David Rees: "Southern Europe: NATO's Crumbling Flank," *Conflict Studies*, No. 60 (1975), 2/3, 13.
14 Tad Szulc, "Washington and Lisbon: Behind the Portuguese Revolution," *Foreign Policy*, No. 21 (Winter 1975/76), 9.
15 Commission of the European Communities, *Beziehungen* (n. 10), ibid.

"our own interest in preserving and stabilizing our political system" whose "credibility and efficiency, confronted with communism..., is at stake in Portugal."[16]

However, a $180 million European Investment Bank loan was only granted Portugal on October 7, after a new, de facto social democratic, provisional government had been in office for three weeks; the first disbursements were not made before April 1976. The trade agreement of 1972 was finally amended in June of the same year. Evidently, aid from Western Europe could not be obtained without a commitment to the West.

General Francisco da Costa Gomes, Spinola's successor to the Portuguese presidency, has made abundantly clear that the EC attitude, from the autumn of 1974 onward, was interpreted by the Portuguese governments not in economic terms, but along political lines as "inimical" foreign pressure.[17]

The Common Market's "power of denial,"[18] demonstrated from May to July 1975, could not have failed to impress, first and foremost, President Costa Gomes, Foreign Minister Major Melo Antunes, and ambassador itinerant Major Vitor Alves (the latter visiting Western European capitals between April and September 1975). One week after the EC Council had been in session, Costa Gomes, in a discourse to the MFA Delegate Assembly, made no secret of his conviction that, because of Portugal's economic "dependence on the West," the country could not endure "Western enmity" as long as its economic ties with Third World and socialist countries had not been further developed. Advancing the revolution was conceivable only after the country's external condition had become such that the global powers' "fields of influence would cancel each other."[19] Antunes and Alves led the MFA officers' "Group of Nine" whose August 7 document, signaling open discord in MFA ranks and sharply criticizing the cabinet's "revolutionary vanguard" politics, was instrumental in ending the short period of left—leaning governments (frequently called "Gonçalvist," after Prime Minister Brigadier Vasco Gonçalves). They were tacitly supported by Costa Gomes, who agreed with their opinions, if not with their methods.[20]

The Group of Nine document contained the first reference to the alleged necessity of "strengthening and deepening the ties with certain economic areas (Common Market, EF'TA)."[21] Elsewhere, too, the European Council's declaration had not gone unremarked in Portugal. Proof is provided by a "revolutionary critique" of the Group of Nine document, published by offic-

---

16   Hans Beck, "Portugal und die EG - Notwendigkeit und Möglichkeit einer Gemeinschafts-
     hilfe für Portugal," *Neue Gesellschaft* 22 (1975), p. 532.
17   Cf. Francisco da Costa Gomes, *Sobre Portugal*, Lisbon 1979, p. 59.
18   Story, "Portugal's Revolution" (n. 8), ibid.
19   Francisco da Costa Gomes, *Discursos Politicos*, Lisbon 1976, p. 201.
20   Costa Gomes, *Sobre Portugal*, p. 81.
21   Cited in Guenter Schroeder (ed.): *Portugal: Materialien und Dokumente*, Vol. 3, Giessen,
     1976, p. 133.

ers close to Brigadier Otelo Saraiva de Carvalho, the April 25 coup's military architect who now commanded the MFA special forces (COPCON). The critique found that the economic perspective of the Nine would "reinforce the country's subjugation under a pernicious dependence. Whoever may still have entertained illusions has now lost them considering the recent conditions tied to 'financial aid for Portugal.'"[22]

Melo Antunes himself – and along with him an important MFA faction – would originally have preferred a "Third World option," the emergence – from a position of nonalignment – of a Lisbon/Maputo/Luanda "axis."[23] This position, as has been demonstrated, proved unattainable, with both sides in the East-West conflict "not prepared or not able to tolerate the withdrawal of an associate."[24]

In 1977, after the new constitution had been promulgated a year before, Mario Soares' First Constitutional Government applied for Portuguese EC membership. Soares went so far as to assert that the application had not been "the decision of a government," but "the decision of a people," "the meeting of a country with its own destiny."[25] (Four years later, 67 percent of the Portuguese population had no exact idea about the Common Market.[26])

For their part, the EC Council of Ministers, the European Parliament, the Commission, and the EC Economic and Social Committee unanimously stressed the political aspect – consolidating democracy in Portugal and Southern Europe – as the "overriding objective" of Portugal's EC accession.[27] Just about everybody in the EC, however, also voiced immediate concern about "the economic, financial, agricultural, and social difficulties Portugal will face."[28]

Thus, as during the preceding periods – the dictatorship and the revolutionary interlude -hesitancies again could be perceived, each time fed by either the politics or the economics of the situation. Once again, political and economic considerations seemed to be at odds with each other – a not unfamiliar experience for both parts in the mutual Portugal—EC involvement before and after Portugal's liberation by *golpe*. What, if any, has been the

---

22 Cited ibid., p. 149.
23 Cf. José Medeiros Ferreira, "Aspectos Intemacionais da Revolugao Portuguesa", paper presented at the II International Meeting on Modern Portugal, Durham, 1979, p. 6.
24 Horst Bieber, „Entwicklungen und Zielsetzungen der Aussenpolitik Portugals seit April 1974", *Berichte zur Entwicklung in Spanien, Portugal und Lateinamerika* 3 (1977), p. 32.
25 Mario Soares, "Portugal and Europe," *European Yearbook*, 24 (1978): 16.
26 Cf. *Diario de Noticias*, December 25, 1981, p. 1.
27 Cf. Commission of the European Communities: "Portugal and the European Community", *Europe Information* 34/80, Brussels, 1980, pp. 2, 3.
28 Cf. Eric N. Baklanoff, *The Economic Transformation of Spain and Portugal*, New York/Lisbon, 1978, p. 156, citing the EC Council of Ministers' 1977 joint position regarding the Portuguese candidacy.

underlying common denominator guiding perceptions on either side of the "hesitant relation-ship"?

The standard of joining the EC was first raised, in 1976, by the PS in a politically motivated attempt to attach Portugal more firmly to Western Europe. "Europa connosco" became the slogan symbolizing the PS project to advance its electoral appeal and, at the same time, to consolidate parliamentary democracy in Portugal.

Even in 1972, however, the Caetano regime, after signing the free trade agreement, had evoked the economic perspective of extending the treaty, via its evolutionary clause, into the fields of technological aid and industrialization.[29]

The MFA, for its part, expressly defined its basic aims in 1974 as "Decolonization – Democratization – Development." It is the notion of development that has increasingly been gaining ground in Portugal: As no endogenous and autonomous process of socioeconomic modernization has occurred in the country, integrating Portugal into the EC ought to mean "priming the pump", mobilizing for a dynamic process of structural transformation which is to be pushed from outside.[30]

Although a case can be made that such transformation is the object that has been emerging into the foreground of official Portuguese aspirations, considerations of military security may be considered to rank paramount if an underlying consistency is looked for in Western European attitudes and behavior toward Portugal.

In 1949, under Salazar, "the capital importance of [Portugal's] geostrategic situation" was already deemed "sufficient to justify its admission into NATO, even if internally it was characterized by a dictatorial and autocratic regime."[31] By the time Caetano was negotiating with the Common Market, the "necessity of harmony in consultations between the EEC and NATO" was being stressed by Joseph Luns, and the "enlargement of the Community" was judged "very important in encouraging closer defense cooperation."[32] Conversely, the EC balked in 1974/75 after Portugal had been de facto excluded from NATO intelligence in general and nuclear contingency planning in particular, and the country's NATO membership had even seemed about to come under review at the NATO summit in May 1975.[33]

---

29 Cf. Guinee, *Portugal and the EEC*, pp. 40, 45.

30 Cf. Emani Rodrigues Lopes, "Desinvolvimento Economico e Social e Integracao Europeia. Dois Desafios para a Decada 80," Manuscript, 1981, pp. 23-24 and passim; excerpts printed in *Diario de Noticias*, May 26, 1981, pp. 17 ss.

31 Cf. Assemblée de l'Atlantique Nord, Commission Economique: "La Situation économique et les besoins d'aide économique et militaire du Portugal", Doc. Y 87-EC/P (81), May l, 1981, p. 2.

32 The latter by the United Kingdom's Geoffrey Rippon; for both quotes, cf. Guinee, *Portugal and the EEC*, p. 81.

33 For details, cf. Szulc, "Washington and Lisbon", pp. 42 ss.

The EC's more affluent "center" is, of course, identical with most of NATO's "core" members, promoting and facilitating joint action. Moreover, the North Atlantic Alliance, to the EC countries, offers a habitual military substitute for a European Defense Community nowhere in sight, and security considerations are rather automatically invoked in arguments about EC policies. In a West German official's discussion of the second EC enlargement's consequences for the Mediterranean, the very first sentence deduced the "special importance, to the EC," of that region from its "strategic situation."[34]

Rather habitually, when considering possible EC solutions for Mediterranean countries' economic problems, the specter has been evoked of a possible "rise in the influence of other, rival, powers", meaning the Soviet Union, "with potentially important strategic implications for the Community".[35] Concerning, more specifically, Portugal's accession demand, it was held that the North Atlantic Alliance also had "to take an active interest in that country's economic development" because "recent events lend even more urgency to enforcing NATO's southern flank", and Portugal's economic stability was seen as a necessary prerequisite for the country "to keep its defense engagements".[36]

Security considerations, however, even if they do not provide the sole explanation for Western European attitudes toward Portugal, may combine with built-in sociopolitical resistances in the country itself against more than minimal structural change. As an alternative to socioeconomic development, a stagnating "marginal" society in Portugal remains more than a mere "figment of imagination",[37] continuing to offer bases to NATO, migrant labor (when and if welcomed again by the more prosperous EC countries), a convenient, if limited outlet for Common Market exports, and attractive resorts for tourism.

Portugal's Polity and Economy: A Persistent Structural Crisis

Between April 1974 and December 1978, Portugal has had 16 governments – 6 of them provisional (until the new constitution's promulgation in 1976), the

---

34 Rudolf Morawitz (FRG Ministry of Economics), "Die Auswirkungen der Süderweiterung der Europäischen Gemeinschaft auf das Mittelmeerbecken", *Europa-Archiv*, No. 6 (1980), p. 179.
35 Robert Taylor, "Implications for the Southern Mediterranean Countries of the Second Enlargement of the European Community", *Europe Information*, Brussels (1980), p. 15. Cf. also the literature cited by Heinz Kramer, "Die Europäische Gemeinschaft und der Mittelmeerraum", *Jahrbuch für Ost-West-Fragen 1979*, Cologne, 1979, p. 317, n. 3.
36 Assemblée de l'Atlantique Nord, "La Situation économique", p. 3.
37 Cf. Lopes, "Desinvolvimento", p. 18.

other 10 constitutional. The most recent parliamentary election – the fifth since 1976 – were held on October 6, 1985. If the popular vote had been moving to the right slowly but steadily until 1980 (from 40 to 47.5 percent of votes cast), the trend was stopped in 1983, after the governing conservative-liberal coalition Alianca Democrática (AD) had fallen apart. However, the de facto social-democratic Socialist Party (Partido Socialista, PS), which polled just above 36 percent and thus a plurality of the vote had, in matters of economic policy, already made clear that it could be expected to look more after business than labor interests.

The Ninth Constitutional Government with Mário Soares as prime minister was based on a bloco central, including the conservative-liberal Partido Social Democrata (PSD), the party that had been, before the 1983 elections, the major AD coalition partner. Following the collapse of the Soares-led coalition in June 1985 and facing the impending loss of his own presidential powers in July, General Eanes dissolved the Assembly on July 10, setting October 6, 1985 for anticipated general elections.

In Portugal, large differences in electoral behavior have persisted, corresponding mainly to deep socioeconomic and sociocultural rifts between the country's North, Center, and South. Thus, the Communist Party (Paitido Comunista Português, PCP) has continued to attract between 14 and 19 percent of the electorate, mainly among the "agnostic" rural and industrial proletariat of the Lisbon-Setubal "industrial belt" and the sparsely populated agrarian South. The PSD and the conservative Social Democratic Center (Centro Democrático Social, CDS) have derived their main electoral strength from among the small and medium peasantry of the populous North; the PSD, at the same time, has been competing with the PS for the vote of the urban white collar strata and part of the more skilled Porto and Lisbon industrial workers.

Apart from socio-cultural differences between Continental Portugal's "two (or even three) nations," electoral movements and governmental instability may be traced, in large part, back to the fact that, while a *social* majority was resolved to break with the Salazarist dictatorship's more extreme political, social, and economic inequalities, deep and continuing rifts have persisted about the scope and direction a transformation of the Portuguese society's hierarchies and values ought to assume. These rifts have made themselves particularly felt among the electorate and membership of the two largest political parties, PS and PSD. Thus, a *political* majority in favor of a distinct alternative did not – in spite of the 1976 constitution's socialist commitments – assert itself, and the "limited" social revolution occurring during 1974/75 immediately after the military coup has been succeeded by what might be termed a "limited" restoration.

The "socialist" PS developed out of the Acao Socialista Portuguésa (ASP), founded during 1964 in Geneva and later admitted into the Socialist

International. With the support of the West German Social Democratic Party (SPD) and the Friedrich Ebert-Stiftung (FES), the ASP was transformed into the PS at Bad Münstereifel (FRG) in 1973. The report of its general secretary Mário Soares at the time found it lacking not only in organizational capacity but also in theoretical training and reflection.[38] While verbally rejecting, in its 1974 program, "social democratic" solutions maintaining, "on purpose or in fact, capitalist structures", it had, by 1976 (strongly influenced and financed by SPD and FES[39], and probably also receiving U.S. money "funneled by the Central Intelligence Agency through Western European Socialist parties and labor unions"[40]) developed into an "orthodox Western party."[41]

Twice, large parts of its left wing seceded from the PS. A recent *International Herald Tribune* commentary described Soares as "probably farthest to the right among Western European socialist party leaders", blaming his autocratic regime for the lack of inner-party democracy.[42] With Soares as prime minister, the PS formed the I Constitutional Government in 1976/77 as a minority cabinet and led, in 1978, the II Constitutional Government under an informal arrangement with the CDS. These two administrations were succeeded in 1978/79, due to lack of a parliamentary majority, by three presidential cabinets of "independents", the first two ranging from liberal to conservative, the third a mere caretaker administration headed by a progressive Catholic, Maria de Lurdes Pintasilgo.

---

38 For details, cf. Partido Socialista, ed., *Destruir o sistema - Construir uma NovaVida*, n. p., 1973, pp. 25, 27, 31, 39.

39 The only SPD statement offering any quantitative information referred, in January 1975, to DM 882,000 in FES aid for political training and organization building (cf. "Sozialdemokraten helfen," *Sozialdemokrat Magazin*, No. 1 [1975]: 21). A news report specified in 1979 that the FES had altogether supported the PS with DM 10-15 mio; in 1977 alone, 2.9 mio of these were paid out of FRG government subsidies (cf. "Immer auf der Sonnenseite des Lebens," *Der Spiegel* 33, No. 16, April 16, 1979, p. 47). When former West German Chancellor Willy Brandt visited Portugal and conferred with the PS during October 19-21, 1974, the SPD did not mince its words, commenting that Brandt's travel made "plain the influence Germany's social democracy is exerting on the development of democracies in Europe" (Friedhelm März, "Solidarität mit Portugal," *Sozialdemokrat Magazin*, No. 11 [1974]: 14). Half a year later, Brandt stated that "ideological export models" in Portugal would "not be tolerated" ("Vor Ideologie-Export gewarnt," *Vorwärts*, July 3, 1975). A press article friendly to the Socialist International has been quite candid in reporting that, as West German trade union officials traveled to Portugal, "it was not uncommon that they carried a suitcase full of money as a gesture of solidarity" (Nina Grunenberg, "Frieden, Freiheit und ein Traum: Die Sozialistische Internationale," *Die Zeit*, Dec. 26, 1980, p. 11). The report's further assertion that "dependencies did not result" may, however, be called into question, considering Soares' own judgment, quoted above, on the PS's initial lack in theoretical training and the party's subsequent 'social democratization.'

40 *New York Times*, September 25, 1975, pp. 1, 25.

41 Tom Gallagher: "Portugal's Bid for Democracy: The Role of the Socialist Party", *West European Politics* 2 (1979), p. 203.

42 Cf. John Darnton, "Soares - The Comeback of a Natural Politician", *International Herald Tribune*, April 27, 1983, p. 5.

The CDS, established in 1974 by public figures from the Caetano regime's economy and bureaucracy, has most consistently appealed to "those groups which [were] most content with the old system."[43] It was the only party to vote against the 1976 constitution.

Also founded in 1974, the PSD experienced even more profound factional strife than the PS. In the course of impassioned internal debates (followed by several splits), whether the party was essentially a moderate-to-progressive group concerned with a selective opposition to post-1974 revolutionary results or a conservative organization fundamentally opposed to the revolution, the PSD, under the direction of Francisco Sá Carneiro (who had led the short-lived "liberal wing" of the Salazarist state party Acçao Nacional Popular and was killed in a 1980 plane crash) moved steadily toward the right.[44] In the 1979 and 1980 parliamentary elections, the Aliança Democrática (AD), a coalition of PSD and CDS with a smaller monarchical group, won an absolute majority of seats. When Sá Carneiro's successor as prime minister, Francisco Pinto Balsemão, attempted to steer a more liberal course, the PSD's internal discords erupted with a vengeance that twice resulted in Balsemão's resignation and finally led to the elections of April 1983.

The PCP, finally, only gained a minority representation in the first six provisional governments. Banned in 1927 and viciously repressed between 1933 and 1974, conditioned by what have been most aptly termed the "traumatic experiences" of a "Hobbesian world",[45] it has rightly been judged still a "party from the times of Dimitrov", with a "hardly fertile theoretical dogmatism.[46] However, it had been the only party to survive in the underground; at least in the Alentejo, by its tradition of resistance, it was firmly established among the exploited rural workers.

It was the rural workers of the Alentejo, as has been indicated, together with the workers of the Lisbon-Setúbal "industrial belt" and the dwellers of the shantytowns or miserable quarters of Porto, Lisbon, and Setubal, that during 1974/75 contributed to the beginnings of a social revolution by occupying latifundist farms, vacant government and private housing, finally industrial firms whose owners were either declaring themselves bankrupt or seeking to close down their factories. Workers', occupants', and residents' commissions were formed to manage cooperatives, voice demands, organize strikes, and push for government support. The PCP, but also smaller, more militant groups of the revolutionary Left (especially PRP, the Partido Revo-

43   Ben Pimlott, "Parties and Voters in the Portuguese Revolution", *Parliamentary Affairs* (Winter 1977), p. 42.

44   Cf. ibid., p. 41; Tom Gallagher: "The 1979 Portuguese General Election", *Luso-Brasilian Review* 18 (1981), p. 256.

45   Tom Gallagher, "The Portuguese Communist Party and Eurocommunism", *Political Quarterly* 50 (1979), pp. 205, 206.

46   Marcio Moreira Alves, *Les Soldats socialistes du Portugal*, Paris, 1975, p. 156.

lucionario do Proletariado, and MES, the Movimento de Esquerda Socialista) came to secure influence among the military, workers committees and trade unions, municipal administrations, and part of the mass media.

Because of prevailing paradigms and even the popular "demonology" of the East-West conflict, scholarly and political assessments of the years 1974-75 have tended to play down the role of Portuguese social movements, as well as of the smaller organized groups on the left. Instead, concentrating on political elites – parties and their leaderships – and arguing along the familiar lines of the "pluralism vs. totalitarianism" approach, interpretations have usually stressed inter-party strife, especially between the PS and PCP, and have tended to cast the latter party in the role of the acting villain, while the PS was pictured as the reacting, finally triumphant martyr. The popularity of that perception was enhanced, of course, by the presentation of the Portuguese situation put forward abroad by Mário Soares and his followers. However, it enormously simplified the realities of a social eruption in which neither the MFA nor the Communist Party were pulling all the strings.[47]

Accordingly, when the MFA *reacted* to the social movement in the South and Center by increasingly intervening directly into the political process, ideological conflicts began to divide the officers into warring factions. At the same time, the conservative peasantry of the North remained opposed and indeed, encouraged by the Catholic Church, became violently hostile to the leftward trend.

After the North had, by sheer numerical weight of its people, decided the 1975 Constituent Assembly elections in favor of the PS (and the PSD), the PS increasingly challenged both the PCP and MFA. A military-political coalition came to unite the MFA's moderate socialist faction, "operational" officers extolling traditional military professionalism over structural social change, and the PS. It proved its effectiveness on and after November 25, 1975, when an uprising of left-wing units was suppressed by measures so carefully prepared that they have been judged equal to a "centrist coup", "coolly planned and executed" by troops under the command of Lieutenant-

---

47 More sober accounts have repeatedly disclaimed the "gross oversimplification to view today's (i.e. Summer 1975) political scene in Portugal exclusively as a forum in the battle between Democratic freedom and Communist dictatorship" (Tad Szulc, "Volatile Portugal", *New Republic*, August 16-23, 1975, p. 18). In contrast to Mário Soares' speech making "as the demagogic defender of socialism and democracy. . . struggling against the forces of totalitarianism" (Robert Harvey, *Portugal: Birth of a Democracy*, London, 1978, p. 39), former PS Agricultural Minister Lopes Cardoso has always insisted that the "hot summer" of 1975 cannot be considered as "um periodo de pre-ditadura comunista" (*Tempo*, November 26, 1981, p. 11). Cardoso had, in 1978, left the PS and joined in establishing the UEDS, or Uniao da Esquerda Democrata Socialista. That small party formed an electoral alliance with the PS in 1980 which was dissolved again a year later.

Colonel Ramalho Eanes",[48] who thereby prepared the ground-work for his later succession to President Costa Gomes.

These events, expanding into a purge of left-wing officers, put an end to the existence of the MFA. The military "returned to the barracks"; only the Council of the Revolution remained as a military constitutional court until it was abolished in 1982.

The new constitution's economic and social parts had already been voted by the Constituent Assembly between August and October 1975. Promulgated on April 25, 1976, it proclaimed as its fundamental principle the "plurality of democratic expression and democratic political organization" in order "to ensure the transition to socialism", emphasizing the rights of workers' committees, trade unions, and self-managed (rural or industrial) cooperatives. The nationalizations of 1975 in industry and finance were confirmed; precedence was given to the further socialization (not, however, nationalization) of the means of production.

Yet political parties and governments did not rally behind the constitutional model of "socialist pluralism" nor attempt to realize its prospects. When the revised constitutional text was voted by the AD and PS in 1982, previous references to the peaceful continuation of the revolutionary process and to the intended realization of a self-management economy (according to Soares, "excessive ideological ideas of more or less utopian character;[49] the "fundamental law's Marxist, collectivist, militarizing orientation," in AD terms[50]) had disappeared. The emphasis on agrarian reform had been reduced, the indicative character of economic planning appropriately strengthened.

In the meantime, the pre-1974 bureaucracy has largely remained in place, "rather than being modernized by the infusion of new people and new ideas."[51] And the "men of April 24," as ironical parlance began to call the former administrative, economic, and military elites, have increasingly regained their ground – not least as a result of the considerable influence in military and civil matters wielded by Ramalho Eanes. Promoted to general after November 25, voted into the president's office in 1976 and again in 1980, Eanes early commenced to press not only for apolitical professionalism and discipline in his military appointments (implying the renewed ascendancy of conservative officers), but also, in forming two presidential cabinets, for a return of "technocrats" linked to the overthrown dictatorship.

48 Cf. Ben Pimlott, "Portugal's Soldiers in the Wings," *New Statesman*, September 24, 1976, p. 393.
49 Cf. Partido Socialista, ed., *Confiar no PS - Apostar em Portugal*, Lisbon, 1979, p. 67.
50 Aliança Democrática, "Programa de Revisão Constitucional - Linhas Gerais," *Povo Livre*, September 17, 1980.
51 Kenneth Maxwell: "A Evoluçao Contemporanea da Sociedade Portuguesa," in: Fundaçao Calouste Gulben-kian, ed., *II International Conference on the Portuguese Economy*, vol. 1, p. 32.

At the same time, Eanes – at the outset nicknamed the "symbol of socialism with a stone face" – by his stem, taciturn manner managed to convey the impression of political integrity, seriousness, and competence. If that made him stand out personally among his political surroundings, the powers conferred on him by the constitution (which he did not hesitate to use) have put him into the role of institutional opponent confronting, among several prime ministers, Soares last though far from least. The latter, who fought an underdog campaign in 1986 against Freitas do Amaral, became Eanes' successor, since constitutional rules bar the general from running for a third term.

In view of growing public disillusionment with party in-fighting, governmental stalling over key issues, mounting corruption, and an overdose of IMF-decreed Social Darwinist austerity policy pursued by Soares, an "eanist" movement provisionally called "ex-CNARPE" (after the 1980 Comissão Nacional de Apoio a Recandidatura do Presidente Eanes) sprang up, crystallizing into the Partido Renovadora Democratica (PRD) during February 1985. Still in its organizational throes and, so far, without Eanes' official blessings, the new "party of the president" did surprisingly well in the October 1985 parliamentary elections. At least part of its potential constituency, however, was preempted by the early declaration of candidacy by the popular Maria de Lurdes Pintasilgo, who supported Eanes in 1980 and has been organizing another politically renovative group, the Movimento para o Aprofundamento da Democracia, or MAD. It may be doubted whether the attempt at an "Eanist alternative" turns out to be the viable political solution it purports to be. The impression left by the "Eanistas'" maneuvering is not unlike that of the Aliança Democrática which, having promised to effect *mudança* – change – instead pursued a policy defined "rather by negation of what it [was] opposed to, than by an affirmation of its own project."[52]

The Eanists' emergence, however, adds to the pall of indecision once more enveloping Portuguese politics. Economically tied to the prescriptions of a renewed "government by the IMF", the Soares administration – the only coalition both, in contrast to a PS/PCP alliance, practically conceivable and not previously tried out—was stymied by the mere perspective of the 1986 presidential elections.[53] If President Eanes may be said to have been the cement holding together the disjointed *bloco central*, the prospect of the presidential candidacy was also sufficient to trigger, between November 1984 and January 1985, first a two-week coalition crisis between the two governing parties and, subsequently, renewed in-fighting among PSD factions that toppled party chairman Mota Pinto. And it was presidential politics which finally broke the coalition apart in June 1985 following the election of a new

52   Mario Raposo, "A AD, O Bloco Central e a Definiçao do Estado," *Diario de Noticias*, Nov. 27, 1981, p. 2.
53   Cf. José Rebelo, "Grandes manoeuvres electorales sur fond d'austérité," *Le Monde diplomatique* (October 1984), p. 22.

leader by the PSD convention, Anibal Cavaco Silva. In spite of a comfortable parliamentary majority, therefore, the *bloco central* became a symbol of the apparent fragility and paralysis of the political system in a country where, "in terms of behavior and psychology, it is not clear how much really changed" after 1974.[54]

During 1983, consumer prices in Portugal rose by 25 percent. Real wages per head fell by 8 percent and by mid-1985 were below 1972 levels, with "official" unemployment standing at 11 percent and mounting. The current account deficit in the balance of payments had, by 1982, widened to $3.2 billion, or more than 10 percent of GDP. Three-fourths of what the Portuguese ate had to be imported. The foreign debt, with approximately $13 billion, had come to surpass the value of foreign exchange reserves. In 1984, Portugal's external debt service was $1.8 billion.[55]

During recent years, the country certainly has been affected domestically by repeated droughts and internationally by a renewed deterioration in its terms of trade. The rate of inflation, however, between 1977 and 1983, already had attained an annual average of 22 percent. The "statistical" unemployment rate has fluctuated around 8 percent over the same period; because of contradictory data and debatable statistical methods, however, annual estimates have run as high as 15 percent. Of the nominally unemployed, only 24 percent are receiving unemployment benefits. Continued and considerable underemployment (especially in agriculture) is a virtual certainty. In 1983, public and private enterprises started stemming losses by ceasing to pay wages on a massive scale, counting on workers to show up to avoid being fired for absenteeism. Portugal is at present the one country in Western Europe where an estimated army of 150,000 workers was owed, during the first half of 1984, some $187 million in back wages, most of which they will probably never receive.[56]

In desperate straits because of its huge external debt and accelerating current account deficit, the country again has had to negotiate for an IMF loan. To obtain a stand-by credit of 445 mio special drawing rights and additional compensatory financing of 258 mio SDRs, the Soares government, in a "letter of intent" to the IMF signed in 1983, had to agree to a rigorous austerity policy. While the current account deficit was halved to $1.6 bio in 1983 (and is expected to be halved again during 1984, running up to an estimated $830 mio), steeply decreasing imports were signaling the economic and social impact of the governmental austerity measures as, once again, food subsidies

54 Maxwell, "A Evolucao," pp. 31-32.
55 For the figures, cf. OECD, *Economic Survey: Portugal*, Paris 1984, pp. 16, 41; "Portugal weiterhin auf Restriktionskurs," *Neue Zürcher Zeitung*, June 27, 1984, p. 19; "Seminário para Banqueiros Estrangeiros Análisa Política Económica Portuguesa," *Diario de Noticias*, Nov. 6, 1984, p. 2.
56 Cf. Frederick Painton, "Portugal: Bare Survival," *Time*, April 30, 1984, p. 10.

were cut, public utility prices raised, new taxes introduced, and credit costs pushed up.

The situation is not novel, neither to the Portuguese nor to their prime minister – with the one exception that the economic "recovery policy" tied, in 1977, to another IMF credit brought down the first Soares administration, admittedly a minority government. After Portugal had raised, during the first eight months of 1976 alone, some $750 mio in loans from Common Market reserve banks and, in 1977, had secured foreign government and commercial credits of $600 mio, a $750 million OECD "package" was made contingent on a Portuguese stand-by agreement with the IMF. Desperate to replace short-term borrowing (still $1.3 bio by mid-1978, after restructuring had already started) by medium-and long-term debt, Soares twice during 1977 introduced austerity measures which, however, failed to satisfy the OECD and the IMF. In the end, Soares went before parliament with a program acceptable to the IMF and was defeated by a vote of no confidence.[57]

Data such as these point not merely to conjunctural disadvantages but to structural distortions of the Portuguese economy, inherited from 40 years of an autocracy traditionalist by intent, colonialist in ideology and economic base, and corporatist in its meshing of business and government operations to a point where the controlling "one hundred families" in industry and agriculture could feel protected, even supported, in their "delayed-capitalist" attitude.[58] Conglomerate holdings, such as Companhia União Fabril (CUF), Champalimaud, Borges/ Quina, and Espirito Santo e Comercial, wielded enormous power by controlling banks, insurance companies, and large parts of refining, shipbuilding, steel, and cement production.[59] The large majority of firms in the manufacturing industry, however, were and are small to medium, with 5-10 or 20-50 employees and a low capital- labor ratio.[60]

For their output, the cartelized large groups – and whole sectors of inefficient industries in their shadow – profited from exploiting the preferences of the colonial "escudo area," from delayed tariff reductions under the EFTA treaty, but especially from "tight controls . . . of the level of industrial wag-

---

57 For the data, cf. Rodrigo Marques Guimaraes, "Die portugiesische Währungspolitik," *ETFA Bulletin*, No. 1, 1977, p. 12; Basil Caplan: "Interview with Rui Vilar, Vice-Governor of the Bank of Portugal," *Banker* (October 1978), p. 54; McCauley, "IMF Troubles" (as in n. 7), pp. 154-55 (the quote is on p. 155); Banco de Portugal, *Report of the Board of Directors for 1979*, Lisbon 1980, p. 101.

58 Cf. Lawrence S. Graham, Portugal: *The Decline and Collapse of an Authoritarian Order*, Beverly Hills/ London, 1975, p. 18; Harry M. Makler: "The Portuguese Industrial Elite and its Corporative Relations," *Economic Development and Cultural Change* 24 (1976), pp. 498, 509.

59 For details, cf. Mario Bacalhau: "Nacionalizações e Socialização" *Vida Mundial*, May 1, 1975, pp. 23/24.

60 Cf. Esser et al., Portugal (as in n. 1), pp. 72-73.

es".[61] Qualified labor was scarce in a country that spent, by 1971, only 2 percent of its GNP on education. The obsolete educational system and shortage of teachers resulted in a labor force where hardly 10 percent had received a secondary and 2 percent a higher education; between 20 and 30 percent were considered illiterate.[62] In agriculture, the corresponding percentages for farmers, by 1968, were 1.3 percent with a secondary or higher education and an illiteracy of 43 percent, which has decisively contributed to their low technological receptiveness and innovatory capacity.[63]

Circumstances such as these further aggravated the drastic deficits of Portuguese agriculture, which still employs one-quarter of the labor force, while contributing less than 10 percent to GDP. This has meant, for instance, that Portugal's agricultural trade deficit quadrupled from 1970 to 1973.[64] The virtual stagnation of agricultural productivity and produce have been "a commonplace of any analysis of the Portuguese economy over the last two decades".[65] In the northern half of the country, subsistence peasant farming has been perpetuated on soils fragmented by hereditary tradition; capitalist farming on medium-sized plots has made only slow headway. In the southern half, traditional absentee ownership of big estates produced extensive farming and – even more so than in industry – chronically underpaid (farm) workers.[66] Thus, by 1968, landholdings from 0.5 to 5 hectares numbered 77.7 percent of all landholdings, but only occupied 14.9 percent of the overall farmed area, while holdings over 100 hectares, numbering 0.6 percent of the total, controlled 45.3 percent of the land under cultivation.[67] The State Secretariat from Agriculture had no rural extension services worth the name.

Legal as well as clandestine migration on a massive scale – especially affecting the districts in the north – became the means to absorb population

61 World Bank, Portugal, p. 1. Cheap and disciplined labor also played a significant role when, after 1963, the Salazar regime decided "to step up the rate of economic development in the face of mounting defense [i.e., colonial war] expenditures" by stimulating foreign direct investment (cf. Baklanoff, Economic Transformation, pp. 105-06): Multinational firms from West Germany, the United Kingdom and the United States responded to an extent that reduced part of the colonial power Portugal's domestic - and, it might be added, overseas - economy to a "state of virtual 'colonisation'" itself (Council of Europe, Report, p. 15).

62 Cf. Maria Emilia Freire, "The Economic Value of Education in Portugal," in Fundação Calouste Gulbenkian, ed., II International Conference on the Portuguese Economy, Vol. 2, p. 1029.

63 Cf. Secretariado Tecnico do Planeamento, "Alguns Aspectos Fundamentais da Economia Portuguesa antes de 25 de Abril," unpubl. manuscript, Lisbon, 1975, p. 30.

64 Cf. Esser et al., Portugal, p. 17.

65 A. Cortez Lobao et al., "Politica Agricola e Integração na CEE," in Fundação Calouste Gulbenkian, ed., II International Conference on the Portuguese Economy, Vol. 2, p. 761.

66 Cf. Albert Silbert, Le Portugal méditerranéen d la fin de l'ancien régime, Vol. 2, Lisbon 1978, pp. 720, 752, 822; José Cutileiro, A Portuguese Rural Society, Oxford, 1971, pp. 13 ss., 59 ss.

67 Cf. Manuel Villaverde Cabral, "Agrarian Structures and Recent Rural Movements in Portugal," Journal of Peasant Studies 5 (1978), p. 438, Table 9a.

increase and avoid military service in Africa. Migration drained undeveloped, already depleted districts "of the most active and dynamic parts of their population... contribut[ing] to a further degradation."[68] Emigrant remittances, together with tourism receipts, helped and are still contributing to cover the external trade deficit. Mainly invested for the purpose of "moving up in the village social ladder through the purchase of prestige symbols", this income provided "the trimmings of modem civilization, without altering the infrastructure", and thus did not promote technological progress but rather helped to perpetuate subsistence farming.[69]

The Salazar-Caetano economy was thus based on a "dependency on the export of labor, reliance on remittances, tourism, and colonial balances to cover metropolitan deficits, [plus] the action of the state to repress collective bargaining and hold down wage rates."[70] These safety valves – including the colonial raw material and the international labor markets – finally closed for Portugal during 1974/75.

A wave of occupation of latifundist farms in the Alentejo by wage laborers during the revolutionary period transformed approximately 1.1 mio hectares into 550 collective production units (UCPs) and cooperatives where the PCP had a strong influence. Governmental decrees in July 1975 legalized these seizures to a large extent; however, the occupied estates never controlled more than 14 percent of the country's cultivated soils.[71] In 1976, the Agrarian Reform Zone was limited substantially to the districts Evora, Beja, Portalegre, and Setubal, but 500,000 additional hectares which fell under the decrees of 1975 never were expropriated; credits initially available for investments and for the payment of wages were increasingly restricted. The Basic Agrarian Reform Law of 1977, which superseded the decrees of 1975, not only expanded "reserves" returned to former landowners, it also accorded considerable discretionary powers to the agricultural ministry for their further augmentation.

Interpreted by both the AD and PS in terms of their attempt to wrest political influence from the PCP, the law has inaugurated a continuing attempt to replace collective farms by individual, small to medium-sized plots. By the end of 1981, altogether 135 UCPs or cooperatives had been disbanded; many more were severely threatened in their existence. Stymied for essentially political reasons, the attempt at agrarian reform in the Alentejo could only

---

68 Heinz-Michael Stahl, "Portuguese Migration and Regional Development," in Fundação Calouste Gulbenkian, ed., II International Conference on the Portuguese Economy, Vol. 1, pp. 391-92.
69 Caroline Brettell, "Emigration from Rural Portugal," Paper presented at the II International Meeting on Modern Portugal, Durham, N.C., 1979, p. 8.
70 Maxwell, "A Evolução Contemporanea" (as in n. 51), pp. 33-34.
71 Cf. Afonso de Barros, "A Reforma Agraria em Portugal e o Desinvolvimento Economico e Social," Revista Crítica de Ciências Sociais 3 (1979), p. 61; Cabral, "Agrarian Structures," p. 427.

contribute in a very limited way to solving the social and economic problems of agricultural employment and productivity. In 1977/78, 73 percent of jobs were permanent and 27 percent seasonal – a net reverse of the 1968 ratio, when only 35 percent of agricultural workers had been permanently employed. However, out of 71,900 workers in 1975/76, only 59,000 remained, representing 13.3 percent of all paid labor in agriculture; they produced but 9 percent of GAP. Three years later, governmental policies in the Alentejo had left a mere 25,000 workers.[72]

Cattle raising and mechanization had at first substantially expanded on the UCPs. In the Agrarian Reform Zone as a whole – of whose cultivated soils, paid agricultural labor, and GAP, UCPs and cooperatives never represented more than 30 to 35 percent – yields of major crops, however, seem to have more or less stagnated during the 1974-78 period. Stagnation of crop yields in Portugal's North was hardly less pronounced during the same period. Severe droughts during and after 1980, as mentioned above, contributed to a further deterioration of agricultural production.[73]

A law alleviating conditions of tenancy (which, in 1968, had accounted for 14 percent of landholdings) was passed in 1975, but partly revoked in 1977. Regionalized extension services, but no agrarian reform centers, have been established north of Castelo Branco. In 1979, an attempt was started to cycle emigrant remittances, by a system of saving-credit, into the installation of agro-pastoral enterprises. General borrowing modalities have only started to become less complex, after the Financing Institute for the Development of Agriculture and Fisheries (IFADAP) was established in 1977/78 as an attempt to centralize credit facilities. Less than 5 percent of overall credit has gone to the agricultural sector,[74] while the World Bank has estimated that more than $400 million in investments would be necessary to solve its most pressing problems.[75]

Further measures would have to include prohibiting further partition, offering incentives for augmenting landholdings, stimulating cooperatives, and presenting a social program for retiring farmers. At the cost of a host of politically influential middlemen, attractive commercial circuits would have to be placed at the farmers' disposal; and the severe lack of secondary, polytechnical, and other advanced education would have to be attacked. However, for fear of meeting resistance and alienating electoral support, successive AD, as well as PS (-led) governments have abstained from any attempt at a comprehensive agrarian reform in the North. .

---

72 Cf. Barros, "A Reforma Agraria," pp. 61, 66; Secretariado e Uniões das UCPs e Cooperativas Agricolas, ed., 6.a Conferéncia da Reforma Agrária, Evora, 1982, pp. 3-4, 12, 17-18.
73 Cf. Barros, "A Reforma Agraria," pp. 61, 64; OECD, Economic Survey: Portugal, Paris, 1980, p. 26.
74 According to Robert Graham, "Portugal - Banking, Finance and Investment", Financial Times, July 2, 1981, p. 1.
75 Cf. Diario de Noticias, July 12, 1981, p. 25.

In industry and finance, banks, insurance, transports, and basic industries – largely controlled by the conglomerate groups listed above – were nationalized in 1975. The enlarged public sector, "instead of being an instrument for the full socialization of the economy," never constituted more than "a partial solution in the frame of a market economy."[76] In 1975, it accounted for 11.5 percent of employment (France, 8.7 percent; Italy, 11.6 percent), 33.6 percent of gross fixed investment (33.5 and 28 percent), and 14 percent of sales (10 and 8.1 percent).[77] In manufacturing, private enterprise predominates even more, with 79.5 percent of sector GDP and 90 percent of employment.[78]

Concentrated in the large, regionally centralized, capital-intensive basic industry firms, the public sector has offered little incentive to the improvement of employment and the regional imbalance. In spite of their control over banking, public authorities never got around to define a coherent investment financing policy. After advent of the austerity policy, nationalized enterprises during 1977/78 began—and have continued—to borrow heavily abroad, so that their financial position has deteriorated very significantly.[79] Moreover, the public sector was used as a pasture for political patronage by successive governments, under whose rapid turnover administrative reform has come nearly nowhere. Few removals from the Salazar-Caetano bureaucracy actually took place, and there has been little change in the traditional operation of economic ministries.[80]

Altogether, no initiative for a comprehensive strategy of restructuring and diversifying the Portuguese economy has come from the public sector. Instead, its existence has merely served to trigger sharp political conflict over public and private sector limits. After the constitutional revision, cement and fertilizer industries, insurance, and banking were opened up to private enterprise in 1983.

For the private sector, the problems of regional imbalance, disadvantageous firm size, and low productivity may conveniently be illustrated by referring to textiles and clothing, with 26.3 percent (1977) the single largest item in an export balance which has continued to concentrate on traditional products highly sensible to changes in consumer income, i.e. , (besides textiles), cork, wood, and leather products, wines, and glassware. In 1974, small firms (less than 10 employees) in the textile and clothing sector numbered 17,

76 Paulo Pitta e Cunha, "Portugal and the European Economic Community", paper presented at the II International Meeting on Modern Portugal, Durham, N.C., 1979, p. 35.
77 Cf. Ivo Pinto: "Sector Publico Empresaria antes e depois do 11 de Marco", *Analise Social* 12 (1976), p. 745.
78 Data for 1977; cf. Celso Ferreira, "Aspectos Economicos do Sector Publico Empresarial," *Economia e Socialismo* 4, No. 40 (1979), pp. 7, 17.
79 Cf. OECD, *Economic Survey: Portugal*, 1984, pp. 27-28.
80 Cf. Lawrence S. Graham, „Problems of Portuguese Bureaucracy and Prospects for Administrative Reform", paper presented at the II International Meeting on Modern Portugal, Durham, N. C., 1979, pp. 8, 19, 23.

and medium—sized (10-50 employees) 45 percent; only 22 percent had more than 100 employees (only 9.7 percent in manufacturing as a whole, where figures were even more reminiscent of mere workshop size). Global industrial productivity has been estimated at one-third to one-fourth of Western European countries[81] In 1981, 40 percent of the textile industry were considered "moribund" and 20 percent "seriously ailing" by the Portuguese Association of Textile Engineers.[82]

Portugal's industry is concentrated excessively along the coast, centering there on the Porto-Braga and Lisbon-Setubal areas. Textiles and clothing again offer only an example: 69 percent of their gross output, in 1975, originated from the districts of Braga and Porto.[83] Inadequate communications, stagnating urbanization, poor social infrastructures, and minimal financial resources continue to function as serious drawbacks of the extensive "hinterland".[84] The 1978 law assigning their own tax receipts and additional allotments of state taxes to mu-nicipal administrations was bitterly fought by the centralized bureaucracy and has become a source of continuous political friction (especially, but not exclusively where a PCP majority exists) between municipal councils and the central government. A new scheme for local authority finance was only adopted in 1984. Regional planning agencies have been established since 1977 but are still embryonic.

The data for the Portuguese economy have been summarized by pointing to a simultaneous "bloqueio estrutural, instabilidade politica e crise económica", fundamentally due to Portugal's transition "from a dependent capitalism, with a determined pattern of accumulation and growth, to a new form of dependency not yet stabilized and internally structured".[85] It is precisely this precarious new dependency of peripheral Portugal with the EC "core" that is at issue when the alternatives of exogenously induced development or further stagnation are envisaged.[86]

---

81 Cf. Esser et al., *Portugal*, pp. 73, 76; Assemblée de l'Atlantique Nord, "La Situation Economique" (as in n. 31), p. 16.
82 Cf. *Diario de Noticias*, November 3, 1981, p. 25.
83 Cf. OECD, *Regional Problems and Policies in Portugal*, Paris, 1978, p. 39; Bodo Freund, *Portugal*, Stuttgart, 1979, p. 93.
84 Cf. OECD, *Regional Problems*, p. 47.
85 Mario Murteira, "Trajectoria de Longo Prazo do Capitalismo Português," *Economia e Socialismo* 3, No. 32/33 (1978), pp. 28, 30.
86 António Inocencio Pereira, "Adesão a CEE: Reflectindo sobre Incertezas", *Diario de Noticias*, January 4, 1982, p. 19.

The Halting Rapprochement: Common Market Policy Constraints and Portuguese Non-Reciprocity

If in 1970 the level of GDP per capita was 5 times higher in Hamburg and 4 times higher in Paris compared to the EC's poorest regions in the west of Ireland, the margin, by 1977/78, of the Community's most prosperous regions (Hamburg, Paris, Brussels) over the Irish west had risen to between 6 and 8. It will increase again drastically to 12:1 between Hamburg and Vila Real-Braganca (or 10:1 for Hamburg over the four poorest Portuguese regions) after Portugal will have joined the Common Market.[87]

Income disparities, however, whether measured at current prices and exchange rates or by comparing purchasing power parities, have been augmenting not only at regional but also at country levels in the Community. If GDP per capita is determined as a percentage of EC average for the EC ten and for the two application countries, a *four-tier community* increasingly emerges, where Denmark and the FRG are leading the upmost group, with Ireland, Italy, Greece, and Spain united at third level, the United Kingdom in between, and *Portugal at a separate bottom tier by 17 to 20 percent.*[88]

Against the background of the general fall and rising disparities in GDP growth, the rise and increasing divergence of inflation rates, the wide differences in exchange rate changes and current account positions in the balance of payments, the absurd common agricultural policy's mounting financial difficulties, and finally, steadily worsening unemployment, "crippling uncertainties"[89] have beset the Common Market. It is faced not just with its second enlargement but with a more profound challenge the Rome Treaty does not seem to be equipped to handle: Inspired "less [by] the Welfare State than [by] a degree of laissez faire which would have dismayed Keynes", that agreement became "a classical statement of the assumption that the free working of the market, if properly policed," would "ensure economic and social progress," promote "the constant improvement of living and working conditions," and "reduce the...backwardness of the less favored regions".[90] The

---

87 Cf. Frieder Schlupp, "Anmerkungen zum Status quo-Europa," *EG-Magazin* 7 (1980), p. 5; Commission of the European Communities, "Wirtschaftliche und sektorielle Aspekte - Analysen der Kommission als Ergänzung zu den Betrachtungen über das Problem der Erweiterung", KOM(78) 220 endg., Brussels, 1978, p. 149.

88 Data for 1976/77; cf. E. C. Hallett, "Economic Convergence and Divergence in the European Community: A Survey of the Evidence", in Michael Hodges and William Wallace, eds., *Economic Divergence in the European Community*, London, 1981, pp. 25 ss.; Loukas Tsoukalis, "Economic Divergence and Enlargement," in Hodges and Wallace, eds., *Economic Divergence*, pp. 152, 153.

89 Commission of the European Communities, "Commission Report on the Mandate of 30 May 1980", COM(81) 300 final, Brussels, 1981, p. 7.

90 The first quote is from Stuart Holland, *The Socialist Challenge*, London, 1975, p. 320; the second is taken from the Preamble of the Rome Treaty.

treaty stresses measures of negative market integration (i.e., the removal of discrimination and trade impediments) at the expense – excepting agriculture – of positive development integration (meaning the introduction and application of common trade cycle, industrial, and social policy instruments), which it treats in a "vague and permissive, instead of definitive and mandatory" manner. The EC, therefore, has remained "bias[ed] against economic union" with its redistributive and welfare aspects, favoring instead a common market limited, essentially, to an industrial and agricultural tax and customs union.[91]

Such a "philosophy" was barely compatible with the Community's functioning as long as the Common Market remained an instrument for drawing together highly developed industrial countries – which, in fact, the EC had originally been designed for, and as long as the business cycle continued to flatten itself out – whereby precisely that environment of sustained economic growth was created that allowed the instruments for implementing the Rome Treaty to be circumscribed in the way they were. Between 1973 and 1975, however, the rug was pulled out from under the EC. The first enlargement augmented the number and area of structurally underdeveloped regions within the Common Market; the oil price-induced recession introduced industrial decline into regions which had been prosperous. With the resulting adjustment problems far from successfully tackled, and with austerity measures persisting in virtually every Western European country, the EC for political and military reasons chose to include, after Ireland. another industrializing society, Greece, while two more countries of the same developmental stage, Spain and Portugal, will enter on January 1, 1986. The Community has not, however, adapted either institutionally or politically to its increasing developmental tasks – and that is the crux of the matter.

In response to the Common Market's first enlargement of 1972, and after a first Council debate in 1971 of "unprecedented inadequacy",[92] the European Regional Development Fund (ERDF) was finally established in 1975. By 1980, the Fund's budget was 1,165 billion EUA (European units of account), or roughly the amount the ERDF had dispensed of during its first three years; by 1983, it had risen to 2 billion ECU (European currency units), still equivalent to only 0.08 percent of the Community's GDP. Until 1984, disbursements were subject to an amended quota system, under which Italy and the United Kingdom received the highest amounts, but France slightly more than Greece and West Germany only a little less than Ireland.

When, in 1979, a quota-free section was introduced for programs in regions "affected by other Community measures" or by especially severe events, the Council limited expenditure to 5 percent of total ERDF endow-

---

91 Cf. Jan Tinbergen, *International Economic Integration*, Amsterdam/London/New York, 1965, pp. 76 ss.; John Pinder, "Positive Integration and Negative Integration", *World Today*, (1968), pp. 90, 97 ss., 100 ss.
92 Walter Hallstein, *Die europäische Gemeinschaft*, Dusseldorf/Wien, 1973, p. 236.

ment. Commission proposals to stock up the quota-free section to 20 percent and shift quotas from states to regions (those with GDP per capita lagging at least 25 percent behind the EC average) were rejected by the Council. Instead, national quotas were merely substituted, in 1984, by ranges indicating the upper and lower limits of member states' shares, without substantially altering the previous allocation (though Ireland's range now surpassed West Germany's by two percentage points, and Greece managed to overtake France by one percentage point). However, the new regulation did stipulate that a part of ERDF appropriations, increasing over three years, up to 20 percent, should be used to finance comprehensive development programs, including multinational Community programs.

Concerning the Mediterranean, the Council during 1979/80 approved the financing of specific measures in the Mezzogiorno and in South-west France both by ERDF quota-free and quota sections, after formally subscribing to the view that the imminent Southern enlargement "could endanger the development of a certain number of weak Community regions".[93] If priorities were thus being established, the Commission in 1983, following demands by Greece, attempted to enlarge the "specific measures" into a package labeled "integrated Mediterranean programs", or IMPs. At a total cost of 6.6 billion ECU (or $4.7 billion), these proposals were to include Greece (approximately 38 percent of appropriations), Italy (nearly 45 percent), and France (17 percent). After the Council failed to react, Greece, at the Dublin EC summit of December 1984, demanded that, as a precondition to continuing negotiations with Spain and Portugal, the IMPs be approved. When other EC governments refused to commit themselves, Greek Prime Minister Andreas Papandreou threatened to veto further accession talks, thus initiating what amounts to a continuing attempt (which Italy has indicated it might join) to pressure the Community into adopting a substantial Mediterranean development program.

At the Dublin summit, in a situation where the established timetable for admitting Spain and Portugal into the EC by January 1, 1986, was at stake, past neglects finally caught up with the Common Market. The developmental challenge it is confronted with by its imminent second enlargement (already underway, as far as Greece is concerned) has become very much apparent since the first EC enlargement. That challenge is now most distinctly typified by the needs of Portugal's – to a substantial part – obsolete industry and agriculture and by corresponding Portuguese hopes for the EC's transformative capacity. Slackening in its economic performance, the EC, however – much like Portugal, if for different reasons – also appears politically weak and structurally stymied.

Under the Free Trade Agreement of 1972 (already referred to in the initial section) as amended in 1976 and 1979, agricultural products – not cov-

---

93   Cf. Commission of the European Communities, *European Regional Development Fund - Fifth Annual Report 1979*, Brussels, 1980, p. 10.

ered by the EFTA Treaty – were included, non-reciprocity for Portugal was retained, and "infant industry" protection was again authorized to be maintained by the country. Tariff preferences, generally around 50 percent, were conceded for several agricultural products, especially tomato concentrates, canned fish, fruit, olives, and certain wines.

However, to the EC, tomato paste, canned sardines, and wines were at the same time "sensitive".products. Their production had been increasing not only in France and Italy, but also in Greece and in the Maghreb and Mashreq countries, which were linked to the Common Market through bilateral cooperation and trade agreements. Consequently, to obtain tariff concessions, Portugal had to accept either floors to its export pricing (sardines), or ceilings to amounts exported (wines), or both (tomato concentrates). Quantitative restrictions, moreover, were also placed on "sensitive" industrial commodities: textiles and clothing, cork and wood (paper) products.

These, however, are exactly the product groups where Portugal is competitive, and if Portugal's trade deficit with the Common Market more than doubled between 1973 and 1978, there is every reason to believe that EC policies have played their part. French, Italian, and Dutch exports of tomato paste into the UK and Denmark, for instance, have been perceptibly subsidized; France and the UK have introduced quotas to protect their textile industries.[94] During accession negotiations with Portugal, the Customs Union "dossier" remained blocked for nine months because the Ten, among themselves, could not agree on howto deal with Portuguese textiles and clothing exports during the (presumably up-to-ten-year) transition period. The formula that finally emerged was that future procedures should be "inspired" by present rules providing for "self-limitation".[95]

The EC pre-accession aid granted to Portugal in 1981 is another case in point. Portugal had asked for 425 million EUA; the Commission, after studying the Portuguese request, proposed 350 million, of which 230 million were to be grants and 120 million loans. The Council reduced the amount by another 75 million and at the same time reversed the ratio between loans and grants (150: 125 million EUA). The final decision was a net result of French-British "in-fighting" over the Community budget.[96]

In the Community, there is a definite tendency during the present recession to try and maintain what remains of social peace "through the prevention

---

94 Cf. Michele Cifarelli, "Stellungnahme des Landwirtschaftsausschusses zum Bericht des Ausschusses fur Aussenwirtschaftsbeziehungen über die Wirtschafts- und Handelsbeziehungen zwischen der Gemeinschaft und Portugal", Europäisches Parlament, Doc. 187/77/rev., September 15, 1977, p. 26; Jimmy Burns, "Le Déficit commercial a doublé durant les quatre premieres années d'application de l'accord de libre-échange", *EFTA-Bulletin*, No. 2 (1980), p. 2.

95 Cf. *Diario de Noticias*, July 12, 1981; author's interviews.

96 Cf. João Vale de Almeida, "Vem ai as Unidades de Conta," *Diario de Noticias*, Oct. 13, 1980, p. 15.

or slowing down of structural adjustment processes",[97] cushioning sectors like textiles, steel, and agriculture against the impact of enlargement. As increasing exports to the Maghreb and Mashreq countries have, moreover, helped the Common Market to offset its huge oil deficit, and as these countries, through their political alignment with the oil-producing states, have gained in geo-strategical (i.e., security) importance, the EC will hardly weaken its position vis a vis them by definitely jeopardizing their export earnings from, again, textile and agricultural products[98] These domestic and foreign policy-induced "sensitivities" apply in a situation where the accession negotiations, to a large part, are "not really negotiations, but rather requests made by Portugal to the Community".[99]

Dilemmas and Risks: Portugal in a Four-Tier European Community

Already by 1977, the EC Commission had concluded that it would be "illusory" to think that the gap in economic development separating Portugal from the Community "could be overcome within the space of a transition period of ten years".[100] Considering available data on the accession's presumable consequences, it moreover stands to reason that (with positive development integration apt to remain, at best, a torso) the country will suffer quite severely from unmitigated negative market integration. The reasons for submitting this argument, apart from those already referred to, may be summed up into the following considerations:

In agriculture, Portugal's main import commodities have been wheat and maize, beef and sugar, roughly 75-90 percent of which have been supplied by the United States and South America. After accession, Portugal will either have to buy these amounts from the EC or pay import levies corresponding to current EC threshold prices. In 1977/78, wheat and maize imports would have cost the country an additional 150 mio units of account (ua) for import levies, or approximately half that sum if trade had been diverted to higher-priced EC cereals. Sugar purchases would have absorbed 47 mio ua and beef imports another 20-25 mio ua.[101]Additional expenditure, therefore, may well

97 E. Guth and H. O. Aeiskens, "Implications of the Second Enlargement for the Mediterranean and ACP Policies of the European Community," *Europe Information* (Brussels) (1980), p. 14.
98 Cf. Taylor, "Implications for the Southern Mediterranean" (as in n. 35), pp. 6 ss.
99 Soares, "Portugal and Europe", ibid. (as in n. 25).
100 As reported by Philippe Le Maitre, *Le Monde*, September 18-19, 1977, cited after Stuart Holland, *Un-Common Market*, London, 1980, p. 168.
101 Cf. Agra Europe, ed., *The Agricultural Implications of EEC Enlargement – Part II: Portugal*, London, 1980, pp. 45 ss., 48 ss., 53 ss., 63 ss. (ua = units of account, now ECU).

run up to double the 75 plus or minus 15 mio ua in Portuguese annual levies to the EC estimated by the Commission in 1978,[102] and sugar, maize, and beef imports are likely to rise further.

This would substantially aggravate the country's serious current account deficit. Through raising consumer prices – by 20-30 percent according to one estimate,[103] although part of the increase might be offset by monetary compensation amounts due to the devalued currency – it would increase runaway inflation, intensify wage demands and labor conflicts, and thereby affect the competitiveness of export industries.[104] Consumer prices would also be hit by the need to progressively dismantle a variety of agricultural (producer and consumer) subsidies inconsistent with EC rules,[105] and following the substitution of the IT (*imposto de transacçoes*) by the VAT, or value-added tax. The latter measure would affect 500,000 instead of the present 90,000 taxpayers, and while the IT touches only roughly 30 percent of total consumption, that percentage may rise, with VAT, to between one-half and two-thirds.[106]

Any possibility of partly offsetting import losses by additional earnings from the export of wines and of tomato paste should suffer from the fact that, for both these products, Spain and Greece (apart from the Maghreb countries) will be directly competing with Portugal. Moreover, the transitional period for tomato concentrates, in the case of Greece, was fixed at seven years; and for wines, measures like preventive obligatory distillation, increased producer responsibility, and stepped-up quality controls are under discussion to prevent the expected surplus, especially from Spain.

In theory, higher Common Market prices for cereals, meat, dairy products, and sugar (for the latter, an additional production quota will have to be negotiated) should stimulate, as they doubtlessly will for wines, Portuguese production. However, not only will crop and livestock husbandry have to be markedly improved, it will also be necessary to disseminate accounting, raise quality control, and develop marketing structures. ("Until very recently, what were sometimes huge increases in agricultural producer prices were not sufficient to bring about an increase in supply because of the inadequacy of factor productivity and also because of the inadequacy of the transport and communications system."[107]) Meat and dairy production, moreover, will suffer from

---

102 Cf. EC Commission, "Wirtschaftliche und sektorielle Aspekte" (as in n. 87), p. 100.
103 Cf. Friedrich Ebert Stiftung, *Portugals Beitritt zur Europäischen Gemeinschaft - Perspektiven und Strategien*, Bonn, 1980, p. 18; also Lobão et al., "Politica Agricola" (as in n. 65), p. 781.
104 Cf. Ebert-Stiftung, *Portugals Beitritt*, p. 781.
105 Cf. *Telex Méditerranée*, May 5, 1981, p. 5.
106 Cf. Xavier de Basto: "O IVA Abrangera 500 mil Contribuintes," *Diario de Noticias*, July 13, 1981; "Preços Podem Agravarse com a Introdução do IVA," *Diario de Noticias*, Nov. 1, 1984, p. 5.
107 OECD, *Economic Survey: Portugal*, 1984, p. 22.

increased feed grain prices, until pasture feeding of livestock is sufficiently increased. Meanwhile, the Common Market farmers' stronger and more aggressive marketing organizations should be able to penetrate urban consumer markets thoroughly, largely crowding out Portuguese competition.[108]

That subsistence peasant farming in the North – the 77.7 percent of landholdings under five hectares referred to earlier – will survive by simply "staying out of the market" is extremely doubtful. Rather, these plots, coming under economic pressure, should continue to diminish as they did, but more rapidly, in favor of medium-sized capitalist farming. This, like any substantial rise in agricultural productivity, will entail a large shift of manpower out of agriculture. A renewed drift from the land into emigration, however, remains impossible. Considering soaring unemployment in the Community, Portugal will not succeed in negotiating anything but a transition period of seven years, as in the case of Greece, for the free movement of its workers. Even after that, persisting technological, i.e., structural, unemployment in the EC "core" countries can be expected to work against a renewed migratory "wave."

The alternative, then, for displaced labor would be to migrate to the already congested Porto-Braga-Lisbon-Setubal coastal region, aggravating housing, infrastructure, and employment problems there. For it is extremely unlikely that a "supply-push" of labor out of agriculture would be met by a sustained "demand-pull" from Portuguese industry. In attempting to assess the impact of accession on Portuguese industry, a strategy of export-led growth relying on comparative wage advantages, similar to that followed in the past by South Korea or Ireland, has been recommended to the country.[109] Still, already now the share of labor-intensive industries in total manufacturing value-added has declined to between 38 and 42 percent. Reliance on export promotion could, moreover, prove a dangerous option in a world economy gripped by stagflation.[110] Alternatively, it has been proposed to combine the development of import substitution and Portugal's domestic market on at least a par or even priority basis, with the attempt at improving the country's export performance: Although Por- tugal should try to diversify and increase exports in, e. g. , machinery, equipment, or petrochemicals, the country should also concentrate on the processing and manufacturing of food products, on the development of basic and investment goods industries ex-

108 Cf. Agra Europe, ed., *Agricultural Implications*, pp. 33, 36, 64; Lobão et al., "Politica Agricola", pp. 784 ss.; Ebert-Stiftung, *Portugals Beitritt*, pp. 18, 19.
109 Cf. Bela Balassa, "Portugal in the Face of the Common Market," in Fundação Calouste Gulbenkian, ed., *II International Conference on the Portuguese Economy*, Vol. II, p. 655.
110 Cf. Jürgen Donges, "On Portugal's Industrial Competitiveness in an Enlarged Community," Paper presented at the Conference on Portugal and the Enlargement of the European Community, Lisbon, 1980, p. 4; Ebert-Stiftung, *Portugals Beitritt*, p. 9; Stuart Holland: "Comentario," in Fundacao Calouste Gulbenkian, ed., *II International Conference on the Portuguese Economy*, Vol. II, pp. 748-49.

ploiting its own pyrite, wolfram, zinc, and iron ore deposits, and on construction to reduce housing and infrastructural deficits.[111]

If these considerations outline, however vaguely, an industrializing strategy, a cautious assessment has estimated that, after joining the EC/Nine, Portugal's annual manufactured imports would increase by 11.6 percent over actual EC imports, with manufactured exports virtually stagnating. Besides, Spain's more diversified and technologically superior industry is expected to penetrate the Portuguese market.[112] A similar argument has been advanced for Greece,[113] and Portugal would also have to face, under existing EC agreements, access to its market of exports from the ACP and Maghreb countries.[114]

This may indeed mean that Portugal, after even gradually introducing the common customs tariff, could fall victim to the two blades of a scissor: new industries with high capital intensity would suffer from the Common Market member states' competition; and traditional, labor-intensive sectors would be undercut by the low-wage supply from developing countries.[115] Not only would no additional employment be forthcoming, but present employment would suffer further. Thus, because of the very long periods involved in the development of both agriculture and industry from their present levels, mere transitional provisions might not prevent Portugal from finding its economy and society quite severely strained.

Successive PS and AD governments have persisted in an "exaggeration of the benefits and minimization of the pains"[116] that will be caused by EC accession. Details about problems and objectives have, to the public, remained "in almost complete nebulosity.[117] Trade unions and parties were late and only rarely consulted by governments. It took a member of the EC Coun-

---

111 Cf. Grant S. McClellan, *Spain and Portugal: Democratic Beginnings*, New York, 1978, p. 208; Klaus Esser, "Portugal in der west-europäischen Arbeitsteilung: Alternative Strategien," *Berichte zur Entwicklung in Spanien, Portugal und Lateinamerika* 3, No. 13 (1977): 37 ff.; Klaus Esser, "Integration zwischen Industrie und teilindustrialisierten Ländern - Portugal in der EG", in Burghard Claus et al., *Zur Erweiterung der Europäischen Gemeinschaft in Südeuropa*, Berlin, 1978, pp. 71 ff; Holland, "Comentario", ibid.

112 Cf. Donges, "Portugal's Industrial Competitiveness," pp. 7 ff.; Christian Deubner, *Der unsichere "europäische Konsens" in den iberischen Ländern*, Ebenhausen, 1981, pp. 74-75.

113 Cf. A. G. Portela, "Exportação Nacional - Mercado Comum," in Fundação Calouste Gulbenkian, ed., *II International Conference on the Portuguese Economy*, Vol. II, pp. 703, 730.

114 Cf. Geoffrey Edwards and William Wallace, *A Wider European Community?*, London, 1976, p. 48. Jürgen Donges et al., *The Second Enlargement of the European Community*, Tübingen, 1982, pp. 127 ss., 131 ss., have argued that Spain and Portugal might come to lead protectionist tendencies against ACP countries, whose position might thereby deteriorate.

115 Cf. Ebert-Stiftung, *Portugals Beitritt*, p. 8.

116 Maxwell, "A Evolução Contemporaneo" (as in n. 51), p. 36.

117 Encarnação Viegas, "As Teses de Natali e a Adesão de Portugal a CEE," *Diario de Noticias*, June 5, 1981, p. 15.

cil of Ministers' General Secretariat to qualify as "not unjustified"[118] the apprehensions expressed by the PCP which would seem to have contributed essentially to that party's position of rejecting accession, proposing instead a series of preferential treaties.[119] That alternative – fundamentally extending the 1972 trade agreement – has again been evoked, as late as 1984, by none other than the Confederação da Industria Portuguesa (CIP).[120]

In 1981, workers reacted against the AD government's social and labor policies by strikes involving 1.5 million employees over the year.[121] During the first week of 1982, another 900,000 workers went on strike, and in March and May of the same year the Confederação Geral dos Trabalhadores Portugueses (CGTP) proclaimed the first general strikes since 1934. These attempts were only partly successful, and strikes since have abated under pressure from the harsh economic squeeze and the daily struggle for survival. Urban and rural workers are still a minority in Portugal, and labor unrest may be muted for some time, even if the misery mounts further. At the same time, however, the lower classes in farming and business may, to a considerable extent, become imperiled in their social existence to the point of being marginalized.[122] Intensely traditionalist, they rose violently in 1975 against the perceived economic and ideological threat from the left. Adversely affected by economic rationalization and Common Market (including, psychologically important, Spanish) competition, they might react to imminent proletarization in a poujadist manner that could destroy the heterogeneous PS constituency, push the conservative parties further to the right, and, by prompting an authoritarian response among the Portuguese military with their established pronunciamiento tradition in a situation where governmental legitimacy is declining,[123] might not even end there.

---

118 Karl H. Buck, "'Europäischer Konsens' in Südeuropa," *Integration* 1 (1982), p. 40.
119 Cf. Carlos Carvalhas, "A Alternative a CEE," in Partido Comunista Português, ed., *Não ao Mercado Comum - Efeitos Globais de Adesão a CEE e Alternativa*, Lisbon, 1980, p. 142. The PCP has published several detailed studies concerning accession problems, e. g., *Não ao Mercado Comum - Agricultura*, Lisbon, 1980.
120 Cf. "Criticas da CIP Visam Retorno ao Estatuto Europeu de 1972," *Diario de Noticias*, Nov. 1, 1984, p. 2.
121 Cf. *Diario de Noticias*, December 25, 1981, pp. 17, 18; December 28, 1981, p. 2; for the subsequent figure, January 4, 1982, p. 3.
122 For the following "educated guesses," cf. Heinz Kramer, "Lagenotiz zur Situation in Portugal zu Beginn der Beitrittsverhandlungen mit der Europäischen Gemeinschaft," Stiftung Wissenschaft und Politik, Dok. SWP-LN 2203, Ebenhausen, 1979, pp. 25, 28; Claus Leggewie, "Die Erweiterung der Europäischen Gemeinschaft nach Süden", *Leviathan* 7 (1979), p. 182; Maxwell, "A Evolução Contemporaneo," p. 37; Ebert-Stiftung, Portugals Beitritt, pp. 14-15; Deubner, *Der unsichere "europäische Konsens"*, pp. 47-48, 86.
123 For the Armed Forces, cf. now Maria Carrilho, *Forças Armadas e Mudança Politica em Portugal no Seculo Vinte*, Lisbon, 1985, summarized in *O Jornal*, November 1, 1984, p. 11.

236

Ex Post Derogation: A Last Resort for Portugal

The Fontainebleau EC summit resolved that accession negotiations should be completed by September 1984. This proved impossible, talks continuing into 1985. In the end, however, almost at the last moment if the planned January 1, 1986 accession date was to be met, a treaty was agreed to and drawn up. On June 12, 1985, in ceremonies in Madrid and Lisbon, the two Iberian countries and the Community signed the accession treaty. The successful completion of the negotiations coincided with a major political crisis in Lisbon. The coalition between the PS and the PSD split apart following the surprise election of Cavaco Silva as leader of the Social Democrats. Both socialists and social democrats claimed policy differences were responsible for the break-up of the "bloco central", but in reality, although such differences certainly existed, the conflict was related more to presidential politics about which Soares and Cavaco Silva took very different positions. Soares sought to promote his own candidacy, Cavaco Silva was more inclined towards attempting to recapture the old AD constituency. The crisis, however, had the immediate effect of forcing an early dissolution of the assembly and the convocation of anticipated general elections; scheduled for October 6, 1985, with the prospect of presidential, municipal, European, and perhaps more general elections over the winter of 1985-86, the prospects for effective government seemed bleak. Moreover, the restrictive policies of the Soares government made it unlikely that the country would overcome its austerity-led recession by the time Portugal joined the EC.

Believing that the "normal" enlargement of 1972 could and should be repeated, the EC Council has insisted, vis a vis Portugal, that adjustment problems would have to be solved not by derogating from the *acquis communautaire* but only by transitional measures.[124] Derogation, in principle, would mean formal acknowledgment of the emerging economic multi-tier community, which cannot be papered over anymore by transitional measures. It would, in fact, be equal to a move in the direction of the institutionalized political multi-tier community introduced as a concept first by Brandt and then, in the context of Economic and Monetary Union proposals, by Tindemans. "Institutionalized" refers to the provision that some member countries, following more or less accurately pre-defined rules, would be either exempt from existing or not participating in newly created common policies (the operation of the so-called snake is a case in point).[125]

---

124 Cf. Klaus von Dohnanyi, "Zur Eröffnung der Verhandlungen zwischen der EG und Portugal", *Bulletin der Bundesregierung*, No. 118, Oct. 19, 1978, p. 1099.

125 For a detailed discussion, cf. Hans-Eckard Scharrer, "Abgestufte Integration - eine Alternative zum herkömmlichen Integrationskonzept?", *Integration*, No. 3 (1981), pp. 123 ss.

Formal, ex ante, derogation, once conceded, would in principle have to apply to every tier of the Community. Because such a solution would impose quite severe institutional strains on the Common Market, it was not considered during accession negotiations. However, Portugal might profit from the experience of Greece: Since the present Greek prime minister's socialist PASOK carried the 1981 elections, the country, as already referred to earlier, has been demanding a special statute – or, at least, massive support for regional and agricultural development – to mitigate the structural impact of accession. By acting likewise, Portugal might proceed to ex post derogation from parts of the *acquis* in an effort to prevent "perverse" consequences, "perverse" in the sense that better-off and more efficient countries would profit from Portuguese EC membership, with conceivably disastrous effects for Portugal's society and polity. This, on the other hand, should not prevent the country from agreeing to the common assignment of specific sets of actions to specific development stages and to provide for joint findings on their implementation. The challenge to Portugal's economy and the calculability of developments for the EC countries may thereby be maintained.

One indisputable result should emerge from any analysis of the "hesitant relationship": Portugal has been and is, economically as well as politically, a weak applicant. It will remain weak during the rest of the 1980s. The European Community cannot prevent that. But contrary to what is commonly said or even assumed, accession might make matters, by its impact, considerably worse for the country.

A Chronology of Events

1949   Portugal founding member of North Atlantic Treaty Organization (NATO)
1951   Signature of Paris Treaty establishing the European Coal and Steel Community (ESCS) – the Six (Belgium, France, West Germany, Italy, Luxembourg, Netherlands)
1957   Signature of Rome Treaty by the Six establishing the European Economic Community (EEC) and the European Atomic Energy Community (EAC, Euratom)
1960   Portugal founding member of the European Free Trade Association (EFTA –the Seven (Austria, Denmark, Norway, Portugal, Sweden, Switzerland, United Kingdom)
1965   Signature of treaty establishing a single Council and a single Commission for ESCS, EEC, and EAC, referred to henceforth as the European Communities (EC)

1972   United Kingdom, Denmark, and Ireland join EC (now the Nine);
        Portugal and EC conclude Free Trade Agreement; Finland and Ice-
        land join "rest-EFTA"
1974   (April 25) Caetano dictatorship overthrown
1975   (July 17) EC Council refuses Community loan during Portuguese
        "hot summer"; (October 7) EC grants $180 mio European Invest-
        ment Bank loan to Portugal
1976   Free Trade Agreement of 1972 is amended; EFTA sets up Industrial
        Development Fund for Portugal ($100 mio over live years)
1977   (March 28) Portugal applies for EC accession, followed by Spain in
        June
1978   (October 17) Commencement of accession negotiations
1979   Second amendment of EC-Portuguese Free Trade Agreement
1981   Greece joins EC (now the Ten); Portugal is granted $275 mio pre-
        accession aid ($150 mio in loans, $125 mio in grants) by EC
1982/83 EC budget problems, mainly revolving around UK contribution,
        continue to block Community policies; in accession negotiations
        with Portugal and Spain, EC pursues "pan-Iberian" approach of ad-
        mitting both countries simultaneously into the Common Market; EC
        reservations over Spanish competition result in slowing of negotia-
        tions with both countries
1984   (June 26) EC Fontainebleau summit resolves conclusion of acces-
        sion negotiations until September 30 to allow for Portuguese-
        Spanish accession by January 1, 1986; negotiations slowed again
        because EC proves unable to agree on common position for re-
        striction of surplus wine production; (October 22) Portugal and EC
        sign preliminary constat d'accord; (December 4) Dublin EC summit
        agrees on wine plan; as proposed Mediterranean aid program is not
        adopted, Greece reserves right to block further accession talks.
1985   (June 12) Treaty signed between Spain, Portugal, and EC
1985   (July 11) Portugal's Assembly of the Republic ratifies Treaty of
        Accession
1986   (January 1) Portugal accedes to the EC

As summed up in 2005 by Carlos Gaspar, Director of the Portuguese Institute of International Relations at Lisbon University, when he talked on „International Dimensions of the Portuguese Transition": „The strategies of the external actors were decisive to determine the final outcome of the Portuguese post-authoritarian transition." 20 years earlier, I had written no less. Gaspar's and my assessments may be expected to be perused today in a fairly detached mood. Impact in 1985 was rather different, at least in Portugal where several of my articles on the „revolution of carnations" and its aftermath – including the following one – were published: The weekly O Jornal, in a one-page write-up, reported on my findings under the caption: „How the Portuguese Revolution Was ‚Tamed'". In the final analysis, that's precisely what happened: International pressure was exerted on a small country's domestic politics.

External Influences on the Portuguese Revolution: The Role of Western Europe[1]

I

On June 21, 1975, the group of officers which had overthrown the dictatorial Caetano regime declared their objective to consist in a „socialist pluralism (which) includes the coexistence, in theory as in practice, of various forms and conceptions of building a socialist society. The MFA repudiates the implantation of socialism by violent or dictatorial means... (This) implies recognition of the existence of various political parties, even though they do not necessarily defend socialist options."[2]

When the Movimento das Forças Armadas (MFA) undertook to thus define its basic program, the original „liberation by golpe" (Philippe Schmitter) had already turned into a social revolution. In April, 1974, the slogan had run: „Decolonization – Democratization – Development". Now it went: „Liberation – Democracy – Socialism". The difference of emphasis was the result,

---

1   Published in Portuguese as „Influências Externas sobre a Revolução Portuguesa: o papel da Europa Ocidental" (cf. sources at the end of this book). For reasons which could not be sorted out afterwards, the concluding paragraph was omitted from the printed text. - This is the revised version of a paper presented at the III International Meeting on Modern Portugal („1974-1984: Portugal and the Portuguese Ten Years After"), Durham NH, May 31-June 3, 1984. I remain grateful to Kenneth Maxwell (New York), Christian Deubner (Ebenhausen), Franz-Wilhelm Heimer (Lisbon) and Uwe Optenhögel (Hamburg) for their critical suggestions.
2   „Plano de Acção Política do MFA", in: Ramiro Correa et al.: *MFA e Luta de Classes*, Lisbon, n. d., p. 176 (author's translation).

241

first, of a series of struggles within the military, resulting from three political crises which had mobilized ever larger parts of the population; and, secondly, of a social mass movement, mainly by the industrial proletariat of the Lisbon-Setúbal region and the rural workers of the Baixo Alentejo, which strongly contributed to accelerating the revolutionary process, but hardly managed to touch the large number of small peasants and medium-sized farmers in the North.

Figurehead of April 25, António de Spínola became the Republic's first president. Counting on the aid of military, economic and political groups, he attempted three times (twice in 1974, the third time on March 11, 1975) to extend or regain his powers – first, by an institutional maneuver, subsequently by appealing to the „silent majority", finally by a military coup. In no case did he succeed. Guinea-Bissau's former military governor stood for „a representative democratic regime similar to others in Western Europe... in which the interests of the propertied would be defended."[3] The first two crises had their major effect on foreign policy, i. e. on the pace of liquidating Portugal's colonial ventures in Africa. The abortive coup of March 11, however, in the wake of which Spínola fled the country, transformed the domestic scene fairly drastically.

Already the general's attempt to win over the „silent majority" had alerted the MFA to the fact that, in vast areas of the country, little had changed with regard to social and ideological structures – hence, the subsequent „cultural dynamization" campaigns in the center and north.[4] Soon it became evident that conglomerate holdings, such as Borges-Quina, Champali-maud, Companhia União Fabril (CUF), and Espírito Santo e Comercial not only wielded enormous economic power by controlling banks, insurance companies, and large parts of refinery, ship building, steel and cement production,[5] but that at least part of them had also supported Spínola.[6] After March 11, banks and insurance were nationalized, followed by transports, basic industries (steel and cement), transports, petrol refinery and distribution, and electricity. Additional decrees in July 1975 legalized to a large extent the occupations of latifundist farms in the Alentejo by wage laborers.

The wave of occupation by seasonally unemployed and – even more so than in industry – chronically underpaid farm workers[7] transformed approximately 1,1 million hectares into 550 collective production units (UCPs) and

3   Graham, Lawrence S.: „The Military in Politics: The Politicization of the Portuguese Armed Forces", in: id./ Harry M. Makler (eds.): *Contemporary Portugal*, Austin/London 1979, p. 234.
4   Cf. Insight Team of the Sunday Times: *Insight on Portugal*, London 1975, pp. 192 ss.
5   See the details in: Bacalhau, Mário: „Nacionalizações e Socialização", *Vida Mundial* No. 1859, May 1, 1975, pp. 22 ss.
6   Cf. Harsgor, Michael: *Portugal in Revolution*, Washington Papers Vol. III No. 32, Beverly Hills/ London 1976, pp. 44 ss.
7   Cf. Cutileiro, José: *A Portuguese Rural Society*, Oxford 1971, pp. 59 ss.

cooperatives.[8] It was only the final stage in a movement of labor unrest which had gotten under way already before the military coup, fueled by accelerated industrialization, agricultural stagnation, internal migration, and increasing inflation. After April 25, this movement erupted in „a series of social struggles for minimum conditions" in fields, factories, and shanty-towns.[9] Vacant state- and later also privately owned buildings were occupied by dwellers of squatter settlements and the most run-down quarters of Lisbon, Setúbal and Porto; occupants' and residents' commissions were established to voice demands and obtain government support;[10] workers' committees, elected by general assemblies, organized strikes to push for national minimum wages, better working conditions and the saneamento of those employers most conspicuously linked to the deposed „corporate state".[11] Around 750, mostly small-and-medium-industry, firms whose owners had declared themselves bankrupt, or had closed down, were occupied and reorganized either as production cooperatives (the majority, over 650) or self-managed enterprises under the control of workers' committees.[12]

Before the Constituent Assembly elections of April 25, 1975, the MFA, „considering the situation resulting from the suppression of the counter-revolutionary coup of March 11", had prevailed upon the political parties „engaged in the... consolidation and enlargement of the hitherto realized democratic accomplishments", to sign a Platform of Constitutional Agreement „which allows for the continuation of the political, economic and social revolution begun on April 25, 1974, in line with political pluralism and the transition to socialism".[13] Concordant with these principles, the new constitution which became effective on April 25, 1976, opted for „a peaceful advance of the revolutionary process", emphasizing the rights of workers' committees, trade unions, production, marketing, and consumer cooperatives. Trade unions were given participatory rights in supervising the implementation of

8 Occupied estates, however, never controlled more than 14% of the country's cultivated soils (cf. Barros, Afonso de: „A Reforma Agrária em Portugal e o Desenvolvimento Económico e Social", Revista Crítica de Ciências Sociais, 1979, No. 3, p. 61). Likewise in industry, the nationalized sector in 1975 accounted for 11.5% of employment (France, 11.2%; Italy, 11.6%), 33.6% of gross fixed investment (France and Italy, respectively, 33.5 and 28%), and 14% of sales (again in France and Italy, 10 and 8.1%). Cf. Pinho, Ivo: „Sector público empresarial: antes e depois do 11 de Março", Análise Social XII (1976), p. 745.

9 Downs, Charles: „Comissões de Moradores and Urban Struggles in Revolutionary Portugal", unpubl. manuscript, II International Meeting on Modern Portugal, Durham 1979, p. 5.

10 Cf. Leitão, Luis et al.: „Mouvement Urbains et Commissions de Moradores au Portugal (1974-1976)", Les Temps Modernes 34 (1978), pp. 660 ss., 670 ss.

11 Cf. Insight Team, op. cit., pp. 120 ss.

12 Cf. Barros, José: „Empresas industriais geridas pelos trabalhadores", Análise Social XIII (1977), p. 687; Costa, Fernando Ferreira da: „Le Coopératisme au Portugal", Révue des Etudes Coopératives, No. 194 (1978), p. 47.

13 Complete text in: Portugal Hoje, Ministério de Comunicação Social, Ano I, No. 50, April 19, 1975 (author's translation).

economic and social plans, the preparation of labor legislation, and the management of social security institutions. Workers' committees elected by general assemblies were entitled to supervise the management of enterprises and to participate in drawing up both labor legislation and economic plans for their respective sectors. Agrarian cooperatives and farmers' organizations, in turn, were to be involved in the planning and implementation of agrarian reform. The constitution directed the state to promote the establishment of agrarian, industrial and consumer cooperatives; it gave precedence to the further socialisation (not, however, nationalisation) of the means of production, based on self-managed enterprise, community property managed by local authorities, and the cooperative sector.[14]

The turn to the left in Portuguese politics, however, was short-lived, lasting only from spring to autumn of 1975. The constitutional text voted during that period triggered no sweeping commitment of political forces aimed at realizing its prospects. Already during 1976-79 (before a liberal-conservative coalition obtained a parliamentary majority),[15] successive administrations conducted a policy which effectively reversed „socialist pluralism" as a constitutional model and an evolutionary process.[16] While, on the one hand, goals and methods different from the „Atlantic" political and socio-economic context failed to take root domestically and, on the other hand, penetrative processes occurred on the international level, those values and institutions prevailed which corresponded to the socio-political systems of the North Atlantic Alliance. The result was a political and economic regime „strongly supported by, and oriented towards the West".[17]

II

In a seminal essay on concept-building in international relations, James N. Rosenau identified a society's penetration as the authoritative allocation of

14 *Constitution of the Portuguese Republic,* Office of the Secretary of State for Mass Communication, Lisbon 1978, Art. 2, 9, 10, 55-58, 61, 81, 84, 90, 96, 100, 1004.
15 None of the first five constitutional administrations (which succeeded the six „provisional" governments between 1974 and 1976) could count on a parliamentary majority. The first was a PS minority cabinet, the second again a PS government that, under an informal arrangement, included „figures from the CDS". The third to fifth were presidential cabinets of „independents" – the first two led by liberal-conservative technocrats –installed by President Ramalho Eanes.
16 Addendum 2011: From 1982, successive constitutional revisions did away with references to the peaceful continuation of the revolutionary process and to the intended realization of a self-management economy, emaciated the chapter on agrarian reform, strengthened the merely indicative character of economic planning, and ended by re-privatizing the public sector.
17 Pimlott, Ben: „Socialism in Portugal: Was it a Revolution?", *Government & Opposition* 12 (1977), p. 349.

socio-political aims and values – including mobilization for the attainment of these goals – by non-members of the penetrated society, acting in concert with some of its members.[18] A society's capacity for penetration results from its „structural" power (Johan Galtung), permitting it to more or less subtly or drastically reduce other societies' autonomy. In the context of an international inter-dependence fundamentally „lopsided" and „asymmetric in power",[19] penetrative activities may serve as efficient tools of a „total diplomacy" pyramiding „labor, diplomacy, intelligence, and business activities in foreign policy".[20]

The arrival of total diplomacy has been facilitated by a development which has added new transnational to traditional international players. Groups such as political parties, trade unions, and multinational corporations, residing in the Warsaw Pact and NATO countries, by transporting ideologies, funds, information, persons and goods across frontiers[21] may turn into instruments of their respective governments' foreign policies[22]

In introducing the concept of penetration, Rosenau emphasized the ultimately binding character of such processes, citing a „shortage of capacities" on the penetrated society's part as underlying reason for the participation of non-members in its politics. Defining that lack „in nonevaluative terms" permitted him to gloss over the fact that, admittedly, „external penetration may not always be gladly accepted by the officials and citizens of a society."[23] As other authors have pointed out, some groups of the penetrated society, by acting as a „bridge-head", may advance their interests and gain „a degree of autonomy" in the process. However, because such additional autonomy „may only evolve within the limits of the strategy pursued by the penetrating society", it is bound to „remain relatively small."[24]

Still, penetration should evidently not be confused with mere manipulation. As the aims and policies of the penetrating society will usually neither be unknown nor without following in the penetrated country, the process of

18 Cf. Rosenau, James N.: „Pre-theories and Theories of Foreign Policy", in: R. Barry Farrell (ed.): *Approaches to Comparative and International Politics*, Evanston 1966, p. 65.

19 Vernon, Raymond: „Multinational Business and National Economic Goals", *International Organization* XXV (1971), p. 705; Morse, Edward L.: „Transnational Economic Processes", *International Organization* XXV (1971), p. 393.

20 Cox, Robert W.: „Labor and Transnational Relations", *International Organization* XXV (1971), p. 555.

21 Cf. Strange, Susan: „The Study of Transnational Relations", *International Affairs* 52 (1976), pp. 334 ss.

22 Cf., e. g., Radosh, Ronald: *American Labor and United States Foreign Policy*, New York 1969, passim; Behrmann, Jack N.: *National Interests and the Multinational Enterprise*, Englewood Cliffs 1970, pp. 101 ss.

23 Rosenau, op. cit., pp. 64, 68.

24 Kiersch, Gerhard/Mettler-Meibom, Barbara: „Die US-Amerikanische Penetration in Frankreich nach dem 2. Weltkrieg", in: Klaus-Jürgen Gantzel (ed.): *Kapitalistische Penetration in Europa*, Hamburg 1976, p. 31.

interaction is both more complex and more dynamic. Domestic controversies (latent or already begun) may be started or fueled by external protagonists through ideological interpretation which takes the effect of „contagion"; external norms, reinforced by enticements or pressures, may be invoked by domestic groups (or even factions of such groups) to generate additional legitimacy for their political strategies; and the original perceptions of these groups may be transformed in the course of such a process as it will be considered here.

Conducive to the North American-Western European interest in Portuguese developments and, subsequently, formal and informal penetration of that NATO member country during 1974/75 was the concern of political and military strategists over what came to be termed „NATO's crumbling Southern flank": Soviet naval build-up in and Communist party strength around the Mediterranean were perceived as two blades of a scissor fragmenting NATO political cohesion and endangering NATO military communications. The revolutionary process in Portugal seemed to pose an immediate threat to both.[25] Accordingly, the threshold was quickly reached after which any real change in the status quo became „intolerable" to NATO.[26]

The Institute for the Study of Conflict in London published a scenario which already envisioned Portugal's „existing obligations" as having been „abrogated", with the Soviet Union attempting to „establish a base" in the Azores and the North-Atlantic forces securing the archipelago „in the defense of its own paramount interests" – an act „evidently facilitated" if it were legitimized „by a democratic Portuguese government in exile".[27] Funds for setting up the London institute and its journal Conflict Studies had come, five years earlier, from Kern House Enterprises, a Delaware-based CIA „front". Leaked documents suggested that the institute continued to work hand in glove with the CIA (and, probably, British intelligence services) by offering „professional and authoritative-sounding analyses".[28] Considering the institute's background, the Conflict Studies scenario illustrates the prevailing

---

25 Cf. Rees, David: *Southern Europe: NATO's Crumbling Southern Flank*, Institute for the Study of Conflict, Conflict Studies No. 60, London 1975, pp. 2 ss., 13.
26 Szulc, Tad: „Washington and Lisbon: Behind the Portuguese Revolution", *Foreign Policy* No. 21, Winter 1975/76, p. 9.
27 Rees, op. cit., p. 16.
28 Cf. Weissman, Steve: „The CIA Makes the News", in: Philip Agee/Louis Wolf (eds.): *Dirty Work: The CIA in Western Europe*, London 1981, pp. 206, 207 ss. Kern House Enterprises had begun by establishing the London-based news (and propaganda) service Forum World Features. This was intended to replace an earlier service which had been operating as part of the Congress for Cultural Freedom, when that group's covert funding by the CIA came under public scrutiny. Forum World Features, in its turn, set up a subsidiary „research services center" which, by 1970, was transformed into the Institute for the Study of Conflict. Addendum 2011: The quote characterizing the Institute's activities may be found on http://www.powerbase.info/ index.php/Institute_for_the_Study_of_Conflict (accessed 6/14/2011).

tendency to put the Portuguese „case" squarely into the context of the Cold War: Portugal was not viewed as a developing polity and society in its own right, but merely in terms of another theater in the East-West conflict.

NATO, US and EC attitudes became particularly important for Portugal because of the country's deteriorating economic situation. While merchandise exports rose only from $1,8 billion (1973) to $2,3 billion (even declining in 1975/76), imports shot up from $2,8 to 4,3 billion in 1974. Because of climbing international prices, the most marked increases were not in amounts but in value of cereal and – especially enormous – of crude oil imports. Income from tourism and emigrant remittances fell drastically. Clandestine capital outflow through the undervoicing of exports alone has been estimated at $108 million for 1975. Labor migration decreased by 45% (barely 45,000 persons as against nearly 80,000 in 1973), after France, West Germany and other countries had reacted to the 1973 oil-price induced world recession by unilaterally suspending the import of labor. Meanwhile, due to returnees from Angola and Mozambique, and to the demobilization of military personnel, continental Portugal's population swelled from 8.43 million in 1973 to 9.09 million in 1975, unemployment and underemployment rising stiffly with it.[29] Judged against the background of worsening terms of trade and international recession, Portuguese revolution and decolonization could hardly have happened in a more unfavorable situation.

As Portugal's accessibility to penetration increased, external attempts at exerting influence intensified to the extent that the leftward trend of the country's social and political power struggles was reflected by the composition of successive „provisional" cabinets and by their socializing measures. During the provisional period, i. e. before promulgation of the new constitution, Portugal had left-leaning – as distinct from moderate or de facto social-democratic – governments, often referred to as „Gonçalvist", only from March to September, 1975. It was during that period that values and means initially inspired by anticommunism, but more and more directed against the entire Left were determinedly pushed from the outside in an effort to reverse the course which seemed set after the events of March 11.

29 For the data, cf. Robert N. McCauley: „A Compendium of IMF Troubles: Turkey, Portugal, Peru, Egypt", in: Lawrence G. Frank/Marilyn Seiber (eds.): *Developing Country Debt*, New York 1979, p. 151; World Bank (ed.): *Portugal: Current and Prospective Economic Trends*, Washington D. C. 1978, p. 34; Manuel Barboza/Luis Miguel P. Beleza: „External Disequilibrium in Portugal 1975-1978", in: Fundação Calouste Gulbenkian (ed.): *II International Conference on the Portuguese Economy*, Vol. 2, Lisbon 1980, pp. 57, 62; information supplied by the Ministry of Social Communication in Lisbon.

III

In a telex of January 27, 1975 (which was partially leaked later),[30] the West German Embassy in Lisbon recommended that the Bonn government should „double funds for Portuguese farmers' organization" – probably the Associação Livre de Agricultores (ALA), predecessor of the militant Confederação des Agricultores de Portugal (CAP). The „DM 50,000 proposed by Vice President [of the German Farmers' Association] v. Feury" were judged „inadequate", because „PCP organises workers and small peasants". The embassy suggested that the funds should be transferred through the German association.

From „confidential sources in the Luso-American community", Rona M. Fields learned in March 1975 that Portuguese immigrants had been sending money to the conservative-liberal Partido Popular Democrático (PPD) and the conservative Centro Democrático Social (CDS), and that „considerable private funds" had been supplemented by „indirect contributions" from the CIA and the State Department.[31] In a circular letter dated December 17, 1975,[32] Kai-Uwe von Hassel, President of the European Union of Christian Democrats, and Christian Democratic Union (CDU) deputy Elmar Pieroth, a board member of that West German party's Small-and-Medium-Business Association, had requested donations to help the CDS „train functionaries, hold conferences and meetings", adding that financial aid was „urgently required" to „facilitate our friends' daily struggle against the strong Communist forces". On February 25, 1976, the CDU announced that it would support the CDS (which was also receiving help from the British Conservatives)[33] in the organisation of its campaign for the April 25 elections.[34]

Founded in 1974 by public figures from the Caetano regime's economy and bureaucracy,[35] the CDS appealed to „those groups which were most content with the old system".[36] The PPD, renamed Partido Social Democráta, PSD, in 1976, experienced profound internal strife over the question whether

---

30 Published by *Berliner Extra-Dienst* IX, No. 21, March 11, 1975, p. 2. The telex had been included in the West German Foreign Ministry's „Yellow Service" distributed to every embassy. Publication in the *Extra-Dienst* seems to have been based on information received from the Cairo Embassy's Press Attache Erich Knapp and Embassy Secretary Peter Lazarek. Knapp was immediately dismissed; Lazarek committed suicide. Cf. subsequent 1975 *Extra-Dienst* issues.

31 Fields, Rona M.: *The Portuguese Revolution and the Armed Forces Movement*, New York/London 1977, p. 230. Also Szulc, op. cit., p. 11.

32 Facsimile reproduction in *Portugal-Nachrichten* No. 18, January 12, 1976, p. 13.

33 Cf. Harvey, Robert: *Portugal: Birth of a Democracy*, London 1978, p. 73.

34 Herzog, Werner: „Staatspräsident wird ein Militär", *Frankfurter Rundschau*, February 26, p. 2.

35 Details in Antunes, Albertino et al.: *Portugal – República Socialista?*, Lisbon 1975, p. 235.

36 Pimlott, Ben: „Parties and Voters in the Portuguese Revolution", *Parliamentary Affairs*, Winter 1977, p. 42.

it was essentially a moderate group, concerned with selective opposition to revolutionary results, or a conservative organization, principally concerned „to protect and to preserve", fundamentally opposed to the revolution.[37]

In any case, not just anti-communism but categorical opposition to the Left were already embedded in the entire conservative-liberal spectrum, from ALA and CAP to PPD and CDS. With regard to these organizations, available indicators point more to limited external support than to penetration in the above-defined sense. Moreover, in spite of the influence wielded by these groups in the Portuguese North during 1974/75, there can be no doubt that the period's principal players, apart from the PCP, were the MFA – including the governments which it headed – and the Socialist Party (Partido Socialista, PS) under the direction of Mário Soares.

The MFA was an „African movement" in more than one sense. The undogmatic Marxism of Amílcar Cabral (PAIGC, Guinea-Bissau) and Agostinho Neto (MPLA, Angola) had impressed the professionally and politically disillusioned captains, who had served in Africa on combat as well as on civil-military („counter-insurgency") missions, and had made them receptive to socialist goals in the widest sense. But while that socialism remained vague in its details, ideological cleavages developed between various military factions to the extent that both foreign and Portuguese parties and foreign governments impressed their political projects on the officers. Domestic and external pressures made themselves felt, to which men like Prime Minister Vasco Gonçalves, Special Forces (COPCON) Commander Otelo Saraiva de Carvalho – the April 25 coup's military architect – and the MFA's political thinker, Foreign Minister Melo Antunes, responded quite differently.

If the MFA was programatically insecure, the PS – as conceded by no less an authority than its general secretary Mário Soares in 1973 – lacked theoretical training, reflection on the Portuguese „way to Socialism" and finally, due to former „tactical ambiguities", political profile.[38] The Acção Socialista Portuguesa, founded during 1964 in Geneva und admitted into the Socialist International in 1972, was transformed into the PS at Bad Münstereifel (Germany) a year later with the support of the West German Social Democratic Party (SPD) and the Friedrich Ebert Foundation (FES). After April 25, the PS (again according to Soares) "lacked more or less everything necessary for making an autonomous impression on the nation's political life: numerous and active members in every town and village, an experienced and solid organization, effective information channels, money..."[39]

---

37 Cf. Pimlott, op. cit., p. 41.
38 Mário Soares, in: Partido Socialista (ed.): *Destruir o Sistema – Construir Uma Nova Vida*, n. p. 1973, pp. 25, 27, 31, 39.
39 Soares, Mário: *Portugal: Que Revolução?*, Lisbon 1976, p. 77 (emphasis added).

During 1975 (and subsequently),[40] Portugal's cabinets (thereby affecting the MFA) and the PS were targeted in a concerted combination of enticements and pressures by the West German and US administrations, the EC and NATO Councils, by SPD and FES, the Socialist International and associations of the international workers' movement. Considering, on the one hand, that this was the period marked in the United States by the ramifications of the Watergate shock and, on the other hand, that the SPD was represented in West Germany's government, one cannot but conclude that the United States were eclipsed, in the pursuit of that strategy, by the EC countries, particularly West Germany.

IV

On April 4, 1975, the Hermes Insurance Agency, managing federal credit guarantees for the protection of West German exporters against economic and political risk, announced it would suspend covering exports to Portugal.[41] Five days later, the West German government postponed a decision on DM 70 million financial assistance. On April 16, the SPD published a joint letter to Vasco Gonçalves by the EC Confederation of Socialist Parties and the European Parliament's Socialist Group, exhorting the MFA to distance itself from the PCP, praising Soares, insinuating the perspective that it might work to promote (or, between the lines, to impede) EC aid. On May 19, the FRG government granted the DM 70 million to Foreign Minister Melo Antunes. But a week later, the EC Foreign Ministers' Council hedged on a Portuguese request already submitted a year earlier.

A mere two months after the coup, on June 27, 1974, the I Provisional Government had asked the EC for economic support. On November 25/26,

---

40 Two examples: Pressing for „apolitical professionalism (and) discipline" (Sen. Edward W. Brooke: „Statement", in: Military and Economic Assistance to Portugal, U.S. Senate, Washington DC 1977, p. 4) in an effort to reorient the Portuguese military toward NATO, a joint U.S.-West German and two U.S. military advisory teams were sent to Portugal in 1976. In the wake of these visits, Portugal received extensive military aid from both countries. – During 1978/79, funds from the Friedrich Ebert Foundation, transferred through the Fundação José Fontana, helped the PS to set up the União Geral dos Trabalhadores (UGT) on a parity basis with the PSD's „Tendência Sindical Reformista Social-Democrata" (TESIRED). The FES/PS/PSD intention was to undercut the largely (by a two thirds majority of its Secretariat) PCP-controlled CGTP (Confederação Geral dos Trabalhadores Portugueses), which had emerged from the Intersindical „umbrella organization" established in opposition to the Caetano regime. The two ideologically polarized trade union confederations have been developing into pliable party instruments, to the detriment of their socioeconomic strength. Cf. Partido Socialista (ed.): *Confiar no PS – Apostar em Portugal*, Lisbon 1979, pp. 37 ss.; author's interview with former Secretary of Labor Francisco Marcelo Curto, February 20, 1980.

41 Details of this chapter are based on reports in *Berliner Extra-Dienst, Süddeutsche Zeitung* and *Frankfurter Rundschau*, and on information published by the EC Commission.

the III Provisional Government presented urgent proposals for new special trade terms (under the Free Trade Treaty concluded in 1972) and for a comprehensive agreement protecting Portuguese emigrant workers in EC member countries (850,000 in France alone by 1974). These proposals, however, were submitted after Spínola had already resigned the presidency and gone on television for his dramatic farewell address to the country. From that moment, „the Community leaders lacked the will...to give rapid satisfaction to the demands put forward by the Portuguese."[42] On May 26, 1975, as already mentioned, and again on June 24, the EC Foreign Ministers' Council hedged on economic aid, voicing its concern with „political stability" and „democratic government" in Portugal. Finally, on July 17, French President Giscard d'Estaing „vetoed a Community loan...for fear of subsidizing a socialist-communist alliance".[43] The EC Council of Heads of State and Government, instead, presented Portugal with what amounted to a „virtual ultimatum":[44] „The EC, because of its political and historical tradition, can grant support only to a pluralist democracy"[45] – evidently referring, by „pluralist", to the North-American-Western European ,public philosophy',[46] rather than to the „socialist-pluralist" creed professed by the MFA four weeks earlier.

A $180 million European Investment Bank loan was only granted Portugal on October 7, after a new, de facto social-democratic – the VI Provisional – government had been in office for three weeks. The first disbursements were not made before April, 1976. The 1972 trade agreement was finally amended in June of the same year. Evidently, aid from Western Europe could not be obtained without a commitment to the West.

General Francisco da Costa Gomes, Spínola's successor to the Portuguese presidency, has made abundantly clear that the EC attitude, from the autumn of 1974 onward, was perceived by the Portuguese government as „inimical" foreign pressure.[47] The Common Market's „power of denial",[48] demonstrated from May to July 1975, could not have failed to impress, first and foremost, Costa Gomes, Melo Antunes, and ambassador itinerant Major Vítor Alves who visited Western European capitals between April and September. One week after the EC Council had given the thumbs down on aid,

---

42 Council of Europe, Parliamentary Assembly: *Report on the Situation in Portugal*, Doc. 3609, Strasbourg, April 21, 1975, p. 18.
43 Story, Jonathan: „Portugal's Revolution of Carnations: Patterns of Change and Continuity", *International Affairs*, Vol. 52 (1976), p. 431.
44 Szulc, Tad: „Hope for Portugal", *The New Republic*, August 30, 1975, p. 9.
45 Commission of the European Communities: *Die Beziehungen zwischen der EG und Portugal*, Brussels 1976, p. 8.
46 The role of the concept of pluralism as a guideline and justification of Western European and U.S. foreign policy has been explored in the author's „A Revolução dos Cravos e a Política Externa: O Fracasso do Pluralismo Socialista em Portugal a seguir a 1974", *Revista Crítica de Ciências Sociais*, Nr. 11 (1983), pp. 95 ss.
47 Costa Gomes, Francisco da: *Sobre Portugal*, Lisbon 1979, p. 59.
48 Story, ibid. (note 43).

Costa Gomes, in a discourse to the MFA Delegate Assembly, made no secret of his conviction that, because of its economic dependence on the West, Portugal could not endure „Western enmity" as long as its economic ties with Third World and socialist countries had not been further developed.[49] Antunes and Alves led the MFA Officers' „Group of Nine" whose August 7 document, signaling open discord in MFA ranks and sharply criticizing the cabinet's „revolutionary vanguard" politics, was instrumental in ending „gonçalvismo". They were tacitly supported by Costa Gomes, who agreed with their opinions, if not with their methods.[50]

Melo Antunes would originally have preferred a „Third World option", the emergence – from a position of non-alignment – of a Lisbon/Maputo/Luanda „axis".[51] This position, however, proved unattainable, and the Group of Nine document contained the first reference to the perceived necessity of „strengthening and deepening the ties with certain economic areas (Common Market, EFTA)".[52] Final proof of the EC Council declaration's significant effect is provided by a „revolutionary critique" of the Group of Nine document, published on August 13, 1975 by COPCON officers close to Otelo Saraiva de Carvalho. The critique included the statement that „whoever may still have entertained illusions has now lost them considering the recent conditions tied to ,financial aid for Portugal'".[53]

V

In January 1975, the PCP, supported by the MFA, had prevailed upon the II Gonçalves Administration to back the principle of unicidade, i. e. of a single national trade union association, which the new constitution would rescind a year later. That meant a legal monopoly for Intersindical, which was largely controlled by the Communist Party.[54] The decision would prove a Pyrrhic victory: For the first time since April 25, the PS confronted the PCP „publicly and by mobilizing the masses":[55] To an Intersindical demonstration of nearly 100,000 workers, the PS responded with a counter-demonstration of 40,000 participants.

---

49   Cf. Costa Gomes, Francisco da: *Discursos Políticos*, Ministry of Social Communication, Lisbon 1976, p. 201.
50   Cf. Costa Gomes, *Sobre Portugal*, p. 81.
51   Cf. Ferreiro, José Medeiros: „Aspectos internacionais da Revolução Portuguesa", unpubl. manuscript, II International Meeting on Modern Portugal, Durham 1979, p. 6.
52   A translation of the document may be found in Schröder, Günter (ed): *Portugal: Materialen und Dokumente*, Vol. 3, Giessen 1976, p. 133.
53   As in Schröder, op. cit., p. 149.
54   However, trade unions were under no obligation to affiliate to Intersindical, and a vote by secret ballot of a union's entire membership on whether or not to affiliate was required. Cf. Insight Team, op. cit., p. 212.
55   Merz, Friedhelm/Rego, Victor Cunha (eds.): *Freiheit für den Sieger*, Zürich 1976, p. 76.

However, the FRG government, West Germany's Social Democrats and the Friedrich Ebert Foundation were not unaware that the PS executive pursued farther-reaching schemes. In the already referred-to telex of January 27 (first denied by Bonn, but later proved authentic), the West German embassy in Lisbon reported that „Soares tends triggering governmental crisis 3 or 2 weeks before [Constituent Assembly] elections... Should c-g. [Costa Gomes] not go along, sp. [Spínola] would emerge from retreat with explicit public statement. Effect demission and statement c-g. or sp. would be coupled to split MFA... Eventual coup Copcon-Carvalho due to obtained majority on election eve...if necessary be thwarted by appeal to NATO. C.-g., sp. or fabião[56] then able to supplement moderate majority Constituent Assembly by government without PC."[57] During a visit, Under-Secretary of State Jorge Campinos (PS) advised his interlocutors at the Friedrich Ebert Foundation on March 10 that „the Portuguese socialists (had) – in conjunction with President Costa Gomes – considered... to obtain a replacement of Prime Minister Vasco Gonçalves even before April 12 [the original date for electing a Constituent Assembly], so that they might be able to secure, after the elections,[58] an even more active participation in political decisions." Spínolas abortive coup attempt by next day, according to the Foundation, „invalidated Campinos' statement".

Following Willy Brandt's visit in Portugal and his discussions with the PS from October 19 to 21, 1974, the SPD did not mince its words, stating that „Brandt's trip has made plain the influence which German Social Democracy is exerting on the evolution of democracies in Europe."[59] No less than the Atlantic Alliance, the party was concerned that popular front governments might emerge in France, Italy and Portugal. Both after World Wars I and II, the SPD had met communism head-on; nevertheless, its experience was that the conservative parties were able to mobilize the electorate's latent anti-communism against social democracy. Now it feared that these parties might benefit if popular front governments should obtain majorities in Southern European countries. Consequently, the SPD tried to prevail in the Socialist International over the French, Italian and Greek socialists led by Mitterrand, and it was also concerned that „our American friends...should not confuse social democracy and communism" (Brandt).[60]

---

56   Major (later Brigadier) Carlos Fabião, originally close to Spínola, Army Chief of Staff subsequent to September 28, 1974, continued to be considered a „moderate".
57   As in n. 30.
58   Esters, Elke: Aktennotiz betr. Portugal vor den Wahlen zur Verfassunggebenden Versammlung, Friedrich Ebert-Stiftung, Bonn, March 17, 1975, p. 1.
59   Merz, Friedhelm: „Solidarität mit Portugal", *Sozialdemokrat Magazin*, No. 11/1974, p. 14. Merz was editor-in-chief of the SPD members' magazine.
60   Brandt quote in Stender, Ralf: *Reaktionen und Einflussnahme der SPD auf die Entwicklung in Portugal vom April 1975 bis zum April 1976*, Thesis, Free University of Berlin 1977, p.

For support, the SPD could count on the Friedrich Ebert Foundation, the trade unions and the West German government. The Foundation's president, Alfred Nau, was SPD Treasurer from 1946 to 1975, and was subsequently made a honorary member of the party's executive. Trade Union Federation (DGB) head Heinz Oskar Vetter sat on the Foundation's Board. His predecessor, Ludwig Rosenberg, belonged to the Foundation's Board of Trustees, which was chaired by Walter Hesselbach, President of the Bank für Gemeinwirtschaft (whose Supervisory Board, in turn, was presided over by Heinz Oskar Vetter). In 1975, the Foundation had 441 employees and a budget of DM 77.4 mio.[61] Like its Christian Democratic, Christian Social and Free Democratic counterparts, the Konrad Adenauer, Hanns Seidel and Friedrich Naumann Foundations, the Friedrich Ebert Foundation continues to be subsized by the Ministries of Economic Cooperation and of the Interior. Outlays are administered confidentially; publication of accounts is not mandatory; and subsidies are assigned globally, allowing foundations a large margin of autonomy in their use.[62]

The Friedrich Ebert Foundation has always interpreted „the legacy of Weimar tied to the name of Friedrich Ebert" as an obligation to „support democrats in the defense of their state against any enemy, whether on the left or on the right". Consequently, the Foundation opposes social-democratic factions „vehemently if they do not adhere to the SPD policy, defined in these terms, as an omnibus party".[63]

Basically, attempts at „exercising influence on social and political processes in [any one] country" (in the words of the Foundation's Annual Report for 1977) are guided by a „communism syndrome" – a syndrome which may lead to „erroneous judgments concerning the possibilities and limits of communist infiltration".[64]

More sober accounts have repeatedly disclaimed the „gross oversimplification to view today's [i. e. the 1975] political scene in Portugal exclusively as a forum in the battle between Democratic freedom and Communist dictatorship",[65] as well as the equally gross affirmation that „freedom of the press died with the caso República".[66] In contrast to Mário Soares, who propound-

---

77. Cf. also Stender, op. cit., pp. 154 ss., and Hübner, Hans: *Portugal – Prüfstein der Demokratie?*, Cologne 1976, pp. 127/128.

61   Cf. Vieregge, Henning von: „Zur politischen Bildungsarbeit der parteinahen Stiftungen", *Aus Politik und Zeitgeschichte*, No. B 7-77, February 19, 1977, pp. 30/31, 36.

62   Ibid., pp. 28/29, 34.

63   Ibid., p. 31.

64   Bley, Helmut/Tetzlaff, Rainer (eds.): *Afrika und Bonn*, Reinbek 1977, pp. 117, 170. The quote from the Foundation's 1977 Report is on p. 62.

65   Szulc, Tad: „Volatile Portugal", *The New Republic*, August 16-23, 1975, p. 18.

66   Szulc, Tad: „Washington and Lisbon" (as above, n. 26), p. 41; cf. also Graham, *The Military in Politics* (as above, n. 2), p. 245. The PCP's participation in occupying the newspaper *República* (affiliated to the PS) by typographical workers was „at best indirect and may have been merely a reaction to the militancy of workers organized in the Maoist UDP"

254

ed that view abroad, former PS Agricultural Minister Lopes Cardoso, who later left the party, has always insisted that the ‚hot summer' of that year cannot be considered as „um período de pré-ditadura communista".[67]

The PCP had certainly secured influence among the military, municipal administrations, the trade unions, and part of the mass media. Obviously, it received continuous financial support from the USSR and several orthodox communist parties. Nevertheless, four points should be considered.

First, the PCP could count on a position of „hegemony" only among the rural proletariat, never among the industrial workers, even less among the armed forces. In the MFA's principal political institutions – the Council of the Revolution and the Delegate Assembly -, the number of its supporters was limited. As regards the military hierarchy, the party could hardly count on any adherents: neither among COPCON or in the Lisbon Military Region commanded by Otelo Saraiva de Carvalho; nor in the North, where „Gonçalvist" commander Eurico Corvacho found himself unable to rely on his own units; nor, finally, in the Military Regions South and Center whose commanders Pedro Pezarat Correia and Franco Charais had signed the Group of Nine document.

Second, the party entered into an unconditional alliance with the MFA. There – or so it seemed to the PCP – lay the „political" power (regulatory and coercive) which the party considered instrumental for consolidating the „social" power it had acquired on the fields of the Alentejo, in the North's municipal administrations, the trade unions, television, and the press.[68] Depending on the MFA's support and cohesion, it limited its capacity for conducting a dialogue with other parties, particularly the PS. That exclusivist strategy failed: On August 10, 1975, PCP Secretary General Álvaro Cunhal admitted to „a certain social and political isolation" of his party, even „among those military whom we may consider as progressive".[69]

Three, at no time was the PCP in a position to „dictate strategy". Having turned more militant with the radicalization of the MFA after March 11, it could only continue to react. In July/August, the party found itself „essentially a marginal spectator to the drama played out in the MFA Assembly and the Council of the Revolution".[70]

Four, globally considered, the policy pursued by the USSR with regard to Portugal and the PCP seems to have been „largely situational, frequently

(Mujal-Léon, Eusebio M.: „The PCP and the Portuguese Revolution", *Problems of Communism*, Vol. XXVI [1977], p. 31).

67 *Tempo*, October 26, 1981, p. 11.
68 Cf. Schmitter, Philippe C.: „Le Parti Communiste Portugais entre le Pouvoir Social et le Pouvoir Politique", *Etudes Internationales*, Vol. VI (1975), pp. 380 ss.
69 Cunhal, Álvaro: „Rede auf der Plenarsitzung des Zentralkomitees der PCP", in: id.: *Zur portugiesischen Revolution. Reden 1974-79*, Frankfurt 1979, pp. 57 ss.
70 Mujal-Léon, op. cit., pp. 30 ss.

contradictory rather than coherent".[71] Recognizing the advantageous commercial and technological aspects of easing tensions with the United States, the Soviet leaders feared that „Portugal could turn into an obstacle for the Conference on Security and Cooperation in Europe".[72] Not wishing to risk „détente", they preferred resorting to a position which has been characterized as „essentially a low-risk, limited-investment operation".[73]

Not so the West German and international Social Democracy, aided and abetted by the United States and the European Community. They gave their complete support to that „first-rate political tactician" Mário Soares, whose rhetoric as „demagogic defender of socialism and democracy... for a while were to give him the air of an authentic Portuguese martyr, struggling against the forces of totalitarianism".[74] Soares had boosted his international prestige by negotiating decolonization in 1974, as Minister of Foreign Affairs. In the period of radicalization, which followed March 11, the U.S. and Western European governments came to place their bets on him; and when his party obtained 38% of the vote in April, 1975, the PS Secretary General concluded it was only proper that he should direct national policy, along lines acceptable to both NATO and EC.

These were elections for the Constituent Assembly, of course, not for Parliament; and during the electoral campaign, the PS had emphasized that it stood for a „socialist" revolution, different from either a „social-democratic" or a „social-bureaucratic" (referring to the PCP) path. Besides, the Platform of Constitutional Agreement specified that the outcome would not affect the composition of governments until parliamentary elections would have been held under the new constitution. Soares, however, argued that his party's „representative" legitimacy now rivaled the MFA's „revolutionary" legitimacy. Nominally challenging the PCP, but in fact the MFA, he did not hesitate „to call his forces onto the streets in their tens of thousands"[75] and to „enter into a tacit alliance with more conservative, and in some cases, open reactionary forces which only now recommenced to show themselves in public."[76]

At this point, the support by the Committe of Friendship and Solidarity with democracy and Socialism in Portugal, an initiative of the Socialist International, was only the final step in „an auxiliary action whose story cannot yet be told".[77] The Committee, established on September 5, 1975 in London,

71 Wettig, Gerhard: *Die sowjetische Portugal-Politik 1974-1975*, Berichte des Bundesinstituts für ost-wissenschaftliche und internationale Studien, no. 60, Cologne 1975, p. 90.
72 Brandt, Willy: *Begegnungen und Einsichten*, Hamburg 1976, p. 632.
73 Szulc, Tad: „Washington and Lisbon" (as above, n. 26), p. 57.
74 Harvey, op. cit. (as in n. 33), p. 39.
75 Gallagher, Tom: „Portugal's Bid for Democracy: The Role of the Socialist Party", *West European Politics*, Vol. 2 (1979), S. 210.
76 Mujal-Léon, op. cit., p. 32.
77 Brandt, op. cit., p. 631.

was chaired by Willy Brandt; Bruno Kreisky, François Mitterrand, Olof Palme, Joop den Uyl and Harold Wilson were also members. While the Committee strove to „contact numerous individuals with political and military responsibilities" in Portugal and to influence „European governments and players of the international political scene",[78] the SPD and its foundation had long begun to grant considerable aid to the PS under the Leitmotiv „explicit rejection of popular front ideology".[79] In April 1974, the PS – as quoted above – had no money and no organization worth mentioning. In April 1975, it was able to outspend any other party during its election campaign. Outside donations to the PS alone equaled the PPD's total election expenses. The sale of publications was reported by the party to have fetched five times more than, again, in the case of the PPD, possibly hiding „laundered" contributions. While the PS claimed 35 971 new members in relation to 1974 (and 44 623 in relation to 1975), membership dues amounted to hardly 1% of its income.[80]

The only SPD statement offering any quantitative information on financial support referred to DM 882,000 in Friedrich Ebert Foundation aid for political training and organization building.[81] A news report specified in 1979 that the Foundation had altogether supported the PS with DM 10-15 mio.; in 1977 alone, 2.9 mio of these were paid out of FRG government subsidies.[82]

The Dutch Partij van de Arbeid reportedly contributed another 3 mio. dollars; further news reports referred to financial aid by the socialist parties of Austria and Sweden.[83] And on September 25, 1975, the New York Times wrote that, according to „four official sources in Washington", the U.S. government, subsequent to the May 30 NATO summit in Brussels and after consultations with the West European governments, had decided to join in supporting the PS. According to the newspaper, the U.S. funds were to be „funneled by the Central Intelligence Agency through Western European socialist parties and labor unions", where the CIA had been reviving „dormant but traditionally existing relations with anti-communist socialist workers' move-

---

78 Brandt, Willy: „Das portugiesische Volk kann sich auf uns verlassen", in: Merz/Rego, op. cit. (as in n. 55), pp. 187 ss.
79 Wagner, R.: „Klare Absage an die Volksfront" (commenting on Brandt's 1974 visit to Portugal), *Vorwärts* (main SPD newspaper), October 24, 1974, cit. by Stender, op. cit. (as in n. 60), p. 15.
80 Figures reported on parties' income and expenses are from Antunes, Albertino et al.: *Portugal – República Socialista?*, op. cit. (as in n. 35), pp. 164 ss., membership numbers from Partido Socialista (ed.): *Confiar no PS – Apostar em Portugal*, Lisbon 1979, p. 73.
81 Cf. „Sozialdemokraten helfen", *Sozialdemokrat Magazin* No. 1/1975, p. 21.
82 Cf. „Immer auf der Sonnenseite des Lebens", *Der Spiegel*, Vol. 33 No. 16, April 16, 1979, p. 47.
83 Cf. *Washington Post*, Aug. 24, 1975, p. A 20; *International Herald Tribune*, Aug. 30, 1975, pp. 1ss.

ments."[84] (The newspaper was referring to the fact that, in France, AFL – the American Federation of Labor – and CIA funds, distributed by the AFL, had contributed in 1947 to splitting the Confédéraion Génerale du Travail, close to the PCF, and establishing the competing Force Ouvrière; it was also referring to West Germany, where both AFL and CIO – Congress of Industrial Organizations – had, in 1947/48, used CIA funds to create anti-communist trade unions.)[85]

It was planned subsequent press article friendly to the Socialist International has been candid in reporting that, as West German trade union officials traveled to Portugal, „it was not uncommon that they carried a suitcase full of money as a gesture of solidarity". What may be called into question is the report's further assertion that „dependencies did not result".[86] In 1973, Soares had found the PS lacking in theoretical training and reflection on socialism. In its 1974 ‚Declaration of Principles', the party had announced that its aim consisted in the „construction of a classless society", opting for a „socialism that includes and develops pluralism", rejecting „social democratic" solutions that would „maintain, on purpose or in fact, capitalist structures". Commencing in that year, the PS not only received massive aid from abroad, but also saw itself confronted with no less massive expectations tied to that aid. In such situations, varieties of informal penetration – particularly if founded in ‚socialist solidarity and friendship' – certainly played their part in the Partido Socialista's „social democratization", its rapid evolution „into an orthodox Western party".[87]

Álvaro Cunhal never left any doubt about his conviction that „Leninism is the Marxism of transition from capitalism to socialism".[88] Conditioned under the dictatorship by what have been aptly termed the „traumatic experiences" of a „Hobbesian world"[89], the PCP had remained a „party from the times of Dimitrov", with a „hardly fertile theoretical dogmatism".[90] By its tactic, the PCP contributed its share to the 1975 wave of anti-communism in Portugal, indirectly favoring a PS whose politics resulted in a weakening of the entire Left, including the Partido Socialista itself.

84 New York Times, No. 42,978, Sept. 25, 1975, pp. 1, 25.
85 Cf. Radosh, American Labor (as in n. 22), pp. 319 ss., 323, 438.
86 Grunenberg, Nina: „Frieden, Freiheit und ein Traum: Die Sozialistische Internationale", Die Zeit, December 12, 1980, p. 11.
87 Gallagher, op. cit. (as in n. 75), p. 203.
88 Cunhal, Álvaro: „Die PCP und der reale Sozialismus", address of May 6, 1978, in: id., op. cit. (as in n. 69), p. 203.
89 Gallagher, Tom: „The Portuguese Communist Party and Eurocommunism", Political Quarterly, Vol. 50 (1979), pp. 205/206.
90 Alves, Márcio Moreira: Les Soldats Socialistes de Portugal, Paris 1975, p. 156.

VI

Drawing attention to the role of formal and informal penetration in its various dimensions, culminating in „total diplomacy", does not mean disputing the importance of domestic developments such as, e. g., the virtual uprising in the rural parts of the North against the leftward shift of the revolutionary process and, more particularly, against the PCP, unleashed in July/August 1975 by the catholic clergy and by CAP, the militant alliance of wealthy farmers, large landowners and middlemen. Or the conflicts which increasingly divided the MFA into ideological factions, lasting until November 25, 1975, when an uprising of left-wing units was suppressed by measures so carefully prepared that they have been judged equal to a „centrist coup", „coolly planned and executed" by ‚operational' officers extolling traditional military professionalism.[91] The golpe expanded into a purge of left-wing officers and terminated the MFA's existence as a „movement".

Internal turmoil contributed to these developments, but even there, the PS struck „political alliances with unlikely political forces".[92] On July 13, 1975, the wave of sacking and burning PCP offices started in Rio Maior, which would soon become the CAP's principal bastion. A month later, with Soares present, PS Secretariat member Manuel Alegre declared that „this soil has become a symbol... Here the people demonstrated what should be done if a minority attempts to manipulate it..."[93]

While ideological and political rifts widened in the MFA Assembly and the Council of the Revolution between adherents of PS, PCP and radical-socialist parties, it was the Group of Nine that chose to bypass both Assembly and Council by circulating its August 7 critique of „revolutionary vanguardism" among military units. Aiming at the collection of further signatures, it was also effectively eroding the political structure introduced into the Armed Forces after March 11. The operation led to a coalition which combined the Nine, the above-mentioned „operationals", and the PS.[94] That coalition proved its effectiveness on and after November 25 – and, as shown above, it had been the Group of Nine which had responded most noticeably to formal penetration, as the PS executive had reacted to the informal variety.

„Ideological export models" would „not be tolerated" in Portugal, Willy Brandt had affirmed that same year. Referring to Portugal, German Chancellor Helmut Schmidt would sum up later that „in this little area of world poli-

---

91   Pimlott, Ben: „Portugal's Soldiers in the Wings", *New Statesman*, September 24, 1976, p. 393.
92   Gallagher, „Portugal's Bid..." (as in n. 75), p. 210.
93   *Portugal Socialista*, August 27, 1975. Cf. also Soares: *Portugal: Que Revolução?* (as in n. 39), p. 152.
94   Cf. Soares, *Portugal – Que Revolução?*, op. cit., p. 163 ss.

tics, the Americans followed our advice. And they have no reason for regret."[95]

From the aborted „revolution of carnations", another lesson was learnt. A decade later, the National Endowment for Democracy (NED) was created in the United States. Designed to finance „democratic institution-building" abroad – i. e. to promote „American-style pluralistic societies" -, it was endowed by Congress, for the first year of its existence, with $26.3 mio. in federal funds: 13.8 mio. were to be spent by the American Institute for Free Labor Develop-ment (jointly directed by the American Federation of Labor and the Congress of Industrial Organizations; since renamed the American Center for International Labor Solidarity), 2.5 mio. by the new Center for International Private Enterprise (set up by the Chamber of Commerce of the United States), and 5 mio. each by the two recently established international offshoots of the Democratic and Republican National Committees. Further annual appropriations would be forthcoming.[96]

The NED project was first mentioned by Ronald Reagan, when he spoke to the British Parliament in 1982, with the U.S. President expressly referring to the West German party foundations as a model. It is highly possible that his advisors[97] acquainted him with the „positive" results obtained by the Friedrich Ebert Foundation in Portugal – at least by those activities which served as instruments of „total diplomacy". In a country with a divided left and political forces – civilian no less than military – lacking a consistent reform program, such diplomacy may well prove decisive for the final outcome.

---

95 Schmidt, Helmut: „Die internationale Verantwortung der Bundesrepublik Deutschland", address of April 9, 1976, cit. in Stender, op. cit. (as in n. 60), p. 77.

96 Cf. „Project Democracy Takes Wing", *New York Times*, No. 56,059, May 29, 1984, p. B 10. – Addendum 2011: For an overview of NED activities and critical assessments („a lot of what NED does today was done covertly 25 years ago by the CIA"), see, e. g., the Wikipedia write-up on the Endowment, with further sources (http://en.wikipedia.org/wiki/ National_ Endowment_for_Democracy, accessed 7/9/2011).

97 In 1981, Frank C. Carlucci was appointed Deputy Defense Secretary by the Reagan Administration; he became the President's National Security Advisor in 1986, and Secretary of Defense a year later. Carlucci had been ambassador to Portugal from 1974 to 1977 and had subsequently served as CIA Deputy Director.

Sources

- „How Political Science Might Regain Relevance and Obtain an Audience: A Manifesto for the 21st Century", *European Political Science,* Vol. 10 (2011), 220-225. Permission to republish by Palgrave Macmillan is gratefully acknowledged.
- „Towards Creating a Discipline With a ‚Regional Stamp': Central-East European Political Science and Ethno-Cultural Diversity", *Lithuanian Foreign Policy Review,* No. 25 (2011), 121-129. Permission to republish by Prof. Tomas Janeliunas, the *Review's* editor, is gratefully acknowledged.
- „Pluralism and Democratic Governance: A Century of Changing Research Frame works", in: Rainer Eisfeld (ed.), *Pluralism: Developments in the Theory and Practic of Democracy,* Opladen & Farmington Hills: Barbara Budrich 2006, 39-57
- „Pluralism as a Critical Political Theory", *Praxis International,* Vol. 6 (1986), 277-293. Original publication by Blackwell Publishers is gratefully acknowledged.
- (with Leslie A. Pal) "Political Science in Central-East Europe and the Impact of Poli-tics: Factors of Diversity, Forces of Convergence", Introduction to: Rainer Eisfeld/ Leslie A. Pal (eds.), *Political Science in Central-East Europe. Diversity and Convergence,* Opladen & Farmington Hills: Barbara Budrich 2010, 9-35 (a slightly shorter version was pre-published in: *European Political Science,* Vol. 9 [2010], 223-243).
- "German Political Science at the Crossroads: The Ambivalent Response to the 1933 Nazi Seizure of Power", in: Rainer Eisfeld/Michael Th. Greven/Hans Karl Rupp: *Political Science and Regime Change in 20th Century Germany,* New York: Nova Science Publishers 1996, 17-53. Permission to republish by Nova Science Publishers is gratefully acknowledged.
- "From Hegelianism to Neo-Pluralism: The Uneasy Relationship Between Private and Public Interests in Germany", *International Review of Sociology,* Vol. 8 (1998), Monographic Section, 389-396. Grateful acknowledgement is made to prior publication in this Taylor & Francis journal.
- "'Mitteleuropa' in Historical and Contemporary Perspective", *German Politics and Society,* No. 28 (1993), 39-52. Original publication by Berghahn Books is gratefully acknowledged.
- "Myths and Realities of Frontier Violence: A Look at the Gunfighter Saga", *Journal of Criminal Justice and Popular Culture,* Vol. 3 (1995), 106–122, reprinted in: Sean E. Anderson/Gregory J. Howard (eds.), *Interrogating Popular Culture: Deviance, Justice, and Social Order,* Alba-

ny: Harrow & Heston (1998), 42 – 54. Original publication by Harrow & Heston is gratefully acknowledged,
- "Projecting Landscapes of the Human Mind onto Another World: Changing Faces of an Imaginary Mars", in: Alexander C. T. Geppert (ed.): *Imagining Outer Space*, Basingstoke: Palgrave Macmillan 2012, 89-105. Permission to republish by Palgrave Macmillan is gratefully acknowledged.
- „Portugal and Western Europe: Shifting Involvements", in: Kenneth Maxwell (ed.): *Portugal in the 1980s: Dilemmas of Democratic Consolidation*, New York/Westport: Greenwood Press 1986, 29-62. Original publication by Greenwood Press is gratefully acknowleged.
- „External Influences on the Portuguese Revolution: The Role of Western Europe", published as "Influências Externas sobre a Revolução Portuguesa: o papel da Europa Ocidental" in: Eduardo de Sousa Ferreira/Walter C. Opello jr. (eds.): *Conflict and Change in Portugal 1974-1984*, Lisbon: Teorema 1985, 79-99. Original publication by Teorema is gratefully acknowleged.

About the author

Rainer Eisfeld was born in Berlin (1941). Educated at the Universities of Heidelberg, Saarbrücken and Frankfurt (Ph. D. 1971), he was Professor of Political Science at the University of Osnabrück, 1974-2006. Now emeritus.

International apppointments: Visiting Scholar, Center for European and Eurasian Studies, UCLA, 1995 and 2000; College of Social and Behavioral Sciences, University of Arizona, 2005. Visiting Professor, Department of Political Science, UCLA, 2002.

Professional activities: Member, International Conference Group on Modern Portugal, 1984-1989. Chair, IPSA Research Committee on Socio-Political Pluralism, 2000-2006. Member, IPSA Executive Committee (as Research Committee Representative), 2006-. Program Co-Chair, IPSA World Conference in Montreal: "International Political Science: New Theoretical and Regional Perspectives", 2008. Member, Board of Trustees, Concentration Camp Memorials Buchenwald and Mittelbau-Dora, 1994-.

Honors: Faculty Dissertation Award (University of Frankfurt), 1971. Volkswagen Foundation Research Grant (Akademie-Stipendium, Research Project: „German Political Science 1920-1945"), 1989. Selection of *Mondsüchtig. Wernher von Braun und die Geburt der Raumfahrt aus dem Geist der Barbarei* by 'Bild der Wissenschaft' as one of the „Year's Outstanding Books on Science", 1997.

Books (international editions): Il pluralismo tra liberalismo e socialismo (Bologna: Il Mulino 1976); *Pluralizam između liberalizma i socijalizma* (Zagreb: Informator 1992); *Touha po měsíci. Wernher von Braun a zrození kosmických letů ze zvěrstev II. světové války* (Brno: Jota 1997).

Books (in English): *Political Science and Regime Change in 20th Century Germany*, New York: Nova 1999 (co-author); *Pluralism. Developments in the Theory and Practice of Democracy* (IPSA World of Political Science Series No. 4), Opladen/Farmington Hills: Barbara Budrich 2006 (editor); *Political Science in Central-East Europe: Diversity and Convergence*, Opladen/Farmington Hills: Barbara Budrich 2010 (co-editor).

Selected lectures: University of the Witwatersrand (Johannesburg) and University of the Western Cape (Capetown), 2003; Lecture Tour (supported by the German Research Foundation, DFG): Columbia University, University of Maryland and UCLA, 2007; Guest Lecturer, Moscow State Institute of International Relations – MGIMO University, 2008; Keynote Lecture, Conference on Political Science Development, Vilnius University, 2009; Panel Speaker, Russian Political Science Association Conference on Ethno-Cultural Diversity and Tolerance (St. Petersburg), 2010.

Peer reviewer: Volkswagen Foundation, 1983-1993; *Political Studies*; *International Political Science Review*; *European Political Science*.

Index

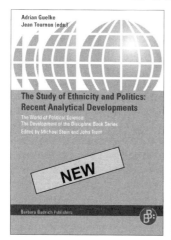